DRUGS, ALCOHOL AND ADDICTION
IN THE LONG NINETEENTH CENTURY

DRUGS, ALCOHOL AND ADDICTION IN THE LONG NINETEENTH CENTURY

Edited by
Dan Malleck

Volume I

Drunks, Fiends and the Roots of Concern

LONDON AND NEW YORK

First published 2020
by Routledge
2 Park Square, Milton Park, Abingdon, Oxon OX14 4RN

and by Routledge
52 Vanderbilt Avenue, New York, NY 10017

Routledge is an imprint of the Taylor & Francis Group, an informa business

© 2020 selection and editorial matter, Dan Malleck; individual owners retain copyright in their own material.

The right of Dan Malleck to be identified as the author of the editorial material, and of the authors for their individual chapters, has been asserted in accordance with sections 77 and 78 of the Copyright, Designs and Patents Act 1988.

All rights reserved. No part of this book may be reprinted or reproduced or utilised in any form or by any electronic, mechanical, or other means, now known or hereafter invented, including photocopying and recording, or in any information storage or retrieval system, without permission in writing from the publishers.

Trademark notice: Product or corporate names may be trademarks or registered trademarks, and are used only for identification and explanation without intent to infringe.

British Library Cataloguing-in-Publication Data
A catalogue record for this book is available from the British Library

Library of Congress Cataloging-in-Publication Data
A catalog record for this book has been requested

ISBN: 978-1-138-34670-3 (set)
eISBN: 978-0-429-43597-3 (set)
ISBN: 978-1-138-35010-6 (Volume I)
eISBN: 978-0-429-43611-6 (Volume I)

Typeset in Times New Roman
by Apex CoVantage, LLC

Publisher's note
References within each chapter are as they appear in the original complete work

CONTENTS

Acknowledgements	viii
Introduction: Drink, drugs, and the creation of addiction in the west	1

VOLUME I Drunks, fiends and the roots of concern	**21**
Introduction to Volume I: Drunks and fiends; users and observers	23

PART 1
The drug habit and its confessionals   **41**

1 Thomas DeQuincey, *Confessions of an English Opium Eater*, 2nd ed. (London: Taylor and Hessey, Fleet St., 1823), pp. 156–73   43

2 Walter Colton, 'Effects of Opium', *The Knickerbocker*, 7, 1836, 421–23   49

3 William Blair, 'An Opium-Eater in America', *The Knickerbocker*, 20, 1842, 47–57   53

4 Sigma, 'Opium-Eating', *Lippincott's Magazine*, 1, 1868, 404–9   63

5 H. G. Cole, *Confessions of an American Opium Eater: From Bondage to Freedom* (Boston: James H. Earle, 1895), pp. 5–7, 8–9, 27–32, 47–50, 107–119   70

6 A. Calkins, 'Opium-Literature in the Reflex View', in *Opium and the Opium Appetite* (Philadelphia: J Lippincott, 1871), pp. 88–98   84

CONTENTS

PART 2
Drug use observed **91**

7 Anon, 'Use of Opiates Among the Operative Population',
Chambers Edinburgh Journal, 3, 1845, 346–48 93

8 Anon, 'The Narcotics We Indulge In', *Blackwood's
Edinburgh Magazine*, 74, 1853, part 1, 129–39, part 2,
605–28 98

PART 3
Cannabis **143**

9 William Brooke O'Shaughnessy, *On the Preparation of
the Indian Hemp, or Gunjah*, 1839, pp. 7–13, 19–20, 36–37 145

10 F. H. Ludlow, 'Introduction', 'The Night Entrance', 'Under
the Shadow of Esculapius', and 'The Kingdom of the
Dream', in *The Hasheesh Eater: Being Passages from the
Life of a Pythagorean* (New York: Harper & Brother, 1857),
pp. ix–xiv; 15–43 152

11 Victor Robinson, *An Essay on Hasheesh, including
Observations and Experiments* (New York: Medical
Review of Reviews, 1912), pp. 38–51, 65–83 170

PART 4
Drink and the dilemma of habit **181**

12 Benjamin Rush, *An Inquiry into the Effects of Ardent Spirits
upon the Human Body and Mind*, 6th ed. (New York:
Cornelius Davis, 1811), pp. 1–32 183

13 Thomas Trotter, 'Introduction' and 'Definition of
Drunkenness', in *An Essay Medical, Philosophical,
and Chemical on Drunkenness and its Effects on the
Human Body* 1st Philadelphia Edition, (Philadelphia:
Anthony Finley, 1813), pp. 11–22 202

14 R. Macnish, *The Anatomy of Drunkenness: An Inaugural
Essay* (Glasgow: W. R. McPhun, 1827), pp. 1–28 207

CONTENTS

PART 5
The virtues of drink — **225**

15 Erasmus Darwin, 'On Drunkenness', *Zoonomia; or the
Laws of Organic Life* (Fourth American edition, 1818),
pp. 191–197 — 227

16 Edward Cutbush, *Observations on the Means of Preserving
the Health of Soldiers and Sailors* (Philadelphia: Thomas
Dobson, 1808), pp. 22–30 — 233

17 Francis E. Anstie, *On the Uses of Wines in Health and
Disease* (New York: J. S. Redfield, 1870), pp. 7–48 — 237

18 G. G. Gervinus, *Art of Drinking: A Historical Sketch* (New
York: United States Brewers' Association, 1890), pp. 5–23 — 259

PART 6
Places and spaces — **273**

19 Charles Dickens, *Barnaby Rudge: A Tale of the Riots
of Eighty* (London: George Routledge and Sons, 1884
[1841]), pp. 172–73 — 275

20 Charles Dickens, 'The Dawn', in *The Mystery of
Edwin Drood* (London: Chapman and Hall, 1870),
pp. 1–3 — 278

21 Anon, 'East London Opium Smokers', *London Society*,
14, 1868, 68–72 — 281

22 J. Platt, 'Chinese London and its Opium Dens',
Gentleman's Magazine, 279, 1895, 272–82 — 287

23 E. C. Moore, 'The Social Value of the Saloon', *American
Journal of Sociology*, 3, July 1897, 1–12 — 296

24 Royal L. Melendy, 'The Saloon in Chicago', *American
Journal of Sociology*, 6, November 1900, 289–306 — 302

25 Anon, 'The Experience and Observations of a New York
Saloon-Keeper as Told by Himself', *McClure Magazine*, 32,
January 1909, 301–12 — 314

26 Hutchins Hapgood, 'McSorley's Saloon', *Harper's Weekly*,
58, 25 October 1913, 15 — 334

ACKNOWLEDGEMENTS

This collection has been a remarkably satisfying voyage of discovery, allowing me to dig deeper into this field than my previous work has permitted and broaden my appreciation for the complexity and nuance of drug and alcohol history. I am therefore grateful to several people for helping to set me on this path. The extended discussions with my first editor, Kimberly Smith, gave me the sense of the value and breadth of this project. Holly Karibo suggested me to Kimberly, and I'm grateful and humbled by the recommendation. My friend and editor Melissa Pitts saw the importance of such a work in the big picture and ardently encouraged me to take up the challenge.

Scholarly colleagues provided insightful support along the way. Carole Lynn Stewart directed me towards the works of Remond and Harper. Pam Lock provided copies of the Lewes and Carpenter spat, and reminded me of the pubs of Dickens. James Kneale's expertise in Anstie was a persistent voice in the back of my head. My brilliant Brock colleague Renee Lafferty-Salhany pointed me towards Edward Cutbush's work on soldiers and drink. Annemarie McAllister and the staff at the Livesey's collection kindly allowed me to include some digitized material. Thembisa Waetjen kindly, enthusiastically, provided me with copies of material from the Transvaal gold fields and some South African medical literature, along with an extensive bibliography, not all of which made it into the final cut. At the last minute Xiufeng Yuan helped with quick, crucial, Chinese translation. The enthusiastic members of the Alcohol and Drugs History Society have provided inspiration over many years of collegiality. They set the foundation upon which this work has been built.

Essential personal support made the long process of writing and assembling this collection possible. Bonnie Tompkins has listened to my meandering ideas, bolstered flagging spirits, and stoked my enthusiasm, while putting up with my absences and need to *get back to work*. Meanwhile, Honey often lay nearby, quietly watching with those beautiful shifting eyes and ever-enthusiastic tail, waiting for the next walk and roll in the snow. Her passing during the last phases of this project has left a space no drug, alcohol, or book will fill. It is to Bonnie and Honey that this work is dedicated.

INTRODUCTION

Drink, drugs, and the creation of addiction
in the west

Between the French Revolution and the beginning of the First World War, the perception of drugs and alcohol changed fundamentally in the Anglo-American world. At the beginning of this period, drug use and alcohol consumption, if discussed at all, were generally considered personal choices and outside of the purview of government intervention. Certainly there were concerns about public drinking and drunkenness, and episodic uprisings like the "Gin Panic" of the eighteenth century in Britain or various condemnations of drink uttered by mostly puritan religious leaders. But there was little expressed concern over drinking as a broad social problem, and drug taking for non-medical purposes (that is, what we might today call recreational drug use) was hardly mentioned. The idea of addiction as a medical problem, meanwhile, was generally missing from the scanty discussions of drug and alcohol use; people might have a habit, a desire, or a craving, but there was little tendency to label repeated, habitual consumption of mind- and behaviour-altering substances as an addiction. Between 1789 and 1914 all of that changed.

Historians have long debated the roots of the concerns about substance use that expanded and diversified over the nineteenth century. Certainly there were puritanical and evangelical perceptions of the physical and moral degradation caused by drink. Classic images such as Bruegel the Elder's "Fight between Carnival and Lent" and the two Hogarth prints "Gin Lane" and "Beer Street" present clear connections between excessive drinking and social disorder. But the tension between Carnival and Lent was a tension between common and divine activity, and although viewed with some concern, it was not something against which authorities normally sought to impose heavy restrictions. The Hogarth drawings, on the other hand, represent the concerns about types of drinking and the excesses of spirits over beer. The community where gin prevailed was degraded and destitute, with only the pawn shop benefitting because people would sell their goods to buy gin. The community where beer prevailed was healthy and orderly; only the pawn shop was destitute.[1] The resulting laws to suppress the gin trade targeted one product, not all forms of consumption.[2] Such regulations themselves demonstrate how profound were the changes in the nineteenth century, because in order to curtail the gin trade the government instituted controls including

INTRODUCTION

taxes and licensing, rather than imposing prohibitions and laws condemning individual consumption. More complex than these secular impressions were the debates among religious leaders. Especially, Puritan ministers railed against public drunkenness, linking it to more substantial problems of individual excess and social deterioration.[3]

Such proclamations are often seen as the roots of the idea that addiction to drink was a social problem requiring more sophisticated social intervention. One classic work on addiction is by Harry Levine, and set the origins of the medical interpretation of addiction in the writings of Philadelphia physician Benjamin Rush. Levine argued that Rush's *An Inquiry into the Effects of Ardent Spirits upon the Human Body and Mind* (reprinted in this collection) was the pivotal document that started the process of medicalizing drunkenness, providing a language upon which subsequent reformers based their concerns. Levine further contended that the push against drunkenness coincided with industrialization in America, and that in a regulated, structured, and mechanized workplace, drunkenness was not only inappropriate, it was positively dangerous. It was no surprise, Levine observes, that the first advocates for some kind of prohibition were drawn from the middle class, the same cohort whose businesses would be negatively affected by the insobriety of their workers.[4] This interpretation set the stage for more nuanced understanding of the origins of the temperance movement, which encouraged first restrictive legislation and later complete prohibition of liquor, most especially in Canada and the United States. There, adherents of Evangelical religions were, in the early part of the nineteenth century, experiencing a series of revivals encouraging individuals to seek personal redemption by renouncing their earthly proclivities in an attempt to prepare for the second coming of Jesus Christ.[5]

Levine's attribution of Rush's primacy in the medicalization of temperance has been criticized and modulated by subsequent scholars, many of whom have noted that the explanation did not recognize the European (or at least British) roots of Rush's perception. Historian James Nicholls points out that *Inquiry* "contains little that was not already commonplace in England prior to its publication, and rather a lot that was anachronistic" and that Rush had also lived in London in the 1770s and was familiar with the work of English physicians such as William Cadogan and John Coakley Lettsom.[6] Rush had studied in Edinburgh in the 1760s under William Cullen, whose student Thomas Trotter wrote a thesis *On Drunkenness* (1788) which set the foundation for his *An Essay, medical, philosophical, and chemical, on Drunkenness and its effects on the human body* (1804), portions of which are reproduced in this collection.[7]

Accurately identifying the origin of the medicalization of a drinking habit is less important here than the fact that, by the beginning of the nineteenth century, more people were considering heavy drinking and drunkenness to be problematic. For some it was a problem that needed social if not political intervention, and for others it remained a personal problem that had solutions in the strengthening of the individual will. So despite the historical dilemmas in finding the origins of a pathologized drinking behaviour, the work of Rush and Trotter are representations

2

of the bridge between earlier ideas of physical and moral decline through drink, and emerging ideas of drink as a problem that needed a broader legislative and social solution. Thus, even if Rush's ideas were not revolutionary, they are certainly representative of a shifting perception of drunkenness that emerged in the Enlightenment and influenced subsequent generations of both medical and non-medical thinkers. They also informed the ideas of the temperance advocates throughout the century.

Liquor was additionally problematic because it functioned not only as a recreational substance, but also as a medicine on its own, and in combination with other medicines. Indeed, the gin of the "Gin Craze" originated as a preparation of distilled grains and infused herbs and botanicals with a distinctly medical application.[8] Gin was not the only such substance, and the intersection of spirits and medicines rendered the distinction between medicinal and recreational substance use difficult to discern. One example may be found in the work of Thomas Syndenham, the seventeenth-century physician, botanist and taxonomist whose preparation of sherry and opium infused with a variety of botanicals including saffron, cinnamon, and cloves became the seemingly ubiquitous form of laudanum.[9] Although Paracelsus is credited with developing laudanum, it was something closer to Sydenham's laudanum that Thomas DeQuincey, the "English Opium Eater," consumed therapeutically before becoming bound physically and associated in perpetuity. This liquid preparation was practical: since opium is not easily soluble in water, it was dissolved in alcohol. Although opium was laudanum's main active ingredient, in both Sydenham and DeQuincey's times, alcohol and botanicals each had their own therapeutic value.

Despite the polypharmaceutical nature of Sydenham's laudanum, by the nineteenth century it was the opium that had captured the attention of medical and social commentators. DeQuincey's memoirs were not *Confessions of an Opium, Sherry, Cinnamon, Cloves, Saffron and Other Botanicals Eater* because the medicinal use of those other substances was not becoming problematized. Opium's importance to medicine cannot be understated. Its properties fit well in a medical system in which symptom management was often the best that physicians could do for a patient. Opium is a pain killer (anodyne) and a sleep inducer (soporific). It dries up pulmonary and gastrointestinal secretions so is helpful in dealing with coughs and diarrhoea, common symptoms in a range of illnesses. Most notably, pain, coughing and gastrointestinal distress were conditions of industrialization, where unclean water and polluted air could combine with other environmental factors to cause any number of problems.[10] The medical issue that launched DeQuincey's opium habit and historical relevance was "a most painful affection of the stomach" and such iatrogenic origins of drug habituation remain an issue of concern for physicians up to the present day.[11] The way that medical practitioners wrestled with their role in creating and treating habitual drug use is a topic addressed in much of the second volume of this collection.

DeQuincey's *Confessions*, which he initially published anonymously, were criticized by contemporaries for the alluring descriptions this romantic author provided of his opium dreams, and it was the recreational use of opium that was first seen to be a problem. Indeed, DeQuincey's habit may have been iatrogenic, but his recreational experience with opium predated the medical intervention. As he confesses in his *Confessions*, "I did occasionally take opium, for the sake of the exquisite pleasure it gave me" but the episodic nature of this recreational indulgence, he argues, "effectually protected" him from long-term effects.[12] Numerous medical writers discussed the therapeutic effects of opium, and in these treatises recreational use appeared only occasionally. John Leigh's *An Experimental Inquiry into the Properties of Opium and its Effects on Living Subjects* (1785); Hastings Handy's *An Inaugural Dissertation on Opium* (1791); Valentine Seaman's *Inaugural Dissertation on Opium* (1793); John Laws' *An Inaugural Dissertation on the Rational of the Operation of Opium* (1797) all present the medical and physical impact of opium on the body, but do not express significant concern about the habit.[13] Leigh's inquiry was a series of dozens of experiments with opium, commenting on its usefulness only at the end. He talked about "dangers of opium" normally to refer to the potential for it to injure the patient. Drawing on the work of Leigh and Cullen, Handy provided an overview of its therapeutic value with no discussion of habit. Seaman discusses the pleasures derived from opium in those "who do not suffer under any particular pain or distress" but sees no problems emerging. Even when patients experience pleasure from opium, he considers this therapeutic since "for as pleasure clearly consists in a certain degree of relaxation of the system, . . . it would be no way surprising that opium in transporting the system over to sleep should carry it through the limits of this pleasurable state."[14] He does however caution that "this pleasant situation is not permitted to be long enjoyed" but only because too much opium could cause too much relaxation of the system, which could cause death.[15] Laws did mention the problems of habit, but it was a problem because the pleasures of opium could make patients prefer it to more useful treatments, or as he wrote "that kind of dependence upon it, which so often proves fatal by generating a laxity in the use of other more efficacious means." This habit he admitted was difficult to eliminate, especially among the "unreflecting and illiterate."[16] Ironically, DeQuincey could be described with neither adjective.

At least into the 1860s, then, the opium habit was familiar in the Anglo-American world, but not a cause of concern in many circles. Physicians saw it as a potential side effect of medical treatment and something to be avoided, and social reformers were much more concerned about the habitual use of alcohol. When opium use as a problematic social habit arose among reform-minded individuals, it was often a growing concern about Chinese opium smoking as witnessed by evangelical missionaries and others writing from China or engaged in speaking engagements to raise funds for ongoing mission activities (this will be discussed further in what follows). There was one industry, however, that took up the concern over the effect of the opium habit in the west well in advance of medical and reform organizations: the growing and increasingly sophisticated life insurance industry.

Habitual opium use was considered a problem to the life insurance industry. Life insurance is a business based upon probabilities, and its profitability depended upon insuring people who would live a long life, during which they could contribute to the coffers of the insurance companies and make investors wealthy.[17] Thus, a condition that could shorten life would be problematic to the industry, and a secret habit that was undisclosed was especially problematic. This is where the death of John Thomas Erksine becomes so important. When Erksine, the Seventh Earl of Mar, died of jaundice in 1828, his life insurance company refused to pay out. It claimed that this habit, which had not been disclosed by either his medical advisor or the applicant himself, voided the policy. His beneficiary begged to differ. In the subsequent trial, a number of physicians were called as witnesses. According to Robert Christison, a noted toxicologist who was one of the main expert witnesses, all of the physicians he consulted figured that the opium habit must have some kind of debilitating effect, but they could think of no concrete examples of a life shortened by the opium habit. That conclusion notwithstanding, the court decided that since the insurance company had not asked about whether the Earl of Mar had such a habit, he did not need to disclose it. The case was thrown out, and the company had to honour his policy.[18]

The Earl of Mar case is important to the history of drug habit and historians have pointed to it as one of the earliest medical discussions of the morbid effect of opium habituation. What is most notable about the case, however, is not that Christison examined the situation and assumed that the opium habit must be problematic even though he had no evidence, but that this conclusion permeated medical textbooks for the next half a century. Even in the 1880s, toxicology textbooks regularly referred to the Earl of Mar case, DeQuincey, and poet and noted opium eater Samuel Taylor Coleridge in discussing the opium habit.[19] These precedents were important because for much of the first half of the century little vigorous research was undertaken on the opium habit as a medical problem, and physicians writing text books usually simply reminded their readers of the Christison's observations on the Earl of Mar, along with the stories of DeQuincey and Coleridge and then moved on to more important topics.

When opium did appear in print during the middle of the nineteenth century, it was more likely to appear as a problematic substance for others. Medicinal use by sick westerners was familiar to many people, given opium's multiple applications, but westerners were also aware of opium as a valuable commercial product sold, indeed forced, upon China, and moreover as an intoxicant for which Chinese people seemed to have an inordinate craving. This craving was not spontaneous, but rather the outcome of the British government and the British East India Company building a market for opium in China despite the Chinese government's opposition. When these efforts faced resistance from the Chinese government, the Anglo-Chinese war, also known as the first Opium War, resulted in the Chinese government being forced to open its borders to British and other companies and allow opium to flow freely.[20] When western missionaries, many evangelical reformers hoping to convert heathen Chinese to Christianity, reported to their conferees back

5

home and detailed the sad scenes of debased opium smokers, they framed it in the same language that drove the temperance movement's anti-drink rhetoric. After all, many of these reformers were also temperance advocates, and the degradation of opium was readily transcribed within a temperance-oriented perspective. So when British people read about the poor Chinese opium smoker, many of them realized that this decrepit soul was the product of a particularly rapacious form of British imperialism, although doubtless their pity was also the product of imperialist paternalism. The result was an increasingly powerful agitation to stop the trade in opium, the vocal and expansive Society for the Suppression of the Opium Trade (SSOT), and a vast movement from well beyond British borders to do something to end a trade that many saw as immoral.

The temperance-orientation of missionaries in China and elsewhere was rooted in the burgeoning temperance movement of the west. As noted earlier, anti-alcohol sentiment had grown from religious and medical notions of the problems with habituation, but these sentiments congealed into more fully formed and articulated opposition to alcoholic beverages as the century unfolded. Evangelicalism was an approach that was distinctively outward reaching, seeing the role of the devout to include good works in the community, which could involve simply spreading the word of God, working to convert non-Christians to a life with Christ, or doing good works, such as caring for and ministering to the poor and sick.[21] Thus Evangelicals found in the campaign against the liquor trade a variety of ways that their need to do good work could be satisfied. Bringing back to Christ people who had taken a wayward path could include helping drunks escape the clutches of the good King Alcohol.

Temperance manifested itself in a variety of ways. Some of the earliest work in the English speaking world is credited to Joseph Livesey, a Lancaster-born weaver whose various moral reform activities in the city of Preston, UK, included extensive work encouraging personal temperance, often called "teetotalism."[22] Livesey's advocacy for total abstinence was apparently rooted in a single experience taking a drink of whiskey, after which he pledged to himself never to touch the stuff again.[23] He founded with some friends the Preston Temperance Society, a group of men who pledged not to drink, although the degree of abstinence was debatable and debated. Livesey himself urged his temperance colleagues to reject beer, an early position that remained a minority viewpoint for some time. The temperance movement was buoyed by Livesey's efforts, and his lecturing and publications expanded the reach of temperance throughout the United Kingdom.[24]

Personal improvement was one element of temperance, but evangelical temperance gained considerable traction. Livesey's work was a personal dedication to the pragmatism of a totally abstinent life, and converged with other liberal values he advocated, including helping the working class, fighting against the poor law, and advocating public health reforms. Throughout the English-speaking world the evangelical impulse drove a growing movement of reformers seeking, along with other changes, to drive liquor from the land in the hopes of preparing the way for the second coming of Jesus Christ. People like Livesey shared their immediate goals, but his expressions of temperance principles did not match the sorts of temperance advocacy that emerged later in the century. Indeed, Brian Harrison notes that later in the century Livesey (who lived to 90, dying in 1884) had become disillusioned with the direction of temperance in the UK, seeing it as elitist and questioning the preoccupation with political prohibitionism which was aloof from the project of helping drunkards.[25]

Although secular liberals were an important part of temperance in the United Kingdom, it was evangelicals in both the UK and North America who took moral reform and moral suasionism to greater heights. Their temperance movement became arguably the largest single issue movement in the world. By the middle of the nineteenth century many evangelicals advocated government action to destroy the liquor trade. This work began with targeting the stronger alcohols, most notably spirits like whisky and rum, but soon even wine and beer was considered problematic. In *Inquiry*, Benjamin Rush's "Moral and Physical Thermometer" included drinks such as small beer, cider, and porter under the category of "Temperance" imbuing drinkers with "serenity of mind," "long life," "happiness," "cheerfulness" and "strength."[26] By the middle of the century, such a perspective was positively antiquated. Nothing short of total prohibition of the manufacture, importation, and sale of alcoholic beverages was the goal of many evangelical temperance organizations. For these often middle-class reformers, this was an evangelical imperative to help the poor and dissipated who were victims of the traffic, and simultaneously to protect their own homes and children from the temptations of the barroom.[27]

Such broad-based reform work is best represented by the activities of the Woman's Christian Temperance Union. Founded in 1874 in the United States, spurred on by the Women's Temperance Crusade of the year before, the WCTU quickly spread beyond that nation's borders, driven by women's concern about the temptations of the saloon, and the evangelical zeal for personal and social reform.[28] The WCTU gained further strength from the philosophy of its second president, Frances E Willard, who advocated a "do everything" policy. Through this approach, women could engage in a wide range of temperance projects, from more traditional work with children, advocacy in church groups, and home visiting of poor to activities that expanded women's role in society, such as engaging more directly in politics. In 1883 the World's WCTU was formed, following the missionary model of evangelical churches to bring temperance principles and teetotalism, as well as some taste for social activism, to women and communities around the world.[29] In this way the WCTU was decidedly paternalistic, bringing its enlightened message to those who were seen as less enlightened or less able to help themselves (or simply not adhering to the values of the western hegemon). Nevertheless, the WCTU has also been credited with introducing many women to political activity, and the "do everything" policy embraced projects that ranged far beyond personal moral suasion, including votes for women. In the countries where it was most active, including the United States, Canada, Australia and New Zealand, the WCTU often partnered with male-led organizations (for example the Anti-Saloon League in the United States, and the Dominion Alliance for the

INTRODUCTION

Total Suppression of the Liquor Traffic in Canada) and its leadership frequently eclipsed male leaders in their public profile.

Evangelicals, however, did not have a monopoly on mass anti-alcohol movements. Both Ireland and Quebec saw Catholic-based popular movements, led by charismatic priests, sweep the population in the nineteenth century. The "crusades" of Father Theobald Mathew in Ireland and Father Charles Chiniquy in Quebec urged Catholics to renounce alcohol and seek personal sanctification in temperance in the 1840s. Mathew's campaign purportedly enrolled over 3 million people in his mass total abstinence movement which is estimated to be nearly half the adult population of Ireland.[30] Chiniquy's campaign was less successful, but arguably more colourful, seeing at its height over 200,000 people pledging total abstinence, an impressive number in a province of about 700,000 people and 550,000 Catholic.[31] Both of these movements attempted to remain distant from secular politics, but neither Mathew nor Chiniquy could avoid various political entanglements. Mathew was urged by his church to distance himself from the abolitionist movement, a decision that upset key allies (many temperance people also worked to abolish slavery) among whom were such luminaries as Frederick Douglass, whose speech lamenting Mathew's apparent "neutrality" is included in Volume III. Chiniquy, after leaving Quebec for Illinois in order, reportedly, to remove him from several personal emotional entanglements, had a very public dispute with the Bishop of Chicago, a further entanglement that led to his excommunication.[32]

What about the drinkers themselves? Much of the history of drink in the nineteenth century has focused on how it appeared through a problem framework: those who wrote about drink tended to view it as a problem. It is not that others did not think about drink, but that with something so commonplace, it was not an issue that demanded much attention. Thus historians, who need documentary evidence and gravitate to well-preserved collections of archival material, have made much of the temperance movements. Nevertheless, this is changing. This collection includes several items by people who refused to parrot the intemperate language of the temperance movement. The virtues of drink, and the pleasures of the pub, were not beyond the ken of thoughtful observers.

It is not until we look to the material in the end of the century that we find what might be called more dispassionate examinations of drinking and drinking behaviour. Research sponsored by the US Committee of Fifty, and studies from academic journals such as the *American Journal of Sociology*, attempted more clinical examination of drinking, and especially the drinking space (the saloon), while other articles place the American saloon in its social and cultural context and find its value in its community connection. This sort of view of the saloon is less bound to the problem framework, although as works of sociology they are subjecting the drinking space to critical analysis. In contrast, as the temperance movement gained traction and the push for prohibition was seeing some success, efforts by the drink industry to push back against these campaigns generated considerable analysis of their own. Several articles in this collection challenged arguments about the negative medical and social impact of alcoholic beverages.

8

INTRODUCTION

Whereas the temperance movement increasingly sought prohibition, and the liquor industry pushed against this threat to their livelihood, legislators and moderates also looked to several middle-ground options, notably rigorous licensing and disinterested management. Licensing has a long but contentious history; disinterested management was even more controversial. Both approaches contradicted the ideal of laissez-faire economics in which the government generally avoided interfering in the market, but both sought ways to mitigate the perceived problems of drunkenness, mollify the temperance movement, and yet still allow the industry to flourish in a not-quite-free but still open market.

Licensing was, in the simplest sense, the process of granting licenses to vendors and manufacturers. To gain the privilege of holding a license an applicant might have to fulfil certain statutory requirements.[33] For example, the 1753 British Licensing Act required licensees to include a signed certificate from a local clergyman and several reputable local householders attesting to the good character of the applicant.[34] The character of the applicant was not enough to prevent the license system from being abused. In the British case, local licensing magistrates who wanted to limit public houses in their jurisdiction could simply refuse to grant licenses. At a time when public houses often were also breweries, or affiliated with them, such limits to licensing detrimentally affected brewers, and could also run afoul of municipal councils who saw brewers as a lucrative source of revenue. By the early nineteenth century, attempts to reduce licensing by magistrates and the desire to increase market share by brewers and revenue by councils came to a head with the 1830 Beer Act. By eliminating the need for beer sellers to apply to magistrates for a license, and introducing a simple and relatively inexpensive license fee, "in one dramatic move," James Nicholls explains, the Beer Act managed to "undo almost three centuries of work towards placing beer retail under magisterial control."[35] The immediate result was an explosion of beer retailers. Over 24,000 beer shops opened within a year of the law passing, and 40,000 by 1835. At the same time, the Beer Act allowed only the holders of alehouse licenses to sell wine and spirits, which ironically encouraged such places to push stronger and more lucrative spirits. It also helped to consolidate an erstwhile disconnected temperance movement; it is not coincidental that the work of people like Joseph Livesey gained a social foothold at this time. The worst excesses of the system remained in place until 1834, when a Select Committee investigated the rise of drunkenness, and recommended a return to magisterial control, the reinstatement of the character reference, and numerous other changes that diversified the types of places that could sell beer, and provided different retail restrictions on each.[36] Yet the free-trade aspects of the Beer Act persisted until replaced by the Wine and Beerhouse Act in 1869.[37]

For many observers, the Beer Act was a victory for laissez-faire market forces, while to others, it illustrated the worst excesses of overly lenient licensure, but it did not end free market attempts to regulate liquor. A powerful example of the challenge of licensing could be found in the experience of Liverpool, England, where the city's licensing magistrates instituted a less

9

INTRODUCTION

liberal but still relatively wide-open system of liquor licensing in 1861. Frustrated with the expectation that they grant licenses based upon a perceived "need" in a neighbourhood, the magistrates decided to grant licenses based solely upon an assessment of "the character of the applicant and the standard of the premises to be licensed."[38] The assumption was that the best way to check rampant drinking was to license only well-apportioned premises, run by relatively well-off, and therefore assumed respectable, proprietors. Like the Beer Act itself, it was a dismal failure, and the "Liverpool experiment" lasted only four years. But in that time, the resulting multiplication of licenses and increase in drinking became notorious, and for years afterwards temperance reformers referred to Liverpool when facing people arguing for easing up on license regulations.

Such stories gave weight to arguments that the potent mix of alcohol and free market economics was ripe for abuse; thus alternatives that removed alcohol from the competitive marketplace grew in appeal. The alternatives offered various forms of what was called "disinterested management" where the profit from alcohol sales was removed from the motivation of the proprietors of liquor outlets. Disinterested management systems varied, but the main feature was that proprietors were not rewarded based upon how much money they made in sales, but rather through other aspects of the business. The most notorious form of disinterested management was introduced in Sweden and Norway in the 1860s. Called the Gothenburg System (or Scheme) after the Swedish city in which it was introduced, the arrangement gave to a trust the right to sell liquor. Shareholders received a maximum 5% annual return, and the remaining profits were used by the city to fund various public amenities like parks and libraries.[39] The Swedish system was designed to redirect customers from spirits drinking into less problematic beverages like beer. Premises were designed to de-emphasize spirits drinking, managers were rewarded for encouraging moderation, and patrons found other activities, such as eating meals, to occupy their time.

Different versions of disinterested management were taken up by various reform-minded individuals. In Britain, the Bishop of Chester and H J Craufurd co-founded the People's Refreshment House Association, based upon the same 5% profit ideal.[40] Similarly, Earl Grey created a Central Public House Trust Association in 1901. When Grey became Governor General of Canada, interested moderates sought input on how they might create something similar in that country. More fascinating was the effort of South Carolina Governor Benjamin Tillman to impose government ownership over retail liquor sales. Faced with a strong prohibitionist movement, and powerful liquor forces, Tillman sought a compromise in 1892 by introducing a state-run "dispensary" system in which a central depot bottled all booze and distributed those bottles to county dispensaries. The South Carolina Dispensary was a step beyond the trust system because the government was in charge of both wholesale and retail liquor. Although reportedly rife with corruption and even after the Supreme Court declared unconstitutional the government's practice of seizing liquor imported by individual citizens, the South Carolina dispensary lasted until 1907.[41] Nevertheless, it became, like Gothenburg and the UK Public House trust system, an example to moderates of viable alternatives to prohibition. Such solutions were appealing to many citizens who believed there should be a sweet spot between wide-open liquor selling, which caused observable problems in the community, and prohibition, which was both an affront to the ideal of liberty and, as many observers argued, simply did not work.

This challenge persisted in addiction circles, even as the scientific primacy began to edge out moralistic impressions of inebriety and inebriates. When the American Association for the Cure of Inebriates (AACI) was founded in 1870, the membership, mostly men with experience in private institution treatment, debated the origins of the condition. Although its founding documents assert that addiction was a physical weakness that was often inherited and could be treated medically, numerous members of the organization presented moralistic arguments. In 1873 Dr. Robert Harris, the attending physician at an asylum in Philadelphia, asserted that drunkenness remained a sin and a crime so any form of medical treatment needed to be accompanied by moral reform.[42] Although this perspective seems to have been the minority opinion among founding members of the AACI, that it was expressed by a medical doctor illustrates how embedded ideas of morality and blame were within addiction treatment, and many would argue those ideas persist.

The AACI was soon joined by a like-minded organization in Britain, the Society for the Study and Cure of Inebriety (1884). Both organizations changed their name, the AACI became the American Association for the Study and Cure of Inebriety in 1888, while the SSCI dropped the optimistic "and Cure" in 1887.[43] These associations provided forums for research exchange across the Anglo-American world, and the resulting research expanded discussions of the nature of habitual use of various substances. Although initially focused mostly on drink, articles in the society journals were essential reading for inebriety physicians. Indeed, whereas the AASCI's *Journal of Inebriety* remained in operation until 1914, the SSI's *Proceedings* had staying power. It became the *British Journal of Inebriety* in 1904, the *British Journal of Addiction* (1947) and *Addiction* (1993).[44]

Medical writers and observers in these journals and elsewhere gave evidence to both drys and wets in their struggle to shape the state's approach to liquor, but medicine was less equivocal when it came to drugs. Unlike the broad social concern presented by alcohol, spurred by the spectacle of the public drunk, and the tropes of the destroyed home, destitute children, and ruined life that were rife in the temperance literature, the use and habitual consumption of drugs was a much more subtle issue. Outside of the concerns over Chinese opium smoking (to which we will return later) the main voices of concern over the use of habit-forming drugs were physicians. While physicians' interest in the debates over liquor might have been personal as well as professional, drawing upon evangelical faith or ideas about the deterioration of the social fabric, their interest in the drug habit was more firmly professional in nature. Physicians were concerned about drug use for two main reasons. First, because habitual drug use often was the result of medical treatment, known as iatrogenic addiction. Second, because an individual's use

INTRODUCTION

of powerful medicines like opium (and later cocaine) was an affront to the professional acumen and authority of physicians. By the end of the century in most jurisdictions, physicians had secured some degree of legislated professional closure, meaning that others could not practice medicine unless licensed by some kind of national, state, or provincial medical licensing body. Within the scope of practice of physicians lay the ability to prescribe drugs, and often to dispense them. This authority was bolstered by pharmacy laws, which often restricted customers' access to substances like opium, cannabis, cocaine other habit-forming drugs like chloral hydrate or certain bromides. Thus personal, individual use of restricted drugs was of considerable professional concern.[45]

Although habitual use of drugs was thus easily viewed as a medical problem, what was less clear for physicians was what caused addiction, and more importantly how to treat it. Indeed, before the 1860s, as noted earlier, physicians tended not to discuss treatment. In an 1869 article in the *Canada Lancet* Dr. D. McGillivray discussed his encounter with a patient who could consume a large quantity of morphine at one time. In its reporting it had the makings of a treatment case study but it lacked any information on how to treat the patient, functioning instead as a sort of cautionary tale to physicians on the challenges of iatrogenesis.[46] The article was published, however, a mere few years before the attention to treatment of drug use took a significant turn. By the middle of the 1870s, physicians were discussing more vigorously and actively the best ways to treat drug addiction. Some of this came via the work of German physician Eduard Levinstein, whose *Die Morphiumsucht* was translated as *The Morbid Craving for Morphia*. It described the conditions under which morphine habit could be considered a disease, and offered physicians with specific, systematic approaches to treating drug addiction. It was at the sharp end of a revisioning of the role of doctors in dealing with drug use.[47]

It is improper, however, to give all the credit to one innovative German physician, however influential his work became among physicians. As the century progressed, a number of other factors affected the way that physicians looked at drug use. The first was a transformation in technology and pharmacology. The isolation of morphine, one of the main components of opium, permitted doctors to have much more precise control over dosages. Raw opium, from which many medicines (such as laudanum) were made, was a natural product and thus had varying levels of the active components, many of which were not isolated until much later in the century. Friedrich Sertürner's isolation of morphine allowed physicians to be much more precise in their dosages (notwithstanding as morphine became more available, overdoses from a misunderstanding of the difference in potencies could result).[48] Along with the pharmacological development, the significant technical innovation of the hypodermic needle provided physicians with a second important therapeutic tool. Up to this point normally physicians would administer drugs orally (although they could score the skin and administer substances subcutaneously, a process that was used, for example, in vaccination).[49] This process allowed patients a degree of control over their medication, and also meant that complications like digestion and expulsion could affect dosage potency. But with the hypodermic needle, the body was no longer able to reject the medicine, and the physician could have more control over treatment. This powerful technology was such an important part of the medical intervention that physicians repeatedly debated the advisability of leaving a needle with the patient.

These technological transformations are also emblematic of the sorts of innovations that added to physicians' concerns over addiction. What might now be called "recreational drug use" was more often referred to as non-medical, which implied that medical drug use was the only appropriate use. Earlier dalliances with what DeQuincey had called the "exquisite pleasures" of opium were now non-medical uses of a valuable drug. Doctors, thus, were more clearly able to argue that such misuse, a violation of the authority of physicians, the potency of medications, and the appropriate attention to the physical integrity of the body, had an impact well beyond the individual's personal interest. Compound this with the fact that many physicians observed drug use not in poor (who often could not afford a doctor's care) but in middle- and upper-class patients, and observations of the damage drug addiction could wreak on the body became metaphors for a danger that drug habituation could pose to the best of society. Now society itself was in danger.

Opium was the classic example of social degradation through upper class drug use, culturally familiar due to the popularity of the "opium eater" (as several articles in this collection attest), but near the end of the century, opium's danger was joined, and arguably eclipsed, by another pharmaceutical innovation: cocaine. Cocaine has several important physiological actions that made it valuable to late nineteenth-century medicine.[50] It is a powerful topical anaesthetic, so helpful in painful procedures like ocular and dental surgery. Its tonic properties meant that it was a useful stimulant, and it also explains its rapid inclusion in many proprietary medicines that purported to function as restoratives or to invigorate the system. Coca-cola was one such product. Cocaine toothpaste to numb tooth pain and cocaine in snuffs were used to reduce sinus irritation and help in hay fever. The ubiquitous advertisements to cure "Catarrh" in late nineteenth-century periodicals, addressed to snotty individuals with extensive nasal discharge owing to a swelling of the mucous membrane, were generally full of cocaine.

The therapeutic promise in the rapid uptake of cocaine had an equally rapid turn to the problems of its misuse. Those catarrh cures did not only shrink the mucous membrane and deal with snot, they also gave the user a buzz. The widespread tonic beverages are not reported to have created any kind of habit, but the pervasiveness of catarrh cures led to an awareness that perhaps this drug could also be problematic. A mere two years after cocaine was lauded in medical literature, it was being criticized. This problematization of cocaine was at least partly because, as a new drug, cocaine was not listed in many pharmacy act poison schedules. Moreover, cocaine's tonic properties had made it useful in treating inebriety. Addicts, especially to opium, needed medical support while they weathered the storm of withdrawal, and a handy stimulant like a cocaine tonic did the job nicely. Unfortunately, it also put cocaine in the hands of an already susceptible patient group, and the opium habit could be replaced, or joined, by the cocaine habit.[51]

Although professional groups were concerned about addiction among their ranks, the broader cultural fear was about addiction among the general population. Even though many people in the west might have experienced addiction among their friends and families, recreational consumption of opiates and cocaine in pursuit of DeQuincey's "exquisite pleasure" was becoming problematic. DeQuincey was unapologetic that he was also seeking pleasure, but by the end of the century pleasure seeking seemed to need restraint. The Victorian rational recreation movement was focused on urging people, especially the urban working class with newly won free time, to channel their energy into what might be called functional pursuits, physical, mental, and moral self-improvement rather than simple pleasure seeking.[52] Bacchanalia, whether through alcohol or drugs, was simply not appropriate. Therefore, although a middle- or upper-class person addicted to opium through medical use, or drawn to cocaine to improve performance and focus in high-stress brainwork might be forgiven for their deviance, pleasure seekers needed to be curtailed. And even though popular culture contained stories of pleasure-seeking elites like Dorian Gray, whose friend Lord Henry Wotton smoked an opium-laced cigarette (a sign of effete upper class indulgence) but Gray himself ended up indulging in the carnal pleasures and morality traps of East London's opium dens, the threat to society was from the fear of a counter-culture of drug users infecting and degrading the general population. David Courtwright's pivotal calculation that by the beginning of the twentieth century the demographics of opiate addicts in the United States was changing to include a more recreational, subculture deviant population has captured historians' imagination about how Gilded Age Americans perceived the threat of drug use.[53] Nevertheless, even without those calculations, and even if the majority of drug users were still middle-class women with an iatrogenic monkey on their backs, the image of recreational use had firmly shifted to one of condemnation of indulgence, and concern about the future of the race, however that race may be construed.

These fears intersected with changed perceptions about the appropriate role of government to interfere in the lives of its citizens. By the end of the nineteenth century a number of changes had shifted public perception of the responsibility of government in regulating behaviour with respect to drug and alcohol use. Around the world the temperance movement secured a variety of legislative initiatives to address drunkenness, which included laws granting municipalities the right to prohibit liquor (called variously local option laws or permissive bills) to outright prohibition. These laws were not without controversy. In liberal democracies, government action that interfered with citizens' freedoms were anathema. Opponents of prohibition normally expressed their ideas in terms of freedom, often combined with the observation that prohibition did not work. Yet drys emphasized the responsibility of government to protect the population from threats, and advocates of local option viewed such laws as allowing municipalities to act on local imperatives for self protection.

INTRODUCTION

Such actions expanded into broader advocacy to prohibit liquor, and less resistance to the role of government in constraining people's lives.

Other events also built a trust in government laws to protect the people. Laws that regulated the profession of pharmacy were based upon a general concern that unfettered access to certain medicines that could also be misused as poisons (such as strychnine, arsenic and opium) established a norm by which governments could legitimately impose restrictions on some forms of trade. Opponents to pharmacy laws saw them as giving a trade monopoly to one subset of vendors (druggists) to the detriment of others, and the detriment of laissez-faire principles.[54] Similar complaints had been launched against other professionalization efforts, but whereas professions such as physicians were selling their skill, pharmacists were selling products. The list of poisons restricted by pharmacy acts expanded, and the understanding of "dangerous" drugs expanded from substances that could kill to substances that could injure. And injury could include forming habits. Such developments adjusted the way people viewed the place of government interference in individual freedom. Former laissez-faire arguments crumbled in the face of idealized arguments about public safety. Broader discussion about the impact of liquor and drugs on the future of the nation also fuelled impetus for change.

Indeed, the very fact that many people who were habitually using drugs were not the dregs of society, but rather some of society's elites, caused additional reasons for worry. Restrictions on access to these drugs might help, but other forms of the drug (especially in proprietary preparations) were easily available. This was the era of the eugenics movement, where activities to improve the physical, moral and intellectual abilities of the "race" were rooted in deep and complex scientific arguments.[55] Drug and alcohol use had been related to ideas of "degeneracy" for decades, and such degeneracy, especially when framed medically, fed into broader concerns about the improvement, or at least the protection of the nation. Added to this discourse of national improvement were tropes about the users of drugs. Whereas alcohol was an Anglo-Saxon intoxicant, opium was seen as Asian, cocaine was South American, and cannabis, in the form of marijuana (a Spanish translation of Mary Jane), was also associated with Hispanics, despite its long history in Asia and Europe.[56] Moreover, cocaine became associated with African Americans. Some evidence exists that people working in hard field labour were taking cocaine, just as Peruvians chewed coca leaves, to provide them with an energy boost in the face of gruelling physical conditions. Such conditions, imposed by white landowners on African American workers, ironically resulted in white people seeing African cocaine use as yet another example of black demoralization, and a threat to white people.[57] Concerned white observers were just as alarmed about the recreational use of opium and investigations of opium dens, where the drug was seen as being consumed exclusively for pleasure, returned to the image of the vulnerable young white person being debased by the predatory Chinese men. Notwithstanding evidence to the contrary, for example presented during visits to opium dens by officials such as the commissioners on the

INTRODUCTION

Canadian Royal Commission on Chinese Immigration (1884), the image of predatory outsiders captured the imagination and fears of westerners. These images joined well-established ideas about iatrogenic drug addiction among elite families to increase an appetite for legislative change.

By the end of the nineteenth century, governments and reformers had become increasingly convinced that not only was the recreational use of drugs a growing problem, but that the only way to address it fully was through international action. Although the SSOT and likeminded organizations had lobbied for an end to the opium trade for much of the century, it was not until the United States obtained the Philippines as a result of the Spanish-American War that persistent diplomatic efforts to curtail the opium trade began. A series of international meetings on the opium traffic created a momentum towards reducing the cultivation and movement of opium. It also included discussion on the trade of other drugs and reinforced the belief that the drug trade needed to be addressed both through domestic laws and international agreements. This idea can be seen in the decision, proposed by the United States and supported by Great Britain, that the Treaty of Versailles recognized the importance of the Hague Opium Convention. Ratification of Versailles would ratify Hague, thereby requiring treaty nations to pass anti-drug legislation.[58] In a little over a century, the way drugs were discussed, from an open market to a highly constrained and internationally sanctioned "traffic" was a fundamental transformation, indeed. The end of the war also saw prohibition and new ways of dealing with the liquor trade, but that is beyond the scope of this collection.

About this collection

This collection assembles some of the key documents in the history of alcohol and drugs in the English-speaking world, and combines with them often obscure documents that represent how these broad ideas manifest themselves in different contexts. Throughout the English-speaking world people presented a variety of views of drugs and alcohol, both their use and habitual consumption, and these are useful both for comparative or reiterative purposes. Discussions of opium use among Chinese gold miners in southern Africa beside Australian discussions of Chinese and a Canadian Royal Commission on Chinese immigration can illustrate and draw out common or disparate themes. Since this collection is intended for the use of student researchers and established scholars alike, such combinations can inspire new and valuable discussions. I have intentionally attempted to find material that came from outside of Britain and the United States, although of course many of the key discussions were initiated there. Thus, we have stories and examples from Canada, Australia and South Africa that provide contrast to and sometimes reinforcement of ideas in some of the more well-known texts.

Given the vast amount of material that was published on drugs and alcohol in the long nineteenth century, there are of course many omissions. For example, Volume II provides a range of medical articles on the topics, but there would be no way to provide all of the articles discussing the topic without making my editors' heads explode and also wading through considerable redundancy. As a result, I have chosen works that represent a variety, but sometimes have included several works that emphasize a theme to show the convergence of ideas. Some articles allude to issues that are discussed specifically in other articles, for example articles on morphine addiction that mention the problem of the hypodermic needle, or two articles that examine Chicago saloons. I will leave it to the reader to interpret the differences and similarities, because we all impose our own understanding upon texts.

When editing some of the long documents my intentions were generally to capture the way certain ideas were presented, while removing redundancy. Many of these documents may be found in digital collections, so, for example, often I have included the introductions to large works that draw out the main arguments of a book and leave it to the readers to pursue that theme if they choose. At other times I have tried to show a general narrative and how it follows similar structures to others. This was especially my intent with the items that were biographies or autobiographies of drug users. The themes of decline and redemption were so stark, and similar, but within such different contexts over a century, that I considered presenting those themes as a useful exercise in viewing the consistency and difference in the way drug use was viewed and presented over the century. In other cases I have removed tables, charts or long discussions that seemed esoteric and distracting from general themes. These editorial decisions are, however, but one interpretation of the stories being told, and I invite readers to make their own interpretation by going beyond the work provided here. It is a curated selection of notable and evocative text; it is meant to be authoritative, but not definitive.

Notes

1 James Nicholls, *Politics of Alcohol: A History of the Drink Question in England* (Manchester: University of Manchester Press, 2009), pp. 46–47.

2 Ibid., pp. 47–48.

3 Roy Porter, "The Drinking Man's Disease: The 'Pre-History' of Alcoholism in Georgian Britain" *British Journal of Addiction* 80 (1985): 385–396; Jessica Warner, "'Resolv'd to Drink No More': Addiction as a Preindustrial Construct" *Journal of Studies on Alcoholism* 55 (November 1994): 685–690; Peter Ferentzy, "From Sin to Disease: Differences and Similarities between Past and Current Conceptions of Chronic Drunkenness" *Contemporary Drug Problems* 28 (Fall 2001): 363–390; James Nicholls, "Vinum Britannicum: The 'Drink Question' in Early Modern England" *Social History of Alcohol and Drugs: An Interdisciplinary Journal* 22 (Spring 2008): 6–25.

4 Harry G. Levine, "The Discovery of Addiction: Changing Conceptions of Habitual Drunkenness in America" *Journal of Studies on Alcohol* 15 (1978): 493–506.

5 On revivals in the US, see William G. McLoughlan, *Revivals, Awakenings and Reform* (Chicago: University of Chicago Press, 1978); Nathan O. Hatch, *The Democratization of American Christianity* (New Haven: Yale University Press, 1989); Jon Butler, *Awash in a Sea of Faith: Christianizing the American People* (Cambridge, MA: Harvard University Press, 1992).

INTRODUCTION

6 James Nicholls, *Politics of Alcohol*, pp. 64–65.

7 Ibid., pp. 69–70.

8 Patrick Dillon, *Gin: The Much-Lamented Death of Madam Geneva* (Boston: Justin Charles & Co, 2002); Jessica Warner, *Craze: Gin and Debauchery in an Age of Reason* (New York: Basic Books, 2002).

9 Henry E. Sigerist, "Laudanum in the Works of Paracelsus" *Bulletin of the History of Medicine* 9 (1941): 530–544; "Laudanum, Sydenham's" in J. Worth Estes, *Dictionary of Protopharmacology: Therapeutic Practices, 1700–1850* (Canton, MA: Science History Publications, 1990), p. 113.

10 Virginia Berridge, *Opium and the People: Opiate Use and Drug Control Policy in Nineteenth and Early Twentieth Century England* (London and New York: Free Association Books, 1999), pp. 62–72; Dan Malleck, *When Good Drugs Go Bad: Opium, Medicine and the Origins of Canada's Drug Laws* (Vancouver: UBC Press, 2015).

11 Thomas DeQuincey, *Confessions of an English Opium Eater* Second Ed (London: Taylor and Hessey, Fleet St., 1823), p. 15.

12 Ibid., pp. 14–15.

13 John Leigh, *An Experimental Inquiry into the Properties of Opium and Its Effects on Living Subjects* (Edinburgh: Charles Elliott, 1785); Hastings Handy, *An Inaugural Dissertation on Opium* (Philadelphia: T Lang, 1791); Valentine Seaman, *Inaugural Dissertation on Opium* (Philadelphia: Johnstone and Justice, 1792); John Laws, *An Inaugural Dissertation on the Rational of the Operation of Opium: On the Animal Economy with Observations on Its Use in Disease* (Wilmington, DE: W C Smyth, 1797).

14 Seaman, *On Opium*, p. 21.

15 Ibid., p. 22.

16 Laws, *Inaugural Dissertation*, p. 12.

17 See Timothy Alborn, *Regulated Lives: Life Insurance and British Society, 1800–1914* (Toronto: University of Toronto Press, 2009).

18 Earl of Mar case is well documented. See Virginia Berridge, "Opium Eating and Life Insurance" *British Journal of Addiction* 72 (1977): 371–377.

19 Dan Malleck, "Between Risk and Medicine: Life Insurance, Authority, and the Medical Perception of the Opium Habit in the Nineteenth Century" presented at "Under Control? Alcohol and Drug Regulation, Past and Present" conference, London School of Hygiene and Tropical Medicine, 23 June 2013.

20 The opium war has been well discussed and researched. See David Edward Owen, *British Opium Policy in China and India* (Cambridge: Yale University Press, 1934); David Anthony Bello, *Opium and the Limits of Empire: Drug Prohibition in the Chinese Interior, 1729–1850* (Cambridge: Harvard University Press, 2005); Harry G. Gelber, *Opium, Soldiers and Evangelicals: Britain's 1840–42 War with China, and Its Aftermath* (Basingstoke, UK: Palgrave Macmillan, 2004); Julia Lovell, *The Opium War: Drugs, Dreams and the Making of China* (London: Picador, 2011).

21 George Marsden, *Understanding Fundamentalism and Evangelicalism* (Grand Rapids, MI: Wm B Eerdmans, 1991).

22 The origins of the term "teetotalism" are debated. The apocryphal roots of the origins of the term include this author's favourite, that people would declare themselves a "capital-T-total abstainer." Other stories include it originating from an individual in Livesey's organization who had a mild stutter and would say he was a "t-t-total abstainer."

23 As reported in *Joseph Livesey: The Story of His Life 1794–1884*, James Weston, ed. (London: S W Partridge & Co, 1884), pp. 49–50.

24 Harrison discusses Livesey throughout Brian Harrison, *Drink and the Victorians: The Temperance Question in England, 1815–1872* (London: Faber and Faber, 1971). See also Brian Harrison, "Livesey, Joseph" *Oxford Dictionary of National Biography*, https://doi.org/10.1093/ref:odnb/16796

INTRODUCTION

25 Harrison, "Livesy, Joseph," *Oxford Dictionary of National Biography*.

26 Rush, "Moral and Physical Thermometer" *Inquiry*, np.

27 Jack S. Blocker, Jr., *American Temperance Movements: Cycles of Reform* (Boston: Twayne Press, 1987); Brian Harrison, *Drink and the Victorians: Women, Evangelism, and Temperance in Nineteenth-Century America* (Middletown, CT: Wesleyan University Press, 1981).

28 Ruth Bordin, *Women and Temperance: The Quest for Power and Liberty, 1873–1900* (Philadelphia: Temple University Press, 1981); Blocker, *American Temperance* Movements; Barbara Epstein, *The Politics of Domesticity: Women, Evangelism, and Temperance in Nineteenth-Century America* (Lebanon, NH: University Press of New England, 1981); Carol Mattingly, *Well Tempered Women: Nineteenth Century Temperance Rhetoric* (Carbondale, IL: Southern Illinois University Press, 1998); Jack S Blocker, Jr., *Give to the Winds Thy Fears: The Women's Temperance Crusade, 1873–1874* (Westport, CT and London, England: Greenwood Press, 1985); Sharon Anne Cook, *Through Sunshine and Shadow: The Woman's Christian Temperance Union, Evangelicalism, and Reform in Ontario, 1874–1930* (Montreal and Kingston: McGill-Queen's University Press, 1995).

29 Ian Tyrrell, *Women's World Women's Empire: The Woman's Christian Temperance Union in International Perspective, 1880–1930* (Chapel Hill, NC and London: University of North Carolina Press, 1991).

30 Elizabeth Malcolm, "Mathew, Father Theobald (1790–1856)" in Jack S. Blocker, David M. Fahey, and Ian R. Tyrrell, eds. *Alcohol and Temperance in Modern History: An International Encyclopedia* (Santa Barbara, CA: ABC-Clio Press, 2003) II:402–404; Elizabeth Malcolm, *Ireland Sober, Ireland Free: Drink and Temperance in Nineteenth-Century Ireland* (Syracuse, NY: Syracuse University Press, 1986).

31 Jan Noel, *Canada Dry: Temperance Crusades before Confederation* (Toronto: University of Toronto Press, 1995), pp. 159–177; Yves Roby, "Chiniquy, Charles" in *Dictionary of Canadian Biography*, vol. 12 (University of Toronto/Université Laval, 2003), www.biographi.ca/en/bio/chiniquy_charles_12E.html.

32 Noel, *Canada Dry*; Roby, "Chiniquy, Charles."

33 See Dan Malleck, "Regulation and Prohibition" in Deborah Toner (ed.), *A Cultural History of Alcohol in the Age of Industry, Empire and War, 1850–1950* (Bloomsbury Academic Press, forthcoming).

34 Nicholls, *Politics of Alcohol*, p. 80.

35 Ibid. quote pp. 80, 91.

36 Ibid., pp. 92–93.

37 Ibid., p. 122.

38 David Beckingham, *The Licensed City: Regulating Drink in Liverpool 1830–1920* (Liverpool: Liverpool University Press, 2017), p. 63.

39 David W. Gutzke, "Gentrifying the British Public House, 1896–1914" *International Labor and Working Class History* No. 45, Drinking and the Working Class (Spring 1994): 29–43.

40 Ibid., p. 31.

41 James Hill Welborn, III, "Dispensing the Progressive State: Benjamin Tillman's South Carolina State Dispensary" *Social History of Alcohol and Drugs* 27 (Winter 2013): 82–101; Joe L. Coker, *Liquor in the Land of the Lost Cause: Southern White Evangelicals and the Prohibition Movement* (Lexington: University of Kentucky Press, 2007).

42 Malleck, "American Association for the Study and Cure of Inebriety" Blocker et al. *Alcohol and Temperance in Modern History* I: 38–39.

43 Virginia Berridge, "Society for the Study of Addiction, 1884–1988" special issue of *British Journal of Addiction* 85 (1990); Arnold Jaffe, "Reform in American Medical Science: The Inebriety Movement and the Origins of the Psychological Disease Theory of Addiction, 1870–1920" *British Journal of Addiction* 73 (1978): 139–147.

44 Berridge, "Society for the Study of Addiction"; Malleck, "Society for the Study of Addiction" Blocker et al. *Alcohol and Temperance in Modern History* II: 564–565.

INTRODUCTION

45 Berridge, *Opium and the People*; Malleck, *When Good Drugs Go Bad*; Courtwright, *Dark Paradise Dark Paradise: A History of Opiate Addiction in America* (Cambridge, MA: Harvard University Press, 1982), pp. 42–55; H. Wayne Morgan, *Drugs in America: A Social History, 1800–1980* (Syracuse, NY: Syracuse University Press, 1981), pp. 40–43.

46 See Malleck, *When Good Drugs Go Bad*, pp. 115–116.

47 Berridge, *Opium and the People*, pp. 150–155.

48 A good illustration is in the iatrogenic deaths of John Blackie and Job Broom as told in Jacalyn Duffin, "'In View of the Body of Job Broom': A Glimpse of the Medical Knowledge and Practice of John Rolph" *Canadian Bulletin of Medical History/Bulletin canadien d'histoire de la médecine* 7 (1990): 9–30 and in Malleck, *When Good Drugs Go Bad*, pp. 43–45.

49 Courtwright, *Dark Paradise*, pp. 46–50; Morgan, *Drug in America*, pp. 24–28.

50 Joseph Spillaine, *Cocaine: From Medical Marvel to Modern Menace in the United States, 1884–1920* (Baltimore: Johns Hopkins University Press, 2000).

51 Musto, *American Disease*, pp. 6–8; Berridge, *Opium and the People*, pp. 218–224; Malleck, *When Good Drugs Go Bad*, pp. 189–193.

52 Peter Bailey, *Leisure and Class in Victorian England: Rational Recreation and the Contest for Control, 1830–1885* (London: Methuen, 1978).

53 Courtwright, Chapter 5 "Transformation of the Opium Addict" *Dark Paradise*, 110–144; For perspective on how attitudes were changing even before demographics, see Malleck, *When Good Drugs Go Bad*, pp. 219–220.

54 Malleck, *When Good Drugs Go Bad*, pp. 54–55, 70–72.

55 On Eugenics, Daniel J. Kevles, *In the Name of Eugenics: Genetics and the Uses of Human Heredity* (New York: Knopf, 1985); Paul A. Lombardo, ed., *A Century of Eugenics in America: From the Indiana Experiment to the Human Genome Era* (Bloomington and Indianapolis: Indiana University Press, 2011); Marius Turda, *Modernism and Eugenics* (Basingstoke, UK: Palgrave MacMillan, 2010); Erika Dyck, *Facing Eugenics: Reproduction, Sterilization, and the Politics of Choice* (Toronto: University of Toronto Press, 2013).

56 See Isaac Campos, *Home Grown: Marijuana and the Origins of Mexico's War on Drugs* (Chapel Hill: University of North Carolina Press, 2012).

57 On the racial construction of African American cocaine use, see Hickman, *Secret Leprosy of Modern Days*, pp. 72–80.

58 Musto, *American Disease*, pp. 50–53; Berridge, *Opium and the People*, pp. 241–245; William B. McAllister, *Drug Diplomacy in the Twentieth Century: An International History* (London and New York: Routledge, 2000), pp. 28–37.

Volume I

DRUNKS, FIENDS AND THE ROOTS OF CONCERN

INTRODUCTION TO VOLUME I
Drunks and fiends; users and observers

The documents in this volume examine the way consumption of drugs and alcohol were represented across the nineteenth century. New drugs, pharmacological innovation and methods of ingestion altered the ability for people to get high. At the same time, and behind the scenes, new technology in distilling and brewing made alcohol cheaper and more interesting. The nineteenth century saw the Coffey still permit whiskey makers to distill a lighter spirit, blending this lighter (and cheaper) whisky to more challenging tipples to make it more palatable for a broader audience. It saw the hydrometer permit more precise measurements of alcohol content (and also permit more precise excise taxation).[1] New malting techniques enabled brewers to diversify their brews, and pale ales travelled literally around the world.[2] Colonization enabled Europeans to exploit new populations and the products of different ecosystems, while creating new markets in, or forcing new markets on, the colonized population. Louis Pasteur's identification of yeast as the key factor in fermentation and development of pasteurization to reduce spoilage improved viticulture and brewing.

When historians examine drugs and alcohol in the nineteenth century, the tendency has been to look at these substances in their problematic forms. The temperance movement was a massive global network of citizens concerned about the dangers society faced from drunkenness and what they saw as a predatory liquor trade. It had roots in evangelical Protestantism and well-meaning liberal concerns for the plight of the poor. The opium trade in Asia, and especially the forceful imposition of opium on China despite its government's concerted attempts to address the overuse of opium among its population, was seen by many like-minded reformers as a horrible injustice, even as they used the trade routes and extraterritoriality concessions wrested from the Chinese government to expand their evangelical mission.[3] All of this activity generated a tremendous amount of literature: pamphlets, magazine, reports, meeting minutes and detailed accounts of meetings from sympathetic newspapers. Yet opium was a valuable medicine— some would argue the most valuable medicine—in the western pharmacopoeia, having effects on the human body that could deal with many of the symptoms of modern life. This utility and the gradual expansion of medical power meant that many people had taken opium, and some, whether through the exigencies of chronic pain or due to the distinct pleasurable effects of the drug, became habitual users.

Only in the past few decades, which is a short time for historians, has the academic study of attempts to restrict been met with research on the consumption of drugs and alcohol from a less problem-based focus. Such an approach is difficult, however, because much of the documentary evidence has come through the material generated by the "antis" who framed drugs and alcohol consumption as a problem, stripped from any potential benefits. Indeed, except for the generation of revenue, governments tend not to concern themselves with a product unless it becomes dangerous or perceived as such. Moreover, social movements rarely arise as a means of celebrating a well-appreciated product.[4] Thus when examining the use of drugs and alcohol in history, we need often to read between the lines.

There have been some valuable attempts to do exactly this. Canadian historian of working class culture, Craig Heron, investigated the place of liquor in the lives of the people from early European settlement to the end of the twentieth century, placing liquor, its consumption and the places where people met to enjoy drinks together into a cultural context that did not ignore the dangers of over-drinking, but did not see the product as an unmitigated problem.[5] Scottish historian Thora Hands's *Drinking in Victorian and Edwardian Britain* has addressed the historical focus on temperance by reconsidering the classic British temperance history, Brian Harrison's *Drink and the Victorians*. Her work (based on a thesis entitled "Re-Framing Drink and the Victorians") was not a critique of Harrison's work but rather a history of drink*ing* rather than the oft problematized "drink" and seeing where drink fit in the lives of Victorians.[6] It is easier to find work on the positive aspects of drink from scholars of literature, whose work places drink within the context of stories being told.[7] For example, Steven Earnshaw's work on "the existential drinker" considers the idea of the drinker, including unrepentant drinkers such as "Mary Thompson." Thompson's story told to the Select Committee on Habitual Drunkards befuddled the committee members, who could not figure out why an habitual seemed to choose to be one, and the story was "a unique individualist bump in that it cannot be ironed flat."[8] Similarly, and driven by contemporary political shifts, histories of cannabis have attempted to balance the drug's suppression against the efforts to extoll its virtues.[9]

One subfield of drink history in which problematization of drinking has not been a central feature is in the studies of drinking spaces. Ironically, the pub, tavern, and saloon were the main villains to nineteenth-century temperance reformers, and yet Perry Duis and Madelon Powers wrote expansive studies of the turn-of-the-twentieth-century saloon in the United States; Julia Roberts placed the rural tavern in nineteenth-century Upper Canada; and historians both academic and popular, including Paul Jennings, Anthony Cooke and Pete Brown have examined the British pub.[10] Australia has seen a number of important books on the pub, most especially on women's work in pubs offering a contrast to the normal gendered perception of the drinking space by seeing it as a contested place of employment and livelihood for women.[11] Historians of other countries and other periods also have explored the drinking space as a place of recreation, socialization, and even revolution. Scott Haine's work on the Parisian Café examines the place of the drinking space, (cafes were not merely for coffee) as a site of intellectual exchange and connection.[12] Works on the early modern tavern are similarly robust, such as found in the *World of the Tavern* essay collection.[13] Apart from the aforementioned works on cannabis, there is little history on drug cultures that does not examine the practice from the perspective of drug taking as problematic.

The documents in this volume present a variety of ways that drugs and alcohol were discussed in the nineteenth century. Rather than present positive accounts of use, which would be a small collection indeed, this material provides a range of perceptions of drug and alcohol consumption in the nineteenth century. It begins with some classic discussions of drugs and includes studies of the variety of drugs and the different contexts in which they were consumed. Since the nineteenth century was an era of colonialization and also of scientific exploration (often these activities went hand in hand), numerous writers attempted to process the information they were collecting about different substances. Thomas DeQuincey's *Confessions of an English Opium Eater* set the field of engagement for this type of literature, and the "opium eater" trope reappears in many forms. Indeed, it became so popular that other books or articles chronicling drug use later in the century often used the "opium eater" or at least the "eater" language, notwithstanding the fact that most of the time the mode of ingestion was not, in fact, eating. DeQuincey drank laudanum, a mixture of brandy and opium. Although DeQuincey's habit was iatrogenic, based upon medical prescription, laudanum was also consumed recreationally. It was linked to such romantic authors as Samuel Taylor Coleridge and Lord Byron, and the association was so well known that medical textbooks would refer to the experiences of Coleridge and DeQuincey rather than attempt to provide descriptions of the opium habit from medical observation.[14] H. G. Cole's *Confessions of an American Opium Eater*, written half a century later, could not avoid framing it as a liberation narrative ("from bondage to freedom") but still retained some of the prurient elements that captured the imagination of moralists and sensualists alike.

At the same time, other drugs were gaining attention. William O'Shaughnessy examines the history and common uses of cannabis extracts, connects them to potential therapeutic value and then, in a method typical of the period, describes his own personal consumption experiments.[15] F. H. Ludlow's classic *The Hasheesh Eater* made no pretense of being scientific, encouraging indulgence and self-exploration.[16] *Blackwood's Edinburgh Magazine*, a somewhat conservative general interest periodical, used the publication of a relatively dry medical textbook, Jonathan Pereira's *Elements of Materia Medical and Therapeutic,* as a way of indulging in an extensive discussion of a variety of drugs. The author intentionally drew upon the stories in DeQuincey's *Confessions* which he called "as fresh and new as ever" as a framework for discussing the "natural wants" of man. Specifically, he sees three orders of wants: food for sustenance, liquor to help "assuage" his cares, and narcotics so that "his enjoyments, intellectual and animal are multiplied and for the time exalted."[17] Even Victor Robinsons's *Essay on Hasheesh*, published in the beginning of the twentieth century when the negative ideas of inebriation and habituation had established themselves within the dominant discourse around drug and alcohol consumption in the west, is a strangely adulatory description of the fantastic and even hilarious experiences of hasheesh users. The descriptions seem more suited to the writings of romantic authors a century earlier. Apart from O'Shaughnessy warning readers of the potential delirium from "hemp inebriation" these accounts did not condemn this behaviour.

The examinations of cannabis and its various extracts vary considerably from the perception of opium. After the middle of the century the opium habit was becoming a problem, most notably observed by physicians. In his extensive *Opium and the Opium Appetite*, American physician Alonzo Calkins condemned the lure of opium presented through the florid works of romantic authors. Calkins, who was a member of a prominent and deeply religious New England family, was especially concerned about how the temptation of opium would reduce individuals to a subhuman state. He did not mince words:

> Let the man deliberately yield himself up to the mastery of a depraved appetite, the soul must perforce become contaminated from the festering virus, the moral sense will be perverted, the finer sensibilities and nobler aspirations will decline and die out until existence itself seems shrunken to the diminutive proportions of a troglodyte semi-creation.[18]

Similar discussions expanded the concern, many presenting images of individuals in this "troglodyte" state.

In the early part of the nineteenth century, opium and cannabis retained an exotic fascination, with the sorts of experimentation designed to determine their usefulness and dangers; less was the case with alcohol, a domestic, and familiar, intoxicant. The work of Benjamin Rush and Thomas Trotter, as discussed earlier, both viewed drink and drunkenness as causing problems. Rush was unrelenting in his criticism, while Trotter sought to modulate the invectives of "the priesthood . . . and the moralists," who have "declaimed against it as a vice degrading to our nature" by offering objective medical evidence of the problems of overdrinking.[19] Yet medical examinations did not always result in unfettered criticism of drunkenness. In his *Anatomy of Drunkenness* Scottish physician Robert MacNish considered the immediate effects of drink, as well as other substances, and classified drunkards in order to enact a more sophisticated understanding of the condition. He attempted to classify drunkards into six types, based upon humoral physiology (sanguineous, melancholy, choleric and phlegmatic) and innovations based upon observation (surly and nervous). MacNish also described variations of drunkenness based upon the type of "inebriating agent" distinguishing opium, tobacco and other non-alcohols from alcoholic beverages, but also observing the different types of drunkenness from different types of beverages: wine, spirits and malt liquors. Yet his is not entirely critical, and he recognizes with more sympathy the pleasures of drink when, prior to drunkenness "the soul is commencing to expand its wings and rise from earth"—doubtless an eloquent description of many student experiences with drink.[20]

The works of Rush, Trotter and MacNish were central to the problematized view of alcohol, but a parallel discourse did exist. Erasmus Darwin's *Zoonomia* included a discussion of drunkenness as a natural and generally unproblematic state. Although he did not shy away from discussing the potential dangers of drunkenness to physical health, this was for Darwin a minor issue. American military surgeon Edward Cutbush was similarly less critical of drink than his compatriot Rush. Although he preferred that soldiers drink only water, he admitted they rarely chose that beverage exclusively and he therefore felt it was important to discuss the various types of alcoholic drinks and their physiological value. Apart from strong spirits, Cutbush finds healthfulness in most alcoholic beverages, mirroring the sentiments of Rush's moral thermometer. Noted British physician Francis Anstie's discussion of wine takes the discussion of the general healthfulness of that beverage for the broader population, introducing the eponymous Anstie's Limit of how much alcohol can be consumed without problem: 1.5 ounces of pure spirit, in case you're counting.

Perhaps alcohol was too common a drink of the common man, or too familiar to western writers, but few spent much time lauding their drunken state. Much more frequent were writers lamenting the drunkenness of themselves and their peers, such as is found in Whitman's *Franklin Evans, or the inebriate* and Jack London's *John Barleycorn*. Other authors also presented drunkenness in a pathologized form, subtly coded for their readers. For example, George Sands included a minor character in *Adam Bede* who, several scholars have argued, bore a behavioural likeness to Sands' own mother, Christiana Evans.[21] More blatantly, Anne Brontë's *Tenant of Wildfell Hall* includes a character that Pam Lock argues represents the author's own brother Branwell, and the book is part of a broader discussion of drunkenness in Victorian literature; Anne's sister Emily presented a dangerous drunkenness in *Wuthering Heights*.[22] Similar representations of drink and drunkenness were replete throughout the nineteenth-century literature, although not always representing real people.

Alcohol consumption in the public space was often a major irritant and motivator for temperance reformers (as will be discussed in more detail in Volume III), but many other observers examined public spaces of both drink and drug consumption in a variety of ways. The pub or tavern as a space of meeting and relaxation was a common trope in British writing, where the ubiquity of the pub doubtless, combined, with many authors' own personal experiences, modulated the often shrill commentary of temperance reformers who saw their job as to destroy that persistent social institution. Renowned author and social commentator Charles Dickens had tremendous sympathy for the conviviality of a bourgeois tavern, and often wrote of a homey and comfortable environment. Later in the century, sociological and anthropological studies such as those of E. C.

Moore and Royal Melendy sought to understand the perception and use of the saloon. Moore and Melendy examined the saloons of Chicago. Although Moore concludes with typical progressive scoffing at the people who find the saloon an important part of their lives, he admits to his readers that these spaces were valued, even if not ideal. Melendy, in contrast, was writing as part of the investigations of the Committee of Fifty, a group of businessmen and liquor interests who sought to present an alternative to temperance histrionics with serious research. His work argues that the negative images of the saloon were merely the exaggerations and myopic perceptions of zealous temperance advocates. The conclusion of the first part of his examination comments on the versatility of the social space of the saloon, even as it remains a "cause of genuine consternation among Christian people."[23] That both of these accounts were published three years apart in the same academic journal illustrates how contentious these spaces were.

Less debatable as a problem was the opium den. It had a place deep in the popular imagination, and many stories from renowned authors included the opium den as a place of degradation. Dickens's Edwin Drood, Wilde's Dorian Gray, and some criminals pursued by Doyle's Sherlock Holmes frequented such places (and of course when his mind wasn't stimulated by a case Holmes was himself a casual cocaine user).[24] Notwithstanding these images of the opium den, the public continued to consume it. Late nineteenth-century yellow journalists embarked on urban adventures to explore the netherworlds of the opium den, cranking out purple prose and reinforcing the discourses of Chinese decadence and the threat of moral decay. Such images may explain why, when Canada's Royal Commission on Chinese Immigration spoke to a white woman in an opium den in Victoria, BC, they were shocked to hear her argue that she had never experienced "one act of rudeness from a Chinaman. . . . In that respect they are far superior to white men."[25] Despite this and other evidence that argued the Chinese workers were not morally degrading to residents of the west coast, such images of Chinese opium dens persisted in the popular imagination, and in policy.

The complex relationship individuals and societies have had with intoxication is difficult to underscore. These selections demonstrate some of the key arguments and perspectives in the historical record of drugs and alcohol during the nineteenth century. Alcohol, ubiquitous in western society and familiar even to those who did not indulge, could attract considerable vilification. It may have been a case that familiarity bred contempt, but more likely that the physical effects of alcohol, the cheapness of the product, the technical innovations that opened-up transportation networks and simultaneously reduced costs, made drink and drunkenness too familiar to individuals. Its familiarity meant that, since it was not so exotic, curious writers and adventurous investigators tended not to spend much time deeply examining their local pub. The same could not be said for opium and other drugs like hasheesh. Opium was a familiar medicine and could be used as an intoxicant; its association with fantastic mental journeys and with the exotic danger of the opium den rendered it a much more appealing topic for investigation. Nevertheless, this unfamiliarity meant that negative tropes and

INTRODUCTION TO VOLUME 1

ideas could persist. As we will see in Volume III, the place of alcohol was debated even as drunkenness was nearly universally condemned, and nobody credible was arguing that the opium habit was worth defending.

Headnotes for Volume I

The drug habit and its confessionals

1   DeQuincey, Thomas, *Confessions of an English Opium Eater* Second Ed (London: Taylor and Hessey, Fleet St., 1823): 156–73
2   Colton, Walter, "Effects of Opium." *Knickerbocker*, 7 (1836): 421–23
3   Blair, William, "An Opium-Eater in America." *Knickerbocker*, 20 (1842): 47–57
4   Sigma, "Opium Habit," *Lippincott's Magazine* 1 (1868): 404–9
5   Cole, H. G., *Confessions of an American Opium Eater: From Bondage to Freedom* (Boston: James H. Earle, 1895): 5–7, 8–9, 27–32, 47–50, 107–119.
6   Calkins, A. Ch IX "Opium-Literature in the Reflex View" in *Opium and the Opium Appetite* (Philadelphia: J Lippincott, 1871): 88–98

Throughout the nineteenth century, numerous writers told of their drug habit and attempts to break it. They drew upon the trope of "opium eater" made popular by Thomas DeQuincey (1785–1859). First published anonymously in *London Magazine* (1821) DeQuincey's reflection on his experience becoming habituated to, and then attempting to break the addiction, is a classic in the history of drug use.[26] One of the criticisms of DeQuincey's work was that, rather than discouraging opium consumption, his vivid descriptions of the hallucinations encouraged people to try it.[27] Whether this was actually the case, DeQuincey, with the eye for detail and talent of a romantic author, definitely described some compelling dreams. The selection of *Confessions* included in this collection provides examples of those dreams, underscoring how a habit considered so problematic could also be remarkably appealing.

We see the allure in subsequent writings in this section. Walter Colton, an American navy chaplain was inspired enough by DeQuincey's writings to investigate opium while in Constantinople. His "Effects of Opium" are notable for the generally positive assessment of opium's intoxicating effects, and his suggestive description that sets opium as preferable, it seems, to liquor. Colton noted that "the juice of the poppy is as harmless as any other source of excitement" and that "it never makes a man foolish, . . . It allows a man to be a gentleman."[28] Such observations were likely intended as a contrast to alcohol which, during the same time, had begun to be the topic of considerable social concern. In contrast, William Blair gives a parallel story to that of DeQuincey, describing a habit that was also inspired by the *Confessions*. Blair's account has a tragic denouement. After a failed attempt at treatment in the City Hospital in New York, which included writing the narrative included here, he left on his own accord. His physician,

29

B. W. M'Cready, surmised that "with his habits it is scarcely probably that he still survives."[29]

Similar accounts with increasingly dire outcomes appeared throughout the century. In an anonymous account in *Lippincott's Magazine* in 1868 (the same year Day's book was published) the author concludes by warning readers against the sort of casual experimentation in which he indulged. H. G. Cole unapologetically lifted DeQuincey's title, Americanizing the protagonist and giving him a more positive outcome in 1895. Cole's drug of choice was morphine, the mode of ingestion was by the hypodermic needle, but the purpose was clear: to dissuade readers from attempting the same reckless career. He explains that he would not have ever written the book "had the Opium Eater come in contact in his younger days with a book that would have served as a beacon light to reveal the terrible hell that lies in the pathway of all men from the use of opium."[30] In a chapter on the influence of opium hallucinations in literature, New York physician Alonzo Calkins (1804–1878) criticizes and condemns writers like DeQuincey and Coleridge for their depraved appetites which seems to have inspired the sub-genre of opium fiend writer.

Drug use observed

7 Anon, "Use of opiates among the operative population" *Chambers Edinburgh Journal* Vol 3 (1845): 346–48
8 Anon, "The Narcotics We Indulge In" *Blackwood's Edinburgh Magazine*, 74 (1853), part 1: 129–39; part 2: 605–28

Chambers Edinburgh Journal looks at the opium use among the urban poor, basing its concern on the evidence of terrible conditions in the urban working class districts that were uncovered in the Health of Towns Commission report. The commission, chaired by noted urban public health reformer Edwin Chadwick, had uncovered unsanitary conditions in British cities and is considered the roots of the public health movement in the United Kingdom.[31] The author, possibly William Chambers, the eponymous editor of the journal, uses that committee's report to springboard into concerns about the dangerous health effects of the use of opium by the poor. Most notable to the author is the practice of doping infants by mothers who have to work in factories, something the author likens to the reports of infanticide in India. The author sees it as an unmitigated evil, but the article, drawing upon the reports from druggists, is also a picture of self-medication and survival in the dire conditions of working-class England.

The three-part article "The Narcotics We Indulge In" originally published in *Blackwoods Edinburgh Magazine*, uses the occasion of the publication of the third edition of Jonathan Pereira's *Elements of Materia Medica and Therapeutics* as an opportunity to describe the drug taking of people around the world. It is generally a non-judgemental account of the types of substances consumed casually and recreationally by cultures, and includes an extensive assessment of tobacco,

INTRODUCTION TO VOLUME 1

"the hop" which he calls "The English narcotic" notwithstanding its origins in the Netherlands, opium, hemp and coca. The third section, not printed here, explores less-familiar substances including betel nut, emetic holly and lettuce, often drawing upon oral reports of indigenous uses. In contrast to the *Chambers* article which focused on the urban working poor, the *Blackwoods* article seemed generally more focused on bourgeois consumption, which was less problematic.

Cannabis

9 O'Shaughnessy, William Brooke, *On the preparation of the Indian hemp, or gunjah*, (Calcutta: Bishop's College Press, 1839)
10 Ludlow, F. H., "Introduction," Chapter 1 "The Night entrance," Chapter 2 "Under the Shadow of Esculapius," Chapter 3 "The Kingdom of the Dream" in *The Hasheesh Eater* (New York: Harper & Brother, 1857): ix–xiv; 15–43
11 Robinson, Victor, *An Essay on Hasheesh* (New York: Medical Review of Reviews, 1912): 39–83

Although opium was the main intoxicating drug of interest and concern through much of the nineteenth century, colonial expansion and general interest in the botany and biology of far-flung regions introduced (or reintroduced) numerous other potent substances to the Anglo-American audience. Especially notable were the leaves, flowers and sap of the hemp plant. Haschish, ganja, bhang, cannabis, marijuana: the terms overlapped and were drawn from different cultures, and incorporating them into the pharmacopoeia or recreational armory of the west included investigations into their properties and use.[32]

William Brooke O'Shaughnessy (1809–1889) was an Irish-born physician who is credited with introducing cannabis sativa into western medical therapy.[33] O'Shaughnessy joined the British East India Company in 1833, moved to Calcutta where his work included serving on the committee of the Materia Medica and chemical examiner for the government. This work brought him in contact with drugs used locally and initiated his investigations into cannabis. Along with describing the therapeutic uses of cannabis, O'Shaughnessy's *On the Preparation of Indian Hemp or Gunjah* also listed the various ways it was consumed for intoxication and, in a process that was not unusual in investigations at the time, his "experiments" of consuming it himself and recounting the experience.

Fitz Hugh Ludlow's *The Hasheesh Eater* took a different approach. As with the various "opium eater" tales, Ludlow (1836–1870) blends the exotic and cautionary, although the cultural concerns about opium's addictive properties do not appear as vividly in Ludlow's accounts of his cannabis use. Ludlow was a journalist and the son of an ardent temperance advocate, and the metaphors and tropes of temperance literature are replete throughout the tale. It tends to make the veracity of the account suspect, and given that it is a story of someone who consumed cannabis chronically, it would not be surprising if some of the elements were less than accurate. Nevertheless, it is a valuable piece given both how popular it was at the

31

time and how it compares to the confessional opium eater literature that was well known in the period.

Victor Robinson's *Essay on Hasheesh* brings the story to the beginning of the twentieth century. Robinson (1886–1947) was born in the Ukraine, was brought to the United States in early childhood, and studied pharmacy in New York. As had O'Shaughnessy nearly a century earlier, Robinson blends the scientific examination with the personal experimentation. Robinson asserts that everyone has heard of opium because so much of it is consumed in the west, but he contends that it is the same of hasheesh in other countries.[34] Although he recognizes the exotic nature of the drug and its prevalence in other cultures, he also entertains the reader with a series of vignettes about the experiences of him and his friends. One cannot help but think it was less a cautionary tale than an invitation to imbibe.

Drink and the dilemma of habit

12 Rush, Benjamin, *An Inquiry into the Effects of Ardent Spirits* Sixth Ed (New York: Cornelius Davis, 1811).
13 Trotter, Thomas, Introduction, Chapter 1 "Definition of Drunkenness" and Chapter 2, "Phenomena and Symptoms of Drunkenness" in *An Essay Medical, Philosophical, and Chemical on Drunkenness and its Effects on the Human Body* First Philadelphia Edition (Philadelphia: Anthony Finley, 1813): 11–22
14 Macnish, R., *The Anatomy of Drunkenness: An Inaugural Essay* (Glasgow: W. R. McPhun, 1827): 1–28

Although physicians and other observers had noted the dire physical consequences of drink prior to the nineteenth century, by the beginning of the century physicians had begun to articulate a more consistent discussion of the damage that the habit could wreak. Sociologist Harry Gene Levine set the origins of this concern in the United States on the work of Dr. Benjamin Rush (1746–1813), physician, signatory to the Declaration of Independence, and national hero who was most lauded for his decision to remain in Philadelphia to treat the sick during a yellow fever epidemic.[35] Rush's *An Inquiry into the effects of Ardent Spirits* certainly inspired early temperance tracts, and just as DeQuincey's *Confessions* was referenced frequently throughout the century, Rush's work was considered to be a foundational discussion of the problems of overindulgence. Rush was not the first to do this but became the most celebrated. Especially notable, and often reproduced, was his thermometer of temperance, which listed alcoholic beverages from healthful to damaging.

Rush and his contemporary Thomas Trotter (1760–1832) trained in Edinburgh under the noted Scottish Enlightenment physician William Cullen, whose nosology of disease based all illness upon disorders of the nervous system. These influences can be seen in both Rush and Trotter's work on alcohol, since the effect of drink could appear as a nervous disorder. Nevertheless, Rush and Trotter differ most especially in the fact that Trotter attempted to remove moral assessment from his medical view, whereas Rush saw morality and physical illness as intertwined.[36]

Also trained in Scotland, which was a hotbed of medical innovation at the beginning of the nineteenth century, Robert MacNish (1802–1837) wrote an inaugural thesis on drunkenness, published as *An Anatomy of Drunkenness* in 1827 and republished five times before his untimely death from typhus in 1837 at the age of 34.[37] Instead of examining the physiology of drinking and the habit, MacNish was interested in the immediate effects of drink (and intoxication from other substances) and the long-term impacts of drink on the body. The text provides a detailed impression of the emergence of a disease nosology prior to any fully formed disease concept of alcoholism, and at the same time is a sympathetic and dispassionate description of a condition many people had experienced. The section included here is what is most unique about MacNish's work, his classification and description of drunkenness.

The virtues of drink

15 Erasmus Darwin, "On drunkenness" *Zoonomia: Or the Laws of organic life*, Fourth American Edition (Philadelphia: Edward Earle, 1818) chapter XXI

16 Edward Cutbush, *Observations on the means of preserving the health of Soldiers and Sailors* (Philadelphia: Thomas Dobson, 1808) 22–31

17 Francis E. Anstie, *On the uses of wines in health and disease* (New York: J. S. Redfield, 1870), 7–48

18 G. G. Gervinus, *Art of Drinking: A Historical sketch* (New York: United States Brewers' Association, 1890): 5–23

In an era dominated by the temperance movement, which generated a tremendous number of tracts, pamphlets, and maudlin dramatic books and plays, writing that presented drinking in a positive light was a niche market. Yet, as MacNish's description of the "etherial emanations" floating around the brain illustrate, there was much to be said about the benefits of drink. Not only was alcohol a valuable medicine, but its intoxicating qualities were, to some, salubrious. The selections in this section demonstrate the range of perspectives on drink, both from a medical and purely recreational perspective.

Erasmus Darwin (1731–1802) was a polymath: physician, philosopher and advocate for the abolition of the slave trade, poet and inventor. Among his many works, *Zoonomia, or the Laws of Organic Life* examined broad principles of the anatomy, physiology and pathology of the body.[38] As MacNish did a generation later, Darwin (who also wrote on opium use) presented drunkenness as a natural and generally unproblematic state.[39] Although this chapter did conclude with an observation of the diseases from drunkenness, the dominant theme was about the pleasurable nature of drunkenness, and the occasional episodic negative outcomes of overindulgence.

Alcoholic drinks were long used in medical treatment, and the passage from Edward Cutbush's textbook on military medicine demonstrates a complex understanding of the properties of alcoholic beverages and their value (or limited value) in sustaining the soldier's body. Philadelphia-born Cutbush (1772–1843) was a surgeon in the United States navy for thirty years, and his book *Observation on the Means of Preserving the Health of Soldiers and Sailors* from which this extract is taken, was an important text on the subject of military medicine.[40] Cutbush advocated water as the principal drink of soldiers, but admitted that "we do not find that they use it when other articles can be procured" and proceeded to condemn "pernicious whiskey or rum" which because it was cheap was "to the great injury of their constitutions." Cutbush instead advocated cider and beer, as well as lemon and orange juice, and vinegar for strictly medicinal purposes.

The value of alcoholic beverages is also emphasized by Francis E. Anstie (1833–1874), a well-respected British physician and editor of the influential medical journal *Practitioner*. Anstie's work on drugs and alcohol in health and disease emphasized moderation in drink, and the text included here is from a pamphlet, *On the Use of Alcohol in Health and Disease*, possibly the only publication by Anstie that was known on both sides of the Atlantic. The section included is a discussion of wine as part of a healthy diet. In this discussion, he introduces what came to be known as "Anstie's Limit" the amount of alcohol that an average person could consume daily without any harmful effects—1.5 ounces of absolute alcohol.[41]

In an entirely different approach, George Gottfried Gervinus (1805–1871) was a German political and literary historian who believed that it was time to develop a historical field of "oinology or potology"—the study of drink.[42] His rationale was that such was necessary to demonstrate that this "partly physical, partly intellectual desire" was entwined with a "satisfaction of the highest needs" of an individual's "striving mind."[43] Although his work on the art of drinking was translated posthumously for the United States Brewers' Association in an effort to provide a counter narrative to the increasingly powerful temperance movement, Gervinus' work appears to have been self-motivated, although he clearly comes to the same conclusions as the brewers, that it would be a shame that such an important experience as drinking might be forbidden by law.

Places and spaces

19   Charles Dickens, *Barnaby Rudge: A tale of the riots of eighty* (London: Chapman and Hall, 1841) Ch 33

20   Charles Dickens, *The Mystery of Edwin Drood* (London: Chapman and Hall, 1870) Chapter 1

21   Anon, "East London Opium Smokers" *London Society* 14 (1868): 68–72

22   Platt, J., "Chinese London and its Opium dens" *Gentleman's Magazine* 279 (1895): 272–82

23   Moore, E. C., "The Social value of the saloon" *American Journal of Sociology* 3 (July 1897)

24   Melendy, Royal L., "The Saloon in Chicago" *American Journal of Sociology* 6 (Nov 1900): 289–306

25 Anon, "The Experience and Observations of a New York Saloon-Keeper as told by himself" *McClure Magazine* 32 (January 1909): 301–21
26 Hapgood, Hutchins, "McSorley's Saloon" *Harper's Weekly* 58 (25 October 1913): 15

This section combines impressions of two types of spaces for consuming intoxicants: the archetype of the opium den and the public house. Public consumption not only allowed people to come together in collective use of intoxicants, but also permitted outsiders to observe and judge. This is most notable in the accounts of the opium dens, which were almost always assessed by non-users, and often cultural and social outsiders to the consumer community, who imposed judgement upon the practice and the people.

Charles Dickens was possibly the most popular writer and social commentator in Victorian England. His accounts of a tavern in *Barnaby Rudge* and an opium den in *The Mystery of Edwin Drood* permit a direct contrast of Dicken's ideas of intoxicating leisure. The tavern was a relaxing place of comfort, where the character lulled sleepily by the fireplace. The opium den was a frightening place of discomfort, where participants lolled sleepily by the flame used to burn opium. The opium den scene was the first chapter in Drood, whereas the tavern scene was simply a setting for a discussion to advance the plot.[44]

The fictional opium den presented by Dickens is reiterated and challenged in descriptions of the dens in the popular magazines *London Society* and *Gentleman's Weekly*. Both authors approach the topic with a mixture of trepidation and wonder at the exoticism, both display an openness to the discovery, but both reiterate the stereotypes and prejudices of the western gaze upon the Chinese opium den. The anonymous author in *London Society* admits of the "strange yearning to make more intimate acquaintance with the miraculous drug concerning which there is so much whispering" while recognizing "a superstitious dread of approaching it." Similarly, American James Platt references Dicken's *Edwin Drood* as one of the inspirations for his visit, but unlike the earlier authors, Platt attempts to contextualize and normalize the activities in the dens, finding them less exotic and more familiar than other writers.[45]

In contrast to the opium den, the saloon, despite targeting by the temperance advocates, had an additional role as a site of socialization and comradery, as found in numerous sociological examinations. Selections in Volume III of this collection will illustrate the various ways that the temperance movement condemned the public drinking space as a site of debauchery, deviance and the source of family discord and destruction. The items in the current section highlight the ways this problematic space were investigated and placed into a much more balanced context. Both E. C. Moore and Royal Melendy undertook sociological investigations of saloons in Chicago at the turn of the century. Moore concluded that the saloon had a social value because there was nowhere else for the working class to pass their time.[46] He recognized that the drinks the saloons sell could be considered problematic "but the poison appears in their abuse and not in their use." Royal

35

Melendy's study was commissioned by the Committee of Fifty.[47] His unsurprising conclusions, that

> the adaptability of the saloon to the needs of a particular locality is a source of constant surprise and admiration, as it is also a cause of genuine consternation among Christian people who reflect at all upon the cautious institutionalism of the churches

reflected the committee's mandate to offer more balanced assessment of the liquor question.[48]

The sentiments of these serious investigations were reflected in more journalistic impressions. The anonymous story of a working-class saloon keeper contrasts the negative stereotypes of the tavernkeeper (predatory, rapacious, immoral), replacing them with the image of a businessman who aspires to respectability, but it is the business itself that is degraded. From the other side of the bar it might look better, as with the description of McSorley's Saloon by Hutchins Hapgood (1869–1944), American journalist and anarchist who built his reputation telling stories of working class life which, brings us back to the tone of Dickens's tavern half a century earlier. In keeping with Hapgood's general themes, the working-class patrons are noble and respectable; drunkenness is hardly seen. In a subtle acknowledgement of the problems found in some taverns, Hapgood muses that if there were more taverns like this one, "there would probably now be no strong temperance movement." Six years later the eighteenth amendment instituted prohibition.

Notes

1 See Kevin R. Kosar, *Whiskey: A Global History* (London: Reaktion Books, 2010).

2 A definitive history of brewing technology is James Sumner, *Brewing Science, Technology and Print, 1700–1880* (Pittsburgh: University of Pittsburgh, 2013). See also C. Anne Wilson, ed., *Liquid Nourishment: Potable Foods and Stimulating Drinks* (Edinburgh: Edinburgh University Press, 1993).

3 Yangwen Zheng, *The Social Life of Opium in China* (Cambridge: Cambridge University Press, 2005), pp. 97–98; Hans Derks, *History of the Opium Problem: The Assault on the East, ca 1600–1950* (Leiden: Brill, 2012), pp. 637–638; Kathleen Lodwick, *Crusaders against Opium: Protestant Missionaries in China, 1874–1917* (Lexington: University of Kentucky Press, 1996); David Hardiman, ed., *"Healing Bodies, Saving Souls": Medical Missions in Asia and Africa* (Amsterdam and New York: Rodolpi, 2006); Meyer and Parssinen note that the American approach to opium laws in China was fuelled by a contradictory impulse: missionaries lamenting the traffic opium and businesses wanting to profit from trade in China when the colonial powers are disavowed in favour of Americans. Kathryn Meyer and Terry Parssinen, *Webs of Smoke: Smugglers, Warlords, Spies, and the History of the International Drug Trade* (Lanham, Boulder, New York, and Oxford: Rowman & Littlefield, 1998), p. 21. On extraterritoriality, see Charles Denby, "Extraterritoriality in China" *American Journal of International Law* 18 (October 1924): 667–675.

4 An exception to this statement might be recent movements to legalize medical and recreational cannabis, but even here we see the inverse of the principle in action. Since

INTRODUCTION TO VOLUME 1

cannabis has not been legal in most jurisdictions, there has been no temperance movement to urge its suppression.

5 Craig Heron, *Booze: A Distilled History* (Toronto: Between the Lines Press, 2003).

6 Thora Hands, *Drinking in Victorian and Edwardian Britain: Beyond the Spectre of the Drunkard* (London: Palgrave Macmillan, 2018).

7 See especially the special issue of the *Social History of Alcohol and Drugs* that focused on the Victorian Drinker, edited by Pam Lock, *Social History of Alcohol and Drugs* 28 (Winter 2015).

8 Steven L. Earnshaw, *The Existential Drinker* (Manchester: University of Manchester Press, 2019), esp pp. 47–50, the story of Mary Thompson. Also Earnshaw, "Habitual Drunkards and Metaphysics: Four Case Studies from the Victorian Period" *The Social History of Alcohol and Drugs* 28 (2015): 143–160. Mary Lester discusses the multifaceted view of drinkers heading home in her "'A Man May Drink Many Pots Therein': Drink and Disorder in Arthur Morrison's 'To Bow Bridge' (1893)" *Social History of Alcohol and Drugs* 28 (Winter 2015): 179–194.

9 Isaac Campos, *Home Grown: Marijuana and the Origins of Mexico's War on Drugs* (Chapel Hill: University of North Carolina Press, 2012); Emily Dufton, *Grass Roots: The Rise and Fall and Rise of Marijuana in America* (New York: Basic Books, 2017); Nick Johnson, *Grass Roots: A History of Cannabis in the American West* (Corvalis, OR: Oregon State University Press, 2017).

10 Perry Duis, *The Saloon: Public Drinking in Chicago and Boston, 1880–1920* (Urbana and Chicago: University of Illinois Press, 1999); Madelon Powers, *Faces along the Bar: Lore and Order in the Workingman's Saloon, 1870–1920* (Chicago: University of Chicago Press, 1998); Julia Roberts, *In Mixed Company: Taverns and Public Life in Upper Canada* (Vancouver: University of British Columbia Press, 2009); Paul Jennings, *The Local: A History of the English Pub* (Stroud: The History Press, 2007); Paul Jennings, *A History of Drink and the English* (New York and London: Routledge, 2017); Pete Brown, *Man Walks into a Pub: A Sociable History of Beer* (London: MacMillan, 2003).

11 Daine Kirkby, *Barmaids: A History of Women's Work in Pubs* (Cambridge: Cambridge University Press, 1997); Clare Wright, *Beyond the Ladies' Lounge: Australia's Female Publicans* (Melbourne: Melbourne University Press, 2003).

12 W. Scott Haine, *The World of the Paris Café: Sociability among the French Working Class, 1789–1914* (Baltimore: Johns Hopkins University Press, 1996).

13 Beat Kumin and B. Ann Tlusly, eds., *The World of the Tavern: Public Houses in Early Modern Europe* (Aldershot, UK and Burlington, VT: Ashgate, 2002).

14 Dan Malleck, *When Good Drugs Go Bad: Opium, Medicine and the Origins of Canada's Drug Laws* (Vancouver: UBC Press, 2015) pp. 48, 113–114.

15 James H. Mills, "Chapter 2: Dr. O'Shaughnessy Appears to Have Made Some Experiments with Charas': Imperial Merchants, Victorian Science, and Hemp to 1842" in *Cannabis Britannica: Empire, Trade, and Prohibition* (Oxford: Oxford University Press, 2003).

16 See Oriana Josseau Kalant, "Ludlow on Cannabis: A Modern Look at a Nineteenth Century Drug Experience" *International Journal of the Addictions* 6 (1971): 309–322.

17 Anon, "The Narcotics We Indulge In (Part 1)" *Blackwood's Edinburgh Magazine* 74 (1853): 130.

18 Alonzo Calkins, "Chapter IX: Opium-Literature in the Reflex View" in *Opium and the Opium Appetite* (Philadelphia: J. Lippincott, 1871), p. 90.

19 Thomas Trotter, *An Essay Medical, Philosophical, and Chemical on Drunkenness and Its Effects on the Human Body*, First Philadelphia Edition (Philadelphia: Anthony Finley, 1813), p. 13.

20 Robert MacNish, *Anatomy of Drunkenness an Inaugural Essay* (Glasgow: W. R. McPhun, 1827), p. 6.

DRUNKS, FIENDS, AND THE ROOTS OF CONCERN

21 Gay Sibley, "Closet addiction in Fiction" *Social History of Alcohol and Drugs: An Interdisciplinary Journal* 21 (Spring 2007): 183–202.

22 Pam Lock, "Death and the Alcoholic: Public Discourses of Alcoholism in Anne Brontë's" *"The Tenant of Wildfell Hall"*, *Social History of Alcohol and Drugs: An Interdisciplinary Journal* 29 (2015): 29–47; Pam Lock, "Hindley's 'Reckless Dissipation': Making Drunkenness Public in Emily Bronte's *Wuthering Heights*" *Bronte Studies* 44 (January 2019): 68–81.

23 Royal L. Melendy, "The Saloon in Chicago" *American Journal of Sociology* 6 (November 1900): 306.

24 Charles Dickens, *The Mystery of Edwin Drood* (London: Chapman & Hall, 1870); Oscar Wilde, *The Picture of Dorian Grey* (London: Ward, Lock and Co, 1891); Arthur Conan Doyle, "The Man with the Twisted Lip" in *The Adventures of Sherlock Holmes* (London: George Newness, 1892); Doyle, *A Study in Scarlet* (London: Ward, Lock & Co, 1888); Doyle, *The Sign of the Four* (London: Spencer Blackett, 1890). Holmes's cocaine use is first noted in *A Study in Scarlet* and more detailed in *A Sign of Four*. See Conan Doyle Info: A Seven-Percent Solution: Sherlock Holmes and Cocaine, www.conandoyleinfo.com/sherlock-holmes/sherlock-homes-and-cocaine/

25 Royal Commission on Chinese Immigration, *Report of the Royal Commission on Chinese Immigration* (Ottawa: Printed by Order of the Commission, 1885), p. 151.

26 Berridge, *Opium and the People*, pp. 51–53; Hayter, *Opium and the Romantic Imagination*, p. 101; Howard Padwa, *Social Poison: The Culture and Politics of Opiate Control in Britain and France*, pp. 22–26.

27 Berridge, *Opium and the People*, p. 53.

28 Walter Colton, "Effects of Opium" *Knickerbocker* 7 (1836): 421.

29 This account was retold in detail taking up a full chapter in Horace B. Day, *The Opium Habit with Suggestions as to the Remedy* (New York: Harper and Brothers, 1868), pp. 179–197. Quotation is on p. 180.

30 H. G. Cole, *Confessions of an American Opium Eater: From Bondage to Freedom* (Boston: James H. Earle, 1895), p. 5.

31 Roger Watson, *Edwin Chadwick, Poor Law and Public Health* (London: Longman, 1971); Dorothy Porter, *Health, Civilisation and the State: A History of Public Health from Ancient to Modern Times* (New York and London: Routledge, 1999).

32 James H. Mills, *Cannabis Britannica: Empire, Trade, and Prohibition* (Oxford: Oxford University Press, 2003); Isaac Campos, *Home Grown*.

33 Mills, *Cannabis Britannica*, p. 39.

34 Victor Robinson, *An Essay on Hasheesh* (New York: Medical Review of Reviews, 1912), p. 39.

35 Levine, "The *Discovery of Addiction*." Carl Binger, *Revolutionary Doctor: Benjamin Rush, 1746–1813* (New York: Norton, 1966), pp. 203–226.

36 Nicholls, *Politics of Alcohol*, p. 69.

37 Michael Bevan, "MacNish, Robert" *Oxford Dictionary of National Biography*, www.oxforddnb.com (published online 23 September 2004).

38 Maureen McNeil, "Darwin, Erasmus" *Oxford Dictionary of National Biography*, www.oxforddnb.com (published online 23 September 2004).

39 Alethea Hayter, *Opium and the Romantic Imagination: Addiction and Creativity in De Quincey, Coleridge, Baudelaire and Others* (Berkeley: University of California Press, 1968), p. 101.

40 Jack E. McCallum, "Cutbush, Edward, (1772–1843)" in *Military Medicine: From Ancient Times to the 21st Century* (Santa Barbara: ABC-Clio Press, 2008), pp. 96–97.

41 Arthur Baldwin, "Anstie's Alcohol Limit: Francis Edmund Anstie, 1833–1874" *American Journal of Public Health* 67 (July 1977): 679–681.

INTRODUCTION TO VOLUME 1

42 "Gervinus, Georg Gottfried (1805–1871)" *Encyclopedia Britannica 1911* Available open access at: https://en.wikisource.org/wiki/1911_Encyclop%C3%A6dia_Britannica/Gervinus,_Georg_Gottfried.

43 Georg Gottfried Gervinus, *The Art of Drinking* (New York: United States Brewers' Association, 1890), p. 6.

44 Joachim Stanley, "Opium and 'Edwin Drood': Fantasy, Reality, and What the Doctors Ordered" *Dickens Quarterly* 21 (March 2004): 12–27; Jeremy Tambling, "Opium, Wholesale, Resale, and for Export: On Dickens and China (Part Two)" *Dickens Quarterly* 21 (June 2004): 104–113.

45 Christopher Freyling, *The Yellow Peril: Dr. Fu Manchu and the Rise of Chinaphobia* (London: Thames and Hudson, 2014).

46 See also John Gilkeson, Jr., *Middle-Class Providence 1820–1940* (Princeton, NJ: Princeton University Press, 1986), p. 245.

47 James H. Timberlake, *Prohibition and the Progressive Movement 1900–1920* Reprint (New York: Atheneum, 1970).

48 Royal Melendy, "The Saloon in Chicago" *American Journal of Sociology* 6 (November 1900): 306.

Part 1

THE DRUG HABIT AND ITS CONFESSIONALS

1

THOMAS DEQUINCEY, *CONFESSIONS OF AN ENGLISH OPIUM EATER*, 2ND ED. (LONDON: TAYLOR AND HESSEY, FLEET ST., 1823), PP. 156–73

I now pass to what is the main subject of these latter confessions, to the history and journal of what took place in my dreams; for these were the immediate and proximate cause of my acutest suffering.

The first notice I had of any important change going on in this part of my physical economy, was from the re-awakening of a state of eye generally incident to childhood, or exalted states of irritability. I know not whether my reader is aware that many children, perhaps most, have a power of painting, as it were, upon the darkness, all sorts of phantoms: in some, that power is simply a mechanic affection of the eye; others have a voluntary, or a semi-voluntary power to dismiss or to summon them; or, as a child once said to me when I questioned him on this matter, "I can tell them to go, and they go; but sometimes they come, when I don't tell them to come." Whereupon I told him that he had almost as unlimited a command over apparitions, as a Roman centurion over his soldiers.—In the middle of 1817, I think it was, that this faculty became positively distressing to me: at night, when I lay awake in bed, vast processions passed along in mournful pomp; friezes of never-ending stories, that to my feelings were as sad and solemn as if they were stories drawn from times before Œdipus or Priam—before Tyre—before Memphis. And, at the same time, a corresponding change took place in my dreams; a theatre seemed suddenly opened and lighted up within my brain, which presented nightly spectacles of more than earthly splendour. And the four following facts may be mentioned, as noticeable at this time:

1. That, as the creative state of the eye increased, a sympathy seemed to arise between the waking and the dreaming states of the brain in one point—that whatsoever I happened to call up and to trace by a voluntary act upon the darkness was very apt to transfer itself to my dreams; so that I feared to exercise this faculty; for, as Midas turned all things to gold, that yet baffled his hopes and defrauded his human desires, so whatsoever things capable of being visually represented I did but think of in the darkness, immediately shaped themselves into phantoms

THE DRUG HABIT AND ITS CONFESSIONALS

of the eye; and, by a process apparently no less inevitable, when thus once traced in faint and visionary colours, like writings in sympathetic ink, they were drawn out by the fierce chemistry of my dreams, into insufferable splendour that fretted my heart.

2. For this, and all other changes in my dreams, were accompanied by deep-seated anxiety and gloomy melancholy, such as are wholly incommunicable by words. I seemed every night to descend, not metaphorically, but literally to descend, into chasms and sunless abysses, depths below depths, from which it seemed hopeless that I could ever reascend. Nor did I, by waking, feel that I *had* reascended. This I do not dwell upon; because the state of gloom which attended these gorgeous spectacles, amounting at least to utter darkness, as of some suicidal despondency, cannot be approached by words.

3. The sense of space, and in the end, the sense of time, were both powerfully affected. Buildings, landscapes, &c. were exhibited in proportions so vast as the bodily eye is not fitted to receive. Space swelled, and was amplified to an extent of unutterable infinity. This, however, did not disturb me so much as the vast expansion of time; I sometimes seemed to have lived for 70 or 100 years in one night; nay, sometimes had feelings representative of a millennium passed in that time, or, however, of a duration far beyond the limits of any human experience.

4. The minutest incidents of childhood, or forgotten scenes of later years, were often revived: I could not be said to recollect them; for if I had been told of them when waking, I should not have been able to acknowledge them as parts of my past experience. But placed as they were before me, in dreams like intuitions, and clothed in all their evanescent circumstances and accompanying feelings, I *recognised* them instantaneously. I was once told by a near relative of mine, that having in her childhood fallen into a river, and being on the very verge of death but for the critical assistance which reached her, she saw in a moment her whole life, in its minutest incidents, arrayed before her simultaneously as in a mirror; and she had a faculty developed as suddenly for comprehending the whole and every part. This, from some opium experiences of mine, I can believe; I have, indeed, seen the same thing asserted twice in modern books, and accompanied by a remark which I am convinced is true; viz. that the dread book of account, which the Scriptures speak of, is, in fact, the mind itself of each individual. Of this, at least, I feel assured, that there is no such thing as *forgetting* possible to the mind; a thousand accidents may, and will interpose a veil between our present consciousness and the secret inscriptions on the mind; accidents of the same sort will also rend away this veil; but alike, whether veiled or unveiled, the inscription remains for ever; just as the stars seem to withdraw before the common light of day, whereas, in fact, we all know that it is the light which is drawn over them as a veil—and that they are waiting to be revealed, when the obscuring daylight shall have withdrawn.

Having noticed these four facts as memorably distinguishing my dreams from those of health, I shall now cite a case illustrative of the first fact; and shall then cite any others that I remember, either in their chronological order, or any other that may give them more effect as pictures to the reader.

I had been in youth, and even since, for occasional amusement, a great reader of Livy, whom, I confess, that I prefer, both for style and matter, to any other of the Roman historians; and I had often felt as most solemn and appalling sounds, and most emphatically representative of the majesty of the Roman people, the two words so often occurring in Livy—*Consul Romanus;* especially when the consul is introduced in his military character. I mean to say, that the words king—sultan—regent, &c. or any other titles of those who embody in their own persons the collective majesty of a great people, had less power over my reverential feelings. I had also, though no great reader of history, made myself minutely and critically familiar with one period of English history, viz. the period of the Parliamentary War, having been attracted by the moral grandeur of some who figured in that day, and by the many interesting memoirs which survived those unquiet times. Both these parts of my lighter reading, having furnished me often with matter of reflection, now furnished me with matter for my dreams. Often I used to see, after painting upon the blank darkness a sort of rehearsal whilst waking, a crowd of ladies, and perhaps a festival, and dances. And I heard it said, or I said to myself, "These are English ladies from the unhappy times of Charles I. These are the wives and the daughters of those who met in peace, and sat at the same tables, and were allied by marriage or by blood; and yet, after a certain day in August, 1642, never smiled upon each other again, nor met but in the field of battle; and at Marston Moor, at Newbury, or at Naseby, cut asunder all ties of love by the cruel sabre, and washed away in blood the memory of ancient friendship."—The ladies danced, and looked as lovely as the court of George IV. Yet I knew, even in my dream, that they had been in the grave for nearly two centuries.—This pageant would suddenly dissolve: and, at a clapping of hands, would be heard the heart-quaking sound of *Consul Romanus:* and immediately came "sweeping by," in gorgeous paludaments, Paulus or Marius, girt round by a company of centurions, with the crimson tunic hoisted on a spear, and followed by the *alalagmos* of the Roman legions.

Many years ago, when I was looking over Piranesi's Antiquities of Rome, Mr. Coleridge, who was standing by, described to me a set of plates by that artist, called his *Dreams*, and which record the scenery of his own visions during the delirium of a fever. Some of them (I describe only from memory of Mr. Coleridge's account) represented vast Gothic halls: on the floor of which stood all sorts of engines and machinery, wheels, cables, pulleys, levers, catapults, &c. &c. expressive of enormous power put forth, and resistance overcome. Creeping along the sides of the walls, you perceived a staircase; and upon it, groping his way upwards, was Piranesi himself: follow the stairs a little further, and you perceive it come to a sudden abrupt termination, without any balustrade, and allowing no step onwards to him who had reached the extremity, except into the depths below. Whatever is to become of poor Piranesi, you suppose, at least, that his labours must in some way terminate here. But raise your eyes, and behold a second flight of stairs still higher: on which again Piranesi is perceived, but this time standing on the very brink of the abyss. Again elevate your eye, and a still more aerial flight of stairs is beheld: and again is poor Piranesi busy on his aspiring labours: and so on, until the unfinished stairs and Piranesi both are lost in the upper gloom of the hall.— With the same power of endless growth and self-reproduction did my architecture proceed in dreams. In the early stage of my malady, the splendours of my dreams were indeed chiefly architectural: and I beheld such pomp of cities and palaces as was never yet beheld by the waking eye, unless in the clouds. From a great modern poet I cite part of a passage which describes, as an appearance actually beheld in the clouds, what in many of its circumstances I saw frequently in sleep:

> The appearance, instantaneously disclosed,
> Was of a mighty city—boldly say
> A wilderness of building, sinking far
> And self-withdrawn into a wondrous depth,
> Far sinking into splendour—without end!
> Fabric it seem'd of diamond, and of gold,
> With alabaster domes, and silver spires,
> And blazing terrace upon terrace, high
> Uplifted; here, serene pavilions bright
> In avenues disposed; there towers begirt
> With battlements that on their restless fronts
> Bore stars—illumination of all gems!
> By earthly nature had the effect been wrought
> Upon the dark materials of the storm
> Now pacified: on them, and on the coves,
> And mountain-steeps and summits, whereunto
> The vapours had receded,—taking there
> Their station under a cerulean sky, &c. &c.

The sublime circumstance—"battlements that on their *restless* fronts bore stars,"—might have been copied from my architectural dreams, for it often occurred.—We hear it reported of Dryden, and of Fuseli in modern times, that they thought proper to eat raw meat for the sake of obtaining splendid dreams: how much better for such a purpose to have eaten opium, which yet I do not remember that any poet is recorded to have done, except the dramatist Shadwell: and in ancient days, Homer is, I think, rightly reputed to have known the virtues of opium.

To my architecture succeeded dreams of lakes—and silvery expanses of water:—these haunted me so much, that I feared (though possibly it will appear ludicrous to a medical man) that some dropsical state or tendency of the brain might thus be making itself (to use a metaphysical word) *objective;* and the sentient organ *project* itself as its own object.—For two months I suffered greatly in my head—a part of my bodily structure which had hitherto been so clear from all touch or taint of weakness (physically, I mean,) that I used to say of it, as the last Lord Orford said of his stomach, that it seemed likely to survive the rest of my person. — Till now I had never felt a headach even, or any the slightest pain, except rheumatic pains caused by my own folly. However, I got over this attack, though it must have been verging on something very dangerous.

The waters now changed their character, — from translucent lakes, shining like mirrors, they now became seas and oceans. And now came a tremendous change, which, unfolding itself slowly like a scroll, through many months, promised an abiding torment; and, in fact, it never left me until the winding up of my case. Hitherto the human face had mixed often in my dreams, but not despotically, nor with any special power of tormenting. But now that which I have called the tyranny of the human face began to unfold itself. Perhaps some part of my London life might be answerable for this. Be that as it may, now it was that upon the rocking waters of the ocean the human face began to appear: the sea appeared paved with innumerable faces, upturned to the heavens: faces, imploring, wrathful, despairing, surged upwards by thousands, by myriads, by generations, by centuries: — my agitation was infinite, — my mind tossed — and surged with the ocean.

May, 1818.

The Malay has been a fearful enemy for months. I have been every night, through his means, transported into Asiatic scenes. I know not whether others share in my feelings on this point; but I have often thought that if I were compelled to forego England, and to live in China, and among Chinese manners and modes of life and scenery, I should go mad. The causes of my horror lie deep; and some of them must be common to others. Southern Asia, in general, is the seat of awful images and associations. As the cradle of the human race, it would alone have a dim and reverential feeling connected with it. But there are other reasons. No man can pretend that the wild, barbarous, and capricious superstitions of Africa, or of savage tribes elsewhere, affect him in the way that he is affected by the ancient, monumental, cruel, and elaborate religions of Indostan, &c. The mere antiquity of Asiatic things, of their institutions, histories, modes of faith, &c. is so impressive, that to me the vast age of the race and name overpowers the sense of youth in the individual. A young Chinese seems to me an antediluvian man renewed. Even Englishmen, though not bred in any knowledge of such institutions, cannot but shudder at the mystic sublimity of *castes* that have flowed apart, and refused to mix, through such immemorial tracts of time; nor can any man fail to be awed by the names of the Ganges, or the Euphrates. It contributes much to these feelings, that Southern Asia is, and has been for thousands of years, the part of the earth most swarming with human life; the great *officina gentium*. Man is a weed in those regions. The vast empires also, into which the enormous population of Asia has always been cast, give a further sublimity to the feelings associated with all Oriental names or images. In China, over and above what it has in common with the rest of Southern Asia, I am terrified by the modes

THE DRUG HABIT AND ITS CONFESSIONALS

of life, by the manners, and the barrier of utter abhorrence, and want of sympathy, placed between us by feelings deeper than I can analyze. I could sooner live with lunatics, or brute animals. All this, and much more than I can say, or have time to say, the reader must enter into before he can comprehend the unimaginable horror which these dreams of Oriental imagery, and mythological tortures, impressed upon me. Under the connecting feeling of tropical heat and vertical sun-lights, I brought together all creatures, birds, beasts, reptiles, all trees and plants, usages and appearances, that are found in all tropical regions, and assembled them together in China or Indostan. From kindred feelings, I soon brought Egypt and all her gods under the same law. I was stared at, hooted at, grinned at, chattered at, by monkeys, by paroquets, by cockatoos. I ran into pagodas: and was fixed, for centuries, at the summit, or in secret rooms; I was the idol; I was the priest; I was worshipped; I was sacrificed. I fled from the wrath of Brama through all the forests of Asia: Vishnu hated me: Seeva laid wait for me. I came suddenly upon Isis and Osiris: I had done a deed, they said, which the ibis and the crocodile trembled at. I was buried, for a thousand years, in stone coffins, with mummies and sphinxes, in narrow chambers at the heart of eternal pyramids. I was kissed, with cancerous kisses, by crocodiles; and laid, confounded with all unutterable slimy things, amongst reeds and Nilotic mud.

I thus give the reader some slight abstraction of my Oriental dreams, which always filled me with such amazement at the monstrous scenery, that horror seemed absorbed, for a while, in sheer astonishment. Sooner or later, came a reflux of feeling that swallowed up the astonishment, and left me, not so much in terror, as in hatred and abomination of what I saw. Over every form, and threat, and punishment, and dim sightless incarceration, brooded a sense of eternity and infinity that drove me into an oppression as of madness. Into these dreams only, it was, with one or two slight exceptions, that any circumstances of physical horror entered. All before had been moral and spiritual terrors. But here the main agents were ugly birds, or snakes, or crocodiles; especially the last. The cursed crocodile became to me the object of more horror than almost all the rest. I was compelled to live with him; and (as was always the case almost in my dreams) for centuries. I escaped sometimes, and found myself in Chinese houses, with cane tables, &c. All the feet of the tables, sofas, &c. soon became instinct with life: the abominable head of the crocodile, and his leering eyes, looked out at me, multiplied into a thousand repetitions: and I stood loathing and fascinated. And so often did this hideous reptile haunt my dreams, that many times the very same dream was broken up in the very same way: I heard gentle voices speaking to me (I hear every thing when I am sleeping); and instantly I awoke: it was broad noon; and my children were standing, hand in hand, at my bed-side; come to show me their coloured shoes, or new frocks, or to let me see them dressed for going out. I protest that so awful was the transition from the damned crocodile, and the other unutterable monsters and abortions of my dreams, to the sight of innocent *human* natures and of infancy, that, in the mighty and sudden revulsion of mind, I wept, and could not forbear it, as I kissed their faces.

2

WALTER COLTON, 'EFFECTS OF OPIUM', *THE KNICKERBOCKER*, 7, 1836, 421–23

THE number of devotees to this drug of delicious delirium has of late very much diminished; not that there is less misfortune or wretchedness to be soothed or forgotten, but that wine, which ever maketh the heart of man glad, has been clandestinely substituted in its place. Whether the intellect, morality or health of the community has profited by the change, I leave to the decision of those who have had wider opportunities of witnessing the effects of both. My own conviction is, that if a man will take to stimulants, the juice of the poppy is as harmless as any other source of excitement; and then it has this strong recommendation, it never makes a man foolish, it never casts a man into a ditch, or under the table; it never deprives him of his wits or his legs. It allows a man to be a gentleman; it makes him visionary, but his visions create no noise, no riots; they deal no blows, blacken no one's eyes, and frighten no one's peace. It is the most quiet and unoffending relief to which the desponding and distressed, who have no higher resource, can appeal.

I should want no stronger evidence of this, than the immediate effects on those whom I once saw using it at Constantinople. The change which diffused itself through the countenance, limbs, and gait, was like the resuscitation of the dying to the energies and happiness of a fresh life. You could hardly persuade yourself that the man who now moved before you with a light elastic tread, and an eye kindling with secret rapture, was the same who a short time since approached with a faltering, feeble step, scarcely able to sustain himself upon his cane, and the arm of a less withered friend, while every feature seemed settled in that unrelieved despair which might make a word of hope sound like a mockery. Such was the change, such the total renovation produced, that one ignorant of the depression and despondency into which this dreaming, delicious excitement, if unrenewed, must ultimately sink, might have supposed that the tree of life had been discovered, and the immortal ambrosia of its fruits enjoyed. But as weariness will the sooner overtake the forced wing of the eagle, so depression will only the deeper weigh down the heart that has thus been too elated. The even stream pursues its way in cheerfulness and light, through smiling valleys to the deeper wave of the ocean and the lake, while the mountain torrent that foams from the cliff, though

THE DRUG HABIT AND ITS CONFESSIONALS

there it may have worn all the hues of heaven, only plunges, perhaps, into some wild and sunless glen, whose solitude is never cheered by the tints of breaking day, or the song of early birds.

Few men, however, pass through life without testing some source of promised health and happiness beyond the quiet motion of the heart. My imagination was once so kindled, by the perusal of a little book called the 'Opium-Eater,' that I resolved to put its pleasing assurances to a practical test. So, sending to an apothecary's shop, I procured two enormous doses of the precious drug. One was taken by my young companion, who had become equally interested in making the experiment, the other by myself.

My comrade began immediately to feel extremely particular about the stomach, and soon in a retching agony parted with all his anodynical expectations. My portion stuck fast as original sin; and I shortly lapsed into a disturbed slumber, in which it appeared to me that I retained my consciousness entire, while visions passed before me which no language can convey, and no symbols of happiness or terror represent. At one time I was soaring on the pinions of an angel among the splendors of the highest heaven, beholding at a glance the beauty of their unveiled mysteries, and listening to harps and choral symphonies over which, time, sorrow, and death have no power; and then my presumption was checked, my cleaving wings, like the waxen plumes of Icarus, were melted away, and I fell down, down, till caught in the bosom of a thunder cloud, from which I was again hurled, linked to its fiercest bolt upon the plunging verge of a cataract, that carried me down, frantic with horror, into the lowest depth of its howling gulf.

Thence again I emerged, with the placidity and power of Neptune over his troubled realm, and driving my watery team over the excited bosom of the ocean, harmonized its elements into the deep bass it sustained in the bursting anthem of the infant world. And then with the fleetness of a disembodied spirit, I seemed to float around just between the incumbent circle of the blue heaven and the sea, discerning within upon the surging plain the motion of innumerable ships skimming the wave with the lightness of the swallow, while without the circle I beheld far down in the twilight and lurid gloom of an immeasurable gulf, the wrecks of worn-out worlds.

Still I floated on upon the frightful verge of the circle, till coming around near the north pole I saw its steadfast star fixed in the darkened change of death; other planets were bending over it; and when they had sung its funeral hymn, they lowered it into a grave so dark, so fathomless and still, that the agonies and convulsions of expiring nature could not disturb its sepulchral sleep. While thinking of the dismayed mariner, rolling his eyes in vain to find his undeviating star, an iceberg with its mountain mass of frozen torrents came rolling on, and catching me in one of its dripping shelves, bore me through seas lashed by the hurricane, convulsed with the war of the whale and sword fish, and where the serpent, struck by lightning, lay troughed between two waves like a huge pine prostrate among the hills.

EFFECTS OF OPIUM

Being benumbed and paralyzed by the stiffening ice, I fell from my tumbling lodgment, and descending through the sea, was carried by the wave of a submarine current quite within a little grotto, reared of coral and lined with pearls, where a mermaid was gently kindling a fire, beneath whose reviving ray I soon felt each frozen vein and limb slowly tingling back to life — when, as if to reclaim my bewildered thoughts, and soothe their delirious excitement, this daughter of the deep, raising her harp, struck one of those soft strains whose liquid flow melts into the heart like fragrant dew into the bosom of the folding rose.

But scarce had the last note of this sweet minstrel died away into the listening stillness of peace, when a call, loud as the summoning trump of the archangel, sent its rending thunder through the hollow caverns of the astounded ocean, and the rent tombs of the shaking earth, starting even death itself from his sleep. The sheeted dead went up from their watery graves to stand on the sea, while the earth, from precipice to plain, from shore to mountain's brow, was covered with the shrouded myriads that had left their couches of clay.

The sun with a changed, despairing aspect disappeared, leaving a huge darkened chasm in the heavens; the moon spun round and round, and slowly receded from view, leaving another fearful blank in the blue vault; the planets fell from their places, and were quenched as they sunk into the lifeless void beneath; and darkness in a thick palpable mass filled all space, save where the forked lightning, arrested in its course, still preserved its terrific form and brightness, and save the lingering light of some loftier star that contended with its doom. The courses and powers of nature were suspended still and motionless; the mariner heard his relaxed sails fall against the idle mast, the breaker cease to lift its warning voice over the fatal reef; while the seabird, unable again to reach the wave, rested upon his immovable pinions; the curling wave lay half broken on the shore; the torrent ceased to plunge from its waveworn steep; the war-horse kneeled down and died; the monarch in his capital, discrowned, stood pale and speechless; the peasant in his field called aloud on his forgotten God; while the imploring shriek of nations went up like the last wail of a ruined world!

> The agony is o'er; nature her debt
>   Has paid; the earth is covered with a clay
> That once was animate, and even yet
>   Is warm with an existence reft away
>   By Him who gave; it were but yesterday
> This clay peopled a happy universe
>   With beings buoyant, beautiful and gay;
> But now alas! — of all things the reverse,
> Earth is their winding sheet, and darkness palls the hearse!

These lines were engraven on my heart at the time by the departing spirit of my dream; and I awoke, after having been lost to all the realities of this world for two days and nights. But O! the faintness, the thirst, and delirious weakness of

THE DRUG HABIT AND ITS CONFESSIONALS

that waking moment! I look back to it as a man who has been skating over the frozen bosom of a lake turns to the yawning chasm which he has miraculously escaped! I could not stand or sit; and even in a most inclined posture, respiration itself seemed an effort beyond the gasping exhaustion of my frame. I should have turned on my pillow and died, but for the kindly efforts of one whom I can never love too much, or remember too long. Let no one test like me, the dreaming ecstacies and terror of opium; it is only scaling the battlements of heaven, to sink into the burning tombs of hell!

3

WILLIAM BLAIR, 'AN OPIUM-EATER IN AMERICA', *THE KNICKERBOCKER*, 20, 1842, 47–57

'Esse quid hoc dicum, quod tam mihi dura videntur
Strata, neque in lecto pallia nôstra sedent?
Et vacuus somno noctem, quam louga, perigi;
Lassaque vessati corporis assa dolent.'

Ovid Amor.

Before I state the results of my experience as an opium-eater, it will perhaps not be uninteresting, and it certainly will conduce to the clearer understanding of such statement, if I give a slight and brief sketch of my habits and history previous to my first indulgence in the infernal drug which has imbittered my existence for seven most weary years.

The death of my father when I was little more than twelve months old made it necessary that I should receive only such an education as would qualify me to pursue some business in my native town of Birmingham; and in all probability I should at this moment be entering orders or making out invoices in that great emporium of buttons and blackguards, had I not (whether fortunately or otherwise I pretend not to decide) at a very early age evinced a decided and absorbing passion for reading, which the free access to a tolerably large library enabled me to indulge, until it had grown to be a confirmed habit of mind, which when the attention of my *friends* was called to the subject, had become too strong to be broken through; and with the usual foolish family vanity they determined to indulge a taste so early and decidedly developed, in the expectation, I verily believe, of some day catching a reflected beam from the fame and glory which I was to win by my genius; for by that mystical name was the mere musty talent of '*ahellico librorum*' called. The consequence was that I was sent, when eight years of age, to a public school. I had however before this tormented my elder brother with ceaseless importunity, until he had consented to teach me Latin; and by secretly poring over my sister's books, I had contrived to gain a tolerable book-knowledge of French.

THE DRUG HABIT AND ITS CONFESSIONALS

From that hour my fate was decided. I applied with unwearied devotion to the study of the classics — the only branch of education attended to in the school; and I even considered it a favor to be allowed to translate, write exercises and themes, and to compose Latin verses for the more idle of my school-fellows. At the same time I devoured all books of whatever description, which came in my way: poems, novels, history, metaphysics, or works of science, with an indiscriminating appetite, which has proved very injurious to me through life. I drank as eagerly of the muddy and stagnant pool of literature, as of the pure and sparkling fountains glowing in the many-hued sun-light of genius. After two years had been spent in this manner, I was removed to another school, the principal of which, although a fair mathematician, was a wretched classical scholar. In fact I frequently construed passages of Virgil, which I had not previously looked at, when he himself was forced to refer to Davidson for assistance. I stayed with him however two years, during which time I spent all the money I could get in purchasing Greek and Hebrew books, of which languages I learned the rudiments, and obtained considerable knowledge without any instruction. After a year's residence at the house of my brother-in-law, which I passed in studying Italian and Persian, the Bishop of Litchfield, examining chaplain, to whom I had been introduced in terms of the most hyperbolical praise, prevailed on his diocesan and the Earl of Calthorpe to share the expense of my farther education.

In consequence of this unexpected good fortune, I was now placed under the care of the Rev. Thomas Fry, Rector of the Village of Emberton in Buckinghamshire, a clergyman of great piety and profound learning, with whom I remained about fifteen months, pursuing the study of languages with increased ardor. During the whole of that period I never allowed myself more than four hours' sleep; and still unsatisfied, I very generally spent the whole night, twice a week, in the insane pursuit of those avenues to distinction to which alone my ambition was confined. I took no exercise, and the income allowed me was so small that I could not afford a meat dinner more than once a week, and at the same time set apart the half of that allowance for the purchase of books, which I had determined to do. I smoked incessantly; for I now required some stimulus, as my health was much injured by my unrelaxing industry. My digestion was greatly impaired; and the constitution of iron which Nature had given me threatened to break down ere long under the effects of the systematic neglect with which I treated its repeated warnings. I suffered from constant head-ache; my total inactivity caused the digestive organs to become torpid; and the innutritious nature of the food which I allowed myself would not supply me with the strength which my assiduous labor required. My nerves were dreadfully shaken; and at the age of fourteen I exhibited the external symptoms of old age. I was feeble and emaciated; and had this mode of life continued twelve months longer, I must have sank under it.

I had during these fifteen months thought and read much on the subject of revealed religion, and had devoted a considerable portion of my time to an examination of the evidences advanced by the advocates of Christianity, which resulted in a reluctant conviction of their utter weakness and inability. No sooner was I aware that so complete a change of opinion had taken place, than I wrote to my patron stating the fact, and explaining the process by which I had arrived at such a conclusion. The reply I received was a peremptory order to return to my mother's house immediately; and on arriving there, the first time I had entered it for some years, I was met by the information that I had nothing more to expect from the countenance of those who had supplied me with the means of prosecuting my studies 'to so bad a purpose.' I was so irritated by what I considered the unjustifiable harshness of this decision, that at the moment I wrote a haughty and angry letter to one of the parties, which of course widened the breach, and made the separation between us eternal.

What was I now to do? I was unfit for any business, both by habit, inclination, and constitution. My health was ruined, and hopeless poverty stared me in the face; when a distinguished solicitor in my native town, who by the way has since become celebrated in the political world, offered to receive me as a clerk. I at once accepted the offer; but knowing that in my *then* condition it was impossible for me to perform the duties required of me, I decided on TAKING OPIUM! The strange confessions of DE QUINCY had long been a favorite with me. The first part had in fact been given me both as a model in English composition, and also as an exercise to be rendered into Pativinian Latin. The latter part, the 'Miseries of Opium,' I had most unaccountably always neglected to read. Again and again, when my increasing debility had threatened to bring my studies to an abrupt conclusion, I had meditated this experiment, but an indefinable and shadowy fear had as often stayed my hand. But now that I knew that unless I could by artificial stimuli obtain a sudden increase of strength I must STARVE, I no longer hesitated. I was desperate. I believed that something horrible would result from it, though my imagination, the most vivid, could not conjure up visions of horror half so terrific as the fearful reality. I knew that for every hour of comparative ease and comfort its treacherous alliance might confer upon me *now*, I must endure days of bodily suffering; but I did not, could not, conceive the mental hell into whose fierce corroding fires I was about to plunge!

All that occurred during the first day is imperishably engraved upon my memory. It was about a week previous to the day appointed for my début in my new character as an attorney's clerk; and when I arose, I was depressed in mind, and a racking pain, to which I had lately been subject, was maddening me. I could scarcely manage to crawl into the breakfast-room. I had previously procured a drachm of opium, and I took two grains with my coffee. It did not produce any change in my feelings. I took two more — still without effect; and by six o'clock in the evening I had taken ten grains. While I was sitting at tea, I felt a strange sensation, totally unlike any thing I had ever felt before; a gradual *creeping thrill*, which in a few minutes occupied every part of my body, lulling to sleep the before-mentioned racking pain, producing a pleasing glow from head to foot, and inducing a sensation of dreamy exhilaration, (if the phrase be intelligible to others as it is to me,) similar in nature but not in degree to the drowsiness caused by wine, though not inclining me to sleep; in fact so far from it, that I longed to engage in some active exercise; to sing, dance, or leap. I then resolved to go to the theatre—the last place I should the day before have dreamed of visiting; for the sight of cheerfulness in others made me doubly gloomy.

I went; and so vividly did I feel my vitality—for in this state of delicious exhilaration even mere excitement seemed absolute elysium—that I could not resist the temptation to break out in the strangest vagaries, until my companions thought me deranged. As I ran up the stairs I rushed after and flung back every one who was above me. I escaped numberless beatings solely through the interference of my friends. After I had been seated a few minutes, the nature of the excitement was changed, and a 'waking sleep' succeeded. The actors on the stage vanished; the stage itself lost its ideality; and before my entranced sight magnificent halls stretched out in endless succession, with gallery above gallery, while the roof was blazing with gems, like stars whose rays alone illumined the whole building, which was thronged with strange gigantic figures, like the wild possessors of a lost globe, such as Lord Byron has described in Cain; as beheld by the Fratracide, when guided by Lucifer he wandered among the shadowy existences of those worlds which had been destroyed to make way for our pigmy earth. I will not attempt farther to describe the magnificent vision which a little pill of 'brown gum' had conjured up from the realm of ideal being. No words that *I* can command would do justice to its Titanian splendor and immensity.

At midnight I was roused from my dreary abstraction; and on my return home the blood in my veins seemed to 'run lightning;' and I knocked down (for I had the strength of a giant at that moment) the first watchman I met: of course there was 'a row,' and for some minutes a battle-royal raged in New-Street, the principal thoroughfare of the town, between my party and the 'Charleys;' who, although greatly superior in numbers, were sadly 'milled;' for we were all somewhat scientific bruisers, that sublime art or science having been cultivated with great assiduity at the public school, through which I had as was customary fought my way. I reached home at two in the morning, with a pair of 'Oxford spectacles' which confined me to the house for a week. I slept disturbedly, haunted by terrific dreams and oppressed by the Night-mare and her nine-fold, and awoke with a dreadful headache; stiff in every joint, and with deadly sickness of the stomach, which lasted for two or three days; my throat contracted and parched, my tongue furred, my eyes bloodshot, and the whole surface of my body burning hot. I did not have recourse to opium again for three days; for the strength it had excited did not till then fail me. When partially recovered from the nausea the first dose had caused, my spirits were good, though not exuberant; but I could eat nothing, and was annoyed by an insatiable thirst. I went to the office, and for six months performed the services required of me without lassitude or depression of spirits; though never again did I experience the same delicious sensations as on that memorable night, which is an 'oasis in the desert' of my subsequent existence; life I cannot call it, for the '*vivido vis animi et corporis*' was extinct.

In the seventh month my misery commenced. Burning heat, attended with constant thirst, then began to torment me from morning till night: my skin became scurfy; the skin of my feet and hands peeled off; my tongue was always furred; a feeling of contraction in the bowels was continual; my eyes were strained and discolored, and I had unceasing head-ache. But internal and external heat was the pervading feeling and appearance. My digestion became still weaker, and my incessant costiveness was painful in the extreme. The reader must not however imagine that all these symptoms appeared suddenly and at once; they came on gradually, though with frightful rapidity, until I became a '*Morburun Mole*,' as a Romanic physician, whose lucubrations I met with and perused with great amusement some years since in a little country alehouse, (God knows how it got there,) poetically expresses it. I could not sleep for hours after I had lain down, and consequently was unable to rise in time to attend the office in the morning, though as yet no visions of horror haunted my slumbers. Mr. P., my employer, bore with this for some months; but at length his patience was wearied; and I was informed that I must attend at nine in the morning. I could not; for even if I rose at seven, after two or three hours' unhealthy and fitful sleep, I was unable to walk or exert myself in any way for at least two hours. I was at this time taking laudanum, and had no appetite for any thing but coffee and acid fruits. I could and did drink great quantities of ale, though it would not, as nothing would, quench my thirst.

Matters continued in this state for fifteen months, during which time the only comfortable hours I spent were in the evening, when freed from the duties of the office, I sat down to study, which it is rather singular I was able to do with as strong zest and as unwearied application as ever; as will appear, when I mention that in those fifteen months I read through in the evenings the whole of Cicero, Tacitus, the Corpus Poetarum, (Latinorum) Boëthius, Scriptores Historiæ Augustinæ, Homer, Corpus Græcarum Tragediarum, great part of Plato, and a large mass of philological works. In fact, in the evening I generally felt comparatively well, not being troubled with many of the above-mentioned symptoms. These evenings were the very happiest of my life. I had ample means for the purchase of books, for I lived very cheap on bread, ale, and coffee; and I had access to a library containing all the Latin classics—Valpy's edition in one hundred and fifty volumes, octavo, a magnificent publication—and about fifteen thousand other books. Toward the end of the year 1829 I established at my own expense and edited myself a magazine (there was not one in a town as large and as populous as New-York!) by which I lost a considerable sum; though the pleasure I derived from my monthly labors amply compensated me. In December of that year my previous sufferings became light in comparison with those which now seized upon me, never completely to leave me again.

One night, after taking about fifty grains of opium, I sat down in my arm-chair to read the confession of a Russian who had murdered his brother because he was the chosen of her whom both loved. It was recorded by a French priest who visited him in his last moments, and was powerfully and eloquently written. I dozed while reading it; and immediately I was present in the prison-cell of the Fratricide; I saw his ghastly and death-dewed features, his despairing yet defying look, the gloomy and impenetrable dungeon; the dying lamp, which served but to render 'darkness visible;' and the horror-struck yet pitying expression of the priest's countenance; *but there I lost my identity*. Though *I* was the recipient of these impressions, yet I was not myself separately and distinctively existent and sentient; but my entity was confounded with that of not only the two figures before me, but of the inanimate objects surrounding them. This state of compound existence I can no farther describe. While in this state I composed the 'Fratricide's Death,' or rather it composed *itself* and forced itself upon my memory without any activity or violation on my part.

And here again another phenomenon presented itself. The images reflected, if the expression be allowable, in the verses rose bodily and with perfect distinctness before me, simultaneously with their verbal representatives; and when I roused myself (I had not been *sleeping* but was only *abstracted*) all remained clear and distinct in my memory. From that night for six months darkness always brought the most horrible fancies and opticular and auricular or acoustical delusions of a frightful nature, so vivid and real, that instead of a blessing, sleep became a curse; and the hours of darkness became hours which seemed days of misery. For many consecutive nights I dared not undress myself nor 'put out the light,' lest the moment I lay down some '*monstrum horrendum, informe ingeus*' should blast my sight with his hellish aspect! I had a double sense of sight and sound; one real, the other visionary; both equally strong and apparently real; so that while I distinctly heard imaginary footsteps ascending the stairs, the door opening, and my curtains drawn, I at the same time as plainly heard any actual sound in or outside the house, and could not remark the slightest difference between them; and while I *saw* an imaginary assassin standing by my bed bending over me with a lamp in one hand and a dagger in the other, I could see any real tangible object which the degree of light that might be then in the room made visible. Though these visionary fears and imaginary objects had presented themselves to me every night for months, yet I never could convince myself of their non-existence; and every fresh appearance caused suffering of as intense and as deadly horror as on the first night! And so great was the confusion of the real with the unreal, that I nearly became a convert to Bishop Berkeley's non-reality doctrines. My health was also rapidly becoming worse; and before I had taken my opium in the morning, I had become unable to move hand or foot, and of course could not rise from my bed until I had received strength from the 'damnable dirt.' I could not attend the office at all in the morning, and was forced to throw up my articles, and as the only chance left me of gaining a livelihood, turn to writing for magazines for support. I left B. and proceeded to London, where I engaged with Charles Knight to supply the chapters on the use of elephants in the wars of the ancients for the 'History of Elephants,' then preparing for publication in the series of the Library of Entertaining Knowledge. For this purpose I obtained permission to use the Library of the British Museum for six months, and again devoted myself with renewed ardor to my favorite studies.

But 'what a falling off was there!' My memory was impaired; and in reading I was conscious of a confusion of mind which prevented my clearly comprehending the full meaning of what I read. Some organ appeared to be defective. My judgment too was weakened, and I was frequently guilty of the most absurd actions, which at the time I considered wise and prudent. The strong common sense which I had at one time boasted of, deserted me. I lived in a dreamy, imaginative state, which completely disqualified me for managing my own affairs. I spent large sums of money in a day, and then starved for a month; and all this while the 'chateaux en espagne,' which had once only afforded me an idle amusement, now usurped the place of the realities of life, and led me into many errors and even unjustifiable acts of immorality, which lowered me in the estimation of my acquaintances and friends, who saw the effect but never dreamed the cause. Even those who knew I was an opium-eater, not being aware of the effects which the habitual use of it produced, attributed my mad conduct to either want of principle or aberration of intellect; and I thus lost several of my best friends, and temporarily alienated many others.

After a month or two passed in this employment, I regained a portion of strength sufficient to enable me to obtain a livelihood by reporting on my own account in the courts of law in Westminster any cause which I judged of importance enough to afford a reasonble chance of selling again; and by supplying reviews and occasional original articles to the periodicals, the Monthly, New Monthly, Metropolitan, etc. My health continued to improve, probably in consequence of my indulging in higher living and taking much more exercise than I had done for two or three years; as I had no need of buying books, having the use of at least five hundred thousand volumes in the Museum. I was at last fortunate enough to obtain the office of parliamentary reporter to a morning paper, which produced about three hundred pounds a year; but after working on an average fourteen or fifteen hours a day for a few months, I was obliged to resign the situation, and again depend for support on the irregular employment I had before been engaged in, and for which I was now alone fit. My constitution now appeared to have completely sunk under the destroying influence of the immense quantity of opium I had for some months taken—two hundred, two hundred and fifty, and three hundred grains a day. I was frequently obliged to repeat the dose several times a day, as my stomach had become so weak that the opium would not remain upon it; and I was beside afflicted with continual vomiting after having eaten any thing. I really believed that I could not last much longer. Tic-doloreux was also added to my other sufferings; constant head-ache, occasional spasms, heart-burn, pains in the legs and back, and a general irritability of the nerves, which would not allow me to remain above a few minutes in the same position. My temper became soured and morose. I was careless of every thing, and drank to excess, in the hope of thus supplying the place of the stimulus which had lost its power.

At length I was compelled to keep my bed by a violent attack of pleurisy, which has since seized me about the same time every year. My digestion was so thoroughly ruined, that I was frequently almost maddened by the suffering which indigestion occasioned. I could not sleep, though I was no longer troubled with visions, which had left me about three months. At last I became so ill that I was forced to leave London and visit my mother in Kenilworth, where I stayed; writing occasionally, and instructing a few pupils in Greek and Hebrew. I was also now compelled to sell my library, which contained several Arabic and Persian MANUSCRIPTS, a complete collection of Latin authors, and nearly a complete one of Greek; a large collection of Hebrew and Rabbinic works, which I had obtained at a great expense and with great trouble — all went; the only relics of it I was able to retain were the 'Corpores Poetarum' and 'Græcorum et Latinorum;' and I have never since been able to collect another library. Idleness, good living, and constant exercise, revived me; but with returning strength my nocturnal visiters returned, and again my nights were made dreadful. I was 'terrified through visions' similar to those which had so alarmed me at first, and I was obliged to drink deeply at night to enable me to sleep at all.

In this state I continued till June, 1833, when I determined once more to return to London; and I left Kenilworth without informing any one of my intention the night before. The curate of the parish called at my lodgings to inform me that he had obtained the gift of six hundred pounds to enable me to reside at Oxford until I could graduate. Had I stayed twenty-four hours longer, I should not now be living in hopeless poverty in a foreign country; but pursuing under more favorable auspices than ever brightened my path before those studies which supported and cheered me in poverty and illness, and with a fair prospect of obtaining that learned fame for which I had longed so ardently from my boyhood, and in the vain endeavor to obtain which I had sacrificed my health and denied myself not only the pleasures and luxuries but even the necessaries of life. I had while at the office in B. entered my name on the books of the Brazen-nose College, Oxford, and resided there one term, not being able to afford the expense attendant on a longer residence. Thus it has been with me through life. Fortune has again and again thrown the means of success in my way, but they have been like the waters of Tantalus, alluring but to escape from my grasp the moment I approached to seize them.

I remained in London only a few days, and then proceeded to Amsterdam, where I stayed a week, and then went to Paris. After completely exhausting my stock of money, I was compelled to walk back to Calais, which I did with little inconvenience, as I found that money was unnecessary; the only difficulty I met with being how to escape from the overflowing hospitality I every where experienced from rich and poor. My health was much improved when I arrived in town, and I immediately proceeded on foot to Birmingham, where I engaged with Doctor Palmer, a celebrated physician, to supply the Greek and Latin synonymes, and correct the press for a dictionary of the terms used by the French in medicine, which he was preparing. The pay I received was so very small that I was again reduced to the poorest and most meagre diet; and an attack of pleurisy produced such a state of debility that I was compelled to leave Birmingham and return to my mother's house in Kenilworth.

I had now firmly resolved to free myself from my fatal habit; and the very day I reached home I began to diminish the quantity I was then taking by one grain per day. I received the most careful attention, and every thing was done that could add to my comfort and alleviate the sufferings I must inevitably undergo. Until I had arrived at seventeen and a half grains a day I experienced but little uneasiness, and my digestive organs acquired or regained strength very rapidly. All constipation had vanished. My skin became moist and more healthy, and my spirits instead of being depressed became equable and cheerful. No visions haunted my sleep. I could not sleep however more than two or three hours at a time; and from about three A. M. until eight, when I took my opium, I was restless, and troubled with a gnawing, twitching sensation in the stomach. From seventeen grains downward my torment (for by that word alone can I characterize the pangs I endured) commenced. I could not rest, either lying, sitting or standing. I was compelled to change my position every moment; and the only thing that relieved me was walking about the country. My sight became weak and dim; the gnawing at my stomach was perpetual, resembling the sensation caused by ravenous hunger; but food, though I ate voraciously, would not relieve me. I also felt a sinking in the stomach, and such pain in the back that I could not straighten myself up. A dull constant aching pain took possession of the calves of my legs; and there was a continual jerking motion of the nerves from head to foot. My head ached; my intellect was terribly weakened and confused. I could not think, talk, read or write; to sleep was impossible, until by walking from morning till night I had so thoroughly tired myself that pain could not keep me awake; although I was so weak that walking was misery to me. And yet under all these désagrémens I did not feel dejected in spirits; although I became unable to walk, and used to lie on the floor and roll about in agony for hours together. I should certainly have taken opium again, if the chemist had not, by my mother's instruction, refused to sell it. I became worse every day; and it was not till I had entirely left off the drug, two months nearly, that any alleviation of my suffering was perceptible. I gradually but very slowly recovered my strength, both of mind and body; though it was long before I could read or write, or even converse. My appetite was too good; for though while an opium-eater I could not endure to taste the smallest morsel of fat, I now could eat at dinner a pound of bacon which had not a hair's breadth of lean in it.

The fifteenth of May was the first day I was entirely free from pain. Previous to my arrival in Kenilworth, an intimate friend of mine had been ruined—reduced at once from affluence to utter penury by the villany of his partner, to whom he had intrusted the whole of his business, and who had committed two forgeries, for which he was sentenced to transportation for life. In consequence of this event, my friend, who was a little older than myself, and had been about twelve months married, determined to leave his young wife and child, and seek to rebuild his broken fortunes in Canada. When he informed me that such was his plan, I resolved to accompany him, and immediately commenced the necessary preparations for my voyage. I was not however ready, not having been able so soon to collect the sum necessary, when he was obliged to leave; and as I could not have him for my *compagnon du voyage*, I altered my course and took my passage for New-York, in the vain hope and expectation of obtaining a better income here, where the ground

61

was comparatively unoccupied, than in London, where there were hundreds of men as well qualified as myself, dependent on literature for their support.

I need not add how lamentably I was disappointed. The first inquiries I made were met by advice to endeavor to obtain a livelihood by some other profession than authorship. I could get no employment as a reporter; and the applications I addressed to the editors of several of the daily newspapers received no answer. My prospects appeared as gloomy as they could well be, and my spirits sunk beneath the pressure of the anxious cares which now weighed so heavily upon me. I was alone in a strange country, without an acquaintance into whose ear I might pour the gathering bitterness of my blighted hopes. I was also much distressed by the intense heat of July, which kept me from morning till night in a state much like that occasioned by a vapor-bath. I was so melancholy and hopeless that I really found it necessary to have recourse to either brandy or opium. I preferred the latter, although to ascertain the difference, merely as a philosophical experiment, I took rather copious draughts of the former also. But observe; I did not intend ever again to become the slave of opium. I merely proposed to take three or four grains a day, until I should procure some literary engagement, and until the weather became more cool. All my efforts to obtain such engagements were in vain; and I should undoubtedly have sunk into hopeless despondency, had not a gentleman, (to whom I had brought an order for a small sum of money, twice the amount of which he had insisted on my taking,) perceiving how deeply and injuriously I was affected by my repeated disappointments, offered me two hundred dollars to write 'Passages from the Life of an Opium-Eater,' in two volumes. I gladly accepted this generous and disinterested offer; but before I had written more than two or three sheets, I became disgusted with the subject. I attempted to proceed, but found that my former facility in composition had deserted me; that in fact I could not write. I now discovered that the attempt to leave off opium again would be one of doubtful result. I had increased my quantum to forty grains. I again became careless and inert; and I believe that the short time that had elapsed since I had broken the habit in England had not been sufficient to allow my system to free itself from the poison which had been so long undermining its powers. I could not at once leave it off; and in truth I was not very anxious to do so, as it enabled me to forget the difficulties of the situation in which I had placed myself; while I knew that with regained freedom the cares and troubles which had caused me again flee to my destroyer for relief would press upon my mind with redoubled weight. I remained in Brooklyn until November. Since then I have resided in the city, in great poverty; frequently unable to procure a dinner; as the few dollars I received from time to time scarcely sufficed to supply me with opium. Whether I shall now be able to leave off opium, God only knows! But whether I do or not, I have no hope whatever of gaining a respectable livelihood in this country; and I shall therefore return to England the moment I can obtain a passage.

WILLIAM BLAIR.

4

SIGMA, 'OPIUM-EATING', *LIPPINCOTT'S MAGAZINE*, 1, 1868, 404–9

SINCE De Quincey gave to the world his famous "Confessions," people have been content to regard opium-eating as a strangely fascinating or as a strangely horrible vice; most imagining that it transports to realms of ideal bliss unsurpassed by all that poet ever penned or dreamt—inducts into reveries that cast into the shade all the promises of an Oriental paradise; while all have undefined and undefinable conceptions regarding it. Indeed, De Quincey's mode of narration (and this is said with all due deference to the memory of that illustrious scholar) is calculated to foster, to some extent, this idea. The mass of persons regard an opium-eater as at best but a mythical being. If they give him any corporeal existence at all, they think of him as they would of a human vampire, or some other creation bordering on the domains of the fabulous. Those who see or hear of him in the flesh, as moving about and performing his duties and functions, either regard what they hear of the evils of the habit with incredulity, or think of these so-called "dreams" and "reveries" as something enviable, and entertain a feeling much akin to making "I dare not wait upon I would." They argue—If he suffers, he also enjoys: he tastes of raptures *they* know not of. They ponder—Here, then, is that which *can* "minister to a mind diseased, pluck from the memory a rooted sorrow, raze out the written troubles of the brain;" and so, by easy steps, to the "sweet oblivious antidote" they go. Again and again have I had said to me, "I should so like to try it, to see what the visions are like." Now, it is notorious that this practice is on the increase in England, and, as I have recently learnt, in this country also. It should be well understood that no man *continues* an opium-eater from choice: he sooner or later becomes the veriest slave; and it is the object of this paper, originally intended for a friend's hand only, to deter intending neophytes—to warn them from submitting themselves to a yoke which will bow them to the earth. In the hope that it may subserve the good proposed, I venture to give a short account of the experiences of one who clasped this phantom "and found it air;" of one who still feels in his tissues the yet slowly smouldering fire of the furnace through which he has passed; of one who, all but too late, has discovered that the idol which he loved and worshiped so was but a poor, mean thing, "with feet of brass and front of clay." That one is the present writer.

I propose to give here a short sketch of my own case, with a few comments thereon. I first took opium in the form of laudanum, nearly ten years ago, for insomnia, or sleeplessness, brought on by overwork at a European university. A late able writer on this subject has observed very aptly that there are certain men to whom opium is as "fire to tow." Of these, it turned out, I was one. It seemed as if my tissues lapped up the drug and reveled in the new and strange delight which had opened up to them. All that winter I took doses of from ten to thirty drops every Friday night, there being but few classes on Saturday of any consequence, so that I had the full, uninterrupted effect of the drug. Then I could set to work with unparalleled energy. Thought upon thought flowed to me in never-ending waves. I had a mad striving after intellectual distinction, and felt I would pay any price for it. I generally felt, on the Sunday, my lids slightly heavy, but with a sense pervading me of one who had been taking champagne. I never, however, during this whole winter, took more than one dose a week, varying from thirty to sixty drops. Toward the close of the session I one day deferred the dose till Sunday evening. On the Monday following, in the afternoon, I was in one of the class-rooms listening to the lecturer on Belle Lettres and Rhetoric. This professor has passed away, but his name, were it mentioned, would be found to take high rank amongst men of letters. One hundred and more young men sat, on that Monday afternoon, listening to his silvery voice as he read, in the course of his lecture, several long extracts from Falconer's "Shipwreck." Not a breath but was held while the splendid conceptions of the poem, its ever-changing images, the dignified mien of the reader, his grand voice and thrilling tones, the mellowed light of the old room, and the opium, to boot, taken on the Sunday evening before, were all doing their work on an imaginative young man of nineteen. My blood seemed to make music in my vessels as it seemed to come more highly oxygenized singing to my brain; and tingled fresher and warmer into the capillaries of the entire surface, leaping and bubbling like a mountain-brook after a shower. I knew not at first what it could be, but I felt as if I could have bounded to the desk and taken the place of the professor. For a while, I say, I could not realize the cause. At last, as with a lightning flash, it came. Yes! It was the opium! Eureka! Eureka!

And at that moment, then and there was signed the bond which was destined to go far to wither all my fairest hopes; to undermine, while seeming to build up, my highest aspirations; to bring disunion between me and those near and dear to me; to frustrate all my plans, and, while "keeping the word of promise to the ear," ever breaking it to my hope. As I trace these very characters, I am suffering from the remote consequences, in a moral point of view, of having set my hand and seal to that bond.

For two years longer that I remained at college I continued to take laudanum three times a week, and I could, at the end of this period, take two drachms (120 drops) at each dose. All this time my appetite, though not actually destroyed, as it now is, was capricious in the extreme, though I did not lose flesh, at least not markedly so. On the other hand, my capability for mental exertion all through this period was something incredible; and let me say here that one of the most fascinating effects of the drug in the case of an intellectual and educated man is the sense it imparts of what might be termed *intellectual* daring: add to this the endowments of a strong frame, high animal spirits, and on such an one opium is the ladder that *seems* to lead to the gates of heaven. But alas for him when at its topmost rung! His wings are burnt, the goal recedes, and crushed by his own guard he falls, and sees beneath a fathomless abyss too surely his—a pit purchased by his own blood, dug by his own hand. After obtaining my degree I gradually eased off the use of the drug for about three months with but little trouble. I was waiting for an appointment in India. At the end of the period named I sailed for my destination, and had almost forgotten the taste of opium; but I found that I was only respited, not redeemed. I found that I had not lost the memory it imparted of the grand self-dependence, the glorious courage to do and dare, the whetting of the intellectual appetite, the over-mastering desire for the exercise of the wit in controversy, the elevation beyond all that was gross or sensual. All this had not passed from my memory, and two months after I had entered upon my duties and found myself quietly among my books, the bond was renewed. After two months, in which I passed from laudanum to crude opium, I finally settled on the alkaloid *morphia*, as being the most powerful of all the preparations of opium. I began with half a grain twice a day, and for the six months ending the last day of September of the just expired year, my daily quantum was sixty grains (a dose sufficient to destroy any two men not habituated)—half taken the instant I awoke, the other half at six o'clock in the evening; and I could no more have avoided putting into my body this daily supply than I could have walked over a burning ploughshare without scorching my feet.

For the first year, five grains, or even two and a half, would suffice for a couple of days; that is to say, there was no craving of the system for it during its deprivation for this space. At the end of this period there would be a sense of depression amounting to little beyond uneasiness. But soon, four hours' deprivation of the drug gave rise to a physical and mental prostration that no pen can adequately depict, no language convey: a horror unspeakable, a woe unutterable takes possession of the entire being; a clammy perspiration bedews the surface, the eye is stony and hard, the nose pointed, as in the hippocratic face preceding dissolution, the hands uncertain, the mind restless, the heart as ashes, the "bones marrowless."

To the opium-consumer, when deprived of this stimulant, there is nothing that life can bestow, not a blessing that man can receive, which would not come to him unheeded, undesired, and be a curse to him. There is but one all-absorbing want, one engrossing desire—his whole being has but one tongue—that tongue syllables but one word—*morphia*.

Place before him all that ever dazzled the sons of Adam since the fall, lay sceptres at his feet and all the prizes that vaulting ambition ever sighed and bled for, unfold the treasures of the earth and call them his; wearily, wearily will he turn aside and barter them all for a little white powder. Let Aphrodite come before him even as she appeared to Paris—

> "Fresh as the foam new bathed,
> In Paphian wells,"

THE DRUG HABIT AND ITS CONFESSIONALS

and regard him with looks that would draw an angel from the spheres, and a corpse would as soon respond: it could not be more cold and impassioned than he, even though

"Her fruitful kisses came thick as autumn rain."

And oh! the vain, vain attempt to break this bondage, the labor worse than useless—a minnow struggling to break the toils that bind a Triton! Like the fabled task of Sisyphus, the effort only redoubles the labor and leaves him farther from its accomplishment.

I pass over all the horrible physical accompaniments that accumulate after some hours' deprivation of the drug when it has been long indulged in, it being borne in mind that it occurs sooner or later according to the constitution it contends against. Suffice it to say that the tongue feels like a copper bolt, and one seems to carry one's alimentary canal in the brain; that is to say, one is perpetually reminded that there is such a canal from the constant sense of pain and uneasiness, whereas the perfection of functional performance is obtained when the mind is unconscious of its operation.

The slightest mental or physical exertion is a matter of absolute impossibility. The winding of a watch I have regarded as a task of magnitude when not under the opium influence, and I was no more capable of controlling, under this condition, the cravings of the system for its pabulum, by any exertion of the *will*, than I, or any one else, could control the dilatation and contraction of the pupils of the eye under the varying conditions of light and darkness. A time arrives when the will is killed absolutely and literally, and at this period you might, with as much reason, tell a man to *will* not to die under a mortal disease as to resist the call that his whole being makes, *in spite of him*, for the pabulum on which it has so long been depending for carrying on its work.

When you can with reason ask a man to aerate his lungs with his head submerged in water; when you can expect him to control the movements of his limbs while you apply an electric current to its motory nerve,—then, but not till then, speak to a *confirmed* opium-eater of "exerting his will;" reproach him with want of "determination," and complacently say to him, "Cast it from you and bear the torture for a time." Tell him, too, at the same time, to "do without atmospheric air, to regulate the reflex action of his nervous system and control the pulsations of his heart." Tell the Ethiopian to change his skin, but do not mock the misery and increase the agony of a man who has taken opium for years by talking to him of "*will*." Let it be understood that after a certain time (varying, of course, according to the capability of physical resistance, mode of life, etc., of the individual) the craving for opium is *beyond the domain of the will*. The desire for it is, so to say, automatic—is entirely involuntary; and this *physical* craving differs in no way from, and may be likened, so far as volition is concerned, to, the appeal of the stomach under the condition of *hunger* and to that of the fauces under thirst. These are local manifestations of a general want, independent of the will, and operating, except under peculiarly exceptional circumstances (and then only for a time), in spite of it. So also is the uncontrollable want of the general system, which results in abstinence from the drug under the circumstances of habitual use, a purely automatic phenomenon, and as purely independent is it of the will as any other involuntary demand made by nature under particular exigencies. And it is just here that the magnitude of the evil and the horrible thraldom is centred. This *bodily necessity* is quite a distinct and separate feeling from that which might be termed the *mental* call which dominates certain temperaments when opium is first indulged in. So intolerant is the system under a protracted deprivation that I know of two suicides resulting therefrom. They were cases of Chinese who were under confinement. They were baffled on one occasion in carrying out a previously-successful device for obtaining the drug. The awful mystery of death which they rashly solved had no terrors for them equal to a life without opium, and the morning found them hanging in their cells, glad to get "anywhere, anywhere out of the world."

I have seen another tear his hair, dig his nails into his flesh, and, with a ghastly look of despair and a face from which all hope had fled, and which looked like a bit of shriveled yellow parchment, implore for it as if for more than life.

I have digressed somewhat from a narration of my individual case to speak generally. This was necessary toward something like an elucidation of the subject. But to return to myself. I attained a daily dose of forty grains, and on more than one occasion I have consumed sixty. It became my bane and antidote; with it I was an *unnatural*—without it, less than man. To sign my name after four hours' abstinence I regarded as an achievement. All this while my hands never shook, nor were they in the slightest degree tremulous, except when abstaining. Nay, I regarded this firmness of hand as a special endowment; and, with twenty grains of the poison in me, I have again and again hit with an Enfield rifle the bull's-eye of a target at four hundred yards. Yet ten minutes before I was prostrate for the want of it. Food, for months previous to the time of my attaining to such a dose as sixty grains, became literally loathsome; its sight would sicken me; my muscles, hitherto firm and well defined, began to diminish in bulk and to lose their contour; my face looked like a hatchet covered with yellow ochre: and this is the best and truest comparison I can institute. It was sharp, foreshortened and indescribably yellow. I had then been taking *morphia* for nearly two years, but only reached and sustained the maximum doses for the six months already indicated.

Finally, even the sixty grains brought no perceptible increase to the *vitality* of which the body seemed deprived during its abstinence. It stimulated me to not one-tenth of the degree to which a quarter of a grain had done at the commencement. Still, I had to keep storing it up in me, trying to extract vivacity, energy, life itself, from that which was killing me; and grudgingly it gave it. Onward, ever onward, increasing, ever increasing, was to be the programme. To go on was death, horrible and debased; to stop was worse than death, worse than the tortures of the damned.

I tried hard to free myself, tried again and again; but I never could at any time sustain the struggle for more than four days at the utmost. At the end of that time

I had to yield to my tormentor—yield, broken, baffled and dismayed—yield to go through the whole struggle over again; forced to poison myself—forced with my own hand to shut the door against hope. When I could think calmly over all this, I felt like one in the constant pursuit of a shadow that was ever eluding his grasp. Under the stimulating effects I was ever *about* to do, and yet never achieving. I was, in truth, a "walking shadow." I felt my own unreality, and when under the spell of the demon I wove plans of ambition, built up hopes of renown. I came at last to feel that it was but tracing characters in the sand—that the waves would soon pass over them and me, and "no man see me more."

With an almost superhuman effort I roused myself to the determination of doing something, of making one last effort, and, if I failed, to look my fate in the face. What, thought I, was to be the end of all the hopes I once cherished, and which were cherished of and for me by others? of what avail all the learning I had stored up, all the aspirations I nourished?—all being buried in a grave dug by my own hand, and laid aside like funereal trappings, out of sight and memory.

I will not detail my struggles nor speak of the *hope* which I had to sustain me, and which shone upon me whenever the face of my Maker *seemed* turned away. Let it suffice that I fought a desperate fight: again and again I recoiled, baffled and disheartened; but *one aim* led me on, and I have come out of the *melée* bruised and broken it may be, but conquering. One month I waged the fight, and I have now been nearly two without looking at the drug. Before, four hours was the longest interval I could endure. Now I am free and the demon is behind me. I must not fail to add that the advantage of a naturally sound and preter-naturally vigorous constitution, and (except in the use of opium) one carefully guarded against any of the causes which impart a vicious state of system and so render it incapable of recuperative effort, was my mainstay, and acted the part of a bower-anchor in restoring my general system. This, and a long sea voyage, aided efforts which would have been otherwise fruitless. On the other hand, let us not too rashly cast a stone at the opium-eater and think of him as a being unworthy of sympathy. If he is not to be envied—as, God knows, he is not—let him not be too much contemned.

I do not now refer to the miserable and groveling Chinese, who are fed on it almost from the cradle, but to the ordinary cases of educated and intellectual men in this country and in Europe; and I assert that, could there be a realization of all the aspirations, all the longings after the pure, the good and the noble that fill the mind and pervade the heart of a cultivated and refined man who takes to this drug, he would be indeed the paragon of animals. And I go further and say that, given a man of cultivated mind, high moral sentiment and a keen sense of intellectual enjoyment, blended with strong imaginative powers, and just in proportion as he is so endowed will the difficulty be greater in weaning himself from it. I mean, of course, before the will is killed. When that takes place, he is of necessity as powerless as any other victim, and his craving for it is as automatic as in the case of any other opium slave. What he becomes then, I have attempted to describe, and in doing so have suppressed much in consideration of the feelings of those who read.

This it is to be an opium-eater; and the boldest may well quail at the picture, drawn not by the hand of fancy, but by one who has supped of its horrors to the full, and who has found that the staff on which he leaned has proven a spear which has wellnigh pierced him to the heart. Who, knowing this, will form a compact with this demon, the penalty for which transcends in horror all the legends ever penned of souls sold to the devil? Let no man believe he will escape: the bond matures at last; he finds himself in the toils, and the siren sings no more; the drug must be taken still, but its sweetness has flown. Well may one thus trapped apply the words described by Dante as written over the gates of hell: "Abandon hope, all ye who enter here."

5

H. G. COLE, *CONFESSIONS OF AN AMERICAN OPIUM EATER: FROM BONDAGE TO FREEDOM* (BOSTON: JAMES H. EARLE, 1895), PP. 5–7, 8–9, 27–32, 47–50, 107–119

Chapter I

Preliminary

THE world today contains untold numbers of noble men and women who, through a lack of knowledge, have become the slaves of some one of the many remedies prescribed by physicians or made enticing by the advertisers' art, to relieve them from an overworked and overtaxed system. It goes without contradiction that physicians are, strange to say,—yet not strange, either, when we recall the exacting duties of their profession,—numbered among opium's ready victims. There is no department of life, no order of society, from the highest to the lowest, that cannot muster a large roll of opium takers. I come in contact with its victims almost everywhere; and that knowledge, and thereby security and immunity from a life of bondage, the power to break from which has not yet been discovered in the realm of medical science by the student or the careful and conscientious practitioner, would in itself alone warrant these "Confessions" being placed before the world.

Had the Opium Eater come in contact in his younger days with a book that would have served as a beacon light to reveal the terrible hell that lies in the pathway of all men from the use of opium, I do not think I should now be recording "The Confessions of an American Opium Eater." If I may be pardoned for criticising so wonderful and prodigious a writer as De Quincy, I have no hesitation in saying that his "Confessions" have done more to create and stimulate a desire in the mind of the indifferent to enter the enchanted realm that he found, than they have to deter; and that the delights, ecstacies and the lofty flights of the imagination therein portrayed, are not warning in character. Well might he have prefaced and ended his work with the inscription which Dante placed over the portal of hell, "All hope abandon, ye who enter here." Effect arises from cause. We look back over our lives and can find an excuse or a reason for being what we are. We lay to some one's charge the misfortunes that have come to us in our existence, and rarely give the credit for the blessings that we have received to any one but ourselves.

The Opium Eater, therefore, brings (nor ever has he) no railing accusation, or curses, or wishes other than the peaceful repose of the soul that first inoculated and opened up the way in his own life whereby the anguish and despair in the opium inferno was brought into it.

In the lives of men who have entered the world's arena to do battle for some great cause of humanity, and who by severe toil, anxiety, and weary days and nights without rest, succumb to this enchanting demon, how readily should all accord to them charity, and pity, and sympathy, and forgiveness.

But, on the other hand, there is a large and growing class throughout the world with no laudable excuse, except, perhaps, ignorance, to a certain extent, whose lives are filled up with seeking sensual pleasures only, and excitement, and dissipation; who turn night into day, live carelessly and recklessly, and with whom anything that affords momentary pleasure and gratification of a sensual character is grasped and indulged in, unmindful of future retribution from transgressed laws; living for the present, unmindful of the morrow, and who pass on and out into the night, unconscious, until too late, of a soul lost, or of such a thing being possible as the salvation of it.

To this latter class I must confess I held allegiance. And well has the poet said, "Fools rush in where angels fear to tread;" and the great mass of humanity today juggle and tipple, young and old alike, the very liquids that bring destruction and despair, and would produce the same undeviating result if indulged in by angels,—for the same trangressed law would produce the same effect.

In my own case, I ascribe the continued use of opium, in great measure, to gambling and associated vices. And yet thousands pass the same way and never come in contact with this form of dissipation. Unlike De Quincy, I have no language to deify the Opium god, although from the bottomless pit of despair he has often lifted me to an exalted physical paradise, but only to hurl me back again—and again—and again!

By apparently slow degrees one reaches the stages of something like perfect growth in all the various pursuits of life. What else could be expected from one whose life-stream was bent in the direction of folly and pleasure, that he should step aside from the swift-running current when his inclinations were bent in that direction? A young man whose life was passed by day in exacting and nerve-destroying employment, and his nights in the society of congenial and fast associates of both sexes of our modern times, the most alluring and fascinating passion with the Opium Eater being the gaming table,—what wonder that he should have become addicted not only to intoxicating beverages, but every other form of soul-destroying narcotics? The laws of morality are so fixed in their eternal round, that

THE DRUG HABIT AND ITS CONFESSIONALS

when a man becomes an habitué of the gambling house, he has almost invariably gathered to himself pretty nearly all the minor vices that lie beneath. And in a farther ascent of this ladder of pleasure and of vice there seems but one rung left, and that is for the "opium eater"; and from his high perch he can obtain an unobstructed view of the teeming thousands indulging in the petty vices that will eventually surge them onward and downward until they, too, may have an unobstructed view of that pit where the rich man was so solicitous of being relieved by drops of water upon his tongue, and for a messenger to warn his five brethren to avoid that place of torment.

Chapter III

My first experiment with opium

ON the 3d of July, 1873, I took for the first time an alkaloid of opium, known as morphia, by hypodermic injection. It was administered under conditions like this: I had been drinking somewhat to excess, and being in the company of those who were habitués to its use, I have no doubt I asked for the privilege of trying it. However, it was administered to me, it being subcutaneously injected in my forearm, a couple of inches above the wrist of the left one. I particularize this circumstance for various reasons; the most important of which is that morphine administered below the elbow or kneejoints, or the under part of the arms or limbs, has the effect of making exceedingly sore places, and the absorption is less effective, and the result generally not so satisfactory. No doubt the student of anatomy can account for this. Morphia thus used above the joints, immediately raises a bunch not dissimilar to that of a mosquito bite, only magnified many fold. Almost instantly it shoots off into little streams upward and instantaneously the nerve centers respond like a galvanic shock to the terrible power, and wave after wave passes over the system, at times the shocks being so frequent and powerful as almost to stop the breath, and make one gasp. They become pleasant when not too precipitous. The same effect may result from an injection below these parts of the body. Of the thousands upon thousands of these hypodermic syringe marks on the Opium Eater's body above the joints, there are comparatively few below. Excruciating agony alone compelled these few exceptions. Further along in my career the pain arising from this form of using the drug would surely have made me resort to these untouched parts of the body had it been even possible without useless torment. My use, in this respect, of these portions of the body have also been the experience of others of my acquaintance, and for similar reasons. Why, I do not know. That it is true, physicians to the contrary, notwithstanding, is a fact.

The effect of this first "hypo" (a term that will be used largely in the remaining pages to designate "hypodermic injections") was so powerful and overwhelming that almost immediately I fell over, and desired to be let alone and sleep. I was not allowed to. For some time—I do not know how long—I was walked up and down the room. I have at this late day no vivid recollection of how the night was passed, except that a dull and heavy stupor permeated my being. And while I can look back to the scenes preceding and immediately following the taking of the drug, the remaining hours of the night remain hopelessly blank. It being the night of all nights the noisiest in America,—that preceding the Fourth of July,—I had been unmindful of it so far as to noise in one of its most noisy strongholds. The next morning I felt compelled to go to my employment, being connected with a Sunday paper. The invisible forces seemed to have conspired with the visible, for no amount of persuasion could induce my foreman to grant me leave of absence, and my pride forbade me humiliating myself, and the drug seemed to still further determine me to penance and to mortification.

Concerning the ecstatic state described by De Quincy, it was anything but realized in this, the Opium Eater's first experience. I was benumbed. I was sick,—dreadfully sick. I was in the world; I did not seem of it. And yet I felt powerless to act. Mechanically I strove to do something. My spirit seemed chained within me. I managed to go through the motions of labor, but accomplished really nothing. An observer, if he did not watch too closely, would have called it work. My arms were like weights. My face was haggard, and pale beyond description. My eyes were full, dead, and almost sightless. Within I was a flaming fire, and nothing I could drink would quench it; for nothing would stay on my stomach hardly longer than swallowing it. My mouth, and throat, and the whole membrane of the stomach seemed to have taken on a coating not unlike fur; water would not penetrate it, nor whiskey cut it. No sooner was it taken in than it would be ejected with the force of a squirt-gun. I was keenly on the alert, above all things, that no one should discover my condition, and the excitement incidental to the day, and the isolated position I occupied in the office helped me out.

It was a long, long day, and a longer night before I got "good night." Now, while I was conscious momentarily of my doings, I could not have told what I had done five minutes previous. When I say that my memory, by constant training, enabled me to remember everything I would do from one week's end to another, even to remembering so trifling a matter as a number of lines, say two or three, scattered through the columns of a paper, I could not remember one solitary thing I did when I came to look for it in the following week. Responsibility was there, however, from the fact that I was conscious of what I was doing at the time, although not remembering it after a lapse of hours.

When finally released early Sunday morning from those long and terrible hours, I sought my couch. I have always been impressed with the thought,—and of course such a thing as recording it never entered my mind,—when looking back to that day (twenty-one years ago) that the following Monday, late in the afternoon, was the time I first awoke from my first opium stupor, some thirty-six to forty hours after retiring.

After such an experience as that, the general reader will say, How could any one ever be so foolish as to again indulge in so cursed a thing? It is passing strange; but, alas, we do! This is only a multiplication of the effect of tobacco on almost

THE DRUG HABIT AND ITS CONFESSIONALS

every delicate, sensitive constitution. Nature resents this invasion of a foreign foe, and fights for her purity with the only weapon at her command against her overthrow; but at last, after repeated assaults, she submits, but never wholly and unreservedly, for all along life's voyage she makes attempts to regain her first estate,—but the battle more often goes against her. A few reconquer themselves; all might.

The indulgence in both liquor and tobacco are entered into too thoughtlessly by parents. Children are brought up in constant contact with father's pipe; and parents there are who thinking it a cunning, boyish trick to see the contaminating thing in a child's mouth, have a little later in life seen him adopt the habit of tobacco using almost as naturally as ducks take to water, with a seemingly natural relish, and with none of those "upside down" and the-earth-flying-up-to-bump-you-in-the-face sensations, and the action of the limbs, too, put in motion as though two-foot obstacles were put in the pathway at every step. Man's whole nature repulses these invasions at first, in the great majority of cases; and when they have become a forced part of his life, will not yield without a fierce battle far more aggressive and desperate than the surrender to them; and even if mastered, the ill effects will cling, and are too often made manifest in broken health and nervous and irritable temperaments.

But how can the Opium Eater make better excuse for a further indulgence in opium than in making use of the following lines of the poet?—

> "Vice is a monster of so frightful mien,
> As, to be hated, needs but to be seen;
> Yet, seen too oft, familiar with her face,
> We first endure, then pity, then embrace."

As time went on, coming in daily contact with the drug and its users, and adjusting the amount taken more to my temperament, or more scientifically, so to speak, I indulged on occasions more particularly where dissipation or excessive hours of labor had exhausted nature, without giving a thought of coming slavery and bondage, and that hopeless despair was my final doom. Chloral, too, another powerful drug, played no inconsiderable part in this game of life and death. There was no more necessity for my using these drugs at that time than has my sleeping child now lying before me. No pains, no aches, no disease, no sad bereavements, no losses of friends or affections of the heart ruthlessly betrayed,—nothing but simply contact incited me to make use of them. They brought to me none of those enchanting and heavenly sensations described by De Quincey to lure me on. Morphia came to me, rather, when in other dissipations I had found the apex of enjoyment. A small quantity of this delusive fluid made of me, for the time being, a new creature, and weariness and fatigue fled, and the animal and carnal nature found expression where it otherwise would have lain dormant.

Chapter VI

I attempt to break away from the opium habit, do not succeed, and return to gambling

LEFT with sufficient property, on the death of my wife, to have kept me for the remainder of my life in comfort, my opium habit did not immediately strike me as needing attention. The gambling mania was again upon me, and I passed many of my waking hours within the haunts of this and kindred sports, and followed out the inclination of a man with no ambition or stated purpose in life. Along in the summer months following my wife's decease (1880), I determined to make an effort to release myself from my opium habit. In New Hampshire there resided a physican who had an "antidote" for the morphine habit. I had consulted him once before, and he had been very frank and confidential with me on that occasion. The patient, however, at that time, was another person,— my wife. He told me then that it was useless to try further for her; that she was beyond help; that neither De Quincy nor any one else had ever left off the use of the drug, and invited me to read De Quincy's "Confessions," and also a work by Dr. Calkins on the opium habit, both of which he loaned me. Alas! I did not read them, however. The latter book might have been read with profit. At least, it would have shown me the end of the road, as found by others, over which I was fast traveling. But now things had changed, and I was in need of assistance. His formula, also, had undergone a change for the better,—they usually do in such cases,—and he thought by a strict conformity to his directions I would come out all right. I tried it, but I almost immediately abandoned it, as it did not sustain me. And yet, in a comparatively short space of time, I came to him again. And again, ashamed to be known by him, under an assumed name I consulted him. "Drowning men catch at straws." Opium users grasp false promises and delusive hopes almost to the very last.

I returned to Boston, and followed a still falser light, if possible,—the gaming table. In the toils of gamblers I put up a "bank roll," and with a finely furnished house in the residential portion of the city, banked a "private game," and on the "inside" saw the operation of the system of "protection," and how immunity from arrest and trouble is carried out by the paid guardians of the public weal. This book being more intimately associated with the Opium Eater's experiences with the drug, he leaves his gambling life for a more enlarged form.

I narrate an incident occurring while engaged in this unrighteous occupation, to show the potency of opium on the mind in cases of anxiety, and how indelibly fixed everything will remain in connection with it. During the early fall I went to Albany, N. Y., in company with my lecherous friends, with the double purpose of "banking" a faro game and attending the races. Gambling seemed an uncheckable vice in that metropolis. It was nearly midnight; in my room at the Delevan House I dropped my hypodermic syringe upon the floor and the glass barrel was broken. This left me stranded, so to speak; and while I might have drank the drug, as many do, I preferred this more torturous way of injecting it under the skin. On account of the lateness of the hour, I apprehended I might have some trouble in getting the instrument and morphia, being a stranger in the city. Groundless fear. In all the years I had been associated with opium takers, in cities of several States, with statutory enactment severe and penalties large for violation of the law, and in innumerable drug stores, the Opium Eater never experienced any more difficulty in obtaining the drug than in buying the most harmless thing. Here it was simplicity itself. I met some one at that late hour with intelligence enough to direct me to such a place as I was looking for, and I easily found it. The druggist had drawn his curtains, to close. Asking in a calm and thoroughly familiar manner for the objects of my visit, and at the same time explaining in an offhand way my accident, he readily showed me his wares, and I as hastily purchased those I was in need of. He volunteered to me, in the conversation that ensued, the information that he had twelve opium patients to whom he daily administered the drug; and the terrible experiences of two others came up before my eyes, as I contemplated the aggregate amount of their misery. I have read since, from newspaper clippings, that Albany has been maligned, perhaps falsely, as having a large number of opium takers. Where are they not? But the effect of that midnight visit was so indelibly fixed on my mind, that although it was my first and only visit to that city, and years have since elapsed, the Opium Eater feels confident he could go from that hotel to that drug store blindfolded.

Much of the dark mystery which surrounds the manifestations of so-called mind-readers, mediums, and hypnotic influences, might be cleared away if one takes into consideration that the best manipulators of the "black art" are not infrequently the users to excess of drugs in some one of the many forms. They thus place themselves in a more placid or receptive state, and throw their powers unrestrained into their "guides'" control.

Anæsthetics, in the form of chloroform and ether, are frequently resorted to and prescribed in critical emergencies to enslaved opium victims; and I affirm whereof I know, when I say that disembodied evil spirits are their controlling power, whereas the "medium" may be largely ignorant of the source from whence they derive their manifestations. It was the intention of the Opium Eater to relate an experience under the mediumistic or hypnotic state produced by ether; an experience so full of evil spirits and mind torture; that I preferred to bear the ills of my cursed existence than resort to this mode of temporary relief ever after. He believes, however, that in stating its source, he renders as valuable a service as though he gave the experience; while, perhaps, on the other hand, it might throw a little light on so-called psychical phenomena.

Israel's king, when forsaken by God's prophet, went to the same unholy source for light, and in the soothsayer of Endor had revealed to him his own calamitous end. There is no God in these revealments from any point of view, and the code of morals established in Jesus Christ are largely ignored in practice if not in precept by those thus fortified in spiritualistic manifestations.

Chapter XVI

My blessed emancipation from morphia

ON MAY 7, 1883, the Opium Eater again went to the services being held in the aforesaid church. I did not hear anything during the meeting that particularly impressed itself upon me, and at its close I lingered a moment to allow the more hurried ones to pass out; and as I followed in the rear, and approached the door, I heard a voice—sweet, musical, and pure. Raising my eyes to see from whence so heavenly a sound proceeded, they beheld the loveliest face they had ever looked upon, with a small, beautifully shaped hand extended toward me, and the welcome sound of "Brother," as she took my emaciated hand in hers. She was attired in deep mourning, and at her side stood another, similarly dressed, older, but not less noble, a sister. The scene was a strange one, and the interest manifested by the younger, who did all the talking, in a soft, inspired, musical tone of voice, with an earnest truthfulness, riveted me to the spot.

I shall relate further on the incidents that led up to this remarkable, and to many it may seem strange, interview.

If the reader shall have discovered any merit in this feeble record of a rescued life, I can unhesitatingly say that the experience of this young woman furnishes one unparalleled in spiritual power, and singularly beautiful in its purity, innocence and exceeding interest. I listened in deep silence to her story of Divine interposition, and the emotion that filled me at its close found vent in an "open confession" of my life as a degraded sinner past hope, and an opium eater.

I could conceive how God could love a pure and spotless woman, innocent and confiding as a child; but for a man, and a sinner like myself, the case was far different. I mentioned to her these doubts in my wretched existence, and closed by saying,—

"I am addicted to the use of morphia; God never can do anything for me."

Why do tears flow unbidden from the eye, and speech become inaudible and the voice beyond control on such occasions? As I parted with this angel of light, her hand was again given to me with an accompanying word of encouragement. In attempting to pass a group of religious people who evidently had been interested spectators to this uncommon scene,—as "Gertrude" was well known in the church as one "wonderfully raised up by the Lord,"—a clergyman "laid hands" on me, and would have further detained me; but the same voice, now like "one having authority," bade him let me pass on.

Out into the cool air of that beautiful May night, my thoughts engrossed in the testimony I had just heard, I walked toward my room, situated more than a mile away. Alone, with characteristic habit, I put my hand into my pocket and brought forth my tobacco as an accompaniment to help my musings, and was about to take a piece of the favorite morsel, when my thoughts were turned on the uncleanliness of this habit in connection with what I had just heard, and I was forced by

THE DRUG HABIT AND ITS CONFESSIONALS

conviction to cast it away. Probably I never desired a "chew" more than I did then; but I threw it away, and I am impressed with the thought that the next morning I procured another piece.

In my room, tired and weary, and deeply perplexed, I knew not what to do. To leave off my morphine meant a death far more horrible than suicide.

The Opium Eater took his "hypo" and retired.

I had made a promise to the young woman that I would come to the meeting the next evening. A series of meetings were being conducted by a revivalist, who made the claim of having been reformed from drink and converted from infidelity. He did not, however, inspire any great expectations or hope in me, believing as I then did that the former habit could be fought and conquered by the individual himself, as I had then done for months past, without claiming reformation or help from God, though I now know I was being sustained by that invisible power. Infidels (unorthodox) there might be, but so far as a disbelief in a Supreme Intelligence, Power or Being are concerned, I did not believe that existed where ordinary intelligence dwelt.

When evening came I reluctantly wended my way toward the church. I found on entering, however, that the order of service had been changed, and instead of being in the vestry, as on the previous evening, the body of the church had been substituted. A little late, intentionally, I cautiously looked about for a place where the Opium Eater would be least likely of being observed, and the gallery being unoccupied, with but one exception, I passed in and took a seat directly behind its solitary occupant. He was a man well nigh threescore and ten years. In connection with the evangelist, the pastor of the church occupied the pulpit. He is a clergyman of repute in the Baptist denomination, and the author of various works, among them being "The Ministry of Healing." At the close of the short preaching or "exhorting" service, a most singular thing happened,—if we do not believe that intelligent forces exist about us. The clergyman stepped down from the pulpit, and ascending a short flight of steps directly opposite, in a moment's time was by the Opium Eater's side. He gazed intently and earnestly for a moment at the emaciated form and sunken countenance of the victim of folly and dissipation, like one who looks with a pitying glance upon a picture wherein only misery and despair lingered, and out of which all hope had fled. Speech failed him, so far as the Opium Eater was concerned, but turning to the old gentleman, he asked, in substance,—

"Are you on the Lord's side, brother?"

"For more than forty years," I heard the old man reply; and then, hesitatingly, the clergyman cast a look of commiseration upon the Opium Eater, and passed down the steps and from view.

Situated as I was, I could not see many of the audience below, and, in general, they interested me very little. I had not seen the "angel of light" who had ministered to me the previous evening, and felt greatly relieved, than otherwise. For how could I be saved? Perhaps she was not there.

CONFESSIONS OF AN AMERICAN OPIUM EATER

But I was mistaken. She had discovered my presence from the first; had witnessed all that had taken place from the moment her pastor had left the sacred desk and abandoned his mission unaccomplished.

It was a trying moment to her. Powers known only to those who have come in direct contact with them, struggled for the mastery. Finally, raised from her seat by power superhuman, she passed out of the main body of the church into the vestibule and up the stairs and along the length of the gallery of the church, as though borne on "the wings of the wind," and like a creature from the world celestial, she took a seat by my side.

What was said related to the surrender of my soul to Him who had created it.

The evangelist was exhorting the unsaved, after the unscriptural methods of modern times, to accept the Saviour. Of course, my companion urged me to comply with the invitation. I lacked not only the courage of a public declaration, but such an act on my part was freighted with far greater consequences than any one could conceive,—an abandonment of opium and an excruciating death, or a worse fate in a drawn-out existence of imbecility.

Then, too, the presence of this beautiful and innocent woman seemed to clearly manifest the gulf that separated me from such a hope. I felt that her character might suffer by lingering longer in my company, and when she volunteered to accompany me down the steps, to lead my faltering soul back to God, I refused the offer solely on these grounds alone.

The old gentleman, however, who had been a willing or unwilling listener,—perhaps both,—kindly proffered to accompany me down to the altar. To this I assented, and we went forward. The evangelist had also selected some verse of Scripture,—to what end, the Opium Eater cannot say,—which the candidate was supposed to repeat after him. But I refrained from this catechising lesson, and instead, I solemnly asked God to have mercy on my soul. I pass over much that took place incidentally, and which was neither helpful nor inspiring, and at the meeting's close, after a short conversation with my deeply interested friend, I was glad of the opportunity to take my departure. And while she could have had no knowledge of what an opium eater's life meant, she knew by discernment that my terrible physical condition meant more than suffering of an ordinary character. Having herself passed through the fiery ordeal of physical agony, she knew the Power that could alone make my burden light!

Did all of these occurrences of this part of the evening happen by chance? Did the Opium Eater, in his studied endeavor to get in as secluded a place as possible, thwart the leading of the Invisible? How account for the act of the clergyman? He is not, I venture to remark, prone to like acts. Then, too, the solitary old man, and the part he took. To the young woman, of course, to many thoughtless minds, not so much attention will be paid. Woman is always doing deeds of goodness and mercy like this. Did you ever note a face that was pinched by suffering or by opium dissipation? My facial expression beggared description; my general

THE DRUG HABIT AND ITS CONFESSIONALS

appearance was that of one in extreme poverty. Pity, you say, prompted her. Nay, not wholly.

The emaciated face, the garments I wore, the rings, even, on my finger, were all familiar to her. She had seen that face—that ghastly, emaciated countenance—a long time before; not once, twice, but thrice it had been shown to her by One who alone makes revelations to whomsoever He will. Hence her acts *are* accounted for. [Not, however, till several years after the occurrences just narrated, when she had become the wife of the redeemed Opium Eater, did she confide these facts to him.]

But the acts of the others, myself included, were they governed and controlled by Him who takes cognizance even of the sparrows, and to whom all things are known and no mystery exists?

*   *   *   *   *   *

But now to my battlefield, where the final contest for freedom in death was to be fought. It was a low-studded room, situated in the L part of the house, and very plainly and scantily furnished.

But to me, then, it was far more palatial and comfortable than any the Opium Eater had ever realized. Appreciation of its meager comforts had taken the place of all desire for those fine adornments and luxuries of other days. I entered that room as calm and tranquil in soul and spirit as an innocent man ascends the scaffold, or a heroic soul faces danger and eternity, with a confiding trust that the revealment beyond is not one to be shunned, but rather one that will far transcend the expectations of those who have lived in this hope of immortal life. I thought on and carefully weighed the words of this young woman's testimony; an unmistakable revelation to me, and one full of hope, and not of fear. The physical agony I felt prepared to undergo until released and set free by death. I was, however, largely ignorant of the terrible manner in which opium or morphine users died under an entire abandonment of all narcotics, as the only case then familiar to me had passed away finally under the influence of sulphuric ether—the last agency to annihilate physical agony. My past efforts in this direction were unthought of. I realized that days must pass in untold distress, but finally, death—the welcome messenger of deliverance—would set me free!

The Opium Eater lay down upon an old lounge in the room, and thoughts passed panoramically across his vision. It seemed as though an invisible yet present voice aided him when he could not think fast enough concerning the individual cases of hypocrisy and inconsistencies that he had witnessed and been made a sufferer by in the lives of professing Christians. And as a final argument to my now persuaded mind that it was all a mistake, words like these seemed to be rung in my ears by a voice clear as a bell: "There is nothing in it (God or Christianity). People go to church to have a good time, the same as you go to the gaming-table, the theatre, the race-track and other places. That is their method of enjoyment; this is yours."

Springing to my feet, I answered these concluding and convincing statements by an expression given vent to in words, as if I was really in the presence of a visible personage,—"That's so!"

Hardly had the words died from my lips, when a voice, quick, and sharp, and piercing, gave utterance to these words: "This is your last opportunity! If you go back on what you have done tonight,—this is your last chance!" As those words rang through my soul, there pervaded my being, from the crown of my head, a power that might be likened to a bolt of fire, and in its effect far more sedative than opium itself! I hesitated no longer. I determined to abandon morphia and all its kindred alliances. I made no agonizing prayer; I committed my soul to the love and tender mercies of a Supreme Being—my Heavenly Father. For the first time in years I disrobed and went to my bed without taking a "hypo" of morphine.

When I awoke it was morning, and I was a "new creation." My sleep had been as sweet and tranquil as that of a babe. No feeling or desire for the drug possessed me; no cold, nauseating sensations and symptoms manifested in the least decrease of the drug was apparent, or anxiety. I knew I was in the world, but I could hardly realize it. None of the signs and terrible agony described in this book accompanying the abandonment of opium were mine, in feeling or in look.

My brother occupied the room and bed with me. He did not know of the step I had taken, and I have no recollection of being awakened when he retired later, nor did I communicate it to one any else save the young woman to whom I have referred. What folly to have thought of finding sympathy from those who were unfamiliar with the habit, and what nonsense to have expected it from those who knew anything about it! The first class would have said it was a trifling affair; the latter, an impossible thing and useless to attempt. My brother, made familiar with it by a number of years of constant contact with myself, knew by observation the utter uselessness of trying to foil this demon by heroic resolution, by artifice, or by antidotes. When he first came to associate intimately with me, and occupy my apartments, he has told me that he had often stood beside my bed and watched intently for signs of life. My face under its deadly power would appear like marble, my arms often raised above my head, and not a muscle giving a perceptible evidence that the inanimate form contained life, the breathing being entirely undistinguishable, and for hours I would lie in this deathlike condition. He expected at any time to find me dead from over-indulgence.

So on that bright May morning he noted the change before I had recovered from my own cause for wonderment.

I was free! That I knew!

"What are you smiling at?" he asked, as he raised a bottle containing medicine to his lips, to take what is vulgarly termed a "smile."

"I am not smiling," I replied; and then I related to him the cause for the expression of happiness he had noted on my countenance. When I had finished, he looked earnestly and pleadingly toward me and said:—

"Hen (he always called me 'Hen'), you are not going to your work without taking your morphine with you, are you?"

THE DRUG HABIT AND ITS CONFESSIONALS

I always carried in my pocket the case containing my "hypo" and a bottle of morphia. It was my life—my existence. He knew that. The last thing at night, on retiring, I would fill the syringe to the amount required and lay it within reach of my hand, in case I awoke in the night and felt in need of it, or to give me strength to rise by in the morning. I could forget everybody and everything, but not this. My brother had learned this by too many experiences; and fearful, no doubt, that I had lost my mind, or surely would, or that some calamity might come to me, he was forewarning me. Had he not asked the question, I should, without doubt, have taken it along with me.

"No," I replied; "I am done. I'm not going to take it any more."

He was one of those set and determined mortals himself, and without commenting further, he left the room and went to his employment.

Left alone, my joy was too great for utterance. I arose, but none of the feelings incident to the abandonment of this terrible habit manifested themselves,—no trembling, no weakness, no nausea, none of the symptoms described as following even the diminution of the drug were now apparent. A calmness supreme reigned within, and no thought or desire for the drug, that had been my waking demand for years, came into my mind.

An intense desire for food, a keen hunger, possessed me. A delicate eater at all times, my light appetite always had made it possible for me to obtain the best, and often in my destitute and wretched plight, my unwelcome presence forced its way into fashionable places of eating, as well as drinking, for this reason alone. More than once has the Opium Eater quietly been informed, by well-intentioned servants, at fashionable bars and hotels where in his profligate days he had been a welcomed guest, that his room would be preferable to his presence.

But this morning I felt an hungered, and as I entered the restaurant my first order to the waiter was that he immediately bring two cups of coffee. Coffee was a drink I had never used to any great extent; for years lager beer was indulged in at meals, as it counteracted some of the injurious effects of morphine. But now, coffee, and two cups at that, were always brought to me by the waiter as soon as I entered. I followed this up but a short time, and finally abandoned it altogether.

In flesh, too, I was frightfully emaciated. Morphine, like liquor, acts differently on different constitutions. Some persons grew stout and dropsical; others, like myself, thin, and emaciated, and bloodless. But now the flesh seemed to fairly drop on to my bones, and I noted a gain of many pounds in a comparatively short time.

As to my first day of emancipation: The reader has been made familiar with the incidents of time in an opium user's life. It never can be overdrawn. Language cannot exaggerate it. But note the change. In more than forty years of life I have never known so fleeting a day. We all know many pleasures in life where Time has taken the swiftest wings of flight. In a prodigal's life, perhaps, a more infinite variety of such occasions may occur, but none flee so swiftly as those where Love is the guest. Love was the Opium Eater's guest that day! The hours passed as though Time had been obliterated. It was evening before I realized it. But to the outward

CONFESSIONS OF AN AMERICAN OPIUM EATER

observer I presented a picture of one in physical distress. Through my chest, and especially the small of the back and loins, it seemed that a conspiracy existed for my overthrow. I had to sit down quite frequently, for a moment, and then I was up and at my work again. I do not now remember, but probably I did not immediately confide to my associates what I had been taken from during the intervening hours. My personal appearance had told its own tale of life, except the opium part of it. I had made no confidant of this to any one except the superintendent, when he gave me employment.

But when the noon hour came, I told those of my fellow-workmen who took interest enough in me to inquire the cause of my apparent physical uneasiness, the reason for for it, and my boundless gratitude to my Deliverer.

The feelings here described must not be confounded as bearing any relationship to those experienced by the Opium Eater in his attempts with antidotes and in his hospital struggle. Everything was clear and light; no disorder of the functions of the body, or excesses in any direction. I might liken the condition I have feebly attempted to describe as not unlike that experienced in an uncomfortably fitting shoe—a desire to get the foot out and give it rest; an expansion to make room for the crowded spirit that had taken possession of the soul!

When I arrived at my room at the end of my day's toil my brother had preceded me. He had passed a day of intense anxiety. He was prepared at any moment to hear of my being dead, or, worse—insane. Finding me all right he soon took his departure, leaving me alone to myself.

6

A. CALKINS, 'OPIUM-LITERATURE IN THE REFLEX VIEW', IN *OPIUM AND THE OPIUM APPETITE* (PHILADELPHIA: J LIPPINCOTT, 1871), PP. 88–98

> "Tibi cum fauces urit sitis, aurea quæris
> Pocula? Num esuriens fastidis omnia præter
> Pavonem rhombumque?" —HORACE.

> "True I talk of dreams,
> Which are the children of an idle brain,
> Begot of nothing but vain fantasy." —ROMEO AND JULIET.

1. THE *intellectual atmosphere* engendered by the fumes of opium is but a confused commixture of sunshine and cloud, which, when intervening between the eye that surveys and the object contemplated, presents a picture as exaggerated or distorted in its proportions as it is confused and grotesque in its colorings. The transformation is as great as we observe in Abou Hassan, son of the Bagdad merchant, in his metamorphosis as Caliph, now giving audience from the throne to arrogant emirs and obsequious viziers, or again feasting in palatial gardens, with Sunshine, and Coral-Lips, and Heart's-Delight, the caterers to his pleasures and his banquet-companions.

2. *Transport the man* to a newly-created visionary sphere, as author he must, in the nature of things, reappear in his novel thought-creations and musings, a veritable evolution of his proper self. The contrary view would involve that Persian paradox, soul dualism; the idea of the soul alternately swayed between Ormuzd the good principle, and Ahriman the bad. Prof. N. Porter has enunciated the true doctrine in this compact sentence: "For the individual to undertake to hide himself behind the mask, is simply impossible; the features of the original will certainly shine through, and invariably." Even of dramatic representation, in which actor and the character personated are for the occasion blended, the same parallelism holds. No more could Kemble or Macready have exhibited the same Hamlet, than they could have reproduced the Garrick in his proper identity.

OPIUM-LITERATURE IN THE REFLEX VIEW

3. *So of the life*, which is but the outgrowth proper of the *spiritus intus*, thought and resolve energized into action. We reverence the "Great Teacher," our ideal exemplar "in all manner of conversation and godliness," for the "sufficient reason" (as Leibnitz would have had it), that in Him the exemplifications of spiritual culture and growth were so harmoniously congruent with his didactic utterances. When the Great Captain made appeal to his army, as it was deploying within the shadows of the Pyramids, in the memorable words—"Du haut de ces pyramides quarante siècles vous contemplent, From the summits of yonder pinnacles there are looking down this day upon your exploits the generations of forty centuries,"—was there a soldier in those ranks but for the moment imagined himself as marshalled into the very presence of those generations? All disclaimers to the contrary notwithstanding, is there a superficial reader only, who, following the "childe" in his wanderings, continues all the while uncognizant of the fact, that he has in company the veritable original, the aberrant youth whilom a dweller in Albion's Isle,

> "Who né in Virtue's ways did take delight?"

Goldsmith in the "Traveller" is Goldsmith *personâ propria;* on every page of the "Table Talk" the conversational poet has unwittingly made some etching of the melancholic enthusiast:

> "'Tis Nature pictured too severely true."

4. *Let the man* deliberately yield himself up to the mastery of a depraved appetite, the soul must perforce become contaminated from the festering virus, the moral sense will be perverted, the finer sensibilities and nobler aspirations will decline and die out, and life's aim become erratic and purposeless, until existence itself seems shrunken to the diminutive proportions of a troglodyte semi-creation. Here and there indeed fancy may kindle into an ephemeral glow and genius sparkle once more in some fitful resuscitation; but in the stead of the joyous sunbeam gloriously shining around in its serene effulgence, there will have succeeded a vapory ignis-fatuus with its blinky flashiness, a phosphorescent fire glimmering athwart the murky horizon,

> "That leads to bewilder and dazzles to blind."

5. *Out of deference* to that impersonal juridicist and literary *arbiter elegantiarum*, "Common Fame," which in its exultant admiration would so persistently hold up and keep before the public view as model-casts of intellectual acumen and æsthetic taste the Aristarchus and the Trismegistus of their tribe, De Quincey and Coleridge, they are here reintroduced in their proper presentable characters. So long as a jejune subtility of thought shall command

THE DRUG HABIT AND ITS CONFESSIONALS

distinction by force of style-ornamentation, or tenuity of fabric shall offer in compensation an "endless thread of verbosity," so long shall these magnates in transcendental criticism continue to be recognized as star-actors on the lists of the *dramatis personæ*. The true key to their speculations must be searched for in their biographies.

6. *De Quincey* made his first essay upon opium during his student-life at Oxford. Some gastric derangement, sheltered under that broad-shouldered patronymic, dyspepsia, offered a plausible excuse; but back of this a more cogent incitement was at work, the longing felt for some sort of artificial excitement for occasions, and particularly in anticipation of the Saturday-evening opera. His maximum for the day, 8000 drops, was attained by the eighth year—a nominal and putative rather than a precisely definite measure, as appears in a declaration recently made by his quondam-friend Sinclair, who had accompanied De Quincey time and again to the apothecary's in Edinburgh where stands Scott's monument, to see him toss off a wine-glass of laudanum and with a *sang-froid* as if the draught had been mere water.

7. *The autobiographer and essayist*, author of "Suspiria de Profundis" (*ex* Profundis is meant), as also of "Letters to Young Men," and the rest, was wont to herald every fresh volume of his "farrago libellorum" with the pretentious announcement, "By Thomas De Quincey, Author of Confessions of an English Opium-Eater." On every successive title-page, along with the conscious confession to an overshadowing infirmity, is thus paraded a palpable yearning after a notoriety that should pre-occupy the public curiosity,* rather than a precatory appeal, in arrest of judgment, to a lenient public sympathy. "Is this a guide to them that sit in darkness, an instructor of the foolish?" He that "gropeth at noonday as in the night" renders but a dubious protection against the moral titubations of inexperienced youth, who, if walking blindly, appear peradventure less blind than their leader. *Quousque tandem?*

> 8. "Shall gentle Coleridge pass unnoticed here,
>   To turgid ode and humid stanza dear?"

S. T. Coleridge, a Cambridge student in 1796, having been confined for some weeks (bed-ridden as his own account was), for œdema of the knees, with rigidity of the same, found his solace in laudanum. The suggestion had been made by a fellow Cantab. The first dose, 20 drops (a bold and ominous setting out truly), produced an effect so satisfactory as to encourage the repeated use. There appears, however, to have been a letting up not long after, for in 1800 he thus writes to a friend: "I have my health now, restored perfectly." Only four years from this he is well-nigh broken down, having succumbed to his habit beyond retracing, for

---

* "Digito monstrari, et dicier, 'Hic est!'
  Pro nihilo pendes?" —PERSIUS.

now he had reached his high-water line, going at the rate of a pint for 3½ days. On some of these days he used up, as was known, a whole pint. Like the *elixir-vitæ* man, Paracelsus, his prototype in this matter, whichever way he went or wherever he tarried, the laudanum-vial was his regular *compagnon de poche.*

9. *To have an appreciative view* of this dreamy sentimentalist in his alternations of indulgence and penitential regrets, we have simply to refer to the gleanings and garnerings as served up by his "next friend" and most estimable confidant, Joseph Cottle, Esq.—

> "Oh, Joseph Cottle!—(Phœbus, what a name
> To fill the speaking-trump of future fame!")—

and we have our subject presented in his pure undress, to be microscopically anatomized with a pertinacity truly Boswellian. Here emerges into view the transcendentalist *ex integro,* Sinon-like,

> "Fidens animi et in utrumque paratus,"

ready with palliatory excuses for stealthily indulging an unbridled appetite while affecting the merit of a severe self-abnegation; one day discoursing from the pulpit upon celestial themes, the next, by an easy transition, junketing upon a biscuit and a bottle of brandy, or hobnobbing with a chum over a brace of port. One time, after the big doses had become established, under the consciousness of a spirit disquieted within, he delivers himself in a jeremiad after this sort; "I have learned what sin is; sin, that is to say, against an infinitely great and imperishable object, the soul of man!"

10. *This soi-disant ethicist* and quixotic epicurean, pseudo-penitent and rampant voluptuary combined, who could talk of opium as "an accursed thing entailing evils worse than death," yet, as if resolved on straining physical endurance to its extreme tension, seemed bent on making a ubiquitous acquaintance with narcotics and stimuli of every name. Taking no warnings from his experiences with a single poison, baleful to him as that was, he must needs have a trial of bang, hyoscyamus, and nitrous-oxide withal. That a man thus "everything by turns and nothing long," who in his every-day life was as "unstable as water," that one who, when unable so much as to rule his own spirit, should arrogate the office of spiritual director to youth in "Essays towards the Formation of Fixed Principles in Politics, Morals, and Religion"—themes than which none more profound can engage the contemplative mind, and all under the pretentious title of "Friend"—verily all this conveys to the chance-reader the apprehended suspicion, that philosophy may by possibility be travestied in sonorous periods of the mock-burlesque.

11. *As representative* exponents of contrarieties in the realm of poesy, Byron and Coleridge may be set in advantageous juxtaposition.

> "*Genevan* ichor,
> Or some such other spiritual liquor,"

(so saith Leigh Hunt) fired the muse of the one, opium befogged the intellect of the other. Byron's pictures glisten like Alcyone and her sister Pleiads in the starry realms; Coleridge shades off into a *chiarooscuro* nebulosity. For verisimilitude of description, picturesque limning and glowing pathos of sentiment, where may we find a recreated scene that shall bear comparison with the "Trinidada and the Shipwreck?" The fond admirers of the Bristol bard need not be chary of their proffered homage—*latreia* or *douleia*, whichever it be—to their quondam idol, from apprehension of incurring penance for any supposed violation of the Decalogue, seeing that the "Mariner," as imaged in the "Rime," knoweth not its analogue in the "likeness of anything that is in the heaven above, or in the earth beneath, or in the water under the earth." As the Edinburgh hath it, "The shadow of something is resolved into the substance of nothing."

12. *Any attempt* to follow along the devious track by which the *outré* fancies of Coleridge would conduct us, were as bewildering as a chase after the giant shadows that loom up from out the mists of the Hartz. Not in the gas-light illuminations of the camera shall we see symmetrical combinations of form and harmonious blendings of tints as produced in the kaleidoscope. Strip Coleridge and De Quincey together of their tinselly word-drapery, enucleate the seed from its pericarp, and apply your magnifier to the residue. Suppose the Suspiria, the Essays, the Confessions, with all their ostentatious train, were dislodged from the alcoves of our libraries, wherein would metaphysics or ethics, political science or œconomics, be shorn of any real strength?*

13. *The autobiographer*, Mr. B., observes, that for a term of three years after he had come under the habitual use of morphine, he was as comfortable in his general health and as vigorous for brain-work as he had ever been. He, for all, while claiming for opium-eaters a certain "method in their madness," makes the significant admission that their speculations are as vagarious as their eccentricities are peculiar. This martyr-votary (for such he had become through a third and final relapse into a bondage dating thirty years back), so versatile in mental adaptiveness, "grammaticus, rhetor, geometres"—preacher, lawyer, and editor, by a sort of *e-pluribus-unum* combination, seemed to present a tangible realization of the poet's conception,—

> "Sometimes he, like Cerberus, would seem
> Three gentlemen at once."

14. *As appertaining* to the history of this species of literature three names renowned in oratory, and representative of three nationalities respectively, claim distinctive notice here.

---

* "Tolle tuum, precor, Hannibalem victumque Syphacem
E castris, et cum tota Carthagine migra."—JUVENAL.

OPIUM-LITERATURE IN THE REFLEX VIEW

15. *Lamartine*, a *Cato redivivus* in his curule-chair before the presence of the Assemblée Nationale, having survived his proper self, sunk in a dotage into which gourmanderie with opium finally conspiring had hopelessly cast him, has at last passed from our sight forever,

> "Hei mihi qualis erat, quantum mutatus ab illo!"

Painfully verified in him was a remark of De Pouqueville—"The opium-eater has ceased to live ere he has ceased to exist."

16. *Robert Hall*, driven to opium as a resource against nervous derangement and general physical prostration, should, in view of his reluctant surrendry to one evil as against a greater, be accounted an exceptional case rather. Inherited constitutional susceptibilities had as early as his sixth year determined in an intense spinal pain; a symptom aggravated undoubtedly by a habit in his boyhood of sitting with his book and perhaps for hours together in the shade of some tree. In 1826 or by twenty years from the first, he was taking 1000 drops of laudanum daily; but this quantity he appears not to have exceeded. His sufferings, at no time less than severe, were some days excruciating. During all this trying period he had not passed so much as a single night in bed, and sometimes he went sleepless the night through. Upon him opium appears to have operated less as a physical excitant than as a neutralizer of pain. The moral sense does not seem to have swayed out of its proper equilibrium here through any disturbing attractions generated by a temulent imagination. The soul within, still self-poised and serene, could say to itself,

> "Retire; the world shut out, thy thoughts call home;
> Imagination's airy wing repress."

17. *John Randolph of Roanoke*—that incarnation of irony and lord of ridicule—that

> "Fiery soul, which working out its way,
> Fretted the pigmy body to decay,"

was from early youth an invalid with a severe spinal malady of some sort, out of which grew an irritability that cleaved to him his lifetime (Garland). It were no extravagance of charity to assume that the capricious exacerbations of temper and the habitual waywardness of demeanor that so obtrusively marked the man, were in large measure ascribable to the all-controlling habit as much as to the inherited physique. In intellectual fire, sarcastic invective, and withering repartee, Randolph loomed up before his peers of the American Congress,

> "Like to some meteor streaming to the wind,
> With gems and golden lustre rich emblazed."

THE DRUG HABIT AND ITS CONFESSIONALS

The halos that in fancy played around those tremulous lips, as words seraphic in tones mellifluous swelled upon enraptured ears,

"The applause of listening senates to command,"

faded with the occasions that had evoked them, fleeting away like "the troubled sea that cannot rest." Fit inscription for the tombstone of the poet-orator were the line—

"Here in the dust the wreck of genius lies."

Part 2

DRUG USE OBSERVED

7

ANON, 'USE OF OPIATES AMONG THE OPERATIVE POPULATION', *CHAMBERS EDINBURGH JOURNAL*, 3, 1845, 346–48

AMONG the numerous causes of disease and death brought to light by the publication of the report of the Health of Towns Committee, there is one to which but little attention has been paid; and yet, as appears from the statements of Dr Lyon Playfair, it is an evil of a most serious character, widely spread, and one that saps the vitals of the labouring population at their very source. The details in great part will appear incredible to those who are unacquainted with the habits of the poorer classes.

We have been accustomed to read with feelings of horror of the prevalence of infanticide in some of our Indian provinces; but what shall we think of the habitual practice of administering opiates to infants from their very birth, to lull them to quietness while their mothers are working in the factories?—in too many cases, unhappily, careless of the appalling consequences of their indiscretion, which show themselves eventually in the deformity, disease, or death of their offspring.

'The custom first originated,' says Dr Playfair, 'according to all concurrent evidence, in the frequency of disorders, having their primary seat either in the stomach or bowels, arising partly from injudicious feeding and improper nursing, but principally from the irritability produced by their continued exposure to a polluted atmosphere, and other physical causes of disease. The children thus disordered were taken to unlicensed practitioners, who prescribed opiates as a general remedy, and their mothers mistook the soothing effects produced by narcotics for proofs of improvement, and themselves continued the practice. They soon discovered that the administration of narcotic drugs prevented restlessness in the child, enabling them to pursue their ordinary avocations; and thus a practice, often originating in disease, has become habitual, even in cases where disease did not exist. Druggists who vend such narcotic preparations speak as to the extent of their use; and their evidence is perhaps the more to be depended upon, as it was their interest to diminish rather than to exaggerate the extent of the evil.' He goes on to give the evidence of 'a respectable druggist in Manchester, whose customers are, however, entirely of the poorer class, among whom it may safely be said that there is scarcely a single family in which this practice does not prevail. The way it is done is this: the mother goes out to her work in the morning, leaving her child in charge either of a woman who cannot be troubled with it, or with another child of perhaps ten years old. A dose of "quietness" is therefore given to the child to prevent it being troublesome. The child thus drugged sleeps, and may waken at dinner-time; so when the mother goes out again, the child receives another dose. Well, the mother and father come home at night quite fatigued, and as they must rise early to begin work for the day, they must sleep undisturbed by the child; so it is again drugged, and in this manner young children are often drugged three times in each day. This druggist states further that he sells, *in retail alone, about five gallons per week of "quietness," and half a gallon of "Godfrey;"* the strength of the former preparation is such as to contain one hundred drops of laudanum in an ounce; a single teaspoonful is the prescribed dose; so that, allowing one ounce weekly to each family, this one druggist supplies 700 families every week.'

A melancholy characteristic of this fatal practice is the unconcern with which it is followed. Another druggist says, there is 'no dread of laudanum now; it is often used for the same purposes as "quietness." The usual dose to produce sleep in a restless child is eight drops, and this being, like the other, gradually increased to three doses a-day, amount to twenty-four drops.' We are informed that '*three* druggists,' whose evidence is just quoted, 'all of acknowledged respectability, are selling respectively five-and-a-half, three-and-a-half, and one—in all ten gallons weekly; two of them testifying that *almost all the families* of the poor in that district habitually drug their children with opiates; and the third, after a lengthened examination of all the customers who attended a pawnbroker's shop, kept by a relative of his own, giving as a statistical result, that five out of six families in his district were in the habitual use of narcotics for children.'

In the report furnished by the Rev. J. Clay, on the sanitary condition of Preston, there is a table illustrative of the proportions of infantile deaths in the dispensary, and in the worst streets: in the former the proportion is, in even numbers, 8 per cent.; in the latter 44 per cent.—a most striking difference, which is accounted for by the fact that, 'if the wretched inhabitants of these worst streets sought medical aid at all, they would seek it most likely where it could be obtained without charge. If the druggist is sometimes applied to for the medicine, which with greater propriety and safety would be prescribed by the medical man, he is too often asked for compounds which no medical man would prescribe; such as "Godfrey's Cordial," "Infants' Preservative," "Soothing Syrup," "Mothers' Blessing," &c. Returns have been obtained from almost all the chemists and druggists in Preston of the quantity of these mixtures sold by each; the aggregate of the whole quantity indicates that, allowing half an ounce per week to each family, upwards of 1600 families are in the habit of using "Godfrey's Cordial," or some other equally injurious compound.' Mr Robert Brown, a surgeon, states, 'A child was brought to me for a little aperient medicine; the mother suspected that the person who nursed it had been in the habit of giving it some narcotic. It had not had more than two or three motions for the space of three weeks. I advised the mother to stay at home and attend to it herself. The advice was followed, and the child recovered in a few days.'

It may be thought that the evils here pointed out being moral rather than physical, admit easily of the application of the proper remedies; but it is observed that 'the thoughtlessness and unreflecting ignorance of many parents, and the callousness towards their offspring of others, is stronger than the parental feeling, which will lead, in numerous instances, to the indiscriminate administration of opiates and spirituous liquors to sick children.'

'Similar evidence as to the prevalence of the custom is given by druggists in all the towns visited. In Wigan, four druggists examined agree in describing the practice as "very prevalent among the lower orders," and in stating that it appears to prevail with all those who have occupations in factories, workshops, and other places at a distance from home, which oblige mothers to leave their children the whole or greatest part of a day.' The same statements were made by druggists at Rochdale and Bury; and Mr Whitehead, the registrar for Ashton-under-Lyne, says, 'I conceive that the practice of administering opiates to children is very prevalent among the working-classes, and I think more particularly where there are natural children born, and left in charge of the keepers of houses where the mothers lodge, while the latter are working in the mill. In going to register deaths, I have frequently remarked children looking very ill, and on observing this to the neighbours, they have said, "It is no wonder that they are so—they are slept to death;" meaning that sleeping stuffs were given to them.'

The same fatal practice prevails also in Liverpool, accompanied, among the Irish population, by the administration of ardent spirits; equally destructive of human life. In fact, in the whole of Lancashire and the factory districts generally, the evil has been adopted with the most reckless disregard of consequences. The painful surprise which the perusal of these statements produces will, however, be diminished when we read that 'it is no uncommon thing to meet with married females at fifteen, and they are frequently mothers at seventeen; the fathers being but little older. To increase the bearing of this cause upon the mortality of children in the manufacturing districts, comes the fact, that in two, three, or four weeks after delivery, the young mother, if she have but one, two, or three children, returns to her work in the mills, leaving the charge of her children either to some old woman or young girl, or puts them out to nurse. The effects of this unnatural treatment are visible upon the infant in a very short time. A child, born apparently strong and healthy, may almost always be known two or three months after birth if it belong to a mother who goes to the factory. Instead of being plump and growing, it is almost invariably emaciated and less than at birth—commonly wasted by continued diarrhœa, brought on by the manner of its diet. The mother suckles it but at meal times and at night; the milk, having been so long secreted, is too stimulating for the child, and the succedaneous food, in quantity and kind, adds to the irritation. The greatest ignorance prevails as to the organisation and requirements of a child as regards diet. It is no uncommon thing to be consulted for emaciated children with extensive mesenteric disease; and on inquiry, to find that the food consists in great part of bacon, fried meat, and fatty potatoes, when the infant has not perhaps two teeth in each jaw to masticate it.* I am convinced of the great bearing of these facts upon the mortality of children, from the circumstance that a greater proportional number of first and second children die before they attain five years of age, than of children born after the mother has relinquished her factory employment.'[†] While much of this great mortality may doubtless be traced to the extremes of poverty so often met with in manufacturing districts, there is ample evidence of the waste of infant life from the causes in question; for in Wiltshire and Dorsetshire, where the wages are notoriously low, only 11 per cent. of all the children born die before they attain one year of age, while 17 per cent. are carried off in Lancashire. Dr Playfair observes that, 'in the small town of Clitheroe, the population of which, amounting to 6765, consisting partly of calico-printers, and partly of factory operatives, I found a weekly sale of four pints of Godfrey's Cordial, and an annual sale of 4000 poppy heads, for making "sleeping tea for children." One druggist describes these drugs as being sold "to an alarming extent among the factory population: not so much so among printers." Another describes the sale "as *decent* for the size of the town." '

The evil is not only serious in its actual effects, but in prospect; all the inquiries made on the subject elicited proofs of its alarming increase, with a tendency upwards to the middle classes; it has been alleged, though without any clear foundation, that the increase arises from the 'temperance movement;' the use of fermented liquors being supplied by that of opiates. But the whole weight of medical testimony is directly opposed to their exhibition. We are told that 'the administration of this class of medicines requires the greatest skill in the physician. Nothing is more uncertain than the effects of opium upon young subjects; and it ought never to be employed, even by medical men, except with the greatest caution, as it sometimes acts with much violence, and has proved deleterious even in very small doses. Half a drachm of genuine syrup of white poppy, and, in some instances, a few drops of "Dalby's Carminative" has proved fatal in the course of a few hours to very young infants.'[‡]

In summing up the evidence, we encounter evils still more fearfully impressive. Who that has felt the endearing relation of infantile existence, can fail of being moved by the statement of a druggist who says, 'it is curious to see the children in the shop; they stretch out their little hands, for they know the bottle, and when they get it, drink it as eagerly as the drunkard does his glass. I have seen the little children in the shop put the neck of the bottle in their mouths and bite the cork, so fond are they of the preparation; for coming to the shop so often, they know the bottle.'

We read of a child who had been so much habituated to the drugs, that it 'took 100 drops of laudanum during the day;' and of parents 'who are in the habit of giving their children these drugs when the child is only three or four weeks old,

---

* See Chambers's Miscellany of Tracts, No. 6, for Management of Infants.
† Dr Strange, Ashton.
‡ Dr John Clarke on the Diseases of Children. London. 1815.

96

and in many instances younger: this is gradually increased to a double dose, until at last some children will take six drachms a-day to produce the same effect as half a drachm did when they first began to take it.'

There is no difference of opinion among the witnesses as to the extent of the evil, which is felt not only in the loss by death, but in the deterioration and destruction of the mental and physical powers of those who survive the treatment. Dr Playfair states that 'instances have been brought before him in which idiocy and insanity have certainly followed as the result of the practice;' and further, 'I have been led by laborious inquiry to the conclusion, that the custom of administering narcotics to children originated primarily in, and is upheld by, the physical causes of disease acting upon the younger portion of the community. On the removal of these causes, the general inducement to the continuance of the system would cease, for the irritability and difficulty of management of children would diminish with their increased health. It is an evil not confined to factory districts, as some have alleged, for the recent trials in Wales have shown it to be very prevalent in rural districts; and numerous inquiries in small towns in agricultural counties have convinced me of its existence there, though to a much less extent. The diffusion of knowledge, and, above all, the removal of the physical causes of disease, will go far to check this great evil.'

We would gladly indulge the hope that our endeavour to set forth the horrible results of this practice, may be the means of directing such attention to it as will tend to diminish or remove it altogether. We agree with Dr Playfair that to education alone are we to look for the *real* remedy; 'much may be done *with* the people as well as *for* them. Health is as dear to the poor as to the rich. The most abject part of the population—creatures who belong to no class, but are the reprobates, unfortunate, fallen of all classes and several races—can understand its value, and, as we know, are capable of making sacrifices for the good of others; what may not then be expected from the great mass of the labouring English population, from the intelligent artisans of towns, who are so apt in acquiring their difficult arts, and are certainly not surpassed by other classes in the facility with which they grasp and carry out a scientific principle clearly announced? To leave many things to the people themselves will be to proceed slowly, because knowledge and new principles can only be communicated slowly, but it will be to proceed surely; and the improvement will not die away or be superficial, for it will be the act of the mind, penetrate the inmost recesses of home, and be imparted to future generations.'*

* Fifth Report—Registrar-General.

8

ANON, 'THE NARCOTICS WE INDULGE IN', *BLACKWOOD'S EDINBURGH MAGAZINE*, 74, 1853, PART 1, 129–39, PART 2, 605–28

WHEN a distinguished man sinks into his grave, from the midst of many rivals in a common race, the strife of opinions in reference to him is instantaneously allayed; personal feelings, if not quenched, are repressed and hushed; and, like the heroism of the triumphant warrior, when he is caught by the anxious eye emerging unscathed from the battle and the smoke, his merits appear now unclouded and confessed. Such, we believe, is the general feeling among the members of his own profession in regard to the author of the valuable work now before us. Snatched suddenly from the midst of his labours, before the third edition of his *Materia Medica* was completed, there are few in any way familiar with the subject who will not regret the sudden extinction of so much learning, and, apart from all private considerations, that the world should have so prematurely lost the benefits of his ripening judgment and experience, and the results of his extended reading and research. Yet how many precious cabinets of collected knowledge do we see thus hurriedly sealed up for ever! How often, when a man appears to have reached that condition of mental culture and accumulated information, in which he is fitted to do the most for the advancement of learning, or for promoting the material comfort of his fellows, how often does the cold hand suddenly and mysteriously paralyse and stop him! He has been permitted to add only a small burden of earth to the rising mound of intellectual elevation, scarcely enough to signify to aftercomers that *his* hand has laboured at the work. Nevertheless, he may have shown a new way of advancing, in some sense, so that to others the toil is easier and the progress faster, because he has gone before. The more, however, the true-hearted worker in the cause of progressive science becomes familiar with its actual condition and its great future, the more he becomes satisfied also of the vanity of attempting to associate with an individual name the merit of this or that advance—the more earnestly he trains himself to find the best reward for individual attempts in the growing conquests and dimensions of the field he cultivates, and in the consciousness that he has not been unhelpful in widening its domain. Such a consciousness Dr Pereira might well entertain, and we trust he found in it something to alleviate the regrets the best of us naturally feel, when compelled to leave a favourite task unfinished.

We should be forsaking widely the field we usually occupy, were we to attempt to lay before our readers any analysis of a work so elaborate and so purely professional as this of Dr Pereira. We propose, however, to take it as our text-book, in considering a subject of great general interest—one scarcely of more importance to the professional physician than it is to the physiologist, the psychologist, and the economical statist. The book is replete with scattered information on the subject of the *Narcotics we Indulge in*, and some of this we propose to bring together in the present article. And among other sources from which we mean to draw the materials necessary to our purpose, are the *Confessions of an English Opium-Eater*, long, long ago noticed in our pages, but, to us who have been reading it to-day, as fresh and new as ever—as full of interest, as suggestive of profound reflection. We who are ourselves somewhat scientific, can scarce restrain a selfish sigh when we think how fresh and new, how sure of human sympathy this actual burning experience of a living man will continue to be when the heavy and toilsome tomes of Pereira shall have become mere records of the progress of science, and be turned up only to illustrate the ignorance of the most learned or trusted in their professions about the middle of the nineteenth century.

In ministering fully to his natural wants, man passes through three successive stages. First, the necessities of his material existence are provided for; next, his cares are assuaged and for the time banished; and lastly, his enjoyments, intellectual and animal, are multiplied and for the time exalted. Beef and bread represent the means by which, in every country, the first end is attained; fermented liquors help us to the second; and the third we reach by the aid of narcotics.

When we examine, in a chemical sense, the animal and vegetable productions which in a thousand varied forms, among various nations, take the place of the beef and pudding of the Englishman in supplying the first necessities of our nature, we are struck with the remarkable general similarity which prevails among them naturally, or which they are made to assume by the artifices of cookery, before they are conveyed into the stomach. And we exclaim, in irrepressible wonder, "by what universal instinct is it that, under so many varied conditions of climate and of natural vegetation, the experience of man has led him everywhere so nicely to adjust the chemical constitution of the staple forms of his diet to the chemical wants of his living body?"

Nor is the lightening of care less widely and extensively attained. Savage and civilised tribes, near and remote—the houseless barbarian wanderer, the

---

1 *The Elements of Materia Medica and Therapeutics*. By JONATHAN PEREIRA, M.D., F.R.S. Third Edition. London, 1849–50. Pp. 1538.

2. *The Confessions of an English Opium-Eater*. Fifth Edition. London.

settled peasant, and the skilled citizen—all have found, without intercommunion, through some common and instinctive process, the art of preparing fermented drinks, and of procuring for themselves the enjoyments and miseries of intoxication. The juice of the cocoa-nut tree yields its *toddy* wherever this valuable palm can be made to grow. Another palm affords a fermented wine on the Andean slopes of Chili—the sugar palm intoxicates in the Indian Archipelago, and among the Moluccas and Philippines—while the best palm wine of all is prepared from the sap of the oil-palms of the African coast. In Mexico the American aloe (*Agave Americana*) gave its much-loved *pulque*, and probably also its ardent brandy, long before Cortez invaded the ancient monarchy of the Aztecs. Fruits supply the cider, the perry and the wine, of many civilised regions—barley and the cereal grains the beer and brandy of others; while the milk of their breeding mares supplies at will to the wandering Tartar, either a mild exhilarating drink, or an ardently intoxicating spirit. And to our wonder at the wide prevalence of this taste, and our surprise at the success with which, in so many different ways, mankind has been able to gratify it, the chemist adds a new wonder and surprise when he tells us, that as in the case of his food, so in preparing his intoxicating drinks, man has everywhere come to the same result. His fermented liquors, wherever and from whatever substances prepared, all contain the same exciting alcohol, producing everywhere, upon every human being, the same exhilarating effects!

It is somewhat different as regards the next stage of human wants—the exalted stage which we arrive at by the aid of narcotics. Of these narcotics, it is remarkable that almost every country or tribe has its own—either aboriginal or imported—so that the universal instinct has led somehow or other to the universal supply of this want also.

The aborigines of Central America rolled up the tobacco leaf, and dreamed away their lives in smoky reveries, ages before Columbus was born, or the colonists of Sir Walter Raleigh brought it within the chaste precincts of the Elizabethan court. The coca leaf, now the comfort and strength of the Peruvian muletero, was chewed as *he* does it, in far remote times, and among the same mountains, by the Indian natives whose blood he inherits. The use of opium and hemp, and the betel nut, among eastern Asiatics, mounts up to the times of most fabulous antiquity, as probably does that of the pepper tribe in the South Sea Islands and the Indian archipelago; while in northern Europe the hop, and in Tartary the narcotic fungus, have been in use from time immemorial. In all these countries the wished-for end has been attained, as in the case of intoxicating drinks, by different means; but the precise effect upon the system, by the use of each substance, has not, in this case, been the same. On the contrary, tobacco, and coca, and opium, and hemp, and the hop, and *Cocculus indicus*, and the toadstool, each exercise an influence upon the human frame, which is peculiar to itself, and which in many respects is full of interest, and deserving of profound study. These differences we so far know to arise from the active substances they severally contain being chemically different.

I. Tobacco.—Of all the narcotics we have mentioned, tobacco is in use over the largest area, and by the greatest number of people. Opium comes next to it; and the hemp plant occupies the third place.

The tobacco plant is indigenous to tropical America, whence it was introduced into Spain and France in the beginning of the sixteenth century by the Spaniards, and into England half a century later (1586) by Sir Francis Drake. Since that time, both the use and the cultivation of the plant have spread over a large portion of the globe. Besides the different parts of America, including Canada, New Brunswick, the United States, Mexico, the Western coast, the Spanish main, Brazil, Cuba, St Domingo, Trinidad, &c., it has spread in the East into Turkey, Persia, India, China, Australia, the Philippine Islands, and Japan. It has been raised with success also in nearly every country of Europe; while in Africa it is cultivated in Egypt, Algeria, in the Canaries, on the Western coast, and at the Cape of Good Hope. It is, indeed, among narcotics, what the potato is among food-plants—the most extensively cultivated, the most hardy, and the most tolerant of changes in temperature, altitude, and general climate.

We need scarcely remark, that the use of the plant has become not less universal than its cultivation. In America it is met with everywhere, and the consumption is enormous. In Europe, from the plains of sunny Castile to the frozen Archangel, the pipe and the cigar are a common solace among all ranks and conditions. In vain was the use of it prohibited in Russia, and the knout threatened for the first offence, and death for the second. In vain Pope Urban VIII. thundered out his bull against it. In vain our own James I. wrote his "Counterblaste to Tobacco." Opposition only excited more general attention to the plant, awakened curiosity regarding it, and promoted its consumption.

So in the East—the priests and sultans of Turkey and Persia declared smoking a sin against their holy religion, yet nevertheless the Turks and Persians became the greatest smokers in the world. In Turkey the pipe is perpetually in the mouth; in India all classes and both sexes smoke; in China the practice is so universal that "every female, from the age of eight or nine years, wears as an appendage to her dress a small silken pocket, to hold tobacco and a pipe." It is even argued by Pallas that the extensive prevalence of the practice in Asia, and especially in China, proves the use of tobacco for smoking to be more ancient than the discovery of the New World. "Amongst the Chinese," he says, "and amongst the Mongol tribes who had the most intercourse with them, the custom of smoking is so general, so frequent, and has become so indispensable a luxury; the tobacco purse affixed to their belt so necessary an article of dress; the form of the pipes, from which the Dutch seem to have taken the model of theirs, so original; and, lastly, the preparation of the yellow leaves, which are merely rubbed to pieces and then put into the pipe, so peculiar—that they could not possibly derive all this from America by way of Europe, especially as India, where the practice of smoking is not so general, intervenes between Persia and China."*

* *M'Culloch's Commercial Dictionary,* edit. 1847, p. 1314.

Leaving this question of its origin, the reader will not be surprised, when he considers how widely the practice of smoking prevails, that the total produce of tobacco grown on the face of the globe has been calculated by Mr Crawfurd to amount to the enormous quantity of two millions of tons. The comparative magnitude of this quantity will strike the reader more forcibly, when we state that the whole of the wheat consumed by the inhabitants of Great Britain—estimating it at a quarter a-head, or in round numbers at twenty millions of quarters—weighs only four and one-third millions of tons; so that the tobacco yearly raised for the gratification of this one form of the narcotic appetite weighs as much as the wheat consumed by ten millions of Englishmen. And reckoning it at only double the market value of wheat, or twopence and a fraction per pound, it is worth in money as much as all the wheat eaten in Great Britain.

The largest producers, and probably the largest consumers, of tobacco, are the United States of America. The annual production, at the last two decennial periods of their census returns, was estimated at

$$1840, \quad . \quad . \quad . \quad 219,163,319 \text{ lb.}$$
$$1850, \quad . \quad . \quad . \quad 199,752,646 \text{ ,,}$$

being about one-twentieth part of the whole supposed produce of the globe.

One of the remarkable circumstances connected with the history of tobacco is, the rapidity with which its growth and consumption have increased, in almost every country, since the discovery of America. In 1662, the quantity raised in Virginia—the chief producer of tobacco on the American shores of the Atlantic—was only 60,000 lb.; and the quantity exported from that colony in 1689, only 120,000 lb. In two hundred and thirty years, the produce has risen to nearly twice as many millions. And the extension of its use in our own country may be inferred from the facts that, in the above year of 1689, the total importation was 120,000 lb. of Virginian tobacco, part of which was probably re-exported; while, in 1852, the quantity entered for home consumption amounted to

$$28,558,753 \text{ lb.}$$

being something over a pound per head of the whole population; and to this must be added the large quantity of contraband tobacco, which the heavy duty of 3s. per lb. tempts the smuggler to introduce. The whole duty levied on the above quantity in 1852, was £4,560,741, which is equal to a poll-tax of 3s. a head.

Tobacco, as every child among us now knows, is used for smoking, for chewing, and for snuffing. The second of these practices is, in many respects, the most disgusting, and is now rarely seen in this country, except among seafaring men. On shipboard, smoking is always dangerous, and often forbidden; while snuffing is expensive and inconvenient; so that, if the weed must be used, the practice of chewing it can alone be resorted to.

For the smoker and chewer it is prepared in various forms, and sold under different names. The dried leaves, coarsely broken, are sold as canaster or knaster.

When moistened, compressed, and cut into fine threads, they form cut or shag tobacco. Moistened with molasses or with syrup, and pressed into cakes, they are called cavendish and negro-head, and are used indifferently either for chewing or smoking. Moistened in the same way, and beaten until they are soft, and then twisted into a thick string, they form the pigtail or twist of the chewer. Cigars are formed of the dried leaves, deprived of their midribs, and rolled up into a short spindle. When cut straight, or truncated at each end, as is the custom at Manilla, they are distinguished as *cheroots*.

For the snuff-taker, the dried leaves are sprinkled with water, laid in heaps, and allowed to ferment. They are then dried again, reduced to powder, and baked or roasted. The dry snuffs, like the Scotch and Irish, are usually prepared from the midribs—the rappees, or moist snuffs, from the soft part of the leaves. The latter are also variously scented, to suit the taste of the customer.

Extensively as it is used, it is surprising how very few can state distinctly the effects which tobacco produces—can explain the kind of pleasure the use of it gives them—why they began, and for what reason they continue the indulgence. In truth, few have thought of these points—have cared to analyse their sensations when under the narcotic influence of tobacco—or, if they have analysed them, would care to tell truly what kind of relief it is which they seek in the use of it. "In habitual smokers," says Dr Pereira, "the practice, when employed moderately, provokes thirst, increases the secretion of saliva, and produces a remarkably soothing and tranquillising effect on the mind, which has made it so much admired and adopted by all classes of society, and by all nations, civilised and barbarous." Taken in excess in any form, and especially by persons unaccustomed to it, it produces nausea, vomiting, in some cases purging, universal trembling, staggering, convulsive movements, paralysis, torpor, and death. Cases are on record of persons killing themselves by smoking seventeen or eighteen pipes at a sitting. With some constitutions it never agrees; but both our author and Dr Christison of Edinburgh agree that "no well-ascertained ill effects have been shown to result from the habitual practice of smoking." The effects of chewing are of a similar kind. Those of snuffing are only less in degree; and the influence which tobacco exercises in the mouth, in promoting the flow of saliva, &c., manifests itself when used as snuff in producing sneezing, and in increasing the discharge of mucus from the nose. The excessive use of snuff, however, blunts the sense of smell, alters the tone of voice, and occasionally produces dyspepsia and loss of appetite. In rarer cases it ultimately induces apoplexy and delirium.

But it is the soothing and tranquillising effect it has on the mind for which tobacco is chiefly indulged in. And amid the teasing paltry cares, as well as the more poignant griefs of life, what a blessing that a mere material soother and tranquilliser can be found, accessible alike to all—to the desolate and the outcast, equally with him who is rich in a happy home and the felicity of sympathising friends! Is there any one so sunk in happiness himself, as to wonder that millions of the world-chafed should flee to it for solace? Yet the question still remains which is to bring out the peculiar characteristic of tobacco. We may take for granted that it acts in some way upon the nervous system; but what is the special effect of tobacco on the brain and nerves, to which the pleasing reverie it produces is to be ascribed? "The pleasure of the reverie consequent on the indulgence of the pipe consists," according to Dr Madden, "in a temporary annihilation of thought. People really cease to think when they have been long smoking. I have asked Turks repeatedly what they have been thinking of during their long smoking reveries, and they replied, 'Of nothing.' I could not remind them of a single idea having occupied their minds; and in the consideration of the Turkish character there is no more curious circumstance connected with their moral condition. The opinion of Locke, that the soul of a waking man is never without thought, because it is the condition of being awake, is, in my mind, contradicted by the waking somnambulism, if I may so express myself, of a Moslem."*

We concede that Dr Madden might find in England, in Germany, and in Holland, many good smokers, who would make excellent Moslems in his sense, and who at the close of long tobacco reveries are utterly unconscious and innocent of a single thought. Yet we restrict our faith in his opinion to the simple belief, that tobacco, with a haze such as its smoke creates, tends to soften down and assuage the intensity of all inner thoughts or external impressions which affect the feelings, and thus to create a still and peaceful repose—such a quiet rest as one fancies might be found in the hazy distance of Turner's landscapes. We deny that, in Europeans in general, smoking puts an end to intellectual exertion. In moderation, our own experience is, that it sharpens and strengthens it; and we doubt very much if those learned Teutonic Professors, who smoke all day, whose studies are perpetually obscured by the fumes of the weed, and who are even said to smoke during sleep, would willingly, or with good temper, concede that the heavy tomes which in yearly thousands appear at the Leipsic book fair, have all been written after their authors had "really ceased to think." Still it is probably true, and may be received as the characteristic of tobacco among narcotics, that its major and first effect is to assuage, and allay, and soothe the system in general; its minor, and second, or after effect, to excite and invigorate, and, at the same time, give steadiness and fixity to the powers of thought.

The active substances, or chemical ingredients of tobacco or tobacco smoke, by which these effects upon the system are produced, are three in number. The *first* is a volatile oil, of which about two grains can be obtained from a pound of leaves, by distilling them with water. This oil or fat "is solid, has the odour of tobacco, and a bitter taste. It excites in the tongue and throat a sensation similar to that of tobacco smoke; and, when swallowed, gives rise to giddiness, nausea, and an inclination to vomit." Small as the quantity is, therefore, which is present in the leaf, this substance must be regarded as one of the ingredients upon which the effects of tobacco depend.

---

* Madden, *Travels in Turkey,* vol. i. p. 16.

The *second* is a volatile *alkali,* as it is called by chemists, which is also obtained by a form of distillation. The substance is liquid, has the odour of tobacco, an acrid burning taste, and is possessed of narcotic and highly poisonous qualities. In this latter quality it is scarcely inferior to Prussic acid. The proportion of this substance contained in the leaf varies from 3 to 8 per cent, so that he who smokes a hundred grains of tobacco *may* draw into his mouth from three to eight grains of one of the most subtle of all known poisons. It will not be doubted, therefore, that some of the effects of tobacco are to be ascribed to this peculiar substance.

The third is an oil—an empyreumatic oil, it is called—which does not exist ready formed in the natural leaf, but is produced along with other substances during the burning. This is supposed to be "the juice of cursed hebenon," described by Shakespeare as a *distilment.** It is acrid, disagreeable to the taste, narcotic, and so poisonous that a single drop on the tongue of a cat causes immediate convulsions, and in two minutes death.

Of these three active ingredients contained in tobacco smoke, the Turkish and Indian pipes, in which the smoke is made to pass slowly through water, arrest a large proportion, and therefore convey the air to the mouth in a milder form. The reservoir of the German meerschaums retains the grosser portions of the oils, &c., produced by burning; and the long stem of the Russian pipe has a similar effect. The Dutch and English pipes retain less; while the cigar, especially when smoked to the end, discharges everything into the mouth of the smoker, and, when he retains the saliva, gives him the benefit of the united action of all the three narcotic substances together. It is not surprising, therefore, that those who have been accustomed to smoke cigars, especially such as are made of strong tobacco, should find any other pipe both tame and tasteless, except the short black *cutty,* which has lately come into favour again among inveterate smokers.

The chewer of tobacco, it will be understood from the above description of its active ingredients, is not exposed to the effects of the oil which is produced during

---

* The effects, real or imaginary, of this "juice" are thus described:—

> "Sleeping within mine orchard,
> My custom always of the afternoon,
> Upon my secure hour thy uncle stole,
> With juice of cursed hebenon in a vial,
> And in the porches of mine ears did pour
> The leperous distilment: whose effect
> Holds such an enmity with blood of man,
> That, swift as quicksilver, it courses through
> The natural gates and alleys of the body;
> And, with a sudden vigour, it doth posset
> And curd, like eager droppings into milk,
> The thin and wholesome blood: so did it mine;
> And a most instant tetter bark'd about,
> Most lazar-like, with vile and loathsome crust,
> All my smooth body."—*Hamlet,* Act i. scene v.

the burning. The natural oil and the volatile alkali are the substances which act upon him. The taker of snuff is in the same condition. But *his* drug is still milder than that of the chewer, inasmuch as the artificial drying or roasting to which the tobacco is subjected in the preparation of snuff, drives off a portion of the natural volatile oil, and a large part of the volatile alkali, and thus renders it considerably less active than the natural leaf.

In all the properties by which tobacco is characterised, the produce of different countries and districts is found to exhibit very sensible differences. At least eight or ten species, and numerous varieties, of the plant are cultivated; and the leaf of each of these, even where they are all grown in the same locality, is found to exhibit sensible peculiarities. To these climate and soil add each its special effects; while the period of growth at which the leaves are gathered, and the way in which they are dried or cured, exercise a well-known influence on the quality of the crop. To these causes of diversity is owing, for the most part, the unlike estimation in which Virginian, Cuban, Brazilian, Peruvian, East Indian, Persian, and Turkish tobaccos are held in the market.

The chemist explains all the known and well-marked diversities of quality and flavour in the unadulterated leaf, by showing that each recognised variety of tobacco contains the active ingredients of the leaf in a peculiar form or proportion; and it is interesting to find science in his hands first rendering satisfactory reasons for the decisions of taste. Thus, he has shown that the natural volatile oil does not exist in the green leaf, but is formed during the drying, and hence the reason why the mode of curing affects the strength and quality of the dried leaf. He has also shown that the proportion of the poisonous alkali (nicotin) is smallest (2 per cent) in the best Havanuah, and largest (7 per cent) in the Virginian tobacco, and hence a natural and sound reason for the preference given to the former by the smokers of cigars.

As to the lesser niceties of flavour, this probably depends upon other odoriferous ingredients not so active in their nature, or so essential to the leaf as those already mentioned. The leaves of plants, in this respect, are easily affected by a variety of circumstances, and especially by the nature of the soil they grow in, and of the manure applied to them. Even to the grosser senses of us Europeans, it is known, for example, that pigs' dung carries its *gout* into the tobacco raised by its means. But the more refined organs of the Druses and Maronites of Mount Lebanon readily recognise, by the flavour of their tobacco, the kind of manure employed in its cultivation, and esteem, above all others, that which has been aided in its growth by the droppings of the goat.

But in countries where high duties upon tobacco hold out a temptation to frand, artificial flavours are given by various forms of adulteration. "Saccharine matter (molasses, sugar, honey, &c.), which is the principal adulterating ingredient, is said to be used both for the purpose of adding to the weight of the tobacco, and of rendering it more agreeable. Vegetable leaves (as those of rhubarb and the beech), mosses, bran, the sproutings of malt, beet-root dregs, liquorice, terra japonica, rosin, yellow ochre, fullers' earth, sand, saltpetre, common salt, sal-ammoniac"*—such is a list of the substances which have been detected in adulterated tobacco. How many more may be in daily use for the purpose, who can tell? Is it surprising, therefore, that we should meet with manufactured tobacco possessing a thousand different flavours for which the chemistry of the natural leaf can in no way account?

There are two other circumstances in connection with the history of tobacco, which, because of their economical and social bearings, are possessed of much interest.

First, Every smoker must have observed the quantity of ash he has occasion to empty out of his pipe, or the large nozzle he knocks off from time to time from the burning end of his cigar. This incombustible part is equal to one-fourth or one-fifth of the whole weight of the dried leaf, and consists of earthy or mineral matter which the tobacco plant has drawn from the soil on which it has grown. Every ton, when dried, of the tobacco leaf which is gathered, carries off, therefore, from four to five hundred-weight of this mineral matter from the soil. And as the substances of which the mineral matter consists are among those which are at once most necessary to vegetation, and least abundant even in fertile soils, it will readily be understood that the frequent growth and removal of tobacco from the same field must gradually affect its fertility, and sooner or later exhaust it.

It has been, and still is, to a great extent, the misfortune of many tobacco-growing regions, that this simple deduction was unknown and unheeded. The culture has been continued year after year upon virgin soils, till the best and richest were at last wearied and worn out, and patches of deserted wilderness are at length seen where tobacco plantations formerly extended and flourished. Upon the Atlantic borders of the United States of America, the best known modern instances of such exhausting culture are to be found. It is one of the triumphs of the chemistry of this century, that it has ascertained what the land loses by such imprudent treatment—what is the cause, therefore, of the barrenness that befalls it, and by what new management its ancient fertility may be again restored.

Second, It is melancholy to think that the gratification of this narcotic instinct of man should in some countries—and especially in North America, Cuba, and Brazil—have become a source of human misery in its most aggravated forms. It was long ago remarked of the tobacco culture by President Jefferson, in his *Notes on Virginia*, that "it is a culture productive of infinite wretchedness. Those employed in it are in a continued state of exertion beyond the powers of nature to support. Little food of any kind is raised by them, so that the men and animals on these farms are badly fed, and the earth is rapidly impoverished."† But these words do not convey to the English reader a complete idea of the misery they allude to. The men employed in the culture, who suffer the "infinite wretchedness," are the slaves on the plantations. And it is melancholy, as we have said, to think that the gratification of the passion for tobacco should not only have been

---

* Pereira, p. 1427.

† English edition, p. 278, quoted in M'Culloch's *Commercial Dictionary,* p. 1314.

an early stimulus to the extension of slavery in the United States, but should continue still to be one of the props by which it is sustained. The exports of tobacco from the United States in the year ending June 1850, were valued at ten millions of dollars. This sum European smokers pay for the maintenance of slavery in these states, besides what they contribute for the same purpose to Cuba and Brazil. The practice of smoking is in itself, we believe, neither a moral nor a social evil; it is merely the gratification of a natural and universal, as it is an innocent instinct. Pity that such evils should be permitted to flow from what is in itself so harmless!

II. The Hop, which may now be called the *English narcotic*, was brought from the Low Countries, and is not known to have been used in malt liquor in this country till after the year 1524, in the reign of Henry VIII. In 1850 the quantity of hops grown in England was 21,668 tons, paying a duty of £270,000. This is supposed to be a larger quantity than is grown in all the world besides. Only 98 tons were exported in that year; while, on the other hand, 320 tons were imported, so that the home consumption amounted to 21,886 tons, or 49 millions of pounds; being two-thirds more than the weight of the tobacco which we yearly consume. It is the narcotic substance, therefore, of which England not only grows more and consumes more than all the world besides, but of which Englishmen consume more than they do of any other substance of the same class.

And who that has visited the hop grounds of Kent and Surrey in the flowering season, will ever forget the beauty and grace of this charming plant? Climbing the tall poles, and circling them with its clasping tendrils, it hides the formality and stiffness of the tree that supports it among the exuberant profusion of its clustering flowers. Waving and drooping in easy motion with every tiny breath that stirs them, and hanging in curved wreaths from pole to pole, the hopbines dance and glitter beneath the bright English sun—the picture of a true English vineyard, which neither the Rhine nor the Rhone can equal, and only Italy, where her vines climb the freest, can surpass.

The hop "joyeth in a fat and fruitful ground," as old Gerard hath it (1596). "It prospereth the better by manuring." And few spots surpass, either in natural fertility or in artificial richness, the hop lands of Surrey, which lie along the out-crop of the green sand measures in the neighbourhood of Farnham. Naturally rich to an extraordinary degree in the mineral food of plants, the soils in this locality have been famed for centuries for the growth of hops; and with a view to this culture alone, at the present day, the best portions sell as high as £500 an acre. And the *highest* Scotch farmer—the most liberal of manure—will find himself outdone by the hop-growers of Kent and Surrey. An average of ten pounds an acre for manure over a hundred acres of hops, makes this branch of farming the most liberal, the most remarkable, and the most expensive of any in England.

This mode of managing the hop, and the peculiar value and rarity of hop land, were known very early. They form parts of its history which were probably imported with the plant itself. Tusser, who lived in Henry VIII.'s time, and in the reigns of his three children, in his *Points of Husbandry* thus speaks of the hop:—

"Choose soil for the hop of the rottenest mould,
Well-doonged and wrought as a garden-plot should:
Not far from the water (but not overfloune),
This lesson well noted, is meet to be knowne.
The sun in the south, or else southlie and west,
Is joy to the hop as welcommed ghest;
But wind in the north, or else northerly east,
To hop is as ill as fray in a feast.
Meet plot for a hop-yard, once found as is told,
Make thereof account, as of jewel of gold;
Now dig it and leave it, the sun for to burne,
And afterwards fense it, to serve for that turne.
The hop for his profit, I thus do exalt:
It strengtheneth drink, and favoureth malt;
And being well brewed, long kep it will last,
And drawing abide, if ye draw not too fast."*

The hops of commerce consist of the female flowers and seeds of the *humulus lupulus*, or common hop plant. Their principal consumption is in the manufacture of beer, to which they give a pleasant, bitter, aromatic flavour, and tonic properties. Part of the soporific quality of beer also is ascribed to the hops, and they are supposed by their chemical properties to check the tendency to become sour. The active principles in the hop consist of a volatile oil, and a peculiar bitter principle to which the name of *lupulin* is given.

When the hop flowers are distilled with water, they yield as much as eight per cent of their weight of a volatile oil, which has a brownish yellow colour, a strong smell of hops, and a slightly bitter taste. In this "oil of hops" it has hitherto been supposed that a portion of the narcotic influence of the flowers resided, but recent experiments render this opinion doubtful. It is probable that in the case both of tobacco and of the hop, a volatile substance distils over in small quantity along with the oil, which has not hitherto been examined separately, and in which the narcotic virtue resides. This is rendered probable by the fact that the rectified hop oil is not possessed of narcotic properties.

The hop has long been celebrated for its sleep-giving qualities. To the weary and wakeful, the hop-pillow has often given refreshing rest, when every other sleep-producer had failed. It is to the escape, in minute quantity, of the volatile narcotic substance we have spoken of, that this soporific effect of the flowers is most probably to be ascribed.

Besides the oil and other volatile matter which distil from them, the hop flowers, and especially the fine powdery grains or dust which, by rubbing, can be

* *Five Hundred Points of Good Husbandry.* London edition of 1812, p. 167.

109

separated from them, yield to alcohol a bitter principle (lupulin) and a resinous substance, both in considerable proportion. In a common tincture of hops these substances are contained. They are aromatic and tonic, and impart their own qualities to our beer. They are also soothing, tranquillising, and in a slight degree sedative and soporific, in which properties well-hopped beer also resembles them. It is certain that hops possess a narcotic virtue which beer derives from them;* but in what part of the female flower, or in what peculiar chemical compound this narcotic property chiefly resides, is still a matter of doubt.

To the general reader it may appear remarkable, that the chemistry of a vegetable production, in such extensive use as the hop, should still be so imperfect— our knowledge of its nature and composition so unsatisfactory. But the well-read chemist, who knows how wide the field of chemical research is, and how rapidly our knowledge of it, as a whole, is progressing, will feel no surprise. He may wish to see all such obscurities and difficulties cleared away, but he will feel inclined rather to thank and praise the many ardent and devoted men, now labouring in this department, for what they are doing, than to blame them for being obliged to leave a part of the extensive field for the present uncultivated.

Among largely used narcotics, therefore, especially in England, the hop is to be placed. It differs, however, from all the others we have mentioned, in being rarely employed alone except medicinally. It is added to infusions like that of malt, to impart flavour, taste, and narcotic virtues. Used in this way, it is unquestionably one of the sources of that pleasing excitement, gentle intoxication, and healthy tonic action, which well-hopped beer is known to produce upon those who drink it. Other common vegetable productions will give the bitter flavour to malt liquor. Horehound and wormwood, and gentian and quassia and strychnia, and the grains of paradise, and chicory, and various other plants, have been used to replace or supplant the hop. But none are known to approach it in imparting those peculiar qualities which have given the bitter beer of the present day so well-merited a reputation.

Among our working classes, it is true, in the porters and humbler beers they consume and prefer, the *Cocculus indicus* finds a degree of favour which has caused it, to a considerable degree, to take the place of the hop. This singular berry possesses an intoxicating property, and not only replaces the hop by its bitterness, but to a certain extent also supplies the deficiency of malt. To weak extracts of malt it gives a richness and *fulness in the mouth*, which usually imply the presence of much malt, with a bitterness which enables the brewer to withhold one-third of

---

* *Ale* was the name given to unhopped malt-liquor before the use of hops was introduced. When hops were added, it was called *beer*, by way of distinction, I suppose, because we imported the custom from the Low Countries, where the word beer was, and is still, in common use. Ground ivy (*Glechoma hederacea*), called also alehoof and tunhoof, was generally employed for preserving ale before the use of hops was known. "The manifold virtues in hops," says Gerard in 1596, "do manifestly argue the holesomeness of *beere* above *ale*, for the hops rather make it physicall drink to keep the body in health, than an ordinary drink for the quenching of our thirst."

his hops, and a colour which aids him in the darkening of his porter. The middle classes in England prefer the thin wine-like bitter beer. The skilled labourers in the manufacturing districts prefer what is rich, full, and substantial in the mouth. With a view to their taste, it is too often drugged with the *Cocculus indicus* by disreputable brewers; and much of the very beastly intoxication which the consumption of malt liquor in England produces, is probably due to this pernicious admixture. So powerful is the effect of this berry on the apparent richness of beer, that a single pound produces an equal effect with a bag of malt. The temptation to use it, therefore, is very strong. The quantity imported in 1850 was 2359 cwt., equal to a hundred and twelve times as many bags of malt; and although we cannot strictly class it among the narcotics we voluntarily indulge in, it may certainly be described as one in which thousands of the humbler classes are compelled to indulge.

It is interesting to observe how men carry with them their early tastes to whatever new climate or region they go. The love of beer and hops has been planted by Englishmen in America. It has accompanied them to their new empires in Australia, New Zealand, and the Cape. In the hot East their home taste remains unquenched, and the pale ale of England follows them to remotest India. Who can tell to what extent the use of the hop may become naturalised, through their means, in these far-off regions? Who can predict that, inoculated into its milder influence, the devotees of opium and the intoxicating hemp may not hereafter be induced to abandon their hereditary drugs, and to substitute the foreign hop in their place? From such a change in one article of consumption, how great a change in the character of the people might we not anticipate?

This leads us to remark, that we cannot as yet very well explain in what way and to what extent the use of prevailing narcotics is connected, as cause or effect, with peculiarities in national character. But there can no longer be any doubt that the soothers and exciters we indulge in, in some measure as the luxuries of life, though sought for at first merely to gratify a natural craving, do afterwards gradually but sensibly modify the individual character. And where the use is general and extended, the influence of course affects in time the whole people. It is a problem of interest to the legislator, not less than to the physiologist and psychologist, to ascertain how far and in what direction such a reaction can go—how much of the actual tastes, habits, and character of existing nations has been created by the prolonged consumption of the fashionable and prevailing forms of narcotics in use among them respectively, and how far tastes and habits have been modified by the changes in these forms which have been introduced and adopted within historic times. The reader will readily perceive that this inquiry has in it a valid importance quite distinct from that which attaches itself to the supposed influence of the different varieties of intoxicating fermented drinks in use in different countries. The latter, as we have said, all contain the same intoxicating principle, and so far, therefore, exercise a common influence upon all who consume them. But the narcotics now in use owe their effects to substances which in each, so far as is known, are chemically different from those which are contained in every one of the others. They must

111

exercise, therefore, each a different physiological effect upon the system, and, if their influence, as we suppose, extend so far, must each in a special way modify also the constitution, the habits, and the character.

Our space does not permit us, in the present Number, to speak of the use of opium and hemp; we shall return to these extensively consumed drugs on a future occasion.

The narcotics we indulge in

Part II

In a previous Number we treated of Tobacco and the Hop, the two narcotics of the most general and acknowledged use among our British population. But there are many others in extensive use in foreign countries, which, though not of so much immediate interest to us in their social relations, are yet of even higher interest in their general, physiological, and psychological bearings. Among these are opium, hemp, coca, the red-thorn apple, the betel-nut, the Siberian fungus, and several others, which we now propose to consider in their order.

III. The Poppy and Opium.—The use of the poppy, as a giver of sleep and a soother of pain, has been familiar from the earliest periods. This is partly shown by the names—*poppy* in English and *papaver* in Latin—said to have been given to the plant because it was commonly mixed with the food of young children (pap or papa) to ease pain and secure sleep. In this country the chief use of the poppy is as a medicine. The Tartars of the Caucasus, who, though they profess Mahomedanism, yet drink wine publicly, make it very heady and inebriating, by hanging the unripe heads of poppies in the casks while the fermentation is going on; and in the coffeehouses of the cities of Persia a decoction of poppies is sold, called *kokemaar*, which is drunk scalding hot Before it begins to operate, the drinkers quarrel with and abuse each other, but without coming to blows; and afterwards, as the drug takes effect, make peace again. One utters high-flown compliments, another tells stories; but all are extremely ridiculous both in their words and actions.—Tavernier.

But it is the concrete juice of the poppy-head that is generally and extensively employed as a narcotic indulgence. The dried juice is called by the Persians *afioun*, and by the Arabs *aphioum*, and hence our name opium.

Numerous as are the substances included in the enlarged list of drugs and medicines of the present day, opium is still the most important of them all. It is obtained by making incisions into the capsules or seed-vessels of the common white poppy (*Papaver somniferum*), when they are nearly ripe, allowing the milky juice which exudes to thicken upon the capsules for twenty-four hours, and then scraping it off. The best opium of commerce is a soft unctuous mass of a reddish or blackish brown colour, a waxy lustre, a strong disagreeable odour, and a bitter, acrid, nauseous taste, which remains long in the mouth. It is collected chiefly in Asiatic

Turkey, in Persia, and in India. That which is most esteemed in the European markets comes from Smyrna. The most extensively used in Eastern countries is that which is grown in India. The maximum produce of good opium in our Indian possessions is stated to be 41 lb. per acre, and the average from 20 to 25 lb.—MEYEN.

When used as a narcotic indulgence, opium is swallowed either in bulk in the form of pills, or in tinctures—such as our common laudanum—or it is smoked in minute pipes after the manner of tobacco. The first practice prevails most, we believe, in Mahomedan countries, especially Turkey and Persia; the second among Christian nations; and the third in China, and the islands of the Indian Archipelago. In preparing it for smoking, the Chinese extract from the Indian opium all that water will dissolve—generally from one-half to three-fourths of its weight—dry the dissolved extract, and make it into pills of the size of a pea. One of these pills they put into a short tiny pipe, often made of silver, inhale a few puffs at a time, or one single long puff, and return the smoke through the nostrils and ears, till the necessary dose has been taken.

In Borneo and Sumatra finely-chopped tobacco is mixed with the moist extract till it absorbs the whole, and the mixture is made into pills about the size of a pea. At convivial parties a dish of these peas is brought in along with a lamp, when the host takes a pipe, puts in one of the pellets, takes two or three long whiffs, returning the smoke through his nostrils, and, if he be an adept, through his eyes and ears. He then passes the pipe round the company, each of whom does the same with the same pipe; and so they continue smoking till all are intoxicated.

Used in any of these three ways, its sensible effects are nearly the same, varying of course with the quantity taken, with the constitution of the taker, and with the frequency of its previous use. The essential and primary action of the drug is upon the nervous system.

When it is taken in a moderate dose, the results of this action are, that

"The mind is usually exhilarated, the ideas flow more quickly, a pleasurable or comfortable condition of the whole system is experienced, which it is difficult to describe. There is a capability of greater exertion than usual, and hence it is taken as a restorative by such persons as the Tartar couriers, who travel for many days and nights continuously, and with great speed. These exciting effects are succeeded by a corresponding depression. The muscular power is lessened, and the susceptibility to external impressions. A desire for repose ensues, and a tendency to sleep. The mouth and throat become dry meanwhile, the thirst is increased, hunger diminished, and constipation succeeds."

When large doses are taken, all these effects are heightened in proportion. The period of depression, which almost always succeeds the excitement at first produced by opium, comes on more quickly the larger the dose; the prostration of energy degenerates into stupor, with or without dreams; the pulse becomes feeble, the muscles exceedingly relaxed, and if enough has been taken, death ensues.

In small doses, opium acts in a similar way to our wines and spirituous liquors; and it is as a substitute for these that the Chinese use it. Like them, also, its effects diminish by use, and therefore those who take it for the purpose of producing a pleasurable excitement must gradually increase the dose. The Turkish opiumeaters generally begin with doses of from half a grain to two grains a-day, and gradually increase the quantity till it amounts to 120 grains, or sometimes more. The effect shows itself in one or two hours after it has been taken, and lasts for five or six. In those accustomed to take it, it produces a high degree of animation, which the Theriakis (opium-eaters) represent as the summit of happiness.

Dr Madden thus describes his own sensations when under the influence of the drug, in one of the coffeehouses at Constantinople:—

"I commenced with one grain. In the course of an hour and a half it produced no perceptible effect. The coffeehouse-keeper was very anxious to give me an additional pill of two grains, but I was contented with half a one; and in another half hour, feeling nothing of the expected reverie, I took half a grain more, making in all two grains in the course of two hours. After two hours and a half from the first dose, my spirits became sensibly excited; the pleasure of the sensation seemed to depend on a universal expansion of mind and matter. My faculties appeared enlarged; everything I looked at seemed increased in volume; I had no longer the same pleasure when I closed my eyes which I had when they were open; it appeared to me as if it was only external objects which were acted on by the imagination, and magnified into images of pleasure: in short, it was 'the faint exquisite music of a dream' in a waking moment. I made my way home as fast as possible, dreading at every step that I should commit some extravagance. In walking, I was hardly sensible of my feet touching the ground; it seemed as if I slid along the street, impelled by some invisible agent, and that my blood was composed of some etherial fluid, which rendered my body lighter than air. I got to bed the moment I reached home. The most extraordinary visions of delight filled my brain all night. In the morning I rose pale and dispirited; my head ached; my body was so debilitated that I was obliged to remain on the sofa all day, dearly paying for my first essay at opium-eating."*

The effects of opium upon the system of the healthy are generally esteemed to be eminently prejudicial. Not only is an indulgence in the use of opium held to be criminal in itself, because of the evil consequences which are supposed to follow it, but it is esteemed a criminal act to make the procuring of it easy, and thus indirectly to minister to its more extensive consumption.

The opinion is now, however, beginning to prevail among medical men, that opium taken in moderation, even for a serious of years, is not necessarily injurious to health. Like spirituous liquors and tobacco, it acts as a sure poison when taken immoderately, but the moderate enjoyment of any of the three has not been proved to be either generally or necessarily, and upon all constitutions, attended by ill effects. It may be that the temptation to excess in the case of opium is greater, and that the habitual users of it are less frequently able to resist its seductive influence. But even this, as a physiological question, has by no means been

* Madden's *Travels in Turkey, &c.,* vol. i. pp. 25, 26, 27.

THE NARCOTICS WE INDULGE IN

satisfactorily established, and we must be cautious in pushing our conclusions farther than known facts will carry us.

Upon *confirmed* opium-eaters, however, as the irreclaimable are called, the evil effects of the drug are both undoubted and extremely melancholy.

"A total attenuation of body, a withered yellow countenance, a lame gait, a bending of the spine, frequently to such a degree as to assume a circular form, and glassy deep-sunken eyes, betray the opium-eater at the first glance. The digestive organs are in the highest degree disturbed; the sufferer eats scarcely anything, and has hardly one evacuation in a week. His mental and bodily powers are destroyed—he is impotent.

"When the baneful habit has become confirmed, it is almost impossible to break it off. His torments when deprived of the stimulant are as dreadful as his bliss is complete when he has taken it. Night brings the torments of hell, day the bliss of paradise; and after long indulgence, he becomes subject to nervous pains, to which opium itself brings no relief. He seldom attains the age of forty, if he have begun the practice early."—OPPENHEIM.

"The coffeehouses," says Dr Madden, "where the Theriakis, or opium-eaters, assemble, are situate in a large square; and on a bench outside the door they await the wished-for reveries, which present to their glowing imagination the forms of the celestial *houris*, and the enjoyments of their own paradise in all its voluptuousness. I had heard so many contradictory reports of the sensations produced by this drug, that I resolved to know the truth, and accordingly took my seat in the coffeehouse with half a dozen Theriakis. Their gestures were frightful; those who were completely under the influence of the opium talked incoherently, their features were flushed, their eyes had an unnatural brilliancy, and the general expression of their countenances was horribly wild. The effect is usually produced in two hours, and lasts four or five; the dose varies from three grains to a drachm. I saw one old man take four pills, of six grains each, in the course of two hours: I was told he had been using opium for five-and-twenty years; but this is a very rare example of an opium-eater passing thirty years of age, if he commence the practice early. The debility, both moral and physical, attendant on its excitement is terrible; the appetite is soon destroyed, every fibre in the body trembles, the nerves of the neck become affected, and the muscles get rigid: several of these I have seen in this place at various times, who had wry necks and contracted fingers; but still they cannot abandon the custom; they are miserable till the hour arrives for taking their daily dose; and when its delightful influence begins, they are all fire and animation. Some of them compose excellent verses, and others address the bystanders in the most eloquent discourses, imagining themselves to be emperors, and to have all the harems in the world at command."—MADDEN, i. p. 23.

Similar effects are described as resulting from the *smoking* of opium to excess in China; and the drinking of landanum in large quantities in England is equally pernicious in its consequences.

The use of this drug, as a narcotic indulgence, appears to be on the increase among the European populations generally. Among the less provident, especially of the working classes in our own large manufacturing towns, the use of laudanum as a care-dispelling, happiness-giving potion—often as a dispeller of hunger—is said to be greatly extending. If so, we should expect that among us, as among the Turks and Chinese, opium will find many who are unable to resist its seductive allurements, and whom it will drag into the extreme of mental and bodily misery.

Of its powers of seduction, indeed, even over the less delicate and susceptible organisation of our northern European races, and of the absolute slavery to which it can reduce even the strongest minds among us, we have two remarkable examples in the celebrated Coleridge, and in the author of the *English Opium-Eater*. For many years Coleridge was a slave to opium, and the way in which he became addicted to it is thus described by himself, in a letter dated April 1814:—

> "I was seduced into the accursed habit ignorantly. I had been almost bedridden for many months with swellings in my knees. In a medical journal I unhappily met with an account of a cure performed in a similar case (or what appeared to me so), by rubbing in laudanum, at the same time taking a given dose internally. It acted like a charm—like a miracle. I recovered the use of my limbs, of my appetite, of my spirits, and this continued for near a fortnight. At length the unusual stimulus subsided, the complaint returned, the supposed remedy was recurred to—but I cannot go through the dreary history. Sufficient to say, that effects were produced which acted on me by terror and cowardice of pain and sudden death, not (so help me God) by any temptation of pleasure, or expectation or desire of exciting pleasurable sensations. On the contrary, the longer I abstained, the higher my spirits were, the keener my enjoyments—till the moment, the direful moment arrived, when my pulse began to fluctuate, my heart to palpitate, and such a dreadful falling abroad, as it were, of my whole frame, such intolerable restlessness and incipient bewilderment, that in the last of my several attempts to abandon the dire poison, I exclaimed in agony which I now repeat in seriousness and solemnity, 'I am too poor to hazard this.'"*

He subsequently put himself into the hands of a medical man when at a friend's house in Bristol; and while he pretended to be gradually lessening the dose under medical instructions, and while his friends thought he was absolutely cured by being brought down to twenty drops a-day, he was all the while obtaining laudanum secretly, and drinking it in large doses as before!

How his moral sense must have been overborne, and by how powerful a fascination, before he could have stooped to such degrading deception! And how fierce his self-upbraidings must have been, when he could add in the same letter from which the above extract is taken: "There is no hope. O God, how willingly would I place myself under Dr Fox in his establishment; for my case is a species of madness, only that it is a derangement, an utter *impotence of the volition*, and not of the intellectual faculties. You bid me rouse myself. Go bid a man, paralytic in both arms, to rub them briskly together, and that will cure him. 'Alas!' he would reply, 'that I cannot move my arms is my complaint and my misery.' "

And his misery he still further paints in a letter, dated June of the same year: "Conceive a poor miserable wretch, who for many years has been attempting to beat off pain, by a constant recurrence to a vice that reproduces it. Conceive a spirit in hell employed in tracing out for others the road to that heaven from which his

---

* COTTLE's *Early Recollections,* vol. ii. p. 157.

crimes exclude him! In short, conceive whatever is most wretched, helpless, and hopeless, and you will form as tolerable a notion of my state as it is possible for a good man to have."*

And yet Coleridge lived twenty years after this letter was written, conquered the evil habit, and enjoyed, it is to be hoped, much happiness, as he wrote many noble works.

Coleridge speaks of his attempts to give up the indulgence. The following graphic passage describes the horrors undergone by Mr de Quincey, in his efforts to abandon the practice:—

"Opium, therefore, I resolved wholly to abjure, as soon as I should find myself at liberty to bend my undivided attention and energy to this purpose. It was not, however, till the 24th of June last (1822) that any tolerable concurrence of facilities for such an attempt arrived. On that day I began my experiment, having previously settled in my own mind that I would not flinch, but 'would stand up to the scratch' under any possible 'punishment.' I must premise that about 170 or 180 drops had been my ordinary allowance for many months; occasionally I had run up as high as 300, and once nearly to 700: in repeated preludes to my final experiment I had also gone as low as 100 drops, but had found it impossible to stand it beyond the fourth day, which, by the way, I have always found more difficult to get over than any of the preceding three. I went off under easy sail—130 drops a-day for three days; on the fourth I plunged at once to 80. The misery which I now suffered 'took the conceit out of me' at once; and for about a month I continued off and on about this mark: then I sunk to 60; and the next day to—none at all. This was the first day for nearly ten years that I had existed without opium. I persevered in my abstinence for ninety hours—*i. e.*, upwards of half a week. Then I took—ask me not how much. Say, ye severest, what would you have done? Then I abstained again; then took about twenty-five drops; then abstained—and so on.

"Meantime the symptoms which attended my case for the first six weeks of the experiment were these—enormous irritability, and excitement of the whole system; the stomach, in particular, restored to a full feeling of vitality and sensibility, but often in great pain; increasing restlessness night and day; sleep—I scarcely knew what it was—three hours out of the twenty-four was the utmost I had, and that so agitated and shallow that I heard every sound that was near me; lower jaw constantly swelling, much ulcerated, and many other distressing symptoms that would be tedious to repeat; amongst which, however, I must mention one, because it had never failed to accompany my attempt to renounce opium— viz., violent sternutation. This now became exceedingly troublesome, sometimes lasting for two hours at once, and returning at least twice or three times a-day. I was not much surprised at this, on recollecting what I had somewhere heard or read, that the membrane which lines the nostrils is a prolongation of that which lines the stomach; whence I believe are explained the inflammatory appearances about the nostrils of dram-drinkers. The sudden restoration of its original sensibility to the stomach expressed itself, I suppose, in this way. It is remarkable, also, that, during the whole period of years through which I had taken opium, I had never once caught cold (as the phrase is), nor even the slightest cough. But now a violent cold attacked me, and a cough soon after. In an unfinished fragment of a letter begun about this time to—, I find these words—: Do you know Beaumont and Fletcher's

---

* Ibid., p. 185.

DRUG USE OBSERVED

play of *Thierry and Theoderet?* then you will see my case as to sleep; nor is it much of an exaggeration in other features. I profess to you I have a greater influx of thoughts in one hour at present, than in a whole year under the reign of opium. It seems as though all the thoughts which had been frozen up for a decade of years by opium had now, according to the old fable, been thawed at once, such a multitude stream in upon me from all quarters. Yet such is my impatience and hideous irritability, that for one which I detain and note down fifty escape me: in spite of my weariness from suffering and want of sleep, I cannot stand still or sit for two minutes together. 'I nunc et versus tecum meditare canoros.' "*—*Confessions*—Appendix.

It was not so much by the pleasure it gave, as by the tortures connected with the attempt to abjure it, that in both these cases opium kept its firmest hold. But both men finally triumphed over it, though after tortures which few will consent to undergo, and with frail and shattered bodies:—

"I triumphed: but think not, reader, that therefore my sufferings were ended. Nor think of me as of one sitting in a *dejected* state. Think of me as of one, even when four months had passed, still agitated, writhing, throbbing, palpitating, shattered; and much in the situation of him who has been racked, as I collect the torments of that state from the affecting account of them by William Lithgow, the most innocent sufferer of the times of James I. Meantime, I derived no benefit from any medicine, except one prescribed for me by an Edinburgh surgeon of great eminence—ammoniated tincture of valerian."—*Confessions*.

After a seventeen years' use, and an eight years' abuse of its powers, he ceased to consume the drug, but he probably still feels the effects of its long use.

Much uncertainty exists as to the extent to which the use of laudanum really prevails among our healthy adult population. According to De Quincey, the opium-eaters were already numerous thirty years ago. "Of this," he says, "I became convinced several years ago, by computing at that time the number of those in one small class of English society (the class of men distinguished for talents or of eminent station) who were known to me, directly or indirectly, as opium-eaters: such, for instance, as the eloquent and benevolent ——; the late Dean of ——; Lord ——; Mr ——, the philosopher; a late under-secretary of state (who described to me the sensation which first drove him to the use of opium in the very same words as the Dean of ——; viz., 'that he felt as though rats were gnawing and abrading the coats of his stomach'); Mr ——, and many others hardly less known, whom it would be tedious to mention." He adds, also, that about the same time he learned in Manchester that "on a Saturday afternoon the counters of the druggist were strewed with pills of one, two, or three grains, in preparation for the known demand of the evening. The immediate occasion of the practice was the lowness of wages, which at that time would not allow them to indulge in ale or spirits; and wages rising, it may be thought that this practice would cease. But as I do not readily believe that

---

* Among external symptoms he mentions that excessive perspiration, even at Christmas, attended in his case any great reduction in the daily dose of opium, and that in July this was so excessive as to oblige him to use a bath five or six times a-day.

any man, having once tasted the divine luxuries of opium, will afterwards descend to the gross and mortal enjoyments of alcohol, I take it for granted—
'That those eat now, who never ate before,
And those who always ate, now eat the more.'"

In regard to the intensity and suddenness of the positive enjoyment which the uninitiated derive from the first use of opium, the experience of De Quincey is very instructive. Like Coleridge, he took it first to dispel pain. He had been affected for three weeks with excruciating rheumatic pains in the head and face, when he was advised to try laudanum, and forthwith purchased some at a druggist's shop.

"Arrived at my lodgings, it may be supposed that I lost not a moment in taking the quantity prescribed. I was necessarily ignorant of the whole art and mystery of opium-taking; and what I took, I took under every disadvantage. But I took it, and in an hour, oh, heavens! what a revulsion! what an upheaving, from its lowest depths, of the inner spirit! what an apocalypse of the world within me! That my pains had vanished was now a trifle in my eyes. This *negative* effect was swallowed up in the immensity of those positive effects which had opened before me—in the abyss of divine enjoyment thus suddenly revealed. Here was a panacea—a φαρμακον νήπενθες for all human woes. Here was the secret of happiness about which philosophers had disputed for so many ages at once discovered! Happiness might now be bought for a penny, and carried in the waistcoat pocket: portable ecstasies might be had corked up in a pint-bottle; and peace of mind could be sent down in gallons by the mail-coach."

Those who understand best and feel most for the sorrows and pains of the poverty-stricken humbler classes of every pursuit, would feel no surprise on learning that the seductions which the above passage describes had led away many of them into the habitual and intemperate use of opium. To live in pain and privation from day to day, to suffer from the agonies of old remembrances, or the fears of future individual and family griefs, and to have a key to paradise at hand! Who can wonder that the key is used, or would exercise severity towards him who uses it? We must add to the health, and comfort, and peace of mind of the tempted, before we exchange compassion or forbearance for reproach.

But accurate statistical information is still wanting to prove that the habit of opium-eating has really extended in any great degree among our full-grown healthy labouring population, either in town or country. Isolated cases of a melancholy kind do now and then occur, and loose conjectural statements are made as to the prevalence of the practice in this district or that, but we are unwilling to admit the wide prevalence of the custom without the most trustworthy testimony. A child died, for example, from the effects of opium in September (1853) at Boxworth in Cambridgeshire, the mother, because it was unwell, having placed a piece of crude opium in its mouth to suck. To the announcement of this fact in the newspapers, it was added, "that the mother and her family are all opium-eaters, and, though labouring people, spend four shillings a-week on the drug!" This statement suggests the idea that the habit may prevail extensively in the district, a conclusion which may in reality do injustice to an industrious peasantry. We refuse to adopt

DRUG USE OBSERVED

it, therefore. It lays, we think, a moral obligation upon the professional men of the county to collect information and make known the truth; and all who feel an interest in the moral reputation of our labouring people should reject such inferences to their prejudice, in the absence of accurate knowledge, which it ought not to be difficult for certain parties to obtain.

But another form of the opium evil has been shown, upon unquestionable evidence, extensively to prevail. In the large manufacturing towns of Lancashire it is a common thing for mothers who work in the factories to put out their children to nurse, and it is equally common for the nurses to dose the children with opium for the purpose of keeping them quiet or of setting them to sleep. It was stated by the Rev. Mr Clay, that in the town of Preston alone, in 1843, "upwards of sixteen hundred families were in the habit of using Godfrey's Cordial, or some other equally injurious compound," and that in one of the burial clubs in that town, "sixty-four per cent of the members die under five years of age."* The obvious conclusion is, that the fatality among the children is connected with the use of the drug.

A writer in the *Morning Chronicle* of the 4th of January 1850 thus describes the effects which this use of opium produces upon the health of the children:—

"The consequences of this system of drugging are suffusion of the brain, and an extensive train of mesenteric and glandular diseases. The child sinks into a low torpid state, wastes away to a skeleton, except the stomach, producing what is known as pot-belly. One woman said, 'The sleeping stuff made them that they were always dozing, and never cared for food. They pined away. Their heads got big, and they died.' "

It cannot be denied, therefore, that in one melancholy form at least the evils of opium-eating are visible amongst us. And it is curious that this should be the very form of drugging from which the poppy is said to have derived its name. The diffusion of knowledge among the, it may be not unfeeling, mothers of the factory districts, is one of the most likely ways to remove these evils.

It is impossible to arrive at anything like an approximate idea of the quantity of opium consumed by the different nations of the world. Meyen asserts that the quantity consumed by the Malays of the Indian Archipelago, in Cochin-China and Siam, as well as India and Persia, is so immense that, if we could obtain an exact statement of it, the amount would be quite incredible. The Rajpoots and other Hindoo tribes present opium at their visits and entertainments, with the same familiarity as the snuff-box is presented in Europe. In some countries it is even given to the horses, to excite them to greater exertions. "A Cutchee horseman shares very honourably his store of opium with his horse, which then makes an incredible stretch, though wearied out before."†

In India at least six and a half millions of pounds of opium are annually bought by the East India Company from the native growers, and manufactured into a

---

* *First Report of the Commissioners of Inquiry into the State of Large Towns,* 1844. Appendix, pp. 46, 48.

† BURNES's *Visit to Scinde,* p. 230, quoted by Meyen. *Geog. of Plants,* p. 360.

marketable condition. To produce this quantity will require upwards of three hundred thousand acres of land. It yields a revenue to the Company of three and a half millions sterling, and is for the greatest part exported.

As to China, we know that, in the season 1837–8, it imported from India three millions of pounds, and the importation from that country has probably increased considerably since that time. To this importation must also be added the opium which China receives by land from the countries which border it towards the west. The consumption of China at the present moment is probably not less than four or five millions of pounds' weight, having a market value of as many pounds sterling. In the same year (1837–8) India exported about a million and a half of pounds to the islands of the Indian Archipelago and other places.

The consumption of the United Kingdom is of course trifling when compared with this, but it is greatly on the increase. Thus, the quantity imported into Great Britain in 1839 was only 41,000 pounds, while in 1852 it amounted to 114,000 pounds; or, it has increased nearly three times within fifteen years. This implies either the application of the drug to new purposes, or a greatly increased demand for the uses to which it was formerly applied.

It is to be observed, however, as a matter of comfort, that we are not to expect either in Christian Europe or in America to see the consumption of opium ever become so universal as in Mahometan countries, where the use of wine is forbidden to the true believer. So long as a freedom of choice is allowed to the people, or a moral compulsion only is exercised over them, there is little fear of their becoming generally addicted to opium. Prohibit the use of fermented liquors by law, and we may hope to increase largely the consumers of this drug. Morehead mentions a young lady of his acquaintance who, being prevented by her friends from indulging in ardent spirits, had accustomed herself to swallow an ounce of crude opium, with as much ease and indifference as a boy would eat as much liquorice.* We apprehend something of this sort from the strict enforcement of the Maine Law in North America; for although the constitution of our Transatlantic connections has considerably altered, especially in the oldest states, since they crossed the sea, still the universal craving exists among them, and if it is denied gratification in one form, it will seek for it in another.

In regard to its chemical history, opium is probably the best known of all the vegetable extracts or inspissated juices used in medicine. It has been the subject of numerous and elaborate experimental and analytical investigations, and the results of these fill many interesting pages in our newest systems of organic chemistry.

How very complicated a substance even the purest opium is, the general reader will infer from the formidable list of peculiar principles which have been found in it. Besides familiar substances, such as gum, mucilage, resin, fat, caoutchouc, &c., it contains morphine, narcotine, codeine, narceine, thebaine, opianine, meconine,

---

* MOREHEAD, *On the Use of Inebriating Liquors,* p. 106. London, 1824.

pseudomorphine, porphyroxine, papaverine, and meconic acid—eleven peculiar organic compounds, which occur in greater or less quantity in nearly every sample of pure opium!

Of all these, the most active is that now almost universally known under the name of morphine or morphia. Of this invaluable medicine the best qualities of opium contain as much as ten per cent. It is colourless, void of smell, and nearly insoluble in water, but possesses an exceedingly bitter unpleasant taste, and what are called by chemists alkaline properties. It is powerfully narcotic and poison-ous, and is described by some as producing upon the system all the effects of the natural opium. This, however, is not generally the case; and hence it has not, we believe, been anywhere attempted to substitute this pure chemical compound—the chemical composition of which is fixed, and the physiological effects constant and certain—for the crude and uncertain opium, in the production of pleasureable excitement and gratification. And the reason of this obviously is, that the full and peculiar effect of the natural drug is due to the combined and simultaneous action of all the numerous substances it contains. Each of these modifies the effect which would be produced by any one of the others taken singly—as the attraction of each planet modifies the course which would be taken by every one of the others, were it the only one which revolved round the sun. It is from the result of all these conjoined actions that the singular pleasure of the opium-consumer is derived.

At least three of the constituents of opium which have been named above are known to be narcotic and poisonous. These are morphine, codeine, and thebaine. The special action of the other substances upon the system is still unknown or undecided. Indeed, it is a remarkable thing in chemico-physiological history, that, long as opium has been known, extensively as it has been, and still is used, both as a medicine and a luxurious indulgence, and numerous as are the opinions in regard to its mode of action which have been promulgated by medical authorities, we are still so unable to say what is the true action of this drug, that, in the words of Dr Pereira, "we shall save ourselves much time and useless speculation by at once confessing our ignorance on this point." So far does physiology appear still to lag behind, when our chemistry is tolerably advanced.

It is no doubt the complicated nature of the problem which renders the physio-logical solution so difficult. Nearly a dozen different substances are mixed up and given at once. Not only do these act in different ways upon the same individual, but each of them probably acts in a somewhat different way upon each different patient, according to his natural constitution, and the state of his health. Is it won-derful that, out of these multiplied sources of diversity, numerously varied phases should appear in the character of its action, and numerous opinions consequently be formed as to the way in which its effects are produced?

Besides, it is a matter of interest, both in connection with this point and with the general chemical history of opium, that the proportions of the several ingredients which are known to be active, vary very much in different samples of the drug. The locality or country in which the plant is grown, the peculiarities of the season during which the opium is collected, and the state of ripeness of the plant—the way in which the juice is dried, and subsequently prepared for the market, and the variety of poppy from which it is obtained,—all these circumstances influence the proportions of its constituents, and consequently modify the action of the mixed substance upon the human system. The Smyrna opium is generally considered the best in the European market, but even in this the morphia varies between four and fourteen per cent. Bengal opium differs from that of Turkey and Egypt, in containing more narcotine in proportion to the morphia. Generally, also, the Indian and Persian samples yield less morphia than those of Turkey.

This latter fact shows that, though it is in warm climates that opium is chiefly collected and used, yet that mere warmth of climate, whatever may be its other effects upon the white poppy, does not alone cause the juice of its capsules to be rich in morphia; and this is supported further by the statement of some English experimenters, that British-grown opium contains more morphia than that of commerce, as well as by the results of French experiments, which showed the presence of 16 to 28 per cent of morphia in some opiums collected in France. These facts are of considerable scientific interest; but they are not likely to lead to any practical results of importance to the rural economy at least of this country. Our poppy plants are probably too slow in their growth, and possess too little juice or succulence, to yield a satisfactory return to the opium-gatherer—were the uncertainty of the climate and the dearness of labour not alone sufficient to preclude the idea of our entering into competition with the Eastern producers of the drug. A different opinion, however, is entertained in France, where the most recent experiments profess to show that the variety which is there cultivated for its seed may be so treated as to yield a harvest of opium at an expense which need not exceed one-fourth of the present market price of the drug, while the seed which ripens uninjured will pay all the ordinary cost of culture; and from these results it is argued, that in the collecting of opium there is the prospect of great advantage to the agriculture of France.

There are three other circumstances in connection with the chemico-physiological history of opium, which will be interesting to the general reader. These are—

First, That its exciting effect is more conspicuous upon some races of men than upon others. This is said to be especially the case with the negroes, the Malays, and the Javanese. "The latter," says Lord Macartney, "under an extraordinary doze of opium, become frantic as well as desperate. They acquire an artificial courage; and, when suffering from misfortune and disappointment, they not only stab the objects of their hate, but sally forth to attack in like manner every person they meet, till self-preservation renders it necessary to destroy them." They shout, as they run, *Amok, amok*, which means "kill, kill;" and hence the phrase, *running a-muck*. Captain Beeckman was told of a Javanese who ran a-muck in the streets of Batavia, and had killed several people, when he was met by a soldier, who ran him through with his pike. But such was the desperation of the infuriated man, that he pressed himself forward on the pike, until he got near enough to stab his adversary with a dagger, when both expired together. On the Malays its effects are described to be very nearly the same. They remind one of the excitement said to have formerly prevailed in a less fatal form at Donnybrook and other Irish fairs, when an unusual dose of poteen had been administered to the *boys*.

The influence of race, as it affects the physiological action either of substances introduced into the stomach, or of ideas presented to the mind, is the same in kind as the influence of individual constitution. It is only greater in degree, and startles us sometimes because of the extent to which it appears exaggerated. The influence of constitution is recognised and considered in every dose of medicine we take or administer, and in the way in which good or evil tidings are communicated to our friends. We more rarely allow for differences of race in dealing with foreign nations, or in criticising their behaviour and actions under given circumstances.

In the Malays and Javanese we have the excitable temperament, accompanied by the unrestrained outward forms of expression, which are characteristic of Eastern nations. What affects us Saxons lightly or slowly, touches them instantly, and penetrates deep. The emotions which, when awakened, we are accustomed to restrain and hide, they openly and vividly display, and by indulgence heighten often to an overpowering degree. The negro tribes partake of a similar organisation. "In this respect," says Mrs Beecher Stowe, "they have an Oriental character, and betray their tropical origin. Like the Hebrews of old, and the Oriental nations of the present day, they give vent to their emotions with the utmost vivacity of expression, and their whole bodily system sympathises with the movements of their minds. When in distress, they actually lift up their voices to weep, and 'cry with an exceeding bitter cry.' When alarmed, they are often paralysed, and rendered entirely helpless." This susceptibility affects all their relations both to living and dead things. Opium affects different individuals among them in different ways, as it does the different individuals of European races, but upon all it produces those more marked and striking effects which, among ourselves, we only see in rare instances, and in persons of uncommonly nervous temperament.

Second, It is a curious fact, that the active narcotic ingredients of opium often escape the decomposing action of the digestive and other organs. They pass unchanged into the milk of the nurse who uses it, and have been known to poison the infant suckled by a female who had been dozing herself largely with opiates. The odour of the drug is to be perceived in the breath and in the perspiration; and morphia and meconic acid are known occasionally to escape through the kidneys, and have been found in the fluid excretions. This character the active ingredients of opium possess in common with many other narcotic principles, such as those of the deadly nightshade, the henbane, the thorn-apple, the intoxicating fungus, and with many other substances used in medicine.—PEREIRA, p. 102.

Third, Opium, as is well known, gradually loses its effect upon the habitual consumer, so that the dose must be increased from time to time, if the influence of the drug is to be maintained. But at length, even this resource fails the inveterate opium-eaters of Constantinople, and no increase of dose will procure for them the desired enjoyment, or even relieve them from bodily pain. In this emergency, they have recourse to the poisonous corrosive sublimate. Mixing at first a minute quantity of this substance with their daily dose of opium, they increase it by degrees, till they reach the limit of ten grains a-day, beyond which it is usually unsafe to pass. This mixture acts upon their long-tortured frames, when neither of the ingredients, taken alone, will either soothe or exhilarate. But the use of the new medicine only protracts a little longer the artificial enjoyment, which has become a necessary of life, finally bringing to a more miserable termination the career of the debilitated and distorted Theriaki.

We have said that, in moderate doses, opium acts in a similar way to our wines and spirituous liquors, and that it is a substitute for these that the Chinese use it. By this we do not mean that its physiological effects are precisely the same, although the main purpose for which they are used by many—that of a care-dispeller—may be the same. On the contrary, there are many points of difference in the effects which alcohol and opium respectively produce. The following somewhat coloured and imaginative picture represents their relative effects on the constitution of the *English opium-eater:*—

"Crude opium, I affirm peremptorily, is incapable of producing any state of body at all resembling that which is produced by alcohol; and not in *degree* only incapable, but even in *kind*. It is not in the *quantity* of its effects merely, but in the *quality*, that it differs altogether. The pleasure given by wine is always mounting, and tending to a crisis, after which it declines; that from opium, when once generated, is stationary for eight or ten hours: the first—to borrow a technical distinction from medicine—is a case of acute, the second of chronic pleasure; the one is a flame, the other a steady and equable glow. But the main distinction lies in this, that whereas wine disorders the mental faculties, opium, on the contrary (if taken in a proper manner), introduces amongst them the most exquisite order, legislation, and harmony. Wine robs a man of his self-possession; opium greatly invigorates it. Wine unsettles and clouds the judgment, and gives a preternatural brightness, and a vivid exaltation to the contempts and the admirations, the loves and the hatreds, of the drinker; opium, on the contrary, communicates serenity and equipoise to all the faculties, active or passive; and with respect to the temper and moral feelings in general, it gives simply that sort of vital warmth which is approved by the judgment, and which would probably always accompany a bodily constitution of primeval or antediluvian health. Thus, for instance, opium, like wine, gives an expansion to the heart and the benevolent affections; but then with this remarkable difference, that, in the sudden development of kind-heartedness which accompanies inebriation, there is always more or less of a maudlin character, which exposes it to the contempt of the bystander. Men shake hands, swear eternal friendship, and shed tears, no mortal knows why; and the sensual creature is clearly uppermost. But the expansion of the benigner feelings, incident to opium, is no febrile access, but a healthy restoration to that state which the mind would naturally recover upon the removal of any deep-seated irritation of pain that had disturbed and quarrelled with the impulses of a heart originally just and good. . . . Wine constantly leads a man to the brink of absurdity and extravagance; and, beyond a certain point, it is sure to volatilise and to disperse the intellectual energies; whereas opium always seems to compose what had been agitated, and to concentrate what had been distracted. In short, to sum up all in one word, a man who is inebriated, or tending to inebriation, is, and feels that he is, in a condition which calls up into supremacy the merely human—too often the brutal—part of his nature; but the opium-eater (I speak of him who is not suffering from any disease, or other remote effects of opium) feels that the diviner part of his nature is paramount; that is, the moral affections are in a state of cloudless serenity; and over all is the great light of the majestic intellect."

After this highly-coloured eulogium upon the comparative virtues of opium and alcohol, drawn from personal experience, who could blame us were we at once to propose the establishment of a national opium-eating, distillery-burning society, and, Father Mathew-like, should take up our staff, and preach everywhere the exceeding virtues of the inestimable drug, and propose for universal imitation the admirable example of the silver-piped Celestials? But it may occur to the reader, as it does to ourselves, that the English opium-eater himself was brought to death's door by the use of his favourite drug, and was compelled to abandon his beloved enjoyment. For the present, therefore, we refrain, and recommend in preference our own bitters practice. Keep your morphia bottle carefully stowed away till a new attack of toothache or sciatica comes on, and your laudanum as a ready friend should the prevailing epidemic approach you.

And yet even grave and matter-of-fact men are to be found—persons who have had large experience of the use of opium in Eastern countries—who not only pronounce the use of the drug as a narcotic indulgence to be far from an unmitigated evil, but who especially prefer its general use to that of alcoholic drinks. Among these we may mention Dr Eatwell, of the East India Company's service, whose knowledge of the history and action of opium is acknowledged to be most extensive. The deliberate opinion of this gentleman is deserving of much attention; and he argues the case as follows:—

"It has been too much the practice with those who have treated this subject to content themselves with drawing the sad picture of the confirmed debauchee, plunged in the last stage of moral and physical exhaustion; and having taken this exception as the premises of their argument, to proceed at once to involve the whole practice in one sweeping condemnation. But this is not the way in which the subject can be fairly treated. As rational would it be to paint the horrors of *delirium tremens*, and upon that evidence to condemn at once the entire use of alcoholic liquors. The question to be determined is not, what are the effects of opium used in excess, but what are its effects on the moral and physical constitution of the mass of individuals who use it habitually, and in *moderation*, either as a stimulant to sustain the frame under fatigue, or as a restorative and sedative after labour, bodily or mental. Having passed three years in China, I can affirm thus far, that the effects of the abuse of the drug do not come very frequently under observation, and that, when cases do occur, the habit is frequently found to have been induced by the presence of some painful chronic disease, to escape from the suffering of which the patient has fled to this resource. That this is not always, however, the case, I am perfectly ready to admit, and there are doubtless many who indulge in the habit to a pernicious extent, led by the same morbid influences which induce men to become drunkards in even the most civilised countries; but these cases do not, at all events, come before the public eye. As regards the effects of the habitual use of the drug on the *mass* of the people, I must affirm that no injurious results are visible. The people are a muscular and well-formed race, the labouring portion being capable of great and prolonged exertion under a fierce sun, in an unhealthy climate. Their disposition is cheerful and peaceable, and quarrels and brawls are rarely heard even amongst the lower orders; whilst in general intelligence they rank deservedly high amongst Orientals.

"I conclude, therefore, with observing that the proofs are still wanting to show that the moderate use of opium produces more pernicious effects upon the constitution than the moderate use of spirituous liquors; whilst, at the same time, it is certain that the consequences of the abuse of the former are less appalling in their effects upon the victim, and less disastrous to society at large, than the consequences of the abuse of the latter. Compare the furious madman, the subject of *delirium tremens*, with the prostrate debauchee, the victim of opium; the violent drunkard with the dreamy sensualist intoxicated with opium. The latter is, at least, harmless to all except his wretched self, whilst the former is but too frequently a dangerous nuisance, and an open bad example to the community at large."*

It strikes us that the tone of this passage is that of an apologist for an evil practice, rather than of a defender of a good one. But we leave our readers to form their own opinion upon the point not unably argued by Dr Eatwell. It may be that the ideas we have generally entertained in this country, hitherto, as to the necessarily evil effects of the use of opium as an indulgence, may be only unfounded prejudices. They may have arisen from drawing too hasty and general conclusions from the manifest evils of extreme cases; and it is possible that more knowledge may compel us materially to alter our present opinions. Meantime the medical missionaries inform us that the confirmed opium-consumers of China use daily from 30 to 200 grains of the pure extract, which is equal to twice as much of the crude opium. We might expect, therefore, a more frequent recurrence of melancholy spectacles arising from the use of the drug, than by the testimony of Dr Eatwell is really the case.

IV. HEMP.—As a general rule, little is popularly known in northern Europe of the use of hemp as a narcotic indulgence; and yet in the East it is as familiar to the sensual voluptuary as the opium we have been considering.

Our common hemp (*Cannabis sativa*), so extensively cultivated for its fibre, is the same plant with the Indian hemp, *Cannabis Indica*, which from the remotest times has been celebrated among Eastern nations for its narcotic virtues. The plant came to Europe from Persia, and is supposed by many to be a native of India; but, like tobacco and the potato, it has a wonderful power of adapting itself to differences in soil and climate. Hence it is cultivated in northern Russia—whence our manufacturers obtain large supplies of its valuable fibre—in Northern America, on the plains of India and Arabia, in Africa, from its northern to its southern extremities, and throughout the whole of Europe. But in hot climates the fibre degenerates in quality, while the narcotic ingredients increase in quantity, and in apparent strength.

In the sap of this plant, probably in all countries, there exists a peculiar resinous substance in which the narcotic quality resides. In northern climates the proportion of this substance is so small as hitherto to have escaped notice. In the warmer regions of the East, however, it is so abundant as to exude naturally from the flowers, from the leaves, and from the bark of the young twigs. This is another of the many interesting facts now known, which show the influence of climate in modifying the chemical changes that take place in the interior of plants, and

* *Pharmaceutical Journal*, vol. xi. p. 364.

the nature and proportions of the several substances which are produced by these changes. We have already seen how the numerous constituents of opium vary with the locality in which it is collected.

In India the resinous exudation of the hemp plant is collected in various ways. In Nepaul it is gathered by the hand in the same way as opium. This variety is very pure and much prized. It is called *Momeea*, or waxen *Churrus*. It has a fragrant narcotic odour, and a slightly hot, bitterish, and acrid taste. In Central India, men covered with leathern aprons run backwards and forwards through the hemp fields, beating the plants violently. By this means the resin is detached and adheres to the leather. This is scraped off, and is the ordinary churrus of commerce, the *chirs* of Caubul. It does not bring so high a price as the momeea. In other places the leathern aprons are dispensed with, and the resin is collected on the naked skins of the coolies. In Persia it is collected by pressing the resinous plant on coarse cloths, and afterwards scraping the resin from these, and melting it in a little warm water. The churrus of Herat is considered as one of the best and most powerful varieties of the drug.

The plant itself is often collected and dried for the sake of the resin it contains. The whole plant collected when in flower, and dried without the removal of the resin, is called *Gunjah*. The larger leaves and capsules without the stalks form *bang, subjee*, or *sidhee*, which is less esteemed than the gunjah.*

The gunjah, when boiled in alcohol, yields as much as one-fifth of its weight of resinous extract, and hence this method of preparing the drug in a pure state has been recommended as the most efficient and economical.

Among the ancient Saracens, the modern Arabs, in some parts of Turkey, and generally throughout Syria, the preparations of hemp in common use were, and are still, known by the names of *haschisch, hashash*, or *husheesh*. The most common form of haschisch, and that which is the basis of all others, is prepared by boiling the leaves and flowers of the hemp with water to which a certain quantity of fresh butter has been added, evaporating the decoction to the thickness of a syrup, and then straining it through cloth. The butter thus becomes charged with the active resinous principle of the plant, and acquires a greenish colour. This preparation retains its properties for many years, only becoming a little rancid. Its taste, however, is very disagreeable, and hence it is seldom taken alone, but is mixed with confections and aromatics, camphor, cloves, nutmegs, mace, and not unfrequently ambergris and musk, so as to form a sort of electuary. The confection used among the Moors is called *el mogen*, and is sold at an enormous price. *Dawamese* is the name given by the Arabs to that which they most commonly use. This is frequently mingled, however, with other substances of reputed aphrodisiac virtues, to enable it to minister more effectually to the sensual gratifications, which appear to be the grand object of life among many of the Orientals.

---

* *Pharmaceutical Journal*, vol. i. p. 490.

The Turks give the names of *Hadschy Malach* and *Madjoun* to the compositions they use for purposes of excitement. According to Dr Madden, the madjoun of Constantinople is composed of the pistils of the flowers of the hemp plant ground to powder, and mixed in honey with powdered cloves, nutmegs, and saffron.

Thus the hemp plant or its products are used in four different forms.

First, The whole plant dried and known by the name of gunjah; or the larger leaves and capsules dried and known as bang, subjee, or sidhee; or the dried flowers, called in Morocco *kief,* a pipe of which, scarcely the size of an English pipe, is sufficient to intoxicate; or the dried pistils of the flower in the madjoun of the Turks. It is possible that these latter parts of the plant may be peculiarly rich in resin.

Second, The resin which naturally exudes from the leaves and flowers, and is, when collected by the hand, called momeea; or the same beaten off with sticks, and sold by the name of churrus.

Third, The extract obtained by means of alcohol from the gunjah, and which is said to be very active.

Fourth, The extract obtained by the use of butter, which, when mixed with spices, forms the dawamese of the Arabs, and is the foundation of the haschisch of many Eastern countries and districts. Other varieties, however, are in use, under the name of haschisch, one of which consists only of the tops and tender parts of the plants collected after they have been in flower.

The dried plant is smoked, and sometimes chewed, while the resin and resinous extracts are generally swallowed in the form of pills or boluses. The newly-gathered plant and leaves have a rapid and energetic action. Their efficacy diminishes, however, by keeping, which is less the case with the natural resin and the extracts.

In one or other of these forms the hemp plant appears to have been used from very remote times. The ancient Scythians are said by Herodotus to have excited themselves "by inhaling its vapour." Homer makes Helen administer to Telemachus, in the house of Menelaus, a potion prepared from the Nepenthes, which made him forget his sorrows. This plant had been given to her by a woman of Egyptian Thebes; and Diodorus Siculus states that the Egyptians laid much stress on this circumstance, arguing that Homer must have lived among them, since the women of Thebes were actually noted for possessing a secret by which they could dissipate anger or melancholy. This secret is supposed to have been a knowledge of the qualities of hemp.

It is curious how common and familiar words sometimes connect themselves with things and customs of which we know absolutely nothing. The word *assassin*—a foreign importation, it is true, but long naturalised among us—is of this kind. M. Sylvester de Sacy, the well-known Orientalist, says that this word was derived from the Arabic name of hemp. It was originally used in Syria to designate the followers of "the old man of the mountain," who were called *Haschischins*, because among them the haschisch was in frequent use, especially during the performance of certain of their mysterious rites. Others say that, during the wars of the Crusaders, certain of the Saracen army, intoxicated with the drug, were in the habit of rushing into the camps of the Christians, committing great havoc, being themselves totally regardless of death; that these men were known as hashasheens, and that thence came our word assassin. The Oriental term was probably in use long before the time of the Crusades, though the English form and use of the word may have been introduced into Europe at that period.

Nor is the use of hemp less extended than it is ancient. All over the East, and in Mahomedan countries generally, it is consumed. In Northern Africa it is used largely by the Moors. In Southern Africa, the Hottentots use it under the name of *Dacha*, for purposes of intoxication; and when the Bushmen were in London, they smoked the dried plant in short pipes made of the tusks or teeth of animals. What is more astonishing, when we consider what broad seas intervene, even the native Indians of Brazil know its value, and delight in its use; so that over the hotter parts of the globe generally, wherever the plant produces in abundance its peculiar narcotic principle, its virtues may be said to be known, and more or less extensively made use of.

Its effects on the system, therefore, we must suppose, are very agreeable. In India it is spoken of as the increaser of pleasure, the exciter of desire, the cementer of friendship, the laughter-mover, and the causer of the reeling gait,—all epithets indicative of its peculiar effects. Linnæus describes its power as "narcotica, phantastica, dementens, anodyna et repellens;" while in the words of Endlicher, "Emollitum exhilarat animum, impotentibus desideriis tristem, stultam lætitiam provocat, et jucundissima somniorum conciliat phantasmata."

The effects of the churrus or natural resin have been carefully studied in India by Dr O'Shaughnessy. He states that when taken in moderation it produces increase of appetite and great mental cheerfulness, while in excess it causes a peculiar kind of delirium and catalepsy. This last effect is very remarkable, and we quote his description of the results of one of his experiments with what is considered a large dose for an Indian patient:—

"At two P.M. a grain of the resin of hemp was given to a rheumatic patient; at four P.M. he was very talkative, sang, called loudly for an extra supply of food, and declared himself in perfect health. At six P.M. he was asleep. At eight P.M. he was found insensible, but breathing with perfect regularity, his pulse and skin natural, and the pupils freely contractile on the approach of light. Happening by chance to lift up the patient's arm, the professional reader will judge of my astonishment when I found it remained in the posture in which I placed it. It required but a very brief examination of the limbs to find that by the influence of this narcotic the patient had been thrown into the strangest and most extraordinary of all nervous conditions, which so few have seen, and the existence of which so many still discredit—the genuine catalepsy of the nosologist. We raised him to a sitting posture, and placed his arms and limbs in every imaginable attitude. A waxen figure could not be more pliant or more stationary in each position, no matter how contrary to the natural influence of gravity on the part! To all impressions he was meanwhile almost insensible."

This extraordinary influence he subsequently found to be exercised by the hemp extract upon other animals as well as upon man. After a time it passes off entirely, leaving the patient altogether uninjured.

In this effect of the hemp in India we see a counterpart of many of the wonderful feats performed by the fakeers and other religious devotees of that country. It indicates probably the true means also by which they are enabled to produce them. How much power a little knowledge gives to the dishonest and designing in every country over the ignorant and unsuspecting masses!

The effects of the haschisch of the Arabians, which probably do not differ from those of hemp in any of its forms, have been described to us from his own personal experience by a French physician, M. Moreau. When taken in small doses, its effect is simply to produce a moderate exhilaration of spirits, or at most a tendency to unseasonable laughter. Taken in doses sufficient to induce the *fantasia*, as its more remarkable effects are called in the Levant, its first influence is the same as when taken in a small dose; but this is followed by an intense feeling of happiness, which attends all the operations of the mind. The sun shines upon every thought that passes through the brain, and every movement of the body is a source of enjoyment. M. Morean made many experiments with it upon his own person—appears indeed to have fallen into the habit of using it even after his return to France—and he describes and reasons upon its effects as follows:—

"It is really *happiness* which is produced by the haschisch; and by this I mean an enjoyment entirely moral, and by no means sensual, as might be supposed. This is a very curious circumstance, and some remarkable inferences might be drawn from it. Among others, for example, that every feeling of joy and gladness, even when the cause of it is exclusively moral—that those enjoyments which are least connected with material objects, the most spiritual, the most ideal—may be nothing else but sensations purely physical developed in the interior of the system, in the same way as those which are produced by means of the haschisch. At least, in so far as relates to that of which we are internally conscious, there is no distinction to be made between these two orders of sensations, in spite of the diversity of causes to which they are due. For the haschisch-eater is happy, not like the gourmand, or the famished man when satisfying his appetite, or the voluptuary in the gratification of his amative desires,—but like him who hears tidings which fill him with joy, or like the miser counting his treasures, the gambler who is successful at play, or the ambitious man who is intoxicated with success."*

This glowing description of the effects of the baschisch, though given by one who had often used it, is yet on that very account, like the picture of the opium-eater, open to suspicion. We feel as if it were intended as a kind of excuse or justification of the indulgence on the part of the writer. Yet apart from this, the metaphysical question raised by M. Moreau is a very interesting one. To pursue it here, as a general question, would be out of place. We may observe, however, that it is intimately connected not only with the peculiar action exercised over the mind by each of the narcotics we are now considering, but with the probable cause of all those mental aberrations we include under the general term—*insanity*. Can we produce, for example, virtual insanity—imaginary happiness,[†] imaginary

---

* See *British and Foreign Medical Review,* vol. xxiii. pp. 217–225.
† "Madness hath imaginary bliss, and most men have no more."—TUPPER.

131

DRUG USE OBSERVED

misery, or the most truth-like delusions—by introducing into the stomach, and thence into the blood which is passing through the hair-like blood-vessels of the brain, a quantity of a foreign body too minute to be recognised by ordinary chemical processes; and may not real natural insanity, in any of its forms, be caused by the natural production within the system itself of minute quantities of analogous substances possessing similar virtues? And, if so produced, will our future chemistry teach us to remove the mental disease, by preventing the production of the cause, or by constantly neutralising its effects? How important are these facts and considerations to a true pathology of insanity in general, and to every rational attempt to bring it, in all its phases, within the domain of the healing art!

When first it begins to act, the peculiar effects of the haschisch may be considerably diminished or altogether checked by a firm exertion of the will, "just as we master the passion of anger by a strong voluntary effort." By degrees, however, the power of controlling at will and directing the thoughts diminishes, till finally all power of fixing the attention is lost, and the mind becomes the sport of every idea which either arises within itself, or is forced upon it from without.

"We become the sport of impressions of every kind. The course of our ideas may be broken by the slightest cause. We are turned, so to speak, by every wind. By a word or a gesture, our thoughts may be successively directed to a multitude of different subjects with a rapidity and lucidity which are truly marvellous. The mind becomes possessed with a feeling of pride, corresponding to the exaltation of its faculties, which it is conscious have increased in energy and power. It will be entirely dependent on the circumstances in which we are placed, the objects which strike the eyes, the words which fall on our ears, whether the most lively sentiments of gaiety or of sadness shall be produced, or passions of the most opposite character excited, sometimes with extraordinary violence. Irritation may rapidly pass into rage, dislike into hatred and desire for revenge, and the calmest affection into the most transporting passion. So fear becomes terror, courage is developed into rashness which nothing checks, and which seems unconscious of danger, and the most unfounded doubt and suspicion becomes a certainty.

"The mind has a tendency to exaggerate everything, and the slightest impulse carries it along. Hence those who make use of the haschisch in the East, when they wish to give themselves up to the intoxication of the *fantasia*, withdraw themselves carefully from everything which could give to their delirium a tendency to melancholy, or excite anything but feelings of pleasurable enjoyment. They profit by all the means which the dissolute manners of the East place at their disposal. It is in the midst of the harem, surrounded by their women, under the charm of music and of lascivious dances performed by the almees, that they enjoy the intoxicating *dawamese;* and with the aid of superstition, they find themselves almost transported to the scene of the numberless marvels which the Prophet has collected in his paradise."*

The errors of perception to which the patient is liable during the period of fantasia, are remarkably experienced in regard to time and place. Minutes seem hours, and hours are prolonged into years, till at last all idea of time seems obliterated,

---

* MOREAU—*Du Haschisch et de l'Alienation Mentale*, p. 67. Paris, 1845.

and the past and the present are confounded together. Every notion, in this curious condition, seems to partake of a certain degree of exaggeration. One evening, M. Moreau was traversing the passage of the Opera when under the influence of a moderate dose of haschisch. He had made but a few steps when it seemed to him as if he had been there for two or three hours; and as he advanced the passage seemed interminable, its extremity receding as he pressed forward.*

The effect produced by hemp in its different forms varies, however, both in kind and in degree, with the individual to whom it is administered. Its general effect upon Orientals is of an agreeable and cheerful character, exciting them to laugh, dance, and sing, and to commit various extravagances—acting as an aphrodisiac, and increasing the appetite for food. Some, however, it renders excitable and quarrelsome, and disposes to acts of violence. It is from the extravagant behaviour of individuals of this latter temperament that the use and meaning of our word assassin have most probably arisen. There are some rare individuals, however, according to Dr Moreau, on whom the drug produces no effect whatever—upon whom, at least, doses are powerless which are usually followed by well-marked phenomena, as is the case with opium, long use making larger doses necessary. To some even a drachm of the churrus is considered a moderate dose, though sufficient to operate upon twenty ordinary men.

Upon Europeans generally, at least in Europe, its effects have been found to be considerably less in degree than upon Orientals. "In India, Dr O'Shaughnessy had seen marked effects from half a grain of the extract, or even less, and had been accustomed to consider one grain and a half a large dose; in England he had given ten or twelve or more grains, to produce the desired effect."—(PEREIRA, p. 1242.) In kind, also, its effects upon Europeans differ somewhat from those produced upon Asiatics. It has never been known, for example, to produce that remarkable cataleptic state, described in a previous page as having been observed in India as the consequence even of a comparatively small dose of the hemp extract.

Of the chemistry of the hemp plant comparatively little is yet known. Had it been as long familiar to Europeans, or used as extensively as in the East, it would probably, like opium, have been the subject of repeated chemical investigations.

When distilled with water, the dried leaves and flowers yield a volatile oil in small quantity. The properties of this volatile oil have not been studied. It is not supposed, however, to have any important connection with the remarkable effects of the plant upon the living animal.

But the whole hemp plant is impregnated, as we have seen, with a resinous substance, in which its active virtues reside. When collected as it naturally exudes, this resin forms the churrus of India. It is extracted when the leaves are boiled with butter to form the basis of the haschisch, or when the dried plant is treated with alcohol to obtain the hemp extract. It is soft, dissolves readily both in alcohol and ether, and is separated from these liquids in the form of a white powder when

---

* *British and Foreign Quarterly Review,* vol. xxiii. p. 225.

the solutions are mixed with water. It has a warm, bitterish, acrid, somewhat balsamic taste, and a fragrant odour, especially when heated.

Both the resin which naturally exudes from the hemp plant, and the extract it yields to spirituous liquids, are probably mixtures of several substances possessed of different properties and relations to animal life. The remarkably complex composition of opium justifies such an opinion. And the analogy of the same substance makes it probable that the produce of the plant will differ in different localities and countries—so that the churrus of India, and the haschisch of Syria, may produce very different effects on the same constitution. But these points have not as yet been investigated either chemically or physiologically. This substance, therefore, holds out the promise of a rich and interesting harvest to future experimenters.

The extract of hemp differs considerably in its effects from opium. It does not lessen, but rather excites the appetite. It does not occasion nausea, dryness of the tongue, constipation, or lessening of the secretions, and is not usually followed by that melancholy state of depression to which the opium-eater is subject. It differs also in causing dilatation of the pupil, and sometimes catalepsy, in stilling pain less than opium does, in less constantly producing sleep, in the peculiar inebriating quality it possesses, in the phantasmata it awakens, and in its aphrodisiac effects. To the intellectual activity imparted by opium, it adds a corresponding sensitiveness and activity of all the feelings and of the senses, both internal and external. It seems, in fact, a source of exquisite and *peculiar* enjoyment, with which, happily, we are in this part of the world still altogether unacquainted.

It is impossible to form any estimate of the quantity of hemp, of hemp resin, or of the artificial extract, which are used for purposes of indulgence. It must, however, be very large, since the plant is so employed, in one form or another, by probably not less than two or three hundred millions of the human race!

V. Coca.—When the Spanish conquerors overcame the Indians of the hilly country of Peru, they found among them plantations of an herb called coca, and the custom extensively prevalent of chewing its leaves during frequent short periods of repose specially set apart for the purpose. So universal, indeed, was the use of it, that it was the common money or medium of exchange of Peru, and after the introduction of gold and silver money, the principal article of traffic. The practice of using it was already ancient among the Indian races, and its origin is lost in the mists of remote antiquity. It continues equally prevalent to the present day among the Indian inhabitants of Bolivia and Peru. Coca is in reality the *Narcotic of the Andes*, and it is not less interesting than hemp, either in its social or in its physiological relations.

The *Erythroxylon coca** is a bush which attains the height of six or eight feet, and resembles the blackthorn in its small white flowers and bright green leaves. It

---

* The word *Coca* is derived from the Aymara word Khoka, signifying "plant," in the same way as in Paraguay the indigenous tea-plant is called *Yerba,* "*the* plant" par excellence.

grows wild in many parts of Bolivia, but that which is used by the people is chiefly the produce of cultivation. Like our common thorn, it is raised in seed-beds, from which it is planted out into regular coca plantations. It is extensively cultivated in the tropical valleys of the eastern slopes of the Andes, in Upper and Lower Peru. The steep sides of these valleys, below the level of 8000 feet, are often covered with plantations of coca, arranged in terraces like the vine-culture of Tuscany and the Holy Land. The leaves, when ripe enough to break on being bent, are collected and dried in the sun. In favourable localities, the bushes yield three, and even four, crops of leaves in a year. When nearly dried, or exposed to the sun, they emit an odour similar to that of new-made hay, in which much mellilot, or sweet-scented vernal grass, is contained; and they give a headache to new-comers, as haymaking does to some persons among ourselves. These dried leaves form the coca of commerce. When of good quality, they are of a pale-green colour. Dampness causes them to become dark coloured, in which state they are less esteemed; and if they heat through dampness, they become altogether useless. Their taste is not unpleasant; it is slightly bitter and aromatic, and resembles that of green tea of inferior quality. It is more piquant and agreeable when a sprinkling of quicklime or plant ashes is chewed along with it.

The use of this herb among the Indians dates, as we have said, from very remote periods. Its cultivation was a care of the native government during the reign of the Incas, and it is still to the Indian of the mountains the delight, the support, and in some measure a necessity of his life. He is never seen without the leathern pouch (his *chuspa*) to contain his coca leaves, and his little gourd-bottle to hold powdered unslacked lime—or, if he is a Bolivian, the alkaline ashes left by the quinoa or the musa root when burned. Always three, and sometimes four times a-day, he rests from his mining or other labour, or pauses in his journey, and lays down his burden to chew in quiet the beloved leaf. When riding, or walking, or labouring, the leaves have little effect. As with opium and hemp, stillness and repose are indispensable to his full enjoyment of the luxury it produces. In the shade of a tree he stretches himself at ease, and from time to time puts into his mouth a few leaves rolled into a ball (an *acullico*), and after each new supply a little unslacked lime on the end of a slip of wood moistened and dipped into his lime-flask. This brings out the *true taste* of the leaf, and causes a copious flow of greenish-coloured saliva, which is partly rejected and partly swallowed. When the ball ceases to emit juice it is thrown away, and a new supply is taken. The interval of enjoyment conceded to the labouring Indian lasts from fifteen minutes to half an hour, and is generally wound up by the smoking of a paper cigar. Repeated three or four times a-day, his average consumption is an ounce or an ounce and a half in the twenty-four hours, and on holidays double that quantity. The owners of mines and plantations have long found it for their interest to allow a suspension of labour three times a-day for the *chaccar*, as it is called; and the Indian speedily quits an employer who endeavours to stint or deprive him of these periods of indulgence. During these periods his *phlegm* is something marvellous. No degree of urgency or entreaty on the part of his master or employer will move him; while the confirmed *coquero*, when under the influence of the leaf, is heedless of the thunder-storm which threatens to drown him where he lies, of the roar of approaching wild beasts, or of the smoking fire which creeps along the grass, and is about to suffocate or scorch him in his lair.

The Indians of the Peruvian Andes are subject to fits of melancholy, or are generally perhaps of a gloomy temperament. "In their domestic relations," says Von Tschudi, "the Indians are unsocial and gloomy. Husband, wife, and children live together with but little appearance of affection. The children seem to approach their parents timidly, and whole days sometimes elapse without the interchange of a word of kindness between them. When not engaged in out-door work, the Indian sits gloomily in his hut, chewing coca and brooding silently over his own thoughts."—*Travels*, p. 481.

It does not appear, however, that the coca adds to his gloom; on the contrary, he takes it to relieve himself for the time from the peculiarities of his temperament. Silence and abstraction are necessary to the enjoyment, but the use of it makes him cheerful; and it is to the unhappy, often oppressed, and always poor Peruvian, the source of his highest pleasures. It has come down to him as a relic of the ancient enjoyments of his people, and during the phantasy it produces, he participates in scenes and pleasures from which in common life he is altogether excluded. Dr Weddell very sensibly remarks, that, as a relic of the past, he attaches "superstitious ideas to the coca, which must triple, in his imagination, the benefits he receives from it," and that its value to him is further enhanced by its being the "sole and only distraction which breaks the incomparable monotony of his existence."

We have no detailed account, by an actual chewer of the leaf, of the special effects which it produces; but these must be very seducing, since, though long stigmatised, and still very generally considered as a degrading, purely Indian, and, therefore, despicable vice, many white Peruvians at Lima and elsewhere retire daily at stated times to chew the coca; and even Europeans in different parts of the country have fallen into the habit. A confirmed chewer of coca is called a "coquero," and he is said to become occasionally more thoroughly a slave to the leaf than the inveterate drunkard is to spirituous liquors.

Sometimes the coquero is overtaken by a craving which he cannot resist, and he betakes himself for days together to the silence of the woods, and there indulges unrestrained in the use of the weed. Young men of the best families in Peru become sometimes addicted to it to this extreme degree of excess, and are then considered as lost. Forsaking cities and the company of civilised men, and living chiefly in woods or in Indian villages, they give themselves up to a savage and solitary life. Hence the term, a *white coquero*, has there something of the same evil sense as irreclaimable drunkard has with us.

The chewing of coca gives "a bad breath (abominable, according to Weddell), pale lips and gums, greenish and stumpy teeth, and an ugly black mark at the angles of the mouth. The inveterate coquero is known at the first glance. His unsteady gait, his yellow skin, his dim and sunken eyes encircled by a purple ring, his quivering lips, and his general apathy, all bear evidence of the baneful effects of the coca juice when taken in excess."—VON TSCHUDI, p. 450.

Its first evil effect is to weaken the digestion; it then gradually induces a disease locally named the *opilacion*. Biliary affections, with all the painful symptoms which attend them in tropical climates, and, above all, gall stones, are frequent and severe. The appetite becomes exceedingly uncertain, till at length the dislike to all food is succeeded by an inordinate appetite for animal excrement. Then dropsical swellings and boils come on; and the patient, if he can get it, flies to brandy for relief, and thus drags out a few miserable years, till death relieves him.*

This description is sufficiently repulsive, but it is only the dark side of the picture. A similar representation could be truthfully made of the evil effects of wine or beer in too numerous cases, without thereby implying that these liquors ought either to be wholly forbidden, or of our own accord entirely given up. "Setting aside all extravagant and visionary notions on the subject, I am clearly of opinion," says Von Tschudi, "that the moderate use of coca is not merely innoxious, but that it may even be very conducive to health. In support of this conclusion, I may refer to the numerous examples of longevity among Indians who, almost from the age of boyhood, have been in the habit of masticating coca three times a-day. Cases are not unfrequent of Indians attaining the great age of 130 years; and these men, at the ordinary rate of consumption, must in the course of their lives have chewed not less than 2700 lb. of the leaf, and yet have retained perfect health." Even the Indian-coquero, who takes it in excess, reaches the age of fifty years. It is consumed both more abundantly, however, and with less baneful results, in the higher Andes than in the lower and warmer regions.

It is certain that the Peruvian Indians ascribe to it the most extraordinary virtues. They regard it even at the present day as something sacred and mysterious. This impression they have inherited as a fragment of their ancient religion, for in all the ceremonies, whether warlike or religious, of the times of the Incas, the coca was introduced. It was used by the priests either for producing smoke at the great offerings to the gods, for throwing in handfuls upon the sacrifice, or as the sacrifice itself.

"During divine worship the priests chewed coca leaves, and unless they were supplied with them, it was believed that the favour of the gods could not be propitiated. It was also deemed necessary that the supplicator for divine grace should approach the priests with an acullico in his mouth. It was believed that any business undertaken without the benediction of coca leaves could not prosper, and to the shrub itself worship was rendered. During an interval of more than 300 years Christianity has not been able to subdue this deep-rooted idolatry, for everywhere we find traces of belief in the mysterious powers of this plant. The excavators in the mines of Cerro de Pasco throw masticated coca on hard veins of metal, in the belief that it softens the ore and renders it more easy to work. The origin of this custom is easily explained, when it is recollected that in the time of the Incas it was believed that

---

* POPPIG, *Reise in Chile, Peru und auf dem Amazon Strôm,* 1827 to 1832, chap. iv.

the *cozas*, or the deities of metals, rendered the mountains impenetrable if they were not propitiated by the odour of coca. The Indians, even at the present time, put coca leaves into the mouths of dead persons, to secure to them a favourable reception on their entrance into another world; and when a Peruvian Indian on a journey falls in with a mummy, he, with timid reverence, presents to it some coca leaves as his pious offering." —VON TSCHUDI, p. 454.

And even Europeans cannot deny that, in addition to the ordinary properties of a narcotic, this leaf possesses two very remarkable properties not known to coexist in any other substance.

First, They lessen, when chewed, the necessity for ordinary food, and not only enable the chewer, as opium does, to put forth a greater nervous energy for a short time, but actually, with the same amount of food, perseveringly to undergo more laborious fatigue or longer-continued labour. With a feeble ration of dried maize, or barley crushed into flour, the Indian, if duly supplied with coca, toils under heavy burdens, day after day, up the steep slopes of the mountain passes, or digs for years in the subterranean mines, insensible to weariness, to cold, or to hunger. He believes, indeed, that it may be made a substitute for food altogether; and an instance given by Von Tschudi seems almost to justify this opinion.

"A cholo of Huari, named Hatan Huamang, was employed by me in very laborious digging. During the five days and nights he was in my service he never tasted any food, and took only two hours' sleep each night. But at intervals of two and a half or three hours he regularly chewed about half an ounce of coca leaves, and he kept an acullico continually in his mouth. I was constantly beside him, and therefore I had the opportunity of closely observing him. The work for which I engaged him being finished, he accompanied me on a two days' journey of twenty-three leagues across the level heights. Though on foot, he kept up with the pace of my mule, and halted only for the *chaccar*. On leaving me he declared he would willingly engage himself again for the same amount of work, and that he would go through it without food, if I would but allow him a sufficient supply of coca. The village priest assured me that this man was sixty-two years of age, and that he had never known him to be ill in his life." —VON TSCHUDI, p. 453.

How this remarkable effect of the coca is to be accounted for, in accordance with the received notions as to animal nutrition, it is not easy to see.

Second, Another striking property of this leaf is, that, either when chewed or when taken in the form of infusion, like tea, it prevents the occurrence of that difficulty of respiration which is usually felt in ascending the long and steep slopes of the Cordillera and the Puna.

"When I was in the Puna," says Von Tschudi, "at the height of fourteen thousand feet above the level of the sea, I drank always, before going out to hunt, a strong infusion of coca leaves. I could then during the whole day climb the heights and follow the swift-footed wild animals, without experiencing any greater difficulty of breathing than I should have felt in similar rapid movements on the coast. Moreover, I did not suffer from the symptoms of cerebral excitement or uneasiness which other travellers have experienced. The reason perhaps is, that I only drank the decoction on the cold Puna, where the nervous system is far less susceptible than in the climate of the forests beneath. However, I always felt a sense of great satiety after taking the coca infusion, and I did not feel a desire for my next meal until after the time at which I usually took it."

The reason of this action of the leaf is not less difficult to perceive than that of its strength-sustaining capabilities.

When the Spanish conquerors took possession of Peru, the Indians, and all their customs, were treated by them with equal contempt; but everything connected with their religion was especially denounced by the Spanish priests. Hence the use of coca was condemned and forbidden. It was considered worthy the consideration of councils of the church, which denounced it in 1567 as a "worthless substance, fitted for the misuse and superstition of the Indians," and of the thunders of a royal decree which, in 1569, condemned the idea that coca gives strength as an "illusion of the devil." But these fulminations were of no avail. The Peruvians still clung to their esteemed national leaf, and the owners of mines and plantations, soon discovering its efficacy in enabling their slaves to perform the heavy tasks they imposed upon them, became its warm defenders. Even churchmen at last came to regard it with indulgence, and, stranger still, to recommend its introduction into Europe.

"One of the warmest advocates of the plant was the Jesuit Don Antonio Julian, who, in a work entitled *Perla de America*, laments that coca is not introduced into Europe instead of tea and coffee. 'It is,' he observes, 'melancholy to reflect that the poor of Europe cannot obtain this preservative against hunger and thirst; that our working people are not supported by this strengthening plant in their long-continued labours.' In the year 1793, Dr Don Pedro Nolasco Crespo pointed out in a treatise the important advantages that would be derived from the use of the coca plant, if introduced into the European navies; and he expresses a wish that experiments of its utility in that way could be tried. Though it is not probable that Dr Crespo's wish will ever be realised, yet there is little doubt that the use of coca as a beverage on board ship would be attended with very beneficial results. It would afford a nutritious refreshment to seamen in the exercise of their laborious duties, and would greatly assist in counteracting the unwholesome effects of salt provisions. As a stimulant, it would be far less injurious than ardent spirits, for which it might be substituted without fear of any of the evil consequences experienced by the *conqueros*." —VON TSCHUDI, p. 456.

It will strike the reader of the present article as somewhat remarkable, that modern, perhaps more impartial and truth-loving inquiry, should strip so many of these narcotic indulgences of the horrid and repulsive aspect they have always hitherto worn. We find now that they have all a fair side as well as a foul, and that it becomes a question for reasonable discussion whether an educated population, trained to the exercise of a reasonable self-control, might not be safely left to avail themselves of the strangely fascinating enjoyments they are capable of affording, without much risk of their becoming the source of any greatly extended after-misery. But when, it may be pertinently asked, can we hope to see the mass of our population so trained to self-denial and self-restraint?

Of the chemical history of the coca leaf we are almost entirely ignorant. The narcotic principle it contains appears to be volatile and evanescent like that of the hemp plant. By keeping, the leaves gradually lose their smell and virtue, and after twelve months are generally considered worthless. We have found, that as they reach this country the leaves are coated with a resinous or waxy substance which is only sparingly soluble in water, but which ether readily dissolves. When digested in ether, the leaves give a dark green solution, which, on evaporation in the open air, leaves a brownish resin, possessed of a powerful, peculiar, and penetrating odour. By prolonged exposure to the air this resinous matter diminishes in quantity, and gradually loses the whole of its smell, leaving a fusible, nearly inodorous, matter behind. Ether, therefore, seems to extract at least two substances from the leaf, one of which is volatile, and has a powerful odour. It is probably in this volatile body that the narcotic qualities of the leaf reside. According to the French chemist, M. Fremy, the leaf contains besides a bitter principle, which dissolves in alcohol but not in ether, on which, as on the *theine* of tea, some of the virtues of the coca may depend. But the chemical and physiological properties of this substance have not yet been determined. A few pounds of fresh leaves, placed in the hands of a capable chemist, might soon furnish us not only with more chemical light, but probably also with some new and valuable remedial agents capable of producing medicinal effects hitherto beyond our reach.

If we attempt to explain, by the aid of the above modicum of chemical knowledge, the remarkable effects produced by the coca leaf, we utterly fail. How the mere chewing of one or two ounces of the leaves in a day, partly rejecting and partly swallowing the saliva,* but wholly rejecting the chewed leaf—how this supports the strength, or can materially nourish the body in the ordinary acceptation of the term, we cannot understand. It cannot *give* much to the body; it must therefore act simply in preventing or greatly diminishing the ordinary and natural waste of the tissues which usually accompanies bodily exertion. As wine acts upon the nervous system of the aged so as to restrain the natural waste to a quantity which the now weakened digestion can readily replace, and thus maintains the weight of the body undiminished,—so it is probably with coca. In the young and middle-aged it lessens the waste of the tissues, and thus enables a smaller supply of food to sustain the weight and strength of the body. All these substances probably operate in a similar way to the partial absence of light, which, as is well known, causes the same amount of fattening food to go farther in increasing the weight of the body.

This explanation is only conjectural, and we hazard it only that some chemical physiologist, into whose hands the drug may fall, may by actual experiment test and amend it. Besides, we are aware that the explanation itself requires explanation; for how either wine or any other substance should have the effect described

---

* Dr Weddell states that the saliva is *never rejected,* and being a later authority than Von Tschudi, whom we have followed in the text, he is probably correct.

is by no means plain. At first sight it seems wholly irreconcilable with the received chemico-physiological doctrine, that the amount of muscular exertion is a measure of the waste of the tissues. We believe, however, that the apparent difficulty is, to a certain extent at least, capable of a purely chemical solution, but the discussion is unfit for this place.

This leaf resembles hemp in the narcotic quality of dilating the pupil, which opium does not possess. But in the proneness of the coca-eater to stillness and solitude we recognise an influence of this herb similar to that which opium exercises upon those who have experienced its highest enjoyments. "Markets and theatres," says De Quincey, "are not the appropriate haunts of the opium-eater, when in the divinest state incident to his enjoyment. In that state crowds become an oppression to him, music even too sensual and gross. He naturally seeks solitude and silence as indispensable conditions of those trances or profoundest reveries, which are the crown and consummation of what opium can do for human nature. At that time I often fell into these reveries on taking opium; and more than once it has happened to me on a summer night, when I have been at an open window, in a room from which I could overlook the sea at a mile below me, and could command a view of the great town of L—— at about the same distance, that I have sat from sunset to sunrise, motionless, and without wishing to move."

This state resembles somewhat the abstracted condition in which the coquero reclines beneath the sheltering tree;—whether his apathy and phlegm ever approached to that of the coquero, the Opium-eater does not inform us.

We have no accurate data from which to form an estimate of the actual weight of coca leaf collected and consumed in Bolivia and Peru. Pöpping estimates the money value of the yearly prodwuce to be about four and a half millions of Prussian dollars, which, at a shilling a pound, the price it yields to the grower, would make the annual produce nearly fifteen millions of pounds. This approximation is sufficient to show us its importance to the higher regions of South America, in an agricultural and commercial, as well as in a social point of view.

Dr Weddell, whose travels in Bolivia we noticed in a recent Number, informs us that the province of Yongas, in Bolivia, in which the coca is much cultivated, alone produces 9,600,000 Spanish pounds. The total produce, therefore, is probably much beyond the fifteen millions of pounds deduced from the statement of Pöppig. The importance of the plant to Bolivia is shown by another fact stated by Dr Weddell, that the revenue of the state of Bolivia in 1850 amounted to ten and a half millions of francs, of which nine hundred thousand, or one-twelfth of the whole, is derived from the tax on coca. Had he told us the amount of the tax per pound, we should have been able to approximate more nearly to the total produce of the state of Bolivia.

Here we close for the present our remarks upon this interesting class of bodies. There are still others, the effects of which are not less surprising, and which are indulged in by large masses of men, to the consideration of which we may hereafter return.

Meanwhile, with such attractive descriptions before him as the history of these narcotics presents, can we wonder that man, whose constant search on earth is after happiness, and who, disappointed here, hopes and longs and strives to fit himself for happiness hereafter—can we wonder that he should at times be caught by the tinselly glare of this corporeal felicity, and should yield himself to habits which, though exquisitely delightful at first, lead him finally both to torture of body and to misery of mind; that, debilitated by the excesses to which it provokes, he should sink more and more under the influence of a mere drug, and become at last a slave to its tempting seductions? We are indeed feeble creatures, and of little bodily strength, when a grain of haschisch can conquer, or a few drops of laudanum lay us prostrate; and how much weaker in mind, when, knowing the evils they lead us to, we cannot resist the fascinating temptation of these insidious drugs.

Note.—The writer of the above, and the previous article on *Narcotics*, assures the critics who have done him the honour to notice his remarks upon tobacco, that he is himself neither a smoker nor an opium-eater. To the kind old lady, Mrs Mary Smith, who has taken the trouble to write him from No. 195 Twelfth Street, New York, he begs to say, that he will be happy to receive the little volume, containing "the results of American experience on the use of tobacco," and will endeavour to consider them with an unprejudiced mind.

Part 3

CANNABIS

9

WILLIAM BROOKE O'SHAUGHNESSY, *ON THE PREPARATION OF THE INDIAN HEMP, OR GUNJAH*, 1839, PP. 7–13, 19–20, 36–37

Section II

Popular uses

The preparations of Hemp are used for the purpose of intoxication as follows.

Sidhee, Subjee, and *Bang* (synonymous) are used with water as a drink, which is thus prepared. About three tola weight, 540 troy grains, are well washed with cold water, then rubbed to powder, mixed with black pepper, cucumber and melon seeds, sugar, half a pint of milk, and an equal quantity of water. This is considered sufficient to intoxicate an habituated person. Half the quantity is enough for a novice. This composition is chiefly used by the Mahomedans of the better classes.

Another recipe is as follows.

The same quantity of *Sidhee* is washed and ground, mixed with black pepper, and a quart of cold water added. This is drank at one sitting. This is the favorite beverage of the Hindus who practice this vice, especially the Birjobassies and many of the Rajpootana soldiery.

From either of these beverages intoxication will ensue in half an hour. Almost invariably the inebriation is of the most cheerful kind, causing the person to sing and dance, to eat food with great relish, and to seek aphrodisiac enjoyments. In persons of a quarrelsome disposition it occasions, as might be expected, an exasperation of their natural tendency. The intoxication lasts about three hours, when sleep supervenes. No nausea or sickness of stomach succeeds, nor are the bowels at all affected; next day there is slight giddiness and vascularity of the eyes, but no other symptom worth recording.

Gunjah is used for smoking alone—one rupee weight, 180 grains, and a little dried tobacco are rubbed together in the palm of the hand with a few drops of water. This suffices for three persons. A little tobacco is placed in the pipe first, then a layer of the prepared *Gunjah*, then more tobacco, and the fire above all.

Four or five persons usually join in this debauch. The hookah is passed round, and each person takes a single draught. Intoxication ensues almost instantly; and

CANNABIS

from one draught to the unaccustomed, within half an hour; and after four or five inspirations to those more practised in the vice. The effects differ from those occasioned by the *Sidhee*. Heaviness, laziness, and agreeable reveries ensue, but the person can be readily roused, and is able to discharge routine occupations, such as pulling the punkah, waiting at table, &c.

The *Majoon*, or Hemp confection, is a compound of sugar, butter, flour, milk, and *Sidhee* or *Bang*. The process has been repeatedly performed before me by Ameer, the proprietor of a celebrated place of resort for Hemp devotees in Calcutta, and who is considered the best artist in his profession. Four ounces of *Sidhee* and an equal quantity of *Ghee* are placed in an earthen or well-tinned vessel, a pint of water added, and the whole warmed over a charcoal fire. The mixture is constantly stirred until the water all boils away, which is known by the crackling noise of the melted butter on the sides of the vessel; the mixture is then removed from the fire, squeezed through cloth while hot—by which an oleaginous solution of the active principles and colouring matter of the Hemp is obtained—and the leaves, fibres, &c., remaining on the cloth are thrown away.

The green oily solution soon concretes into a buttery mass, and is then well washed by the hand with soft water so long as the water becomes coloured. The colouring matter and an extractive substance are thus removed, and a very pale green mass, of the consistence of simple ointment, remains. The washings are thrown away;—Ameer says that these are intoxicating, and produce constriction of the throat, great pain, and very disagreeable and dangerous symptoms.

The operator then takes two pounds of sugar, and adding a little water places it in a pipkin over the fire. When the sugar dissolves and froths, two ounces of milk are added; a thick scum rises and is removed—more milk and a little water are added from time to time, and the boiling continued about an hour, the solution being carefully stirred until it becomes an adhesive clear syrup, ready to solidify on a cold surface; four ounces of tyre (new milk dried before the sun) in fine powder are now stirred in, and lastly the prepared butter of Hemp is introduced, brisk stirring being continued for a few minutes. A few drops of uttur of roses are then quickly sprinkled in, and the mixture poured from the pipkin on a flat cold dish or slab. The mass concretes immediately into a thin cake, which is divided into small lozenge-shaped pieces. A seer thus prepared sells for four rupees: one drachm by weight will intoxicate a beginner; three drachms one experienced in its use. The taste is sweet, and the odour very agreeable.

Ameer states that there are seven or eight *Majoon* makers in Calcutta;—that sometimes by special order of customers he introduces stramonium seeds, but never nux-vomica;—that all classes of persons, including the lower Portuguese or "Kala Feringhees," and especially their females, consume the drug;—that it is most fascinating in its effects, producing extatic happiness, a persuasion of high rank, a sensation of flying, voracious appetite, and intense aphrodisiac desire. He denies that its continued use leads to madness, impotence, or to the numerous evil

146

consequences described by the Arabic and Persian physicians. Although I disbelieve Ameer's statements on this point, his description of the immediate effects of *Majoon* is strictly and accurately correct.

Most carnivorous animals eat it greedily, and very soon experience its narcotic effects, becoming ludicrously drunk, but seldom suffering any worse consequences.

Section III

Historical details—Notices of Hemp, and its popular uses, by the Sanscrit, Arabic, and Persian writers

The preceding notice suffices to explain the subsequent historical and medicinal details. I premise the historical, in order to shew the exact state of our knowledge of the subject, when I attempted its investigation.

Although the most eminent of the Arabic and Persian authors concur in referring the origin of the practice of Hemp intoxication to the natives of Hindoostan, it is remarkable that few traces can be detected of the prevalence of the vice at any early period in India.

The Pandit Moodoosudun Gooptu finds that the "Rajniguntu," a standard treatise on Materia Medica, which he estimates vaguely at 600 years date, gives a clear account of this agent. Its synonymes are *"Bijoya," "Ujoya,"* and *"Joya,"*—names which mean, promoters of success; *"Brijputta,"* or the strengthener, or the strong-leaved; *"Chapola,"* the causer of a reeling gait; *"Ununda,"* or the laughter-moving; *"Hursiní,"* the exciter of sexual desire. Its effects on man are described as excitant, heating, astringent. It is added that it "destroys phlegm, expels flatulence, induces costiveness, sharpens the memory, increases eloquence, excites the appetite, and acts as a general tonic."

The "Rajbulubha," a Sanscrit treatise of rather later date, alludes to the use of Hemp in gonorrhœa, and repeats the statements of the "Rajniguntu." In the Hindu Tantra, or a religious treatise, teaching peculiar and mystical formulæ and rites for the worship of the deities, it is said, moreover, that *Sidhee* is more intoxicating than wine.

In the celebrated "Susruta," which is perhaps the most ancient of all Hindu medical works, it is written, that persons labouring under catarrh should, with other remedies, use internally the *Bijoya* or *Sidhee*. The effects however are not described.

The learned Kamalakantha Vidyalanka has traced a notice of Hemp in the 5th chapter of *Menu*, where Brahmins are prohibited to use the following substances, *Palandoo* or onions, *Gunjara* or *Gunjah*, and such condiments as have strong and pungent scents.

The Arabic and Persian writers are however far more voluminous and precise in their accounts of these fascinating preparations. In the 1st vol. of De Sacy's "Crestomathie Arabe" we find an extremely interesting summary of the writings of Takim Eddin Makrizi on this subject. Lane has noticed it too with his usual ability

CANNABIS

in his admirable work "the Modern Egyptians." From these two sources, the MS. notes of the Syed Keramut Ali and Mr. DaCosta, and a curious paper communicated by our friend Mirza Abdul Razes, a most intelligent Persian physician, the following epitome is compiled.

Makrizi treats of the Hemp in his glowing description of the celebrated Canton de la Timbaliere, or ancient pleasure grounds, in the vicinity of Cairo. This quarter, after many vicissitudes, is now a heap of ruins. In it was situated a cultivated valley named Djoneina, which we are informed was the theatre of all conceivable abominations. It was famous above all for the sale of the *Hasheeha*, which is still greedily consumed by the dregs of the populace, and from the consumption of which sprung the excesses which led to the name of "Assassin" being given to the Saracens in the Holy Wars. The history of the drug the author treats of thus:—The oldest work in which Hemp is noticed is a treatise by Hasan, who states that in the year 658, M. E. the Sheikh Djafar Shirazi, a monk of the order of Haider, learned from his master the history of the discovery of Hemp. Haider, the chief of ascetics and self-chasteners, lived in rigid privation on a mountain between Nishabor and Ramah, where he established a monastery of Fakirs. Ten years he had spent in this retreat without leaving it for a moment, till one burning summer's day when he departed alone to the fields. On his return an air of joy and gaiety was imprinted on his countenance; he received the visits of his brethren and encouraged their conversation. On being questioned, he stated that struck by the aspect of a plant which danced in the heat as if with joy, while all the rest of the vegetable creation was torpid, he had gathered and eaten of its leaves. He led his companions to the spot,—all ate and all were similarly excited. A tincture of the Hemp leaf in wine or spirit seems to have been the favorite formula in which the Sheikh Haider indulged himself. An Arab poet sings of Haider's *emerald* cup—an evident allusion to the rich green colour of the tincture of the drug. The Sheikh survived the discovery ten years, and subsisted chiefly on this herb, and on his death his disciples by his desire planted it in an arbour about his tomb.

From this saintly sepulchre the knowledge of the effects of Hemp is stated to have spread into Khorasan. In Chaldea it was unknown until 728 M. E. during the reign of the Khalif Mostansir Billah: the kings of Ormus and Bahrein then introduced it into Chaldea, Syria, Egypt, and Turkey.

In Khorasan however, it seems that the date of the use of Hemp is considered to be far prior to Haider's era. Biraslan, an Indian pilgrim, the contemporary of Cosröes,* is believed to have introduced and diffused the custom through Khorasan and Yemen. In proof of the great antiquity of the practice, certain passages in the works of Hippocrates may be cited, in which some of its properties are

---

* By this term is probably meant the first of the Sassanian dynasty, to whom the epithet "of Khusrow" or Cosröes, equivalent to Káiser, Cæsar, or Czar, has been applied in many generations. This dynasty endured from A. D. 202 to A. D. 636—*Vide note* 50 *to Lane's translation of the Arabian Nights, vol.* ii. p. 226.

clearly described—but the difficulty of deciding whether the passages be spurious or genuine, renders the fact of little value. Dioscorides (lib. ij. cap. 169,) describes Hemp, but merely notices the emollient properties of its seeds—its intoxicating effects must consequently be regarded as unknown to the Greeks prior to his era, which is generally agreed to be about the second century of the Christian epoch, and somewhat subsequent to the lifetime of Pliny.

In the narrative of Makrizi we also learn that oxymel and acids are the most powerful antidotes to the effects of this narcotic; next to these, emetics, cold bathing, and sleep; and we are further told that it possesses diuretic, astringent, and especially aphrodisiac properties. Ibn Beitar was the first to record its tendency to produce mental derangement, and he even states that it occasionally proves fatal.

In 780 M. E. very severe ordinances were passed in Egypt against the practice: the Djoneina garden was rooted up, and all those convicted of the use of the drug were subjected to the extraction of their teeth; but in 799 the custom re-established itself with more than original vigour. Makrizi draws an expressive picture of the evils this vice then inflicted on its votaries—"As its consequence, general corruption of sentiments and manners ensued, modesty disappeared, every base and evil passion was openly indulged in, and nobility of external form alone remained to these infatuated beings."

Section V

Experiments by the author—inferences as to the action of the drug on animals and man

Such was the amount of preliminary information before me, by which I was guided in my subsequent attempts to gain more accurate knowledge of the action, powers, and possible medicinal applications of this extraordinary agent.

There was sufficient to show that Hemp possessed in small doses an extraordinary power of stimulating the digestive organs, exciting the cerebral system, of acting also on the generative apparatus. Larger doses, again, were shewn by the historical statements to induce insensibility, or to act as a powerful sedative. The influence of the drug in allaying pain was equally manifest in all the memoirs referred to. As to the evil sequelæ so unanimously dwelt on by all writers, these did not appear to me so numerous, so immediate, or so formidable, as many which may be clearly traced to over-indulgence in other powerful stimulants or narcotics, viz. alcohol, opium, or tobacco.

The dose in which the Hemp preparations might be administered, constituted of course one of the first objects of inquiry. Ibn Beitar had mentioned a *direm*, or 48 grains of *Churrus*, but this dose seemed to me so enormous, that I deemed it expedient to proceed with much smaller quantities. How fortunate was this caution, the sequel will sufficiently denote.

CANNABIS

An extensive series of experiments on animals, was in the first place undertaken, among which the following may be cited:

Expt. 1.—Ten grains of Nipalese *Churrus*, dissolved in spirit were given to a middling sized dog. In half an hour he became stupid and sleepy, dozing at intervals, starting up, wagging his tail as if extremely contented, he ate some food greedily, on being called to he staggered to and fro, and his face assumed a look of utter and helpless drunkenness. These symptoms lasted about two hours, and then gradually passed away; in six hours he was perfectly well and lively.

Expt. 2.—One drachm of *Majoon* was given to a small sized dog, he ate it with great delight, and in twenty minutes was ridiculously drunk; in four hours his symptoms passed away, also without harm.

Expts. 3, 4, & 5.—Three kids had ten grains each of the alcoholic extract of *Gunjah*. In one no effect was produced; in the second there was much heaviness, and some inability to move; in the third a marked alteration of countenance was conspicuous, but no further effect.

Expt. 6.—Twenty grains were given, dissolved in a little spirit, to a dog of very small size. In a quarter of an hour he was intoxicated; in half an hour he had great difficulty of movement; in an hour he had lost all power over the hinder extremities, which were rather stiff but flexible; sensibility did not seem to be impaired, and the circulation was natural. He readily acknowledged calls by an attempt to rise up. In four hours he was quite well.

In none of these or several other experiments was there the least indication of pain, or any degree of convulsive movement observed.

It seems needless to dwell on the details of each experiment; suffice it to say that they led to one remarkable result—That while carnivorous animals and fish, dogs, cats, swine, vultures, crows, and adjutants, invariably and speedily exhibited the intoxicating influence of the drug, the graminivorous, such as the horse, deer, monkey, goat, sheep, and cow, experienced but trivial effects from any dose we administered.

Encouraged by these results, no hesitation could be felt as to the perfect safety of giving the resin of Hemp an extensive trial in the cases in which its apparent powers promised the greatest degree of utility.

Delirium occasioned by continued Hemp Inebriation

Before quitting this subject, it is desirable to notice the singular form of delirium which the incautious use of the Hemp preparations often occasions, especially among young men who try it for the first time. Several such cases have presented themselves to my notice. They are as peculiar as the "delirium tremens," which succeeds the prolonged abuse of spirituous liquors, but are quite distinct from any other species of delirium with which I am acquainted.

This state is at once recognized by the strange balancing gait of the patient, a constant rubbing of the hands, perpetual giggling, and a propensity to caress and chafe the feet of all bystanders of whatever rank. The eye wears an expression of cunning and merriment which can scarcely be mistaken. In a few cases, the patients are violent; in many, highly aphrodisiac; in all that I have seen, voraciously hungry. There is no increased heat or frequency of circulation, or any appearance of inflammation or congestion, and the skin and general functions are in a natural state.

A blister to the nape of the neck, leeches to the temples, and nauseating doses of tartar emetic with saline purgatives have rapidly dispelled the symptoms in all the cases I have met with, and have restored the patient to perfect health.

The preceding cases constitute an abstract of my experience on this subject, and which has led me to the belief that in Hemp the profession has gained an anti-convulsive remedy of the greatest value. Entertaining this conviction, be it true or false, I deem it my duty to publish it without any avoidable delay, in order that the most extensive and the speediest trial may be given to the proposed remedy. I repeat what I have already stated in a previous paper—that were individual reputation my object, I would let years pass by, and hundreds of cases accumulate before publication; and in publishing I would enter into every kind of elaborate detail. But the object I have proposed to myself in these inquiries is of a very different kind. To gather together a few strong facts, to ascertain the limits which cannot be passed without danger, and then pointing out these to the profession, to leave their body to prosecute and decide on the subject of discussion, such seems to me the fittest mode of attempting to explore the medicinal resources which an untried Materia Medica may contain.

It may be useful to add a formula for making the preparations which I have employed.

The *resinous extract* is prepared by boiling the rich, adhesive tops of the dried *Gunjah* in spirit (Sp: gr. 835,) until all the resin is dissolved. The tincture thus obtained is evaporated to dryness in a vessel placed over a pot of boiling water. The extract softens at a gentle heat, and can be made into pills without any addition.

The *tincture* is prepared by dissolving three grains of the extract in one drachm of proof spirit.

Doses, &c.—In *Tetanus* a drachm of the tincture every half hour until the paroxysms cease, or catalepsy is induced. In *Hydrophobia* I would recommend the resin in soft pills, to the extent of ten to twenty grains to be chewed by the patient, and repeated according to the effect. In *Cholera* ten drops of the tincture every half hour will be often found to check the vomiting and purging, and bring back warmth to the surface. My experience would lead me to prefer *small* doses of the remedy in order to excite rather than narcotise the patient.

10

F. H. LUDLOW, 'INTRODUCTION', 'THE NIGHT ENTRANCE', 'UNDER THE SHADOW OF ESCULAPIUS', AND 'THE KINGDOM OF THE DREAM', IN *THE HASHEESH EATER: BEING PASSAGES FROM THE LIFE OF A PYTHAGOREAN* (NEW YORK: HARPER & BROTHER, 1857), PP. IX–XIV; 15–43

Introduction

THE singular energy and scope of imagination which characterize all Oriental tales, and especially that great typical representative of the species, the Arabian Nights, were my ceaseless marvel from earliest childhood. The book of Arabian and Turkish story has very few thoughtful readers among the nations of the West, who can rest contented with admiring its bold flights into unknown regions of imagery, and close the mystic pages that have enchanted them without an inquiry as to the influences which have turned the human mind into such rare channels of thought. Sooner or later comes the question of the producing causes, and it is in the power of few—very few of us—to answer that question aright.

We try to imitate Eastern narrative, but in vain. Our minds can find no clew to its strange, untrodden by-ways of speculation; our highest soarings are still in an atmosphere which feels heavy with the reek and damp of ordinary life. We fail to account for those storm-wrapped peaks of sublimity which hover over the path of Oriental story, or those beauties which, like rivers of Paradise, make music beside it. We are all of us taught to say, "The children of the East live under a sunnier sky than their Western brethren: they are the repositors of centuries of tradition; their semi-civilized imagination is unbound by the fetters of logic and the schools." But the Ionians once answered all these conditions, yet Homer sang no Eblis, no superhuman journey on the wings of genii through infinitudes of rosy ether. At one period of their history, France, Germany, and England abounded in all the characteristics of the untutored Old-world mind, yet when did an echo of Oriental music ring from the lute of minstrel, minnesinger, or trouvére? The difference can not be accounted for by climate, religion, or manners. It is not the supernatural in Arabian story which is inexplicable, but the peculiar phase of the supernatural both in beauty and terror.

I say inexplicable, because to me, in common with all around me, it bore this character for years. In later days, I believe, and now with all due modesty assert, I unlocked the secret, not by a hypothesis, not by processes of reasoning, but by journeying through those self-same fields of weird experience which are dinted by the sandals of the glorious old dreamers of the East. Standing on the same mounts of vision where they stood, listening to the same gurgling melody that broke from their enchanted fountains, yes, plunging into their rayless caverns of sorcery, and imprisoned with their genie in the unutterable silence of the fathomless sea, have I dearly bought the right to come to men with the chart of my wanderings in my hands, and unfold to them the foundations of the fabric of Oriental story.

The secret lies in the use of hasheesh. A very few words will suffice to tell what hasheesh is. In northern latitudes the hemp plant (Cannabis Sativa) grows almost entirely to fibre, becoming, in virtue of this quality, the great resource for mats and cordage. Under a southern sun this same plant loses its fibrous texture, but secretes, in quantities equal to one third of its bulk, an opaque and greenish resin. Between the northern and the southern hemp there is no difference, except the effect of diversity of climate upon the same vegetable essence; yet naturalists, misled by the much greater extent of gummy secretion in the latter, have distinguished it from its brother of the colder soil by the name Cannabis Indica. The resin of the Cannabis Indica is hasheesh. From time immemorial it has been known among all the nations of the East as possessing powerful stimulant and narcotic properties; throughout Turkey, Persia, Nepaul, and India it is used at this day among all classes of society as an habitual indulgence. The forms in which it is employed are various. Sometimes it appears in the state in which it exudes from the mature stalk, as a crude resin; sometimes it is manufactured into a conserve with clarified butter, honey, and spices; sometimes a decoction is made of the flowering tops in water or arrack. Under either of these forms the method of administration is by swallowing. Again, the dried plant is smoked in pipes or chewed, as tobacco among ourselves.

Used in whatever preparation, hasheesh is characterized by the most remarkable phenomena, both physical and spiritual. A series of experiments made with it by men of eminent attainments in the medical profession, principally at Calcutta, and during the last ten years, prove it to be capable of inducing all the ordinary symptoms of catalepsy, or even of trance.

However, from the fact of its so extensive daily use as a pleasurable stimulus in the countries where experiments with it have been made, it has doubtless lost interest in the field of scientific research, and has come to be regarded as only one more means among the multitude which mankind in all latitudes are seeking for

CANNABIS

the production of a sensual intoxication. Now and then a traveler, passing by the bazar where it was exposed for sale, moved by curiosity, has bought some form of the hemp, and made the trial of its effects upon himself; but the results of the experiment were dignified with no further notice than a page or a chapter in the note-book of his journeyings, and the hasheesh phenomena, with an exclamation of wonder, were thenceforward dismissed from his own and the public mind. Very few even of the permanently domesticated foreign residents in the countries of the East have ever adopted this indulgence as a habit, and of those few I am not aware of any who have communicated their experience to the world, or treated it as a subject possessing scientific interest.

My own personal acquaintance with this drug, covering as it did a considerable extent of time, and almost every possible variety of phenomena, both physical and psychological, proper to its operation, not only empowers, but for a long time has been impelling me to give it a publicity which may bring it in contact with a larger number of minds interested in such researches than it could otherwise hope to meet. As a key to some of the most singular manifestations of the Oriental mind, as a narrative interesting to the attentive student of the human soul and body, and the mysterious network of interacting influences which connect them, I therefore venture to present this experience to the investigation of general readers, accompanying it with the sincere disavowal of all fiction in my story, and the assurance that whatever traits of the marvelous may appear in its gradual development are inherent in the truth as I shall simply delineate it. I am aware that, without this disavowal, much—nay, even most that I shall say, will be taken "cum grano salis." I desire it, therefore, to be distinctly understood at the outset that my narrative is one of unexaggerated fact, its occurrences being recorded precisely as they impressed themselves upon me, without one additional stroke of the pencil of an after-fancy thrown in to heighten the tone or harmonize the effect. Whatever of the wonderful may appear in these pages belongs to the subject and not to the manner.

The progress of my narration will be in the order of time. I shall begin with my first experiment of the use of hasheesh, an experiment made simply from the promptings of curiosity; it will then be my endeavor to detail the gradual change of my motive for its employment from the desire of research to the fascinated longing for its weird and immeasurable ecstasy; I shall relate how that ecstasy by degrees became daily more and more flecked with shadows of as immeasurable pain, but still, in this dual existence, assumed a character increasingly apocalyptic of utterly unpreconceived provinces of mental action. In the next succeeding stage of my experience, torture, save at rare intervals, will have swallowed up happiness altogether, without abating in the least the fascination of the habit. In the next and final one will be beheld my instantaneous abandonment of the indulgence, the cause which led to it, and the discipline of suffering which attended the self-denial.

The aim of this relation is not merely æsthetic nor scientific: though throughout it there be no stopping to moralize, it is my earnest desire that it may teem with suggestions of a lesson without which humanity can learn nothing in the schools. It is this: the soul withers and sinks from its growth toward the true end of its being beneath the dominance of any sensual indulgence. The chain of its bondage may for a long time continue to be golden—many a day may pass before the fetters gall—yet all the while there is going on a slow and insidious consumption of its native strength, and when at last captivity becomes a pain, it may awake to discover in inconceivable terror that the very forces of disenthralment have perished out of its reach.

The Hasheesh Eater

I

The night entrance

ABOUT the shop of my friend Anderson the apothecary there always existed a peculiar fascination, which early marked it out as my favorite lounging-place. In the very atmosphere of the establishment, loaded as it was with a composite smell of all things curative and preventive, there was an aromatic invitation to scientific musing, which could not have met with a readier acceptance had it spoken in the breath of frankincense. The very gallipots grew gradually to possess a charm for me as they sat calmly ranged upon their oaken shelves, looking like a convention of unostentatious philanthropists, whose silent bosoms teemed with every variety of renovation for the human race. A little sanctum at the inner end of the shop, walled off with red curtains from the profane gaze of the unsanative, contained two chairs for the doctor and myself, and a library where all the masters of physic were grouped, through their sheep and paper representatives, in more friendliness of contact than has ever been known to characterize a consultation of like spirits under any other circumstances. Within the limits of four square feet, Pereira and Christison condensed all their stores of wisdom and research, and Dunglison and Brathwaite sat check by jowl beside them. There stood the Dispensatory, with the air of a business-like office, wherein all the specifics of the materia medica had been brought together for a scientific conversazione, but, becoming enamored of each other's society, had resolved to stay, overcrowded though they might be, and make an indefinite sitting of it. In a modest niche, set apart like a vestibule from the apartments of the medical gentlemen, lay a shallow ease, which disclosed, on the lifting of a cover, the neatly-ordered rank of tweezers, probe, and lancet, which constituted my friend's claim to the confidence of the plethoric community; for, although unblessed with metropolitan fame, he was still no

"Cromwell guiltless of his country's blood."

Here many an hour have I sat buried in the statistics of human life or the history of the make-shifts for its preservation. Here the details of surgical or medical experiment have held me in as complete engrossment as the positions and crises of romance; and here especially, with a disregard to my own safety which would have done credit to Quintus Curtius, have I made upon myself the trial of the effects of every strange drug and chemical which the laboratory could produce. Now with the chloroform bottle beneath my nose have I set myself careering upon the wings of a thrilling and accelerating life, until I had just enough power remaining to restore the liquid to its place upon the shelf, and sink back into the enjoyment of the delicious apathy which lasted through the few succeeding moments. Now ether was substituted for chloroform, and the difference of their phenomena noted, and now some other exhilarant, in the form of an opiate or stimulant, was the instrument of my experiments, until I had run through the whole gamut of queer agents within my reach.

In all these experiences research and not indulgence was my object, so that I never became the victim of any habit in the prosecution of my headlong investigations. When the circuit of all the accessible tests was completed, I ceased experimenting, and sat down like a pharmaceutical Alexander, with no more drug-worlds to conquer.

One morning, in the spring of 185–, I dropped in upon the doctor for my accustomed lounge.

"Have you seen," said he, "my new acquisitions?"

I looked toward the shelves in the direction of which he pointed, and saw, added since my last visit, a row of comely pasteboard cylinders inclosing vials of the various extracts prepared by Tilden & Co. Arranged in order according to their size, they confronted me, as pretty a little rank of medicinal sharpshooters as could gratify the eye of an amateur. I approached the shelves, that I might take them in review.

A rapid glance showed most of them to be old acquaintances. "Conium, taraxacum, rhubarb—ha! what is this? Cannabis Indica?" "That," answered the doctor, looking with a parental fondness upon his new treasure, "is a preparation of the East Indian hemp, a powerful agent in cases of lock-jaw." On the strength of this introduction, I took down the little archer, and, removing his outer verdant coat, began the further prosecution of his acquaintance. To pull out a broad and shallow cork was the work of an instant, and it revealed to me an olive-brown extract, of the consistency of pitch, and a decided aromatic odor. Drawing out a small portion upon the point of my penknife, I was just going to put it to my tongue, when "Hold on!" cried the doctor; "do you want to kill yourself? That stuff is deadly poison." "Indeed!" I replied; "no, I can not say that I have any settled determination of that kind;" and with that I replaced the cork, and restored the extract, with all its appurtenances, to the shelf.

The remainder of my morning's visit in the sanctum was spent in consulting the Dispensatory under the title "Cannabis Indica." The sum of my discoveries there may be found, with much additional information, in that invaluable popular work, Johnston's Chemistry of Common Life. This being universally accessible,

THE HASHEESH EATER

I will allude no further to the result of that morning's researches than to mention the three following conclusions to which I came.

First, the doctor was both right and wrong; right, inasmuch as a sufficiently large dose of the drug, if it could be retained in the stomach, would produce death, like any other narcotic, and the ultimate effect of its habitual use had always proved highly injurious to mind and body; wrong, since moderate doses of it were never immediately deadly, and many millions of people daily employed it as an indulgence similarly to opium. Second, it was the hasheesh referred to by Eastern travelers, and the subject of a most graphic chapter from the pen of Bayard Taylor, which months before had moved me powerfully to curiosity and admiration. Third, I would add it to the list of my former experiments.

In pursuance of this last determination, I waited till my friend was out of sight, that I might not terrify him by that which he considered a suicidal venture, and then quietly uncapping my little archer a second time, removed from his store of offensive armor a pill sufficient to balance the ten grain weight of the sanctorial scales. This, upon the authority of Percira and the Dispensatory, I swallowed without a tremor as to the danger of the result.

Making all due allowance for the fact that I had not taken my hasheesh bolus fasting, I ought to experience its effects within the next four hours. That time elapsed without bringing the shadow of a phenomenon. It was plain that my dose had been insufficient.

For the sake of observing the most conservative prudence, I suffered several days to go by without a repetition of the experiment, and then, keeping the matter equally secret, I administered to myself a pill of fifteen grains. This second was equally ineffectual with the first.

Gradually, by five grains at a time, I increased the dose to thirty grains, which I took one evening half an hour after tea. I had now almost come to the conclusion that I was absolutely unsusceptible of the hasheesh influence. Without any expectation that this last experiment would be more successful than the former ones, and indeed with no realization of the manner in which the drug affected those who did make the experiment successfully, I went to pass the evening at the house of an intimate friend. In music and conversation the time passed pleasantly. The clock struck ten, reminding me that three hours had elapsed since the dose was taken, and as yet not an unusual symptom had appeared. I was provoked to think that this trial was as fruitless as its predecessors.

Ha! what means this sudden thrill? A shock, as of some unimagined vital force, shoots without warning through my entire frame, leaping to my fingers' ends, piercing my brain, startling me till I almost spring from my chair.

I could not doubt it. I was in the power of the hasheesh influence. My first emotion was one of uncontrollable terror—a sense of getting something which I had not bargained for. That moment I would have given all I had or hoped to have to be as I was three hours before.

CANNABIS

No pain any where—not a twinge in any fibre—yet a cloud of unutterable strangeness was settling upon me, and wrapping me impenetrably in from all that was natural or familiar. Endeared faces, well known to me of old, surrounded me, yet they were not with me in my loneliness. I had entered upon a tremendous life which they could not share. If the disembodied ever return to hover over the hearth-stone which once had a seat for them, they look upon their friends as I then looked upon mine. A nearness of place, with an infinite distance of state, a connection which had no possible sympathies for the wants of that hour of revelation, an isolation none the less perfect for seeming companionship.

Still I spoke; a question was put to me, and I answered it; I even laughed at a bon mot. Yet it was not my voice which spoke; perhaps one which I once had far away in another time and another place. For a while I knew nothing that was going on externally, and then the remembrance of the last remark which had been made returned slowly and indistinctly, as some trait of a dream will return after many days, puzzling us to say where we have been conscious of it before.

A fitful wind all the evening had been sighing down the chimney; it now grew into the steady hum of a vast wheel in accelerating motion. For a while this hum seemed to resound through all space. I was stunned by it—I was absorbed in it. Slowly the revolution of the wheel came to a stop, and its monotonous din was changed for the reverberating peal of a grand cathedral organ. The ebb and flow of its inconceivably solemn tone filled me with a grief that was more than human. I sympathized with the dirge-like cadence as spirit sympathizes with spirit. And then, in the full conviction that all I heard and felt was real, I looked out of my isolation to see the effect of the music on my friends. Ah! we were in separate worlds indeed. Not a trace of appreciation on any face.

Perhaps I was acting strangely. Suddenly a pair of busy hands, which had been running neck and neck all the evening with a nimble little crochet-needle over a race-ground of pink and blue silk, stopped at their goal, and their owner looked at me steadfastly. Ah! I was found out—I had betrayed myself. In terror I waited, expecting every instant to hear the word "hasheesh." No, the lady only asked me some question connected with the previous conversation. As mechanically as an automaton I began to reply. As I heard once more the alien and unreal tones of my own voice, I became convinced that it was some one else who spoke, and in another world. I sat and listened; still the voice kept speaking. Now for the first time I experienced that vast change which hasheesh makes in all measurements of time. The first word of the reply occupied a period sufficient for the action of a drama; the last left me in complete ignorance of any point far enough back in the past to date the commencement of the sentence. Its enunciation might have occupied years. I was not in the same life which had held me when I heard it begun.

And now, with time, space expanded also. At my friend's house one particular arm-chair was always reserved for me. I was sitting in it at a distance of hardly three feet from the centre-table around which the members of the family were grouped. Rapidly that distance widened. The whole atmosphere seemed ductile,

158

and spun endlessly out into great spaces surrounding me on every side. We were in a vast hall, of which my friends and I occupied opposite extremities. The ceiling and the walls ran upward with a gliding motion, as if vivified by a sudden force of resistless growth.

Oh! I could not bear it. I should soon be left alone in the midst of an infinity of space. And now more and more every moment increased the conviction that I was watched. I did not know then, as I learned afterward, that suspicion of all earthly things and persons was the characteristic of the hasheesh delirium.

In the midst of my complicated hallucination, I could perceive that I had a dual existence. One portion of me was whirled unresistingly along the track of this tremendous experience, the other sat looking down from a height upon its double, observing, reasoning, and serenely weighing all the phenomena. This calmer being suffered with the other by sympathy, but did not lose its self-possession. Presently it warned me that I must go home, lest the growing effect of the hasheesh should incite me to some act which might frighten my friends. I acknowledged the force of this remark very much as if it had been made by another person, and rose to take my leave. I advanced toward the centre-table. With every step its distance increased. I nerved myself as for a long pedestrian journey. Still the lights, the faces, the furniture receded. At last, almost unconsciously, I reached them. It would be tedious to attempt to convey the idea of the time which my leave-taking consumed, and the attempt, at least with all minds that have not passed through the same experience, would be as impossible as tedious. At last I was in the street.

Beyond me the view stretched endlessly away. It was an unconverging vista, whose nearest lamps seemed separated from me by leagues. I was doomed to pass through a merciless stretch of space. A soul just disenthralled, setting out for his flight beyond the farthest visible star, could not be more overwhelmed with his newly-acquired conception of the sublimity of distance than I was at that moment. Solemnly I began my infinite journey.

Before long I walked in entire unconsciousness of all around me. I dwelt in a marvelous inner world. I existed by turns in different places and various states of being. Now I swept my gondola through the moonlit lagoons of Venice. Now Alp on Alp towered above my view, and the glory of the coming sun flashed purple light upon the topmost icy pinnacle. Now in the primeval silence of some unexplored tropical forest I spread my feathery leaves, a giant fern, and swayed and nodded in the spice-gales over a river whose waves at once sent up clouds of music and perfume. My soul changed to a vegetable essence, thrilled with a strange and unimagined ecstasy. The palace of Al Haroun could not have bought me back to humanity.

I will not detail all the transmutations of that walk. Ever and anon I returned from my dreams into consciousness, as some well-known house seemed to leap out into my path, awaking me with a shock. The whole way homeward was a series of such awakings and relapses into abstraction and delirium until I reached the corner of the street in which I lived.

CANNABIS

Here a new phenomenon manifested itself. I had just awaked for perhaps the twentieth time, and my eyes were wide open. I recognized all surrounding objects, and began calculating the distance home. Suddenly, out of a blank wall at my side a muffled figure stepped into the path before me. His hair, white as snow, hung in tangled elf-locks on his shoulders, where he carried also a heavy burden, like unto the well-filled sack of sins which Bunyan places on the back of his pilgrim. Not liking his manner, I stepped aside, intending to pass around him and go on my way. This change of our relative position allowed the blaze of a neighboring street-lamp to fall full on his face, which had hitherto been totally obscured. Horror unspeakable! I shall never, till the day I die, forget that face. Every lineament was stamped with the records of a life black with damning crime; it glared upon me with a ferocious wickedness and a stony despair which only he may feel who is entering on the retribution of the unpardonable sin. He might have sat to a demon painter as the ideal of Shelley's Cenci. I seemed to grow blasphemous in looking at him, and, in an agony of fear, began to run away. He detained me with a bony hand, which pierced my wrist like talons, and, slowly taking down the burden from his own shoulders, laid it upon mine. I threw it off and pushed him away. Silently he returned and restored the weight. Again I repulsed him, this time crying out, "Man, what do you mean?" In a voice which impressed me with the sense of wickedness as his face had done, he replied, "You *shall* bear my burden with me," and a third time laid it on my shoulders. For the last time I hurled it aside, and, with all my force, dashed him from me. He reeled backward and fell, and before he could recover his disadvantage I had put a long distance between us.

Through the excitement of my struggle with this phantasm the effects of the hasheesh had increased mightily. I was bursting with an uncontrollable life; I strode with the thews of a giant. Hotter and faster came my breath; I seemed to pant like some tremendous engine. An electric energy whirled me resistlessly onward; I feared for myself lest it should burst its fleshly walls, and glance on, leaving a wrecked frame-work behind it.

At last I entered my own house. During my absence a family connection had arrived from abroad, and stood ready to receive my greeting. Partly restored to consciousness by the naturalness of home-faces and the powerful light of a chandelier which shed its blaze through the room, I saw the necessity of vigilance against betraying my condition, and with an intense effort suppressing all I felt, I approached my friend, and said all that is usual on such occasions. Yet recent as I was from my conflict with the supernatural, I cast a stealthy look about me, that I might learn from the faces of the others if, after all, I was shaking hands with a phantom, and making inquiries about the health of a family of hallucinations. Growing assured as I perceived no symptoms of astonishment, I finished the salutation and sat down.

It soon required all my resolution to keep the secret which I had determined to hold inviolable. My sensations began to be terrific—not from any pain that

THE HASHEESH EATER

I felt, but from the tremendous mystery of all around me and within me. By an appalling introversion, all the operations of vitality which, in our ordinary state, go on unconsciously, came vividly into my experience. Through every thinnest corporeal tissue and minutest vein I could trace the circulation of the blood along each inch of its progress. I knew when every valve opened and when it shut; every sense was preternaturally awakened; the room was full of a great glory. The beating of my heart was so clearly audible that I wondered to find it unnoticed by those who were sitting by my side. Lo, now, that heart became a great fountain, whose jet played upward with loud vibrations, and, striking upon the roof of my skull as on a gigantic dome, fell back with a splash and echo into its reservoir. Faster and faster came the pulsations, until at last I heard them no more, and the stream became one continuously pouring flood, whose roar resounded through all my frame. I gave myself up for lost, since judgment, which still sat unimpaired above my perverted senses, argued that congestion must take place in a few moments, and close the drama with my death. But my clutch would not yet relax from hope. The thought struck me, Might not this rapidity of circulation be, after all, imaginary? I determined to find out.

Going to my own room, I took out my watch, and placed my hand upon my heart. The very effort which I made to ascertain the reality gradually brought perception back to its natural state. In the intensity of my observations, I began to perceive that the circulation was not as rapid as I had thought. From a pulseless flow it gradually came to be apprehended as a hurrying succession of intense throbs, then less swift and less intense, till finally, on comparing it with the second-hand, I found that about 90 a minute was its average rapidity. Greatly comforted, I desisted from the experiment. Almost instantly the hallucination returned. Again I dreaded apoplexy, congestion, hemorrhage, a multiplicity of nameless deaths, and drew my picture as I might be found on the morrow, stark and cold, by those whose agony would be redoubled by the mystery of my end. I reasoned with myself; I bathed my forehead—it did no good. There was one resource left: I would go to a physician.

With this resolve, I left my room and went to the head of the staircase. The family had all retired for the night, and the gas was turned off from the burner in the hall below. I looked down the stairs: the depth was fathomless; it was a journey of years to reach the bottom! The dim light of the sky shone through the narrow panes at the sides of the front door, and seemed a demon-lamp in the middle darkness of the abyss. I never could get down! I sat me down despairingly upon the topmost step.

Suddenly a sublime thought possessed me. If the distance be infinite, I am immortal. It shall be tried. I commenced the descent, wearily, wearily down through my league-long, year-long journey. To record my impressions in that journey would be to repeat what I have said of the time of hasheesh. Now stopping to rest as a traveler would turn aside at a wayside inn, now toiling down through the lonely darkness, I came by-and-by to the end, and passed out into the street.

CANNABIS

II

Under the shadow of Esculapius

On reaching the porch of the physician's house, I rang the bell, but immediately forgot whom to ask for. No wonder; I was on the steps of a palace in Milan—no (and I laughed at myself for the blunder), I was on the staircase of the Tower of London. So I should not be puzzled through my ignorance of Italian. But whom to ask for? This question recalled me to the real bearings of the place, but did not suggest its requisite answer. Whom shall I ask for? I began setting the most cunning traps of hypothesis to catch the solution of the difficulty. I looked at the surrounding houses; of whom had I been accustomed to think as living next door to them? This did not bring it. Whose daughter had I seen going to school from this house but the very day before? Her name was Julia—Julia—and I thought of every combination which had been made with this name from Julia Domna down to Giulia Grisi. Ah! now I had it—Julia H.; and her father naturally bore the same name. During this intellectual rummage I had rung the bell half a dozen times, under the impression that I was kept waiting a small eternity. When the servant opened the door she panted as if she had run for her life. I was shown up stairs to Dr. H.'s room, where he had thrown himself down to rest after a tedious operation. Locking the door after me with an air of determined secrecy, which must have conveyed to him pleasant little suggestions of a design upon his life, I approached his bedside.

"I am about to reveal to you," I commenced, "something which I would not for my life allow to come to other cars. Do you pledge me your eternal silence?"

"I do; what is the matter?"

"I have been taking hasheesh—Cannabis Indica, and I fear that I am going to die."

"How much did you take?"

"Thirty grains."

"Let me feel your pulse." He placed his finger on my wrist and counted slowly, while I stood waiting to hear my death-warrant. "Very regular," shortly spoke the doctor; "triflingly accelerated. Do you feel any pain?" "None at all." "Nothing the matter with you; go home and go to bed." "But—is there—is there—no—danger of—apoplexy?" "Bah!" said the doctor; and, having delivered himself of this very Abernethy-like opinion of my case, he lay down again. My hand was on the knob, when he stopped me with, "Wait a minute; I'll give you a powder to carry with you, and if you get frightened again after you leave me, you can take it as a sedative. Step out on the landing, if you please, and call my servant."

I did so, and my voice seemed to reverberate like thunder from every recess in the whole building. I was terrified at the noise I had made. I learned in after days that this impression is only one of the many due to the intense susceptibility of the sensorium as produced by hasheesh. At one time, having asked a friend to check

162

me if I talked loudly or immoderately while in a state of fantasia among persons from whom I wished to conceal my state, I caught myself shouting and singing from very ecstasy, and reproached him with a neglect of his friendly office. I could not believe him when he assured me that I had not uttered an audible word. The intensity of the inward emotion had affected the external through the internal ear.

I returned and stood at the foot of the doctor's bed. All was perfect silence in the room, and had been perfect darkness also but for the small lamp which I held in my hand to light the preparation of the powder when it should come. And now a still sublimer mystery began to enwrap me. I stood in a remote chamber at the top of a colossal building, and the whole fabric beneath me was steadily growing into the air. Higher than the topmost pinnacle of Bel's Babylonish temple—higher than Ararat—on, on forever into the lonely dome of God's infinite universe we towered ceaselessly. The years flew on; I heard the musical rush of their wings in the abyss outside of me, and from cycle to cycle, from life to life I careered, a mote in eternity and space. Suddenly emerging from the orbit of my transmigrations, I was again at the foot of the doctor's bed, and thrilled with wonder to find that we were both unchanged by the measureless lapse of time. The servant had not come.

"Shall I call her again?" "Why, you have this moment called her." "Doctor," I replied solemnly, and in language that would have seemed bombastic enough to any one who did not realize what I felt, "I will not believe you are deceiving me, but to me it appears as if sufficient time has elapsed since then for all the Pyramids to have crumbled back to dust." "Ha! ha! you are very funny to-night," said the doctor; "but here she comes, and I will send her for something which will comfort you on that score, and reestablish the Pyramids in your confidence." He gave the girl his orders, and she went out again.

The thought struck me that I would compare *my time* with other people's. I looked at my watch, found that its minute-hand stood at the quarter mark past eleven, and, returning it to my pocket, abandoned myself to my reflections.

Presently I saw myself a gnome imprisoned by a most weird enchanter, whose part I assigned to the doctor before me, in the Domdaniel caverns, "under the roots of the ocean." Here, until the dissolution of all things, was I doomed to hold the lamp that lit that abysmal darkness, while my heart, like a giant clock, ticked solemnly the remaining years of time. Now, this hallucination departing, I heard in the solitude of the night outside the sound of a wondrous heaving sea. Its waves, in sublime cadence, rolled forward till they met the foundations of the building; they smote them with a might which made the very topstone quiver, and then fell back, with hiss and hollow murmur, into the broad bosom whence they had arisen. Now through the street, with measured tread, an armed host passed by. The heavy beat of their footfall and the griding of their brazen corslet-rings alone broke the silence, for among them all there was no more speech nor music than in a battalion of the dead. It was the army of the ages going by into eternity. A godlike sublimity swallowed up my soul. I was overwhelmed in a fathomless barathrum of time, but I leaned on God, and was immortal through all changes.

CANNABIS

And now, in another life, I remembered that far back in the cycles I had looked at my watch to measure the time through which I passed. The impulse seized me to look again. The minute-hand stood half way between fifteen and sixteen minutes past eleven. The watch must have stopped; I held it to my ear; no, it was still going. I had traveled through all that immeasurable chain of dreams in thirty seconds. "My God!" I cried, "I am in eternity." In the presence of that first sublime revelation of the soul's own time, and her capacity for an infinite life, I stood trembling with breathless awe. Till I die, that moment of unveiling will stand in clear relief from all the rest of my existence. I hold it still in unimpaired remembrance as one of the unutterable sanctities of my being. The years of all my earthly life to come can never be as long as those thirty seconds.

Finally the servant reappeared. I received my powder and went home. There was a light in one of the upper windows, and I hailed it with unspeakable joy, for it relieved me from a fear which I could not conquer, that while I had been gone all familiar things had passed away from earth. I was hardly safe in my room before I doubted having ever been out of it. "I have experienced some wonderful dream," said I, "as I lay here after coming from the parlor." If I had not been out, I reasoned that I would have no powder in my pocket. The powder was there, and it steadied me a little to find that I was not utterly hallucinated on every point. Leaving the light burning, I set out to travel to my bed, which gently invited me in the distance. Reaching it after a sufficient walk, I threw myself down.

III

The Kingdom of the dream

THE moment that I closed my eyes a vision of celestial glory burst upon me. I stood on the silver strand of a translucent, boundless lake, across whose bosom I seemed to have been just transported. A short way up the beach, a temple, modeled like the Parthenon, lifted its spotless and gleaming columns of alabaster sublimely into a rosy air—like the Parthenon, yet as much excelling it as the godlike ideal of architecture must transcend that ideal realized by man. Unblemished in its purity of whiteness, faultless in the unbroken symmetry of every line and angle, its pediment was draped in odorous clouds, whose tints outshone the rainbow. It was the work of an unearthly builder, and my soul stood before it in a trance of ecstasy. Its folded doors were resplendent with the glory of a multitude of eyes of glass, which were inlaid throughout the marble surfaces at the corners of diamond figures from the floor of the porch to the topmost moulding. One of these eyes was golden, like the midday sun, another emerald, another sapphire, and thus onward through the whole gamut of hues, all of them set in such collocations as to form most exquisite harmonies, and whirling upon their axes with the rapidity of thought. At the mere vestibule of the temple I could have sat and drunk in

164

ecstasy forever; but lo! I am yet more blessed. On silent hinges the doors swing open, and I pass in.

I did not seem to be in the interior of a temple. I beheld myself as truly in the open air as if I had never passed the portals, for whichever way I looked there were no walls, no roof, no pavement. An atmosphere of fathomless and soul-satisfying serenity surrounded and transfused me. I stood upon the bank of a crystal stream, whose waters, as they slid on, discoursed notes of music which tinkled on the ear like the tones of some exquisite bell-glass. The same impression which such tones produce, of music refined to its ultimate ethereal spirit and borne from a far distance, characterized every ripple of those translucent waves. The gently sloping banks of the stream were luxuriant with a velvety cushioning of grass and moss, so living green that the eye and the soul reposed on them at the same time and drank in peace. Through this amaranthine herbage strayed the gnarled, fantastic roots of giant cedars of Lebanon, from whose primeval trunks great branches spread above me, and interlocking, wove a roof of impenetrable shadow; and wandering down the still avenues below those grand arboreal arches went glorious bards, whose snowy beards fell on their breasts beneath countenances of ineffable benignity and nobleness.

They were all clad in flowing robes, like God's high-priests, and each one held in his hand a lyre of unearthly workmanship. Presently one stops midway down a shady walk, and, baring his right arm, begins a prelude. While his celestial chords were trembling up into their sublime fullness, another strikes his strings, and now they blend upon my ravished ear in such a symphony as was never heard elsewhere, and I shall never hear again out of the Great Presence. A moment more, and three are playing in harmony; now the fourth joins the glorious rapture of his music to their own, and in the completeness of the chord my soul is swallowed up. I can bear no more. But yes, I am sustained, for suddenly the whole throng break forth in a chorus, upon whose wings I am lifted out of the riven walls of sense, and music and spirit thrill in immediate communion. Forever rid of the intervention of pulsing air and vibrating nerve, my soul dilates with the swell of that transcendent harmony, and interprets from it arcana of a meaning which words can never tell. I am borne aloft upon the glory of sound. I float in a trance among the burning choir of the seraphim. But, as I am melting through the purification of that sublime ecstasy into oneness with the Deity himself, one by one those pealing lyres faint away, and as the last throb dies down along the measureless ether, visionless arms swiftly as lightning carry me far into the profound, and set me down before another portal. Its leaves, like the first, are of spotless marble, but ungemmed with wheeling eyes of burning color.

Before entering on the record of this new vision I will make a digression, for the purpose of introducing two laws of the hasheesh operation, which, as explicatory, deserve a place here. First, after the completion of any one fantasia has arrived, there almost invariably succeeds a shifting of the action to some other stage entirely different in its surroundings. In this transition the general character of the emotion may remain unchanged. I may be happy in Paradise and happy

165

at the sources of the Nile, but seldom, either in Paradise or on the Nile, twice in succession. I may writhe in Etna and burn unquenchably in Gehenna, but almost never, in the course of the same delirium, shall Etna or Gehenna witness my torture a second time.

Second, after the full storm of a vision of intense sublimity has blown past the hasheesh-eater, his next vision is generally of a quiet, relaxing, and recreating nature. He comes down from his clouds or up from his abyss into a middle ground of gentle shadows, where he may rest his eyes from the splendor of the seraphim or the flames of fiends. There is a wise philosophy in this arrangement, for otherwise the soul would soon burn out in the excess of its own oxygen. Many a time, it seems to me, has my own thus been saved from extinction.

This next vision illustrated both, but especially the latter of these laws. The temple-doors opened noiselessly before me, but it was no scene of sublimity which thus broke in upon my eyes. I stood in a large apartment, which resembled the Senate-chamber at Washington more than any thing else to which I can compare it. Its roof was vaulted, and at the side opposite the entrance the floor rose into a dais surmounted by a large arm-chair. The body of the house was occupied by similar chairs disposed in arcs; the heavy paneling of the walls was adorned with grotesque frescoes of every imaginable bird, beast, and monster, which, by some hidden law of life and motion, were forever changing, like the figures of the kaleidoscope. Now the walls bristled with hippogriffs; now, from wainscot to ceiling, toucans and maccataws swung and nodded from their perches amid emerald palms; now Centaurs and Lapithæ elashed in ferocious tumult, while crater and eyathus were crushed beneath ringing hoof and heel. But my attention was quickly distracted from the frescoes by the sight of a most witchly congress, which filled all the chairs of that broad chamber. On the dais sat an old crone, whose commanding position first engaged my attention to her personal appearance, and, upon rather impolite scrutiny, I beheld that she was the product of an art held in preeminent favor among persons of her age and sex. She was *knit* of purple yarn! In faultless order the stitches ran along her face; in every pucker of her reentrant mouth, in every wrinkle of her brow, she was a yarny counterfeit of the grandam of actual life, and by some skillful process of stuffing her nose had received its due peak and her chin its projection. The occupants of the seats below were all but reproductions of their president, and both she and they were constantly swaying from side to side, forward and back, to the music of some invisible instruments, whose tone and style were most intensely and ludicrously Ethiopian. Not a word was spoken by any of the woolly conclave, but with untiring industry they were all knitting, knitting, knitting ceaselessly, as if their lives depended on it. I looked to see the objects of their manufacture. They were knitting old women like themselves! One of the sisterhood had nearly brought her double to completion; earnestly another was engaged in rounding out an eyeball; another was fastening the gathers at the corners of a mouth; another was setting up stitches for an old woman in petto.

With marvelous rapidity this work went on; ever and anon some completed crone sprang from the needles which had just achieved her, and, instantly vivified, took up the instruments of reproduction, and fell to work as assiduously as if she had been a member of the congress since the world began. "Here," I cried, "here, at last, do I realize the meaning of endless progression!" and, though the dome echoed with my peals of laughter, I saw no motion of astonishment in the stitches of a single face, but, as for dear life, the manufacture of old women went on unobstructed by the involuntary rudeness of the stranger.

An irresistible desire to aid in the work possessed me; I was half determined to snatch up a quartette of needles and join the sisterhood. My nose began to be ruffled with stitches, and the next moment I had been a partner in their yarny destinies but for a hand which pulled me backward through the door, and shut the congress forever from my view.

For a season I abode in an utter void of sight and sound, but I waited patiently in the assurance that some new changes of magnificence were preparing for me. I was not disappointed. Suddenly, at a far distance, three intense luminous points stood on the triple wall of darkness, and through each of them shot twin attenuated rays of magic light and music. Without being able to perceive any thing of my immediate surroundings, I still felt that I was noiselessly drifting toward those radiant and vocal points. With every moment they grew larger, the light and the harmony came clearer, and before long I could distinguish plainly three colossal arches rising from the bosom of a waveless water. The mid arch towered highest; the two on either side were equal to each other. Presently I beheld that they formed the portals of an enormous cavern, whose dome rose above me into such sublimity that its cope was hidden from my eyes in wreaths of cloud. On each side of me ran a wall of gnarled and rugged rock, from whose jutting points, as high as the eye could reach, depended stalactites of every imagined form and tinge of beauty, while below me, in the semblance of an ebon pavement, from the reflection of its overshadowing crags, lay a level lake, whose exquisite transparency wanted but the smile of the sun to make it glow like a floor of adamant. On this lake I lay in a little boat divinely carved from pearl after the similitude of Triton's shelly shallop; its rudder and its oarage were my own unconscious will, and, without the labors of especial volition, I floated as I list with a furrowless keel swiftly toward the central giant arch. With every moment that brought me nearer to my exit, the harmony that poured through it developed into a grander volume and an intenser beauty.

And now I passed out.

Claude Lorraine, freed from the limitations of sense, and gifted with an infinite canvas, may, for aught I know, be upon some halcyon island of the universe painting such a view as now sailed into my vision. Fitting employment would it be for his immortality were his pencil dipped into the very fountains of the light. Many a time in the course of my life have I yearned for the possession of some grand old master's soul and culture in the presence of revelations of Nature's loveliness which I dared not trust to memory; before this vision, as now in the remembrance of it, that longing became a heartfelt pain. Yet, after all, it was well; the mortal limner would have fainted in his task. Alas! how does the material in which we must embody the spiritual cramp and resist its execution! Standing before windows where the invisible spirit of the frost had traced his exquisite algæ, his palms and his ferns, have I said to myself, with a sigh, Ah! Nature alone, of all artists, is gifted to work out her ideals!

Shall I be so presumptuous as to attempt in words that which would beggar the palette and the pencil of old-time disciples of the beautiful? I will, if it be only to satisfy a deep longing.

From the arches of my cavern I had emerged upon a horizonless sea. Through all the infinitudes around me I looked out, and met no boundaries of space. Often in after times have I beheld the heavens and the earth stretching out in parallel lines forever, but this was the first time I had ever stood un-"ringed by the azure world," and I exulted in all the sublimity of the new conception. The whole atmosphere was one measureless suffusion of golden motes, which throbbed continually in cadence, and showered radiance and harmony at the same time. With ecstasy vision spread her wings for a flight against which material laws locked no barrier, and every moment grew more and more entranced at further and fuller glimpses of a beauty which floated like incense from the pavement of that eternal sea. With ecstasy the spiritual car gathered in continually some more distant and unimaginable tone, and grouped the growing harmonies into one sublime chant of benediction. With ecstasy the whole soul drank in revelations from every province, and cried out, "Oh, awful loveliness!" And now out of my shallop I was borne away into the full light of the mid firmament; now seated on some toppling peak of a cloud-mountain, whose yawning rifts disclosed far down the mines of reserved lightning; now bathed in my ethereal travel by the rivers of the rainbow, which, side by side, coursed through the valleys of heaven; now dwelling for a season in the environment of unbroken sunlight, yet bearing it like the eagle with undazzled eye; now crowned with a coronal of prismatic beads of dew. Through whatever region or circumstances I passed, one characteristic of the vision remained unchanged: peace—everywhere godlike peace, the sum of all conceivable desires satisfied.

Slowly I floated down to earth again. There Oriental gardens waited to receive me. From fountain to fountain I danced in graceful mazes with inimitable houris, whose foreheads were bound with fillets of jasmine. I pelted with figs the rare exotic birds, whose gold and crimson wings went flashing from branch to branch, or wheedled them to me with Arabic phrases of endearment. Through avenues of palm I walked arm-in-arm with Hafiz, and heard the hours flow singing through the channels of his matchless poetry. In gay kiosks I quaffed my sherbet, and in the luxury of lawlessness kissed away by drops that other juice which is contraband unto the faithful. And now beneath citron shadows I laid me down to sleep. When I awoke it was morning—actually morning, and not a hasheesh hallucination. The first emotion that I felt upon opening my eyes was happiness to find things again wearing a natural air. Yes; although the last experience of which

I had been conscious had seemed to satisfy every human want, physical or spiritual, I smiled on the four plain white walls of my bedchamber, and hailed their familiar unostentatiousness with a pleasure which had no wish to transfer itself to arabesque or rainbows. It was like returning home from an eternity spent in loneliness among the palaces of strangers. Well may I say an eternity, for during the whole day I could not rid myself of the feeling that I was separated from the preceding one by an immeasurable lapse of time. In fact, I never got wholly rid of it.

I rose that I might test my reinstated powers, and see if the restoration was complete. Yes, I felt not one trace of bodily weariness nor mental depression. Every function had returned to its normal state, with the one exception mentioned; memory could not efface the traces of my having passed through a great mystery. I recalled the events of the past night, and was pleased to think that I had betrayed myself to no one but Dr. H. I was satisfied with my experiment.

Ah! would that I had been satisfied! Yet history must go on.

11

VICTOR ROBINSON, *AN ESSAY ON HASHEESH, INCLUDING OBSERVATIONS AND EXPERIMENTS* (NEW YORK: MEDICAL REVIEW OF REVIEWS, 1912), PP. 38–51, 65–83

Up to this period we have considered hasheesh from the historic, botanic, microscopic, chemic, physiologic, therapeutic and pharmacologic viewpoints: what then remains? Why, friends, the best is yet to be, the last for which the first was made—as Browning would say.

Why has everyone heard of opium? Because of its somnifacient and myotic properties? No, but because sixty million pounds are consumed by people for the purpose of pleasure. It is the same with hasheesh. All heathens use it to increase their joys: Moors, Mohammedans, Malays, Burmese, Siamese, Hindoos, Hottentots, Australian Bushmen and Brazilian Indians—three hundred millions of them. The grateful Orientals have endowed their hasheesh with such epithets as exciter of desire, increaser of pleasure, cementer of friendship, leaf of delusion, the laughter-mover, causer of the reeling gait. "It is real happiness," says Monsieur Moreau, and Herbert Spencer quotes the sentence in his *Principles of Psychology,*—"It is real happiness which hasheesh causes."

It is unreasonable to suppose that a powerful narcotic like cannabis will produce uniform results in all instances, when it is notorious that even coffee affects different people in different ways; one lady drinks tea to keep her awake at night, and her neighbor drinks it to put her asleep; an Havana cigar irritates Brown and tranquillizes Jones; a glass of grog causes one man to beat his children, and induces another to give away his coat to strangers. The constitutional peculiarity of the subject must always be taken into consideration: some folks are so absurd as to become afflicted with nettle-rash after partaking of delicious strawberries; others are poisoned by an egg; some become ill in the presence of the violet, and others faint when they smell the lily; Tissot mentions a person who vomited if he took a grain of sugar; Louis XIV had grand manners, but he preferred the odor of cat's urine to that of the red rose. "Jack Sprat could eat no fat, his wife could eat no lean." Idiosyncrasy may not be the star performer, but it certainly plays an important rôle in the therapeutic drama.

AN ESSAY ON HASHEESH

No drug in the entire Materia Medica is capable of producing such a diversity of effects as cannabis indica. "Of the action of hasheesh," writes Professor Stillé, "many and various descriptions have been given which differ so widely among themselves that they would scarcely be supposed to apply to the same agent, had we not every day a no less remarkable instance of the same kind before us in the case of alcohol. As the latter enlivens or saddens, excites or depresses, fills with tenderness, or urges to brutality, imparts vigor and activity, or nauseates and weakens, so does the former give rise to even a still greater variety of phenomena, according to the natural disposition of the person, and his existing state of mind, the quantity of the drug, and the combinations in which it is taken."

And not only is there a contrariety and dissimilarity of action, but sometimes there is no action at all. Cannabis is certainly the coquette of drugdom. Take agaric, and it will stop your perspiration—take jaborandi, and it will sweat you half to death; take creosote, and it will prevent emesis—take ipecac, and it will vomit you till your very guts cry out for mercy; take eserine, and your pupils will contract—take atropine, and they will dilate; veratrine will make you sneeze, the dust of sanguinaria will give you a bloody nose, aloes will act on your lower bowel, podophyllum will work on the upper, squill will make you pass water by the quart, an injection of strychnine will stimulate you, a dose of morphine will put you in the arms of Morpheus,—but take cannabis, and who can predict the result? It may do wondrous things to you, and it may let you strictly alone.

To a worker on the Associated Press named I. M. Norr, I gave 30 minims of the fluidextract. There were no results. To a law student named Aaron Wolman, I gave 40 minims. There was no more effect than if he had taken 40 drops of water. It must be added, however, that these experimenters, instead of putting themselves in a receptive state, had determined beforehand to fight the influence of the drug. On the evening of May 18th, 1910, I gave 25 minims to Dr. Anna Mercy, and altho she threw herself at the shrine of science in a way that must have astonished the sober old altar of experiment, there were no results worth mentioning, except that while in the evening she looked respectable, in the morning she looked disreputable.

Had all my experiments turned out thus, this essay would never have been written. But I have had results fully as interesting as those achieved by O'Shaughnessy, Moreau, Mabillat, Reidel, Schroff, Wood, Bell, Christison, Aubert, and many others, including our gifted traveler-poet Bayard Taylor.

My brother Frederic Robinson took 25 minims in the presence of some ladies whom he had invited to witness the fun. An hour passed without results. A second hour followed, but—to use the slang of the street—there was nothing doing. The third hour promised to be equally fruitless, and as it was already late in the evening, the ladies said good-by. No sooner did they leave the room, than I heard the hasheesh-laugh. The hemp was doing its work. In a shrill voice my brother was exclaiming, "What foo-oolish people, what foo-oo-ool-ish people to leave just when the show is beginning." The ladies came back. And it was a show. Frederic made Socialistic

171

CANNABIS

speeches, and argued warmly for the cause of Woman Suffrage. He grew most affectionate and insisted on holding a lady's hand. His face was flushed, his eyes were half closed, his abdomen seemed uneasy, but his spirit was happy. He sang, he rhymed, he declaimed, he whistled, he mimicked, he acted. He pleaded so passionately for the rights of Humanity that it seemed he was using up the resources of his system. But he was tireless. With both hands he gesticulated, and would brook no interruption.

Peculiar ideas suggested themselves. For instance, he said something was "sheer nonsense," and then reasoned as follows: "Since shears are the same as scissors, instead of sheer nonsense I can say scissors nonsense." He also said, "I will give you a kick in the tickle"—and was much amused by the expression.

At all times he recognized those about him, and remained conscious of his surroundings. When the approach of dawn forced the ladies to depart, Frederic made a somewhat unsavory joke, and immediately exclaimed triumphantly, "I wouldn't have said that if the ladies were here for a million dollars." Someone yawned deeply, and being displeased by the unexpected appearance of a gaping orifice, Frederic melodramatically gave utterance to this Gorky-like phrase: "From the depths of dirtiness and despair there rose a sickly odorous yawn"—and instantly he remarked that the first portion of this sentence was alliterative! Is it not strange that such consciousness and such intoxication can exist in the same brain simultaneously?

The next day he remembered all that occurred, was in excellent spirits, laughed much and easily, and felt himself above the petty things of this world.

On May 19th, 1910, this world was excited over the visit of Halley's comet. It is pleasant to remember that the celestial guest attracted as much attention as a political campaign or a game of baseball. On the evening of this day, at 10 o'clock, I gave 45 minims to a court stenographer named Henry D. Demuth. At 11.30 the effects of the drug became apparent, and Mr. Demuth lost consciousness of his surroundings to such an extent that he imagined himself an inhabitant of Sir Edmund Halley's nebulous planet. He despised the earth and the dwellers thereon; he called it a miserable little flea-bite, and claimed its place in the cosmos was no more important than a flea-jump. With a scornful finger he pointed below, and said in a voice of contempt, "That little joke down there, called the earth."

"Victor," he said, "you're a fine fellow, you're the smartest man in Harlem, you've got the god in you, but the best thoughts you write are low compared to the things we think up here." A little later he condescended to take me up with him, and said, "Victor, we're up in the realm now, and we'll make money when we get down on that damned measly earth again; they respect Demuth on earth."

He imitated how Magistrate Butts calls a prisoner to the bar. "Butts," he explained, "is the best of them. Butts—Buts—cigarette-butts." If this irrelevant line should ever fall beneath the dignified eyes of His Honor, instead of fining his devoted stenographer for contempt of court, may he bear in his learned mind the fact that under the influence of narcotics men are mentally irresponsible.

By this time Mr. DeMuth's vanity was enormous. "God, Mark Twain and I are chums," he remarked casually. "God is wise, and I am wise. And to think that people *dictate* to me!"

He imagined he had material for a great book. "I'm giving you the thoughts; slap them down, we'll make a fortune and go whacks. We'll make a million. I'll get half and Vic will get half. With half a million we'll take it easy for a while on this damned measly earth. We'll live till a hundred and two, and then we'll skedaddle didoo. At one hundred and two it will be said of Henry Disque Demuth that he shuffled off this mortal coil. We'll skip into the great idea—hooray! horray! Take down everything that is signif*cant*—with an accent on the *cant*—Immanuel Kant was a wise man, and I'm a wise man; I am wise, because I'm wise."

It is to be regretted that in spite of all the gabble concerning the volume that was to make both of us rich, not even one line was dictated by the inspired author. In fact he got no further than the title, and it must be admitted that of all titles in the world, this is the least catchy. It is as follows: "Wise is God; God is Wise."

Later came a variation in the form of a hissing sound which was meant to be an imitation of the whizzing of Halley's comet; there was a wild swinging of the sheets as a welcome to the President; a definition of religion as the greatest joke ever perpetrated; some hasheesh-laughter; and the utterance of this original epigram: Shakespeare, seltzer-beer, be cheerful.

A little later all variations ceased, for the subject became a monomaniac, or at any rate, a fanatic. He became thoroly imbued with the great idea that the right attitude to preserve towards life is to take all things on earth as a joke. Hundreds and hundreds and hundreds of times he repeated: "The idea of the great idea, the idea of the great idea, the idea of the great idea." No question could steer him out of this track. "Who's up on the comet? Any pretty girls there?" asked Frederic. "The great idea is up there," was the answer.

"Where would you fall if you fell off the comet?"

"I'd fall into the great idea."

"What do you do when you want to eat and have no money?"

"You have to get the idea."

"When will you get married?"

"When I get the idea."

Midnight came, and he was still talking about his great idea. At one o'clock I felt bored. "If you don't talk about anything else except the idea, we'll have to quit," I said.

"Yes," he replied, "we'll all quit, we'll all be wrapped up in the great idea." He took out his handkerchief to blow his nose, remarking, "The idea of my nose." I approached him. "Don't interfere," he cried, "I'm off with the great idea."

I began to descend the stairs. When half way down I stopped to listen. He was still a monomaniac. Had he substituted the word thought or theory or conception or notion or belief or opinion or supposition or hypothesis or syllogism or tentative conjecture, I would have returned. But as I still heard only the idea of the great idea, I went to bed.

In the morning his countenance was ashen, which formed a marked contrast to its extreme redness the evening before. He should have slept longer, but I thought of the duties to be performed for Judge Butts, and determined to arouse him, altho

CANNABIS

I knew my touch would cast him down from the glorious Halley's comet to the measly little flea-bite of an earth, besides jarring the idea of the great idea.

So I shook him, but instead of manifesting anger, he smiled and extended his hand cordially, as if he had not seen me for a long time. The effects of the drug had not entirely disappeared, and his friends at work thought him drunk, and asked with whom he had been out all night. Mr. Demuth was in first-class spirits, he bubbled over with idealism, and felt a contempt for all commercial transactions. He was the American Bernard Shaw, and looked upon the universe as a joke of the gods. While adding some figures of considerable importance—as salaries depended upon the results—a superintendent passed. Mr. Demuth pointed to the column that needed balancing, and asked, "This is all a joke, isn't it?" Not appreciating the etiology of the query, the superintendent nodded and passed on.

There yet remains my own case. On March 4th, 1910, I came home, feeling very tired. I found that some cannabis indica which I had expected had arrived. After supper, while finishing up an article, I began to debate with myself whether I should join the hasheesh-eaters that night. The argument ended in my taking 20 minims at 9 o'clock. I was alone in the room, and no one was aware that I had yielded to temptation. An hour later I wrote in my memoranda book: Absolutely no effect. At 10.30, I completed my article, and entered this note: No effect at all from the hemp. By this time I was exhausted, and being convinced that the hasheesh would not act, I went to bed in disappointment. I fell asleep immediately.

I hear music. There is something strange about this music. I have not heard such music before. The anthem is far away, but in its very faintness there is a lure. In the soft surge and swell of the minor notes there breathes a harmony that ravishes the sense of sound. A resonant organ, with a stop of sapphire and a diapason of opal, diffuses endless octaves from star to star. All the moon-beams form strings to vibrate the perfect pitch, and this entrancing unison is poured into my enchanted ears. Under such a spell, who can remain in a bed? The magic of that melody bewitches my soul. I begin to rise horizontally from my couch. No walls impede my progress, and I float into the outside air. Sweeter and sweeter grows the music, it bears me higher and higher, and I float in tune with the infinite—under the turquoise heavens where globules of mercury are glittering.

I become an unhindered wanderer thru unending space. No air-ship can go here, I say. I am astonished at the vastness of infinity. I always knew it was large, I argue, but I never dreamt it was as huge as this. I desire to know how fast I am floating thru the air, and I calculate that it must be about a billion miles a second.

I am transported to wonderland. I walk in streets where gold is dirt, and I have no desire to gather it. I wonder whether it is worth while to explore the canals of Mars, or rock myself on the rings of Saturn, but before I can decide, a thousand other fancies enter my excited brain.

I wish to see if I can concentrate my mind sufficiently to recite something, and I succeed in correctly quoting this stanza from a favorite poem which I am perpetually re-reading:

"Come into the garden, Maud,
    For the black bat, night, has flown,
Come into the garden, Maud,
    I am here at the gate alone;
And the woodbine spices are wafted abroad,
    And the musk of the rose is blown."

It occurs to me that it is high honor for Tennyson to have his poetry quoted in heaven.

I turn, I twist, I twirl. I melt, I fade, I dissolve. No diaphanous cloud is so light and airy as I. I admire the ease with which I float. My gracefulness fills me with delight. My body is not subject to the law of gravitation. I sail dreamily along, lost in exquisite intoxication.

New scenes of wonder continually unravel themselves before my astonished eyes. I say to myself that if I could only record one one-thousandth of the ideas which come to me every second, I would be considered a greater poet than Milton.

I am on the top of a high mountain-peak. I am alone—only the romantic night envelops me. From a distant valley I hear the gentle tinkling of cow-bells. I float downwards, and find immense fields in which peacock's tails are growing. They wave slowly, to better exhibit their dazzling ocelli, and I revel in the gorgeous colors. I pass over mountains and I sail over seas. I am the monarch of the air.

I hear the songs of women. Thousands of maidens pass near me, they bend their bodies in the most charming curves, and scatter beautiful flowers in my fragrant path. Some faces are strange, some I knew on earth, but all are lovely. They smile, and sing and dance. Their bare feet glorify the firmament. It is more than flesh can stand. I grow sensual unto satyriasis. The aphrodisiac effect is astonishing in its intensity. I enjoy all the women of the world. I pursue countless maidens thru the confines of heaven. A delicious warmth suffuses my whole body. Hot and blissful I float thru the universe, consumed with a resistless passion. And in the midst of this unexampled and unexpected orgy, I think of the case reported by the German Dr. Reidel, about a drug-clerk who took a huge dose of hasheesh to enjoy voluptuous visions, but who heard not even the rustle of Aphrodite's garment, and I laugh at him in scorn and derision.

I sigh deeply, open my eyes, and find myself sitting with one foot in bed, and the other on my desk. I am bathed in warm sweat which is pleasant. But my head aches, and there is a feeling in my stomach which I recognize and detest. It is nausea. I pull the basket near me, and await the inevitable result. At the same time I feel like begging for mercy, for I have traveled so far and so long, and I am tired beyond limit, and I need a rest. The fatal moment approaches, and I lower my head for the easier deposition of the rising burden. And my head seems monstrously huge, and weighted with lead. At last the deed is done, and I lean back on the pillow.

I hear my sister come home from the opera. I wish to call her. My sister's name is Ellen. I try to say it, but I cannot. The effort is too much. I sigh in despair. It occurs to me that I may achieve better results if I compromise on Nell, as this contains one syllable instead of two. Again I am defeated. I am too weary to exert myself to any extent, but I am determined. I make up my mind to collect all my strength, and call out: Nell. The result is a fizzle. No sound issues from my lips. My lips do not move. I give it up. My head falls on my breast, utterly exhausted and devoid of all energy.

Again my brain teems. Again I hear that high and heavenly harmony, again I float to the outposts of the universe and beyond, again I see the dancing maidens with their soft yielding bodies, white and warm. I am excited unto ecstasy. I feel myself a brother to the Oriental, for the same drug which gives him joy is now acting on me. I am conscious all the time, and I say to myself in a knowing way with a suspicion of a smile: All these visions because of 20 minims of cannabis indica. My only regret is that the trances are ceaseless. I wish respite, but for answer I find myself floating over an immense ocean. Then the vision grows so wondrous, that body and soul I give myself up to it, and I taste the fabled joys of paradise. Ah, what this night is worth!

The music fades, the beauteous girls are gone, and I float no more. But the black rubber covering of my typewriter glows like a chunk of yellow phosphorus. By one door stands a skeleton with a luminous abdomen and brandishes a wooden sword. By the other door a little red devil keeps guard. I open my eyes wide, I close them tight, but these spectres will not vanish. I know they are not real, I know I see them because I took hasheesh, but they annoy me nevertheless. I become uncomfortable, even frightened. I make a superhuman effort, and succeed in getting up and lighting the gas. It is two o'clock. Everything is the way it should be, except that in the basket I notice the remains of an orange—somewhat the worse for wear.

I feel relieved, and fall asleep. Something is handling me, and I start in fright. I open my eyes and see my father. He has returned from a meeting at the Academy of Medicine, and surprised at seeing a light in my room at such a time, has entered. He surmises what I have done, and is anxious to know what quantity I have taken. I should have answered, with a wink, *quantum sufficit*, but I have no inclination for conversation; on hearing the question repeated, I answer, "Twenty minims." He tells me I look as pale as a ghost, and brings me a glass of water. I drink it, become quite normal, and thus ends the most wonderful night of my existence.

In the morning my capacity for happiness is considerably increased. I have an excellent appetite, the coffee I sip is nectar, and the white bread ambrosia. I take my camera, and walk to Central Park. It is a glorious day. Everyone I meet is idealized. The lake never looked so placid before. I enter the hot-houses, and a gaudy-colored insect buzzing among the lovely flowers fills me with joy. I am too languid to take any pictures; to set the focus, to use the proper stop, to locate the image, to press the bulb—all these seem herculean feats which I dare not even attempt. But I walk and walk, without apparent effort, and my mind eagerly dwells on the brilliant pageantry of the night before. I do not wish to forget my frenzied nocturnal revelry upon the vast dome of the broad blue heavens. I wish to remember forever, the floating, the mercury-globules, the peacock-feathers, the colors, the music, the women. In memory I enjoy the carnival all over again.

"For the brave Meiamoun," writes Theophile Gautier, "Cleopatra danced; she was apparalled in a robe of green, open at either side; castanets were attached to her alabaster hands . . . Poised on the pink tips of her little feet, she approached swiftly to graze his forehead with a kiss; then she recommenced her wondrous art, and flitted around him, now backward-leaning, with head reversed, eyes half-closed, arms lifelessly relaxed, locks uncurled and loose-hanging like a bacchante of Mount Maenalus; now again active, animated, laughing, fluttering, more tire-less and capricious in her movements than the pilfering bee. Heart-consuming love, sensual pleasure, burning passion, youth inexhaustible and ever-fresh, the promise of bliss to come—she expressed all. . . . The modest stars had ceased to contemplate the scene; their golden eyes could not endure such a spectacle; the heaven itself was blotted out, and a dome of flaming vapor covered the hall."

But for me a thousand Cleopatras caroused—and did not present me a vase of poison to drain at a draught. Again I repeated to myself: "And all these charming miracles because of 20 minims of *Fluidextractum Cannabis Indicæ*, U. S. P."

By the afternoon I had so far recovered as to be able to concentrate my mind on technical studies. I will not attempt to interpret my visions psychologically, but I wish to refer to one aspect. Spencer, in *Principles of Psychology*, mentions hasheesh as possessing the power of reviving ideas. I found this to be the case. I spoke about air-ships because there had been a discussion about them at supper; I quoted from Tennyson's *Maud* because I had been re-reading it; I saw mercury-globules in the heavens because that same day I had worked with mercury in preparing mercurial plaster; and I saw the peacock-tails because a couple of days previous I had been at the Museum of Natural History and had closely observed a magnificent specimen. I cannot account for the women.

All poets—with the possible exception of Margaret Sangster—have celebrated Alcohol, while Rudyard Kipling has gone so far as to solemnize delirium tremens; B. V. has glorified Nicotine; DeQuincy has immortalized Opium; Murger is full of praise for Caffeine; Dumas in *Monte Cristo* has apotheosized Hasheesh, Gautier has vivified it in *Club des Hachicins*, Baudelaire has panegyrized it in *Artificial Paradises*, but as few American pens have done so, I have taken it upon myself to write a sonnet to the most interesting plant that blooms:

Near Punjab and Pab, in Sutlej and Sind,
Where the cobras-di-capello abound,
Where the poppy, palm and the tamarind,

With cummin and ginger festoon the ground—
And the capsicum fields are all abloom,
From the hills above to the vales below,
Entrancing the air with a rich perfume,
There too does the greenish Cannabis grow:
Inflaming the blood with the living fire,
Till the burning joys like the eagles rise,
And the pulses throb with a strange desire,
While passion awakes with a wild surprise:—
O to eat that drug, and to dream all day,
Of the maids that live by the Bengal Bay!

Appendix

Mr. Courtenay Lemon has written the following memorandum of the subjective features of his experience:

The first symptom which told me that the drug was beginning to take effect was a feeling of extreme lightness. I seemed to be hollowing out inside, in some magical manner, until I became a mere shell, ready to float away into space. This was soon succeeded, in one of the breathless intervals of my prodigious laughter, by a diametrically opposite sensation of extreme solidity and leaden weight. It seemed to me that I had changed into metal of some sort. There was a metallic taste in my mouth; in some inexplicable way the surfaces of my body seemed to communicate to my consciousness a metalliferous feeling; and I imagined that if struck I would give forth a metallic ring. This heavy and metallic feeling travelled rapidly upwards from the feet to the chest, where it stopped, leaving my head free for the issuance of the storms of laughter. Most of the time my arms and legs seemed to be so leaden that it required Herculean effort to move them, but under any special stimulus, such as the entrance of a third person, the vagrant conception of a new idea, or an unusually hearty fit of laughing, this feeling of unliftable heaviness in the limbs and torso would be forgotten and I would move freely, waving my arms with great vigor and enthusiasm.

Thruout the experiment I experienced a peculiar double consciousness. I was perfectly aware that my laughter, etc., was the result of having taken the drug, yet I was powerless to stop it, nor did I care to do so, for I enjoyed it as thoroly as if it had arisen from natural causes. In the same way the extension of the sense of time induced by the drug was in itself indubitable and as cogent as any normal evidence of the senses, yet I remained able to convince myself at any moment by reflection that my sense of time was fallacious. I divided these impressions into hasheesh-time and real time. But in their alternations, so rapid as to seem simultaneous, both these standards of time seemed equally valid. For instance, once or twice when my friend spoke of something I had said a second before, I was impatient and replied: "What do you want to go back to that for? That was a long time ago. What's the use of going back into the past?" At the next moment, however, I would recognize, purely as a matter of logic, that he was replying to the sentence before the last that I had uttered, and would thus realize that the remark to which he referred was separated from the present only by a moment's interval. I did not, however, at any time on this occasion, attain the state sometimes reached in the second stage of hasheesh intoxication in which mere time disappears in an eternity wherein ages rush by like ephemera; nor did I experience any magnification of the sense of space, my experiences in regard to such extensions being confined to an intermittent multiplication of the sense of time.

When my laughter began it seemed for an instant to be mechanical, as if produced by some external power which forced air in and out of my lungs; it seemed for an instant to proceed from the body rather than from the mind; to be, in its inception, merely physical laughter without a corresponding psychic state of amusement. But this was only momentary. After the first few moments I enjoyed laughing immensely. I felt an inclination to joke as well as to laugh, and I remember saying: "I am going to have some reason for this laughing, so I will tell a story; if I have to laugh anyway, I'm going to supply good reasons for doing so, as it would be idiotic to laugh about nothing." I thereupon proceeded to relate an anecdote. Altho I knew that my condition was the result of the drug, I was nevertheless filled with a genuine sense of profound hilarity, an eager desire to impart similar merriment to others, and a feeling of immense geniality and mirth, accompanied by sentiments of the most expansive good-will.

Against the effects of the drug, much as I enjoyed and yielded to it, there was opposed a preconceived intention. I had determined to tell my friend Victor Robinson, who was taking notes of my condition, just how I felt; had determined to supply as much data as possible in regard to my sensations. The result was that I repeatedly summoned all the rational energy that remained to me, and fought desperately to express the thoughts that came to me, whether riduculous or analytical. Sometimes when I felt myself slipping away again into laughter or dreaminess I summoned all my strength to say what I had in mind, and would lose the thread of my thought and could not remember what I wanted to say, but would return to it again and again with the utmost determination and tenacity until I succeeded in saying what I wished to—sometimes an observation about my sensations, often only a jest about my condition. I believe that this acted as a great resistant to the effect of the drug. The energy of the drug was dissipated, I think, in overcoming my will to observe and analyze my sensations, and it was probably for this reason that I did not pass very far on this occasion into the second stage in which laughter gives place to grandiose visions and charming hallucinations.

After my friend Victor and his father turned out the light and left the room, my laughter gradually subsided into a few final gurgles of ineffable mirth and benevolence, and after a period of the amorous visions sometimes induced by this philtre from the land of harems, I fell into a sound sleep after my three hours of continuous and exhausting laughter.

CANNABIS

I awoke next morning after seven hours sleep, with a ravenous appetite, which I think was probably as much due to the great expenditure of energy in laughing as to any direct effect of the drug itself. I was also very thirsty and my skin was parched and burning. Altho I immediately dressed and went down to breakfast, I felt very drowsy and disinclined to physical exertion or mental concentration. And while no longer given to causeless laughter, I felt a lingering merriment and was easily moved to chuckling. I slept several hours in the afternoon and after dinner I slept all evening, awaking at 11 P. M., when I arose feeling very much refreshed and entirely normal, and went out to get another meal, being still hungry. I should say that the immediate after-effect, the reaction from the stimulation of hasheesh, is not much greater, except for the drowsiness, than that following the common or beer garden variety of intoxication. My memory of what I said and did while under the hasheesh was complete and accurate.

Part 4

DRINK AND THE DILEMMA OF HABIT

12

BENJAMIN RUSH, *AN INQUIRY INTO THE EFFECTS OF ARDENT SPIRITS UPON THE HUMAN BODY AND MIND*, 6TH ED. (NEW YORK: CORNELIUS DAVIS, 1811), PP. 1–32

A moral and physical thermometer

A scale of the progress of Temperance and Intemperance.—Liquors with effects in their usual order.

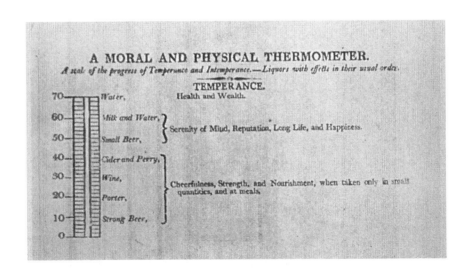

INTEMPERANCE.

	VICES.	DISEASES.	PUNISH-MENTS.
Punch,	Idleness,	Sickness,	Debt.
Toddy and Egg Rum,	Gaming, Peevishness, Quarrelling,	Tremors of the hands in the morning, puking, bloatedness,	Jail.
Grog—Brandy and Water,	Fighting, Racing,	Inflamed eyes, red nose and face,	Black Eyes, and Rags.
Flip and Shrub,	Lying and Swearing,	Sore and swelled legs, jaundice,	Hospital or Poor House.
Bitters infused in Spirits and Cordials.	Stealing and Swindling,	Pains in the hands, burning in the hands, and feet,	Bridewell.
Drams of Gin, Brandy, and Rum, in the morning,	Perjury,	Dropsy, Epilepsy,	State Prison.
The same morning and evening, *The same during day and night,*	Burglary, Murder,	Melancholy, palsy, appoplexy, Madness, Despair,	GALLOWS.

0
10
20
30
40
50
60
70

An inquiry, &c

Part I

By ardent spirits, I mean those liquors only which are obtained by distillation from fermented substances of any kind. To their effects upon the bodies and minds of men, the following inquiry shall be exclusively confined. Fermented liquors contain so little spirit, and that so intimately combined with other matters, that they can seldom be drunken in sufficient quantities to produce intoxication, and its subsequent effects, without exciting a disrelish to their taste, or pain, from their distending the stomach. They are moreover, when taken in a moderate quantity, generally innocent, and often have a friendly influence upon health and life.

The effects of ardent spirits divide themselves into such as are of a prompt, and such as are of a chronic nature. The former discover themselves in drunkenness, and the latter, in a numerous train of diseases and vices of the body and mind.

1. I shall begin by briefly describing their prompt, or immediate effects, in a fit of drunkenness.

This odious disease (for by that name it should be called) appears with more or less of the following symptoms, and most commonly in the order in which I shall enumerate them.

1. Unusual garrulity.
2. Unusual silence.
3. Captiousness, and a disposition to quarrel.
4. Uncommon good humour, and an insipid simpering, or laugh.
5. Profane swearing, and cursing.
7. A disclosure of their own, or other people's secrets.
8. A rude disposition to tell those persons in company whom they know, their faults.
9. Certain immodest actions. I am sorry to say, this sign of the first stage of drunkenness, sometimes appears in women, who, when sober, are uniformly remarkable for chaste and decent manners.
10. A clipping of words.
11. Fighting; a black eye, or a swelled nose, often mark this grade of drunkenness.
12. Certain extravagant acts which indicate a temporary fit of madness. These are singing, hallooing, roaring, imitating the noises of brute animals, jumping, tearing off clothes, dancing naked, breaking glasses and china, and dashing other articles of household furniture upon the ground, or floor. After a while the paroxysm of drunkenness is completely formed. The face now becomes flushed, the eyes project, and are somewhat watery, winking is less frequent than is natural; the under lip is protruded,—the head inclines a little to one shoulder;—the jaw falls;—belchings and hiccup take place;—the limbs totter;—the whole body staggers:—The unfortunate subject of this history next falls on his seat,—he looks around him with a vacant countenance, and mutters inarticulate sounds to himself;—He attempts to rise and walk. In this attempt, he falls upon his side, from

which he gradually turns upon his back. He now closes his eyes, and falls into a profound sleep, frequently attended with snoring, and profuse sweats, and sometimes with such a relaxation of the muscles which confine the bladder and the lower bowels, as to produce a symptom which delicacy forbids me to mention. In this condition, he often lies from ten, twelve, and twenty-four hours, to two, three, four, and five days, an object of pity and disgust to his family and friends. His recovery from this fit of intoxication, is marked with several peculiar appearances. He opens his eyes, and closes them again;—he gapes and stretches his limbs,—he then coughs and pukes,—his voice is hoarse,—he rises with difficulty, and staggers to a chair; his eyes resemble balls of fire,—his hands tremble,—he loathes the sight of food;—he calls for a glass of spirits to compose his stomach—now and then he emits a deep fetched sigh, or groan, from a transient twinge of conscience, but he more frequently scolds, and curses every thing around him. In this state of languor and stupidity, he remains for two or three days, before he is able to resume his former habits of business and conversation.

Pythagoras we are told maintained that the souls of men after death, expiated the crimes committed by them in this world, by animating certain brute animals; and that the souls of those animals in their turns, entered into men, and carried with them all their peculiar qualities and vices. This doctrine of one of the wisest and best of the Greek Philosophers, was probably intended only to convey a lively idea of the changes which are induced in the body and mind of man by a fit of drunkenness. In folly, it causes him to resemble a calf,—in stupidity, an ass,—in roaring, a mad bull,—in quarrelling, and fighting, a dog,—in cruelty, a tyger,—in fetor, a skunk,—in filthiness, a hog,—and in obscenity, a he-goat.

It belongs to the history of drunkenness to remark that, its paroxysms occur, like the paroxysms of many diseases, at certain periods, and after longer or shorter intervals. They often begin with annual, and gradually increase in their frequency, until they appear in quarterly, monthly, weekly, and quotidian or daily periods. Finally they afford scarcely any marks of remission either during the day or the night. There was a citizen of Philadelphia many years ago in whom drunkenness appeared in this protracted form. In speaking of him to one of his neighbours, I said, "does he not *sometimes* get drunk?" "You mean" said his neighbour, "is he not *sometimes* sober?"

It is further remarkable, that drunkenness resembles certain hereditary, family, and contagious diseases. I have once known it to descend from a father to four out of five of his children. I have seen three, and once four, brothers who were born of sober ancestors, affected by it, and I have heard of its spreading through a whole family composed of members not originally related to each other. These facts are important, and should not be overlooked by parents, in deciding upon the matrimonial connexions of their children.

Let us next attend to the chronic effects of ardent spirits upon the body and mind. In the body, they dispose to every form of acute disease; they moreover *excite* fevers in persons predisposed to them, from other causes. This has been remarked in all the yellow fevers which have visited the cities of the United

INQUIRY INTO THE EFFECTS OF ARDENT SPIRITS

States. Hard drinkers seldom escape, and rarely recover from them. The following diseases are the usual consequences of the habitual use of ardent spirits, viz.

1. A decay of appetite, sickness at stomach, and a puking of bile or a discharge of a frothy and viscid phlegm by hawking, in the morning.

2. Obstructions of the liver. The fable of Prometheus, on whose liver a vulture was said to prey constantly, as a punishment for his stealing fire from heaven, was intended to illustrate the painful effects of ardent spirits upon that organ of the body.

3. Jaundice and dropsy of the belly and limbs, and finally of every cavity in the body. A swelling in the feet and legs is so characteristic a mark of habits of intemperance, that the merchants in Charleston, I have been told, cease to trust the planters of South Carolina, as soon as they perceive it. They very naturally conclude industry and virtue to be extinct in that man in whom that symptom of disease, has been produced by the intemperate use of distilled spirits.

4. Hoarseness, and a husky cough, which often terminate in consumption, and sometimes in an acute and fatal disease of the lungs.

5. Diabetes, that is, a frequent and weakening discharge of pale, or sweetish urine.

6. Redness, and eruptions on different parts of the body. They generally begin on the nose, and after gradually extending all over the face, sometimes descend to the limbs in the form of leprosy. They have been called "Rum-buds," when they appear in the face. In persons who have occasionally survived these effects of ardent spirits on the skin, the face after a while becomes bloated, and its redness is succeeded by a deathlike paleness. Thus the same fire which produces a red colour in iron, when urged to a more intense degree, produces what has been called a white heat.

7. A fetid breath composed of every thing that is offensive in putrid animal matter.

8. Frequent and disgusting belchings. Dr. Haller relates the case of a notorious drunkard, having been suddenly destroyed in consequence of the vapour discharged from his stomach by belching, accidentally taking fire by coming in contact with the flame of a candle.

9. Epilepsy.

10. Gout in all its various forms of swelled limbs, colick, palsy, and apoplexy.

Lastly, 11. Madness. The late Dr. Waters, while he acted as house pupil and apothecary of the Pennsylvania Hospital, assured me, that in one third of the patients confined by this terrible disease, it had been induced by ardent spirits.

Most of the diseases which have been enumerated are of a mortal nature. They are more certainly induced, and terminate more speedily in death, when spirits are taken in such quantities, and at such times, as to produce frequent intoxication; but it may serve to remove an error with which some intemperate people console themselves, to remark, that ardent spirits often bring on fatal diseases without producing drunkenness. I have known many persons destroyed by them who were never completely intoxicated during the whole course of their lives. The solitary instances of longevity which are now and then met with in hard drinkers, no more disprove the deadly effects of ardent spirits, than the solitary instances of recoveries from apparent death by drowning, prove that there is no danger to life from a human body lying an hour or two under water.

The body after its death, from the use of distilled spirits, exhibits by dissection certain appearances which are of a peculiar nature. The fibres of the stomach and bowels are contracted;—abscesses,—gangrene,—and schirri are found in the viscera.—The bronchial vessels are contracted,—the blood vessels and tendons in many parts of the body are more or less ossified, and even the hair of the head possesses a crispness which renders it less valuable to wig-makers than the hair of sober people.

Not less destructive are the effects of ardent spirits upon the human mind. They impair the memory, debilitate the understanding, and pervert the moral faculties. It was probably from observing these effects of intemperance in drinking, upon the mind, that a law was formerly passed in Spain which excluded drunkards from being witnesses in a court of justice. But the demoralizing effects of distilled spirits do not stop here. They produce not only falsehood, but fraud, theft, uncleanliness and murder. Like the demoniac mentioned in the New Testament, their name is "legion," for they convey into the soul, a host of vices and crimes.

A more affecting spectacle cannot be exhibited than a person into whom this infernal spirit, generated by habits of intemperance, has entered. It is more or less affecting according to the station the person fills in a family, or in society, who is possessed by it. Is he a husband? How deep the anguish which rends the bosom of his wife! Is she a wife? Who can measure the shame and aversion which she excites in her husband? Is he the father, or is she the mother of a family of children? See their averted looks from their parent, and their blushing looks at each other! Is he a magistrate? or has he been chosen to fill a high and respectable station in the councils of his country? What humiliating fears of corruption in the administration of the laws, and of the subversion of public order and happiness, appear in the countenances of all who see him! Is he a minister of the gospel?—Here language fails me.—If angels weep—it is at such a sight.

In pointing out the evils produced by ardent spirits, let us not pass by their effects upon the estates of the persons who are addicted to them. Are they inhabitants of cities?—Behold! their houses stripped gradually of their furniture, and pawned, or sold by a constable, to pay tavern debt. See! their names upon record in the dockets of every court, and whole pages of newspapers filled with advertisements of their estates for public sale. Are they inhabitants of country places? Behold! their houses with shattered windows,—their barns with leaky roofs,—their gardens overrun with weeds,—their fields with broken fences, their hogs without yokes, their sheep without wool,—their cattle and horses without fat,—and their children filthy and half clad, without manners, principles, and morals. This picture of agricultural wretchedness is seldom of long duration. The farms and property thus neglected, and depreciated, are seized and sold for the benefit of a group of creditors. The children that were born with the prospect of inheriting

INQUIRY INTO THE EFFECTS OF ARDENT SPIRITS

them, are bound out to service in the neighbourhood; while their parents, the unworthy authors of their misfortunes, ramble into new and distant settlements, alternately fed on their way by the hand of charity, or a little casual labour.

Thus we see poverty and misery, crimes and infamy, diseases and death, are all the natural and usual consequences of the intemperate use of ardent spirits.

I have classed death among the consequences of hard drinking. But it is not death from the immediate hand of the Deity, nor from any of the instruments of it which were created by him. It is death from SUICIDE. Yes—thou poor degraded creature, who art daily lifting the poisoned bowl to thy lips—cease to avoid the unhallowed ground in which the self-murderer is interred, and wonder no longer that the sun should shine, and the rain fall, and the grass look green upon his grave. Thou art perpetrating gradually, by the use of ardent spirits, what he has effected suddenly by opium—or a halter. Considering how many circumstances from surprise, or derangement, may palliate his guilt, or that (unlike yours) it was not preceded and accompanied by any other crime, it is probable his condemnation will be less than yours at the day of judgment.

I shall now take notice of the occasions and circumstances which are supposed to render the use of ardent spirits necessary, and endeavour to shew that the arguments in favour of their use in such cases are founded in error, and that in each of them, ardent spirits instead of affording strength to the body, increase the evils they are intended to relieve.

1. They are said to be necessary in very cold weather. This is far from being true; for the temporary warmth they produce, is always succeeded by a greater disposition in the body to be affected by cold. Warm dresses, a plentiful meal just before exposure to the cold, and eating occasionally a little gingerbread, or any other cordial food, is a much more durable method of preserving the heat of the body in cold weather.

2. They are said to be necessary in very warm weather. Experience proves that they increase, instead of lessening the effects of heat upon the body, and thereby dispose to diseases of all kinds. Even in the warm climate of the West-Indies Dr. Bell asserts this to be true. "Rum (says this author) whether used habitually, moderately, or in excessive quantities in the West-Indies, always diminishes the strength of the body, and renders men more susceptible of disease, and unfit for any service in which vigour or activity is required."* As well might we throw oil into a house, the roof of which was on fire, in order to prevent the flames from extending to its inside, as pour ardent spirits into the stomach, to lessen the effects of a hot sun upon the skin.

3. Nor do ardent spirits lessen the effects of hard labour upon the body. Look at the horse; with every muscle of his body swelled from morning till night in the plough, or a team, does he make signs for a draught of toddy, or a glass of spirits

---

* Inquiry into the causes which produce, and the means of preventing diseases among British officers, soldiers and others in the West-Indies.

to enable him to cleave the ground, or to climb a hill?—No—he requires nothing but cool water and substantial food. There is no nourishment in ardent spirits. The strength they produce in labour is of a transient nature, and is always followed by a sense of weakness and fatigue.

But are there no conditions of the human body in which ardent spirits may be given? I answer—there are. 1st. When the body has been suddenly exhausted of its strength, and a disposition to faintness has been induced. Here a few spoon-fuls, or a wine-glassful of spirits, with or without water, may be administered with safety and advantage. In this case we comply strictly with the advice of Solomon, who restricts the use of "strong drink" only "to him who is ready to perish."— 2dly. When the body has been exposed for a long time to wet weather, more especially, if it be combined with cold. Here a moderate quantity of spirits is not only safe, but highly proper to obviate debility, and to prevent a fever. They will more certainly have those salutary effects, if the feet are at the same time bathed with them, or a half pint of them poured into the shoes or boots. These I believe are the only two cases in which distilled spirits are useful or necessary to persons in health.

Part II

BUT it may be said, if we reject spirits from being a part of our drinks, what liquors shall we substitute in their room? I answer in the first place,

1. SIMPLE WATER. I have known many instances of persons who have fol-lowed the most laborious employments for many years, in the open air, and in warm and cold weather, who never drank any thing but water, and enjoyed uninterrupted good health. Dr. Mosely, who resided many years in the West Indies, confirms this remark. "I aver, (says the Doctor) from my own knowl-edge and custom, as well as the custom and observations of many other peo-ple, that those who drink nothing but water, or make it their principal drink, are but little affected by the climate, and can undergo the greatest fatigue without inconvenience, and are never subject to troublesome or dangerous diseases."

Persons who are unable to relish this simple beverage of nature, may drink some one, or of all the following liquors in preference to ardent spirits.

2. CYDER. This excellent liquor contains a small quantity of spirit, but so diluted, and blunted by being combined with a large quantity of saccharine matter, and water, as to be perfectly wholesome. It sometimes disagrees with persons subject to the rheumatism, but it may be made inoffensive to such people, by extinguish-ing a red hot iron in it, or by mixing it with water. It is to be lamented that the late frosts in the spring so often deprive us of the fruit which affords this liquor. The effects of these frosts have been in some measure obviated by giving an orchard a north west exposure, so as to check too early vegetation, and by kindling two or three large fires of brush, or straw, to the windward of the orchard, the eve-ning before we expect a night of frost. This last expedient has in many instances

INQUIRY INTO THE EFFECTS OF ARDENT SPIRITS

preserved the fruit of an orchard to the great joy and emolument of the ingenious husbandman.

3. MALT LIQUORS. The grain from which these liquors are obtained, is not liable, like the apple, to be affected by frost, and therefore they can be procured, at all times, and at a moderate price. They contain a good deal of nourishment; hence we find many of the poor people in Great Britain endure hard labour with no other food than a quart or three pints of beer, with a few pounds of bread in a day. As it will be difficult to prevent small beer from becoming sour in warm weather, an excellent substitute may be made for it by mixing bottled porter, ale, or strong beer, with an equal quantity of water; or a pleasant beer may be made by adding to a bottle of porter, ten quarts of water, and a pound of brown sugar or a pint of molasses. After they have been well mixed, pour the liquor into bottles and place them loosely corked, in a cool cellar. In two or three days, it will be fit for use. A spoonful of ginger added to the mixture, renders it more lively, and agreeable to the taste.

3. WINES. These fermented liquors are composed of the same ingredients as cyder, and are both cordial and nourishing. The peasants of France who drink them in large quantities, are a sober and healthy body of people. Unlike ardent spirits, which render the temper irritable, wines generally inspire cheerfulness and good humour. It is to be lamented that the grape has not as yet been sufficiently cultivated in our country, to afford wine for our citizens; but many excellent substitutes may be made for it, from the native fruits of all the states. If two barrels of cyder fresh from the press, are boiled into one, and afterwards fermented, and kept for two or three years in a dry cellar, it affords a liquor which, according to the quality of the apple from which the cyder is made, has the taste of Malaga, or Rhenish wine. It affords when mixed with water, a most agreeable drink in summer. I have taken the liberty of calling it POMONA WINE. There is another method of making a pleasant wine from the apple, by adding four and twenty gallons of new cyder to three gallons of syrup made from the expressed juice of sweet apples. When thoroughly fermented, and kept for a few years, it becomes fit for use. The blackberry of our fields, and the raspberry, and currant of our gardens, afford likewise an agreeable and wholesome wine, when pressed, and mixed with certain proportions of sugar and water, and a little spirit, to counteract the disposition to an excessive fermentation. It is no objection to these cheap and home-made wines, that they are unfit for use until they are two or three years old. The foreign wines in common use in our country, require not only a much longer time to bring them to perfection, but to prevent their being disagreeable even to the taste.

4. MOLASSES and WATER, also VINEGAR and WATER sweetened with sugar, or molasses, form an agreeable drink in warm weather. It is pleasant and cooling, and tends to keep up those gentle and uniform sweats on which health, and life often depend. Vinegar and water constituted the only drink of the soldiers of the Roman republic, and it is well known they marched and fought in a warm climate, and beneath a load of arms which weighed sixty pounds. Boaz, a wealthy farmer in Palestine, we find treated his reapers with nothing but bread dipped in vinegar.

To such persons as object to the taste of vinegar, sour milk, or buttermilk, or sweet milk diluted with water, may be given in its stead. I have known the labour of the longest and hottest days in summer supported by means of these pleasant and wholesome drinks with great firmness, and ended, with scarcely a complaint of fatigue.

5. The SUGAR MAPLE affords a thin juice which has long been used by the farmers in Connecticut as a cool, and refreshing drink in the time of harvest. The settlers in the Western counties of the middle states will do well to let a few of the trees which yield this pleasant juice, remain in all their fields. They may prove the means not only of saving their children and grand children many hundred pounds, but of saving their bodies from disease and death, and their souls from misery beyond the grave.

6. COFFEE possesses agreeable and exhilarating qualities, and might be used with great advantage to obviate the painful effects of heat, cold and fatigue upon the body. I once knew a country physician who made it a practice to drink a pint of strong coffee previously to his taking a long or cold ride. It was more cordial to him than spirits, in any of the forms in which they are commonly used.

The use of the cold bath in the morning, and of the warm bath in the evening, are happily calculated to strengthen the body the former part of the day, and to restore it in the latter, from the languor and fatigue which are induced by heat and labour.

Let it not be said, ardent spirits have become necessary from habit in harvest, and in other seasons of uncommon and arduous labour. The habit is a bad one, and may be easily broken. Let but half a dozen farmers in a neighbourhood combine to allow higher wages to their labourers than are common, and a sufficient quantity of *any* of the pleasant and wholesome liquors I have recommended, and they may soon, by their example, abolish the practice of giving them spirits. In a little while they will be delighted with the good effects of their association. Their grain and hay will be gathered into their barns in less time, and in a better condition than formerly, and of course at a less expense, and an hundred disagreeable scenes from sickness, contention and accidents will be avoided, all of which follow in a greater or less degree the use of ardent spirits.

Nearly all diseases have their predisposing causes. The same thing may be said of the intemperate use of distilled spirits. It will, therefore, be useful to point out the different employments, situations, and conditions of the body and mind which predispose to the love of those liquors, and to accompany them with directions to prevent persons being ignorantly and undesignedly seduced into the habitual and destructive use of them.

1. Labourers bear with great difficulty, long intervals between their meals. To enable them to support the waste of their strength, their stomachs should be constantly, but moderately stimulated by aliment, and this is best done by their eating four or five times in a day, during the seasons of great bodily exertion. The food at this time should be *solid*, consisting chiefly of salted meat. The vegetables used with it should possess some activity, or they should be made savoury by a mixture

of spices. Onions and garlick are of a most cordial nature. They composed a part of the diet which enabled the Israelites to endure in a warm climate, the heavy tasks imposed upon them by their Egyptian masters, and they were eaten, Horace and Virgil tells us, by the Roman farmers, to repair the waste of their strength, by the toils of harvest. There are likewise certain sweet substances which support the body under the pressure of labour. The negroes in the West Indies become strong, and even fat by drinking the juice of the sugar cane in the season of grinding it. The Jewish soldiers were invigorated by occasionally eating raisins and figs. A bread composed of wheat flower, molasses, and ginger (commonly called gingerbread) taken in small quantities during the day, is happily calculated to obviate the debility induced upon the body by constant labour. All these substances, whether of an animal or vegetable nature, lessen the desire, as well as the necessity for cordial drinks, and impart equable, and durable strength, to every part of the system.

2. Valetudinarians, especially those who are afflicted with diseases of the stomach and bowels, are very apt to seek relief from ardent spirits. Let such people be cautious how they make use of this dangerous remedy. I have known many men and women of excellent characters and principles, who have been betrayed by occasional doses of gin and brandy, into a love of those liquors, and have afterwards fallen sacrifices to their fatal effects. The different preparations of opium are much more safe and efficacious than distilled cordials of any kind, in flatulent or spasmodic affections of the stomach and bowels. So great is the danger of contracting a love for distilled liquors by accustoming the stomach to their stimulus; that as few medicines as possible should be given in spirituous vehicles, in chronic diseases. A physician of great eminence, and uncommon worth, who died towards the close of the last century, in London, in taking leave of a young physician of this city, who had finished his studies under his patronage, impressed this caution with peculiar force upon him, and lamented at the same time in pathetic terms, that he had innocently made many sots by prescribing brandy and water in stomach complaints. It is difficult to tell how many persons have been destroyed by those physicians who have adopted Dr. Brown's indiscriminate practice in the use of stimulating remedies, the most popular of which is ardent spirits, but it is well known, several of them have died of intemperance in this city, since the year 1790. They were probably led to it, by drinking brandy and water to relieve themselves from the frequent attacks of debility and indisposition to which the labours of a physician expose him, and for which rest, fasting, a gentle purge, or weak diluting drinks would have been more safe and more certain cures.

None of these remarks are intended to preclude the use of spirits in the low state of short, or what are called acute diseases, for in such cases, they produce their effects too soon, to create an habitual desire for them.

3. Some people, from living in countries subject to intermitting fevers, endeavour to fortify themselves against them, by taking two or three wine-glasses of bitters, made with spirits, every day. There is great danger of contracting habits of intemperance from this practice. Besides, this mode of preventing intermittents, is far from being a certain one. A much better security against them, is a teaspoonful

of the Jesuits bark, taken every morning during a sickly season. If this safe and excellent medicine cannot be had, a gill or half a pint of a strong watery infusion of centaury, camomile, wormwood, or rue, mixed with a little of the calamus of our meadows, may be taken every morning with nearly the same advantage as the Jesuits bark. Those persons who live in a sickly country, and cannot procure any of the preventatives of autumnal fevers, which have been mentioned, should avoid the morning and evening air;—should kindle fires in their houses, on damp days, and in cool evenings, throughout the whole summer, and put on winter clothes, about the first week in September. The last part of these directions, applies only to the inhabitants of the middle states.

4. Men who follow professions, which require constant exercise of the faculties of their minds, are very apt to seek relief, by the use of ardent spirits, from the fatigue which succeeds great mental exertions. To such persons, it may be a discovery to know, that TEA is a much better remedy for that purpose. By its grateful and gentle stimulus, it removes fatigue, restores the excitement of the mind, and invigorates the whole system. I am no advocate for the excessive use of tea. When taken too strong, it is hurtful, especially to the female constitution; but when taken of a moderate degree of strength, and in moderate quantities, with sugar and cream, or milk, I believe it is in general innoxious, and at all times to be preferred to ardent spirits, as a cordial for studious men. The late Anthony Benezet, one of the most laborious schoolmasters I ever knew, informed me, he had been prevented from the love of spirituous liquors, by acquiring a love for tea in early life. Three or four cups, taken in an afternoon, carried off the fatigue of a whole day's labour in his school. This worthy man lived to be seventy-one years of age, and died of an acute disease, with the full exercise of all the faculties of his mind. But the use of tea, counteracts a desire for distilled spirits, during great *bodily*, as well as mental exertions. Of this, Captain Forest has furnished us with a recent, and remarkable proof in his history of a voyage from Calcutta, to the Marqui Archipelago. "I have always observed, (says this ingenious mariner) when sailors drink tea, it weans them from the thoughts of drinking strong liquors, and pernicious grog; and with this, they are soon contented. Not so with what ever will intoxicate, be it what it will. This has always been my remark! I therefore, always encourage it, without their knowing why."

5. Women have sometimes been led to seek relief from what is called breeding sickness, by the use of ardent spirits. A little gingerbread, or biscuit, taken occasionally, so as to prevent the stomach being empty, is a much better remedy for that disease.

6. Persons under the pressure of debt, disappointments in worldly pursuits, and guilt, have sometimes sought to drown their sorrows in strong drink. The only radical cure for those evils, is to be found in Religion; but where its support is not resorted to, wine and opium should always be preferred to ardent spirits. They are far less injurious to the body and mind, than spirits, and the habits of attachment to them, are easily broken, after time and repentance have removed the evils they were taken to relieve.

INQUIRY INTO THE EFFECTS OF ARDENT SPIRITS

7. The sociable and imitative nature of man, often disposes him to adopt the most odious and destructive practices from his companions. The French soldiers who conquered Holland, in the year 1794, brought back with them the love and use of brandy, and thereby corrupted the inhabitants of several of the departments of France, who had been previously distinguished for their temperate and sober manners. Many other facts might be mentioned, to shew how important it is to avoid the company of persons addicted to the use of ardent spirits.

8. Smoking and chewing tobacco, by rendering water and simple liquors insipid to the taste dispose very much to the stronger stimulus of ardent spirits. The practice of smoking segars, has in every part of our country, been more followed by a general use of brandy and water, as a common drink, more especially by that class of citizens who have not been in the habit of drinking wine, or malt liquors. The less, therefore, tobacco is used in the above ways the better.

9. No man ever became suddenly a drunkard. It is by gradually accustoming the taste and stomach to ardent spirits, in the forms of GROG and TODDY, that men have been led to love them in their more destructive mixtures and in their simple state. Under the impression of this truth, were it possible for me to speak, with a voice so loud as to be heard from the river St. Croix, to the remotest shores of the Mississippi, which bound the territory of the United States, I would say,— Friends and Fellow-Citizens! avoid the habitual use of those two seducing liquors, whether they be made with brandy, rum, gin, Jamaica spirits, whiskey, or what is called cherry bounce. It is true, some men, by limiting the strength of those drinks, by measuring the spirit and water, have drunken them for many years, and even during a long life, without acquiring habits of intemperance or intoxication, but many more have been insensibly led by drinking weak toddy, and grog first at their meals, to take them for their constant drink, in the intervals of their meals; afterwards to take them, of an increased strength, before breakfast in the morning, and finally to destroy themselves by drinking undiluted spirits, during every hour of the day and night. I am not singular in this remark. "The consequences of drinking rum and water, or *grog* as it is called, (says Dr. Mosely) is, that habit increases the desire of more spirit, and decreases its effects; and there are very few grog drinkers, who long survive the practice of debauching with it without acquiring the odious nuisance of dram drinker's breath, and downright stupidity and impotence."* To enforce the caution against the use of those two apparently innocent and popular liquors still further, I shall select one instance, from among many, to shew the ordinary manner, in which they beguile and destroy their votaries. A citizen of Philadelphia, once of a fair and sober character, drank toddy for many years, as his constant drink. From this he proceeded to drink grog. After a while, nothing would satisfy him, but slings made of equal parts of rum and water, with a little sugar. From slings, he advanced to raw rum, and from common rum, to Jamaica spirits. Here he rested for a few months, but at length finding even

---

* Treatise on Tropical Diseases.

DRINK AND THE DILEMMA OF HABIT

Jamaica spirits were not strong enough to warm his stomach, he made it a constant practice to throw a table-spoonful of ground pepper into each glass of his spirits, in order, to use his own words, "to take off their coldness." He soon afterwards died a martyr to his intemperance.

Ministers of the gospel of every denomination, in the United States!—aid me with all the weight you possess in society, from the dignity and usefulness of your sacred office, to save our fellowmen from being destroyed by the great destroyer of their lives and souls. In order more successfully to effect this purpose, permit me to suggest to you, to employ the same wise modes of instruction, which you use in your attempts to prevent their destruction by other vices. You expose the evils of covetousness, in order to prevent theft; you point out the sinfulness of impure desires, in order to prevent adultery; and you dissuade from anger, and malice, in order to prevent murder. In like manner, denounce by your preaching, conversation and examples, the seducing influence of toddy and grog when you aim to prevent all the crimes and miseries, which are the offspring of strong drink.

We have hitherto considered the effects of ardent spirits upon individuals, and the means of preventing them. I shall close this head of our inquiry, by a few remarks on their effects upon the population and welfare of our country, and the means of obviating them.

It is highly probable, not less than 4000 people die annually, from the use of ardent spirits, in the United States. Should they continue to exert this deadly influence upon our population, where will their evils terminate? This question may be answered, by asking, where are all the Indian tribes, whose numbers and arms formerly spread terror among their civilized neighbours? I answer in the words of the famous Mingo Chief, "the blood of many of them flows not in the veins of any human creature." They have perished, not by pestilence, nor war, but by a greater foe to human life than either of them,—Ardent Spirits. The loss of 4000 American citizens, by the yellow fever, in a single year, awakened general sympathy and terror, and called forth all the strength and ingenuity of laws, to prevent its recurrence. Why is not the same zeal manifested in protecting our citizens from the more general and consuming ravages of distilled spirits?—Should the customs of civilized life, preserve our nation from extinction, and even from an increase of mortality, by those liquors; they cannot prevent our country being governed by men, chosen by intemperate and corrupted voters. From such legislators, the republic would soon be in danger. To avert this evil;—let good men of every class unite and besiege the general and state governments, with petitions to limit the number of taverns—to impose heavy duties upon ardent spirits—to inflict a mark of disgrace, or a temporary abridgement of some civil right, upon every man, convicted of drunkenness; and finally to secure the property of habitual drunkards, for the benefit of their families, by placing it in the hands of trustees, appointed for that purpose, by a court of justice.

To aid the operation of these laws, would it not be extremely useful for the rulers of the different denominations of Christian churches to unite, and render the sale and consumption of ardent spirits, a subject of ecclesiastical jurisdiction?—The

Methodists, and society of Friends, have for some time past, viewed them as contraband articles, to the pure laws of the gospel, and have borne many public and private testimonies, against making them the objects of commerce. Their success in this benevolent enterprise, affords ample encouragement for all other religious societies, to follow their example.

Part III

WE come now to the third part of this Inquiry, that is, to mention the remedies for the evils which are brought on by the excessive use of distilled spirits. These remedies divide themselves into two kinds.

I. Such as are proper to cure a fit of drunkenness, and

II. Such as are proper to prevent its recurrence, and to destroy a desire for ardent spirits.

I. I am aware that the efforts of science and humanity, in applying their resources to the cure of a disease induced by an act of vice, will meet with a cold reception from many people. But let such people remember, the subjects of our remedies, are their fellow creatures, and that the miseries brought upon human nature, by its crimes, are as much the objects of divine compassion, (which we are bound to imitate) as the distresses which are brought upon men, by the crimes of other people, or which they bring upon themselves, by ignorance or accidents. Let us not then, pass by the prostrate sufferer from strong drink, but administer to him the same relief, we would afford to a fellow creature, in a similar state, from an accidental and innocent cause.

1. The first thing to be done to cure a fit of drunkenness, is to open the collar, if in a man, and remove all tight ligatures from every other part of the body. The head and shoulders should at the same time be elevated, so as to favour a more feeble determination of the blood to the brain.

2. The contents of the stomach should be discharged, by thrusting a feather down the throat. It often restores the patient immediately to his senses and feet. Should it fail of exciting a puking,

3. A napkin should be wrapped round the head, and wetted for an hour or two with cold water, or cold water should be poured in a stream upon the head. In the latter way, I have sometimes seen it used when a boy, in the city of Philadelphia. It was applied, by dragging the patient, when found drunk in the street, to a pump, and pumping water upon his head for ten or fifteen minutes. The patient generally rose, and walked off, sober and sullen, after the use of this remedy.

Other remedies, less common, but not less effectual for a fit of drunkenness are,

4. Plunging the whole body into cold water. A number of gentlemen who had drunken to intoxication, on board of a ship in the stream, near Fell's point, at Baltimore, in consequence of their reeling in a small boat, on their way to the shore, in the evening, overset it, and fell into the water. Several boats from the shore hurried to their relief. They were all picked up, and went home, perfectly sober to their families.

DRINK AND THE DILEMMA OF HABIT

5. Terror. A number of young merchants, who had drunken together, in a compting house, on James river, above thirty years ago, until they were intoxicated, were carried away by a sudden rise of the river, from an immense fall of rain. They floated several miles with the current, in their little cabin, half filled with water. An island in the river arrested it. When they reached the shore that saved their lives, they were all sober. It is probable terror assisted in the cure of the persons who fell into the water at Baltimore.

6. The excitement of a fit of anger. The late Dr. Witherspoon, used to tell a story of a man in Scotland, who was always cured of a fit of drunkenness, by being made angry. The means chosen for that purpose, was a singular one. It was talking against religion.

7. A severe whipping. This remedy acts by exciting a revulsion of the blood from the brain, to the external parts of the body.

8. Profuse sweats. By means of this evacuation, nature sometimes cures a fit of drunkenness. Their good effects are obvious in labourers, whom quarts of spirits taken in a day, will seldom intoxicate, while they sweat freely. If the patient be unable to swallow warm drinks, in order to produce sweats, they may be excited by putting him in a warm bath, or wrapping his body in blankets, under which should be placed half a dozen hot bricks, or bottles filled with hot water.

9. Bleeding. This remedy should always be used, where the former ones have been prescribed to no purpose, or where there is reason to fear from the long duration of the disease, a material injury may be done to the brain.

It is hardly necessary to add, that each of the above remedies, should be regulated by the grade of drunkenness, and the greater or less degree, in which the intellects are affected in it.

II. The remedies which are proper to prevent the recurrence of fits of drunkenness, and to destroy the desire for ardent spirits, are religious, metaphysical, and medical. I shall briefly mention them.

1. Many hundred drunkards have been cured of their desire for ardent spirits, by a practical belief in the doctrines of the Christian religion. Examples of the divine efficacy of Christianity for this purpose, have lately occurred in many parts of the U. States.

2. A sudden sense of the guilt contracted by drunkenness, and of its punishment in a future world. It once cured a gentleman in Philadelphia, who in a fit of drunkenness, attempted to murder a wife whom he loved. Upon being told of it when he was sober, he was so struck with the enormity of the crime he had nearly committed that he never tasted spiritous liquors afterwards.

3. A sudden sense of shame. Of the efficacy of this deep seated principle in the human bosom, in curing drunkenness, I shall relate three remarkable instances.

A farmer in England, who had been many years in the practice of coming home intoxicated, from a market town, one day observed appearances of rain, while he was in market. His hay was cut, and ready to be housed. To save it, he returned in haste to his farm, before he had taken his customary dose of grog. Upon coming into his house, one of his children, a boy of six years old, ran to his mother, and cried out, "O! mother, father is come home, and he is not drunk." The father, who heard this exclamation, was so severely rebuked by it, that he suddenly became a sober man.

A noted drunkard was once followed by a favourite goat, to a tavern, into which he was invited by his master, and drenched with some of his liquor. The poor animal staggered home with his master, a good deal intoxicated. The next day he followed him to his accustomed tavern. When the goat came to the door, he paused: his master made signs to him to follow him into the house. The goat stood still. An attempt was made to thrust him into the tavern. He resisted, as if struck with the recollection of what he suffered from being intoxicated the night before. His master was so much affected by a sense of shame in observing the conduct of his goat to be so much more rational than his own, that he ceased from that time to drink spiritous liquors.

A gentleman in one of the southern states, who had nearly destroyed himself by strong drink, was remarkable for exhibiting the grossest marks of folly in his fits of intoxication. One evening, sitting in his parlour, he heard an uncommon noise in his kitchen. He went to the door, and peeped through the key hole, from whence he saw one of his negroes diverting his fellow servants, by mimicking his master's gestures and conversation when he was drunk.—The sight overwhelmed him with shame and distress, and instantly became the means of his reformation.

4. The association of the idea of ardent spirits, with a painful or disagreeable impression upon some part of the body has sometimes cured the love of strong drink. I once tempted a negro man, who was habitually fond of ardent spirits, to drink some rum (which I placed in his way) and in which I had put a few grains of tartar emetic.—The tartar sickened and puked him to such a degree, that he supposed himself to be poisoned. I was much gratified by observing he could not bear the sight, nor smell of spirits, for two years afterwards.

I have heard of a man, who was cured of the love of spirits, by working off a puke, by large draughts of brandy and water, and I know a gentleman, who, in consequence of being affected with a rheumatism, immediately after drinking some toddy, when overcome with fatigue and exposure to the rain, has ever since loathed that liquor, only because it was accidentally associated in his memory with the recollection of the pain he suffered from his disease.

This appeal to that operation of the human mind, which obliges it to associate ideas, accidentally or otherwise combined, for the cure of vice, is very ancient. It was resorted to by Moses, when he compelled the children of Israel, to drink the solution of the golden calf (which they had idolized) in water. This solution, if made as it most probably was, by means of what is called hepar sulphuris, was extremely bitter, and nauseous, and could never be recollected afterwards, without bringing into equal detestation, the sin which subjected them to the necessity of drinking it. Our knowledge of this principle of association upon the minds and conduct of men, should lead us to destroy, by means of other impressions, the influence of all those circumstances, with which the recollection and desire of spirits are combined. Some men drink only in the *morning*, some at *noon*, and some at *night*. Some men drink only on a *market day*, some at *one* tavern only, and some only in *one kind* of company. Now by finding a new and interesting employment, or subject of conversation for drunkards at the usual times in which they have been accustomed to drink, and by restraining them by the same means from those places and companions, which suggested to them the idea of ardent spirits, their habits of intemperance may be completely destroyed. In the same way the periodical returns of appetite, and a desire of sleep have been destroyed in an hundred instances. The desire for strong drink, differs from each of them, in being of an artificial nature, and therefore not disposed to return, after being chased for a few weeks from the system.

5. The love of ardent spirits has sometimes been subdued, by exciting a counter passion in the mind. A citizen of Philadelphia, had made many unsuccessful attempts to cure his wife of drunkenness. At length, despairing of her reformation, he purchased a hogshead of rum, and after tapping it, left the key in the door of the room in which it was placed, as if he had forgotten it, His design was to give his wife an opportunity of drinking herself to death. She suspected this to be his motive, in what he had done, and suddenly left off drinking. Resentment here became the antidote to intemperance.

6. A diet consisting wholly of vegetables cured a physician in Maryland, of drunkenness, probably by lessening that thirst, which is always more or less excited by animal food.

7. Blisters to the ankles, which were followed by an unusual degree of inflammation, once suspended the love of ardent spirits, for one month, in a lady in this city. The degrees of her intemperance, may be conceived of, when I add, that her grocer's accompt for brandy alone, amounted annually, to one hundred pounds, Pennsylvania currency, for several years.

8. A violent attack of an acute disease, has sometimes destroyed a habit of drinking distilled liquors. I attended a notorious drunkard, in the yellow fever, in the year 1798, who recovered with the loss of his relish for spirits, which has, I believe, continued ever since.

9. A salivation has lately performed a cure of drunkenness in a person in Virginia. The new disease excited in the mouth and throat, while it rendered the action of the smallest quantity of spirits upon them, painful, was happily calculated to destroy the disease in the stomach which prompts to drinking, as well as to render the recollection of them disagreeable, by the laws of association formerly mentioned.

10. I have known an oath taken before a magistrate, to drink no more spirits, produce a perfect cure of drunkenness. It is sometimes cured in this way in Ireland. Persons who take oaths for this purpose, are called affidavit men.

11. An advantage would probably arise from frequent representations being made to drunkards, not only of the certainty, but of the *suddenness* of death, from habits of intemperance. I have heard of two persons being cured of the love of ardent spirits, by seeing death suddenly induced by fits of intoxication; in the one case in a stranger and in the other, in an intimate friend.

INQUIRY INTO THE EFFECTS OF ARDENT SPIRITS

12. It has been said, that the disuse of spirits should be gradual, but my observations authorize me to say, that persons who have been addicted to them, should abstain from them *suddenly*, and *entirely*. "Taste not, handle not, touch not," should be inscribed upon every vessel that contains spirits in the house of a man, who wishes to be cured of habits of intemperance. To obviate for a while, the debility which arises from the sudden abstraction of the stimulus of spirits, laudanum, or bitters infused in water, should be taken, and perhaps a larger quantity of beer or wine, than is consistent with the strict rules of temperate living. By the temporary use of these substitutes for spirits, I have never known the transition to sober habits, to be attended with any bad effects but often with permanent health of body, and peace of mind.

THE END.

13

THOMAS TROTTER, 'INTRODUCTION' AND 'DEFINITION OF DRUNKENNESS', IN *AN ESSAY MEDICAL, PHILOSOPHICAL, AND CHEMICAL ON DRUNKENNESS AND ITS EFFECTS ON THE HUMAN BODY* 1ST PHILADELPHIA EDITION, (PHILADELPHIA: ANTHONY FINLEY, 1813), PP. 11–22

Introduction

——Dulce periculum est,
O Lenæe? sequi Deum
Cingentem viridi tempora pampino.   Hor.

MANKIND, ever in pursuit of pleasure, have reluctantly admitted into the catalogue of their diseases, those evils which were the immediate offspring of their luxuries. Such a reserve is indeed natural to the human mind: for of all deviations from the paths of duty, there are none that so forcibly impeach their pretentions to the character of rational beings as the inordinate use of spirituous liquors. Hence, in the writings of medicine, we find drunkenness only cursorily mentioned among the powers that injure health, while the mode of action is entirely neglected and left unexplained. This is the more to be wondered at, as the state of ebriety itself exhibits some of the most curious and interesting Phænomena that are to be met with in the history of animated nuture. The potent stimulus of vinous spirit, as if by magical influence, so disturbs, or operates on the animal functions, that new affections of mind, latent, or unknown before, are produced; and the drunkard appears to act the part of a man of deranged intellect, and altogether foreign to the usual terror of his sober reflections.

AN ESSAY ON DRUNKENNESS

But a long train of the most dangerous diseases are the certain consequence of habitual intoxication: the body and mind equally suffer. Sudden death, apoplexy, palsy, dropsy, madness, and a hideous list of mental disquietudes and nervous failings, prey upon the shattered frame of the inebriate, and prove fatal in the end. These sufficiently point out the subject as highly important in a medical view, and worthy of the nicest investigation. But as I have not any precursor in my labours, nor example in the records of physic, to direct my steps, I shall need the less apology for the manner I mean to pursue; and must claim indulgence where I appear singular in my method.

Most instances of casual or sudden death, and suspended animation, have obtained rules for recovery; while the drunkard, exposed in the street and highway, or stretched in the kennel, has been allowed to perish, without pity and without assistance; as if his crime were inexpiable, and his body infectious to the touch. Our newspapers give us too frequent accounts of this kind. The habit of inebriation, so common in society, to be observed in all ranks and stations of life, and the source of inexpressible affliction to friends and relatives, has seldom been the object of medical admonition and practice. The priesthood hath poured forth its anathemas from the pulpit; and the moralist, no less severe, hath declaimed against it as a vice degrading to our nature. Both have meant well; and becomingly opposed religious and moral arguments to the sinful indulgence of animal appetite. But the physical influence of custom, confirmed into habit interwoven with the actions of our sentient system, and reacting on our mental part, have been entirely forgotten. The perfect knowledge of those remote causes which first induced the propensity to vinous liquors, whether they sprung from situation in life, or depended on any peculiar temperament of body, is also necessary for conducting the cure. A due acquaintance with the human character will afford much assistance; for the objects of our care are as diversified as the varieties of corporeal structure. Pleasure, on one hand, presents the poisonous bowl: low spirits, on the other, call for the cheering draught. There business and the duties of office have plunged one man into frequent hard drinking; while cares and misfortunes have goaded on another. The soldier and the sailor get drunk while narrating the dangers of the battle and the storm: the huntsman and the jockey, by describing the joys of the chase and the course. Here genius and talent are levelled with the dust, in trying to forget, in wine, the outrages of fortune, and the ingratitude of the world; while more ponderous and stupid mortals, in attempting to seek in the bottle the feelings and sentiments of exalted beings, gravitate to their original clay, or sink deeper into their parent mud.

In treating these various descriptions of persons and characters, it will readily appear to a discerning physician, that very different methods will be required. The patient already knows, as well as the priest and moralist that the indulgence is pernicious, and ultimately fatal: he is also aware, without the reasonings of the physician, that the constant repetition will destroy health; but it is not so easy to convince him that you possess a charm that can recompence his feelings for the want of a grateful stimulus, or bestow on his nervous system sensations equally soothing and agreeable as he has been accustomed to receive from the bewitching spirit. *Hic labor, hoc opus est:* this is the difficulty; this is the task, that is to prove your discernment, patience, and address. That little has been done hitherto with success, we may be assured, by very rarely meeting with a reformed drunkard. The habit, carried to a certain length, is a gulph, from *whose bourne no traveller returns:* where fame, fortune, hope, health, and life perish.

Amidst the evils which flow from modern wars, is to be reckoned the vast consumption of spirituous liquors. The tax on distilled spirits forms so large a part of finance, and fills up so great chasm in the annual budget of any minister, who may strive more to retain his place than to reform the morals, or check the diseases of his countrymen, that we cease to wonder at its continuance. A few years ago, the crops of grain were so deficient over this island, that the distillation of spirits from malt was prohibited: and thus scarcity, bordering on famine, became a blessing to the human race. But no sooner had fruitful seasons, and the bounty of Providence, covered the earth with plenty, than the first gift of Heaven, abundance of corn, was again, for the sake of taxation, converted into poisonous spirits, by opening the stilleries. Might not other taxes be devised that would be equally productive? and would it not be a virtuous act of the Legislature to abolish the practice for ever?

In order to treat my subject philosophically, and, for the sake of method, I propose dividing it into the following heads, viz.

1st, Definition of Drunkenness.

2d, The Phænomena, or Symptoms of Drunkenness.

3d, In what Manner Vinous Spirit affects the living Body.

4th, The Catalogue of Diseases induced by Drunkenness. And,

5th, The Method of correcting the Habit of Drunkenness, and of treating the Drunken Paroxysm.

Into these heads I shall occasionally introduce such practical remarks as may arise out of the subjects; but which are too desultory for methodical arrangement.

Chap. I

Definition of drunkenness

O! thou invisible spirit of wine, if thou hast no name to be known by let us call thee
——Devil!

Shakspeare.

IN medical language, I consider drunkenness, strictly speaking, to be a disease; produced by a remote cause, and giving birth to actions and movements in the living body, that disorder the functions of health. This being the case, besides the value of an accurate definition for the sake of system, it may be of some practical utility to point out the affinity which the paroxysm has with other affections. In assigning the character formerly, I was well aware of the difficulty of fixing any symptom, or even concourse of symptoms, that are invariably present. For this reason *delirium* seemed to be the most certain, as it is the most prominent and general. But objections may yet be made to this; for difference of age, and varieties of temperament and constitution, influence the accession and progress of wavering intellect during intoxication. Again, although the animal functions are evidently deranged, exhibited by all the shades and gradations of *delirium*, such as imbecility of mind or fatuity, erroneous judgment, imaginary perceptions, false relations, violent emotions called ravings, &c. yet at the same time, the paroxysm is so generally attended with a partial or total abolition of the powers of sense and motion, that it assumes very much the nature of a *comatose* condition. Indeed the most frequent fatal termination of the drunken fit is *apoplexy*. It is certainly no uncommon occurrence to see an inebriate who can neither walk or speak, exercise so considerable a degree of mental power, as to recollect every circumstance that passes; yet so conscious of his inability to move without staggering, that he cunningly watches the opportunity, when unperceived by his companions, to take his leave. The character of this disease therefore, partakes both of *delirium* and *coma*.

To avoid confusion, I take the *remote cause* into my definition. Drunkenness is the delirium occasioned by fermented liquors. It is true that other narcotics, particularly *opium* and *bang*, produce nearly the same phænomena, and their habitual use almost the same diseases; yet, for obvious reasons, the chief of which is the common occurrence of drunkenness in this country, I am induced to separate them here, and consider this subject by itself.—Our definition is briefly this:

Post Vinun immodice assumptum, Delirium et Coma.—Which may be thus translated:—"Imbecility of intellect, erroneous judgment, violent emotions; and loss of sense and motion after the immoderate use of vinous liquors."

The Latin word "Vinum," has been preferred as being the most concise, and best conveying the meaning of vinous spirit, the product of fermentation, and on which the inebriating power of all fermented liquors depends; such as wine, malt-liquors, cyder, perry, mum, mead, koumiss, &c. all of which by distillation yield "*alkohol*."

The *carbonic acid gas, or fixed air*, which is evolved in great quantity during the vinous fermentation, that gives a sparkling and pungency to certain liquors, such as champaigne, bottled beer and cyder, is known to produce a kind of stupefaction resembling intoxication, independent of the spirit. This kind of ebriety is but momentary; as the action of the gas on the nerves of the stomach is of short duration. Very different are the effects of this *gas* when breathed. Brewers have frequently been suffocated in taking out their ale or beer from the vat, as the air lies on the surface of the fermenting liquor. Nay it has sometimes accumulated in such quantites in those cellars, as to prove fatal to several people before the cause was detected, and the air expelled by ventilation. In mines, wells, and the holds of ships, this vapour has often proved lethalic.

Dr. Cullen, in his order of *Vesaniæ*, or mental derangement, has given five genera: but the paroxysm of ebriety more particularly exemplifies the mixed character of *amentia, insania et mania*, or ideotism, agreeable emotions, and violent emotions. *Oneirodynia*, disturbed sleep, which comprehends sleep-walking and night-mare, perhaps only occurs during the decline of the drunken paroxysm. And *melancholia*, melancholy, would appear to be suspended during the stimulant power of wine. This disease is rather the offspring of habitual intoxication; it is probably confined to a peculiar temperament of body, that is little disposed to be excited, and can endure excessive stimulus without proportional action, as well in the functions of the *sensorium commune*, as in the circulating system.

There is a species of delirium that often attends the early accession of *typhus fever*, from contagion that I have known to be mistaken for ebriety. Among seamen and soldiers, where habits of intoxication are common, it will sometimes require nice discernment to decide; for the vacant stare in the countenance, the look of ideotism, incoherent speech, faultering voice, and tottering walk, are so alike in both cases, that the naval and military surgeon ought at all times to be very cautious, how he gives up a man to punishment under these suspicious appearances. Nay, the certainty of his having come from a tavern, with even the effluvium of liquor about him, are signs not always to be trusted: for these haunts of seamen and soldiers are often the sources of infection. In all doubtful cases of this kind, let the members of our profession be guarded in their opinions; it is safe to lean to the humane side.

There is another species of intoxication that follows the inhalation of inflammable spirit, by the nose and mouth, without being swallowed. This species of ebriety is common to coopers, porters, and other workmen employed in cellars and distilleries. The most volatile part of the spirit, or purest alkohol, which arises in pouring it from one vessel to another, probably acts by directly stimulating the nerves of the *membrana Shneideriana* spread about the nose and frontal sinuses; and also the inside of the mouth, trachea and lungs, and thus produces delirium. This ebriety is likewise transitory, and soon disappears when the patient is moved into the open air. It frequently happens in ships, in pumping spirits from a large cask into a smaller, in the confined space of a spirit room: but the practice is dangerous, as vessels have often been set on fire by a lighted candle touching the spirits; and it is now strictly forbidden in all well regulated ships in his Majesty's navy.

14

R. MACNISH, *THE ANATOMY OF DRUNKENNESS: AN INAUGURAL ESSAY* (GLASGOW: W. R. MCPHUN, 1827), PP. 1–28

Causes of drunkenness

To discuss the subject of drunkenness at length, would require a large volume. Its physiology, the diseases to which it gives rise, and its treatment, are of so extensive a character, that any attempt to detail them fully, within the compass of an ordinary essay, would be fruitless. The former topic, therefore, has been totally omitted, and the others merely glanced at in the present sketch, which is less a history of intoxication than an outline of such points as have been slightly touched upon by former writers. I have fixed, more particularly, upon the phenomena and modifications of drunkenness; because, in such of the works as I have seen, these subjects are but briefly noticed, and in some of them altogether overlooked. The first, though sufficiently obvious, are, for the most part, faintly and inaccurately delineated; and the modifications produced by temperament, and the various intoxicating agents, are either entirely neglected, or described in a manner so vague and unsatisfactory, that the mind derives from their imperfect detail neither pleasure nor information.

The causes of drunkenness are so obvious, that few authors have thought it necessary to point them out: we shall merely say a few words upon the subject. There are some persons who will never be drunkards, and others who will be so in spite of all that can be done to prevent them. Some are drunkards by choice, and others by necessity. The former have an innate and constitutional fondness for liquor, and drink *con amore*. Such men are usually of a sanguineous temperament, of coarse unintellectual minds, and of low and animal propensities. They have, in general, a certain rigidity of fibre, and a flow of animal spirits which other people are without. They delight in the roar and riot of drinking clubs; and with them, in particular, all the miseries of life may be referred to the bottle.

DRINK AND THE DILEMMA OF HABIT

The drunkard by necessity was never meant by nature to be dissipated. He is perhaps a person of amiable dispositions, whom misfortune has overtaken, and who, instead of bearing up manfully against it, endeavours to drown his sorrows in liquor. It is an excess of sensibility, a partial mental weakness, an absolute misery of the heart, which drives him on. Drunkenness, with him, is a consequence of misfortune; it is a solitary dissipation preying upon him in silence. Such a man frequently dies broken-hearted, even before his excesses have had time to destroy him by their own unassisted agency.

Some become drunkards from excess of indulgence in youth. There are parents who have a common custom of treating their children to wine, punch, and other intoxicating liquors. This, in reality, is regularly bringing them up in an apprenticeship to drunkenness. Others are taught the vice by frequenting drinking clubs and masonic lodges. These are the genuine academies of tippling. Two-thirds of the drunkards we meet with, have been there initiated in that love of intemperance and boisterous irregularity which distinguish their future lives. Men who are good singers are very apt to become drunkards, and, in truth, most of them are so, more or less, especially if they have naturally much jovialty or warmth of temperament. A fine voice to such men is a fatal accomplishment.

Ebriety prevails to an alarming degree among the lower orders of society. It exists more in towns than in the country, and more among mechanics than husbandmen. Most of the misery to be observed among the working classes springs from this source. No persons are more addicted to the habit, and all its attendant vices, than the pampered servants of the great. Innkeepers, musicians, actors, and men who lead a rambling and eccentric life, are exposed to a similar hazard. Husbands sometimes teach their wives to be drunkards by indulging them in toddy, and such fluids, every time they themselves sit down to their libations.

Women frequently acquire the vice by drinking porter and ale while nursing. These stimulants are usually recommended to them from well meant but mistaken motives, by their female attendants. Many fine young women are ruined by this detestable practice. Their persons become gross, their milk unhealthy, and a foundation is too often laid for future indulgence in liquor.

The frequent use of cordials, such as noyau, shrub, kirsch-waser, curaçoa, and anissette, sometimes leads to the practice. The active principle of these liqueurs is neither more nor less than ardent spirits.

Among other causes, may be mentioned the excessive use of spirituous tinctures for the cure of hypochondria and indigestion. Persons who use strong tea, especially green, run the same risk. The latter species is singularly hurtful to the constitution, producing hysteria, heartburn, and general debility of the chylopoetic viscera. Some of these bad effects are relieved for a time by the use of spirits; and what was at first employed as a medicine, soon becomes an essential requisite.

Some writers allege, that unmarried women, especially if somewhat advanced in life, are more given to liquor than those who are married. This point I am unable, from my own observation, to decide.

Drunkenness appears to be in some measure hereditary. We frequently see it descending from parents to their children. This may undoubtedly often arise from bad example and imitation, but there can be little question that, in many instances at least, it exists as a family predisposition.

Men of genius are often unfortunately addicted to drinking. Nature, as she has gifted them with greater powers than their fellows, seems also to have mingled with their cup of life more bitterness. There is a melancholy which is apt to come like a cloud over the imaginations of such characters. Their minds possess a susceptibility and a delicacy of structure which unfit them for the gross atmosphere of human nature; wherefore, high talent has ever been distinguished for sadness and gloom. Genius lives in a world of its own: it is the essence of a superior nature—the loftier imaginings of the mind, clothed with a more spiritual and refined verdure. Few men endowed with such faculties enjoy the ordinary happiness of humanity. The stream of their lives runs harsh and broken. Melancholy thoughts sweep perpetually across their souls; and if these be heightened by misfortune, they are plunged into the deepest misery.

To relieve these feelings, many plans have been adopted. Dr. Johnson fled for years to wine under his habitual gloom. He found that the pangs were removed while its immediate influence lasted, but he also found that they returned with double force when that influence passed away. He saw the dangerous precipice on which he stood, and, by an unusual effort of volition, gave it over. In its stead he substituted tea; and to this milder stimulus had recourse in his melancholy. Voltaire and Fontenelle, for the same purpose, used coffee. The excitements of Newton and Hobbes were the fumes of tobacco, while Demosthenes and Haller were sufficiently stimulated by drinking freely of cold water. Such are the differences of constitution.

"As good be melancholy still, as drunken beasts and beggars." So says old Burton, in his Anatomy of Melancholy, and there are few who will not subscribe to his creed. The same author quaintly, but justly, remarks, "if a drunken man gets a child, it will never, likely, have a good brain." Dr. Darwin, a great authority on all subjects connected with life, says, that he never knew a glutton affected with the gout, who was not at the same time addicted to liquor. He also observes, "it is remarkable that all the diseases from drinking spirituous or fermented liquors are liable to become hereditary, even to the third generation, gradually increasing, if the cause be continued, till the family becomes extinct."*

We need not endeavour to trace farther the remote causes of drunkenness. A drunkard is rarely able to recall the particular circumstances which made him so. The vice creeps upon him insensibly, and he is involved in its fetters before he is aware. It is enough that we know the proximate cause, and also the certain consequences. One thing is certain, that a man who addicts himself to intemperance

---

* Botanic Garden.

can never be said to be sound in mind or body. The former is in a state of partial insanity, while the effects of the liquor remain; and the latter is always more or less diseased in its actions.

Phenomena of drunkenness

THE consequences of drunkenness are dreadful, but the pleasures of getting drunk are certainly ecstatic. While the illusion lasts, happiness is complete; care and melancholy are thrown to the wind, and Elysium, with all its glories, descends upon the dazzled imagination of the drinker.

Some authors have spoken of the pleasure of being completely drunk: this, however, is not the most exquisite period. The time is when a person is neither "drunken nor sober, but neighbour to both," as Bishop Andrews says in his "Ex—ale—tation of Ale." The moment is when the etherial emanations begin to float around the brain—when the soul is commencing to expand its wings and rise from earth—when the tongue feels itself somewhat loosened in the mouth, and breaks the previous taciturnity, if any such existed.

What are the sensations of incipient drunkenness? First, an unusual serenity prevails over the mind, and the soul of the votary is filled with a placid satisfaction. By degrees he is sensible of a soft and not unmusical humming in his ears, at every pause of the conversation. He seems, to himself, to wear his head lighter than usual upon his shoulders. Then a species of obscurity, thinner than the finest mist, passes before his eyes, and makes him see objects rather indistinctly. The lights begin to dance, and appear double. A gaiety and warmth are felt at the same time about the heart. The imagination is expanded, and filled with a thousand delightful images. He becomes loquacious, and pours forth, in enthusiastic language, the thoughts which are born, as it were, within him.

Now comes a spirit of universal contentment with himself and all the world. He thinks no more of misery: it is dissolved in the bliss of the moment. This is the acme of the fit—the ecstacy is now perfect. As yet the sensorium is in tolerable order: it is only shaken, but the capability of thinking with accuracy still remains. About this time, the drunkard pours out all the secrets of his soul. His qualities, good or bad, come forth without reserve; and now, if at any time, the human heart may be seen into. In a short period, he is seized with a most inordinate propensity to talk nonsense, though he is perfectly conscious of doing so. He also commits many foolish things, knowing them to be foolish. The power of volition, that faculty which keeps the will subordinate to the judgment, seems totally weakened. The most delightful time seems to be that immediately before becoming very talkative. When this takes place, a man turns ridiculous, and his mirth, though more boisterous, is not so exquisite. At first, the intoxication partakes of sentiment, but, latterly, it becomes merely animal.

ANATOMY OF DRUNKENNESS: AN INAUGURAL ESSAY

After this the scene thickens. The drunkard's imagination gets disordered with the most grotesque conceptions. Instead of moderating his drink, he pours it down more rapidly than ever: glass follows glass with reckless energy. His head becomes perfectly giddy. The candles burn blue, or green, or yellow; and where there are perhaps only three on the table, he sees a dozen. According to his temperament, he is amorous, or musical, or quarrelsome. Many possess a most extraordinary wit; and a great flow of spirits is a general attendant. In the latter stages, the speech is thick, and the use of the tongue in a great measure lost. His mouth is half open, and idiotic in the expression; while his eyes are glazed, wavering, and watery. He is apt to fancy that he has offended some one of the company, and is ridiculously profuse with his apologies. Frequently he mistakes one person for another, and imagines that some of those before him are individuals who are, in reality, absent or even dead. The muscular powers are, all along, much affected: this, indeed, happens before any great change takes place in the mind, and goes on progressively increasing. He can no longer walk with steadiness, but totters from side to side. The limbs become powerless, and inadequate to sustain his weight. He is, however, not always sensible of any deficiency in this respect: and, while exciting mirth by his eccentric motions, imagines that he walks with the most perfect steadiness. In attempting to run, he conceives that he passes over the ground with astonishing rapidity. The last stage of drunkenness is total insensibility. The man tumbles perhaps beneath the table, and is carried away in a state of stupor to his couch. In this condition he is said to be *dead drunk*.

When the drunkard is put to bed, let us suppose that his faculties are not totally absorbed in apoplectic stupor; let us suppose that he still possesses consciousness and feeling, though these are both disordered; then begins "the tug of war;" then comes the misery which is doomed to succeed his previous raptures. No sooner is his head laid upon the pillow than it is seized with the strangest throbbing. His heart beats quick and hard against the ribs. A noise like the distant fall of a cascade, or rushing of a river, is heard in his ears. Sough—sough—sough, goes the sound. His senses now become more drowned and stupified. A dim recollection of his carousals, like a shadowy and indistinct dream, passes before the mind. He still hears, as in echo, the cries and laughter of his companions. Wild fantastic fancies accumulate thickly around the brain. His giddiness is greater than ever; and he feels as if in a ship tossed upon a heaving sea. At last he drops insensibly into a profound slumber.

In the morning he awakes in a high fever. The whole body is parched; the palms of the hands, in particular, are like leather. His head is often violently painful. He feels excessive thirst; while his tongue is white, dry, and stiff. The whole inside of the mouth is likewise hot and constricted, and the throat often sore. Then look at his eyes—how sickly, dull, and languid. The fire, which first lighted them up the evening before, is all gone. A stupor, like that of the last stage of drunkenness, still clings about them, and they are affected by the light. The complexion sustains as great a change: it is no longer flushed with gaiety and excitation, but pale and wayworn, indicating a profound mental and bodily exhaustion. There is probably sickness, and the appetite is totally gone. Even yet the delirium of intoxication has not left him, for his head still rings, his heart still throbs violently; and if he attempt getting up, he stumbles with giddiness. The mind also is sadly depressed, and the proceedings of the previous night are painfully remembered. He is sorry for his conduct, promises solemnly never again so to commit himself, and calls impatiently for something to quench his thirst. Such are the usual phenomena of a fit of drunkenness.

In the beginning of intoxication we are inclined to sleep, especially if we indulge alone. In companies, the noise and opportunity of conversing prevent this; and when a certain quantity has been drunk, the drowsy tendency wears away. A person who wishes to stand out well, should never talk much. This increases the effects of the liquor, and hurries on intoxication. Hence, every experienced drunkard holds it to be a piece of prudence to keep his tongue under restraint.

The giddiness of intoxication is always greater in darkness than in the light. I know of no rational way in which this can be explained; but, certain it is, the drunkard never so well knows his true condition as when alone and in darkness. Possibly the noise and light distracted the mind, and made the bodily sensations be, for the time, in some measure, unfelt.

There are some persons who get sick from drinking even a small quantity; and this sickness is, upon the whole, a favourable circumstance, as it proves an effectual curb upon them, however much they might be disposed to intemperance.

Intoxication, before it proceeds too far, has a powerful tendency to increase the appetite. Perhaps it would be more correct to say, that inebriating liquors, by stimulating the stomach, have this power. We often see gluttony and drunkenness combined together at the same time. This continues till the last stage, when, from overloading, and excess of irritation, the stomach expels its contents by vomiting.

All along the action of the kidneys is much increased, especially at the commencement of intoxication.

When a large quantity of intoxicating fluid has been suddenly taken into the stomach, the usual preliminary symptoms of drunkenness do not appear. An instantaneous stupefaction ensues; and the person is at once knocked down. This cannot be imputed to distention of the cerebral vessels, but to a sudden operation on the nervous branches of the stomach. The brain is thrown into a state of collapse, and many of its functions suspended. In such cases, the face is not, at first, tumid and ruddy, but pale and contracted. The pulse is likewise feeble, and the body cold and powerless. When re-action takes place, these symptoms wear off, and those of sanguineous apoplexy succeed; such as turgid countenance, full but slow pulse, and strong sterterous breathing. The vessels of the brain have now become filled, and there is a strong determination to that organ.

Persons of tender or compassionate minds are particularly subject, during intoxication, to be affected to tears at the sight of any distressing object, or even on hearing an affecting tale. Drunkenness, in such characters, may be said to melt the heart, and open up the fountains of sorrow. Their sympathy is often ridiculous, and aroused by the most trifling causes. Those who have a lively imagination, combined with this tenderness of heart, sometimes conceive fictitious cases of distress, and weep bitterly at the woe of their own creating.

During a paroxysm of drunkenness, the body is much less sensible to external stimuli than at other times: it is particularly capable of resisting cold. Seamen, when absent on shore, are prone to get intoxicated; and they will frequently lie for hours on the highway, even in the depth of winter, without any bad consequences. A drunk man seldom shivers from cold. His frame seems steeled against it, and he holds out with an apathy which is astonishing. The body is, in like manner, insensible to injuries, such as cuts, bruises, &c. He frequently receives, in fighting, the most severe blows, without seemingly feeling them, and without, in fact, being aware of the matter till sobered. Persons in intoxication have been known to chop off their fingers, and otherwise disfigure themselves, laughing all the while at the action. But when the paroxysm is off, and the frame weakened, things are changed. External agents are then withstood with little vigour, with even less than in the natural state of the body. The person shivers on the slightest chill, and is more than usually subject to fevers and all sorts of contagion.

External stimuli frequently break the fit. Men have been instantly sobered by having a bucket of cold water thrown upon them, or by falling into a stream. Strong emotions of the mind produce the same effect, such as a sense of danger, or a piece of good or bad news, suddenly communicated.

There are particular situations and circumstances in which a man can stand liquor better than in others. In the close atmosphere of a large town, he is soon overpowered; and it is here that the genuine drunkard is to be met with in the greatest perfection. In the country, especially in a mountainous district, or on the seashore, where the air is cold and piercing, a great quantity may be taken with impunity. The Highlanders drink largely of ardent spirits, and they are often intoxicated, yet, among them, there are comparatively few who can be called habitual drunkards. A keen air seems to deaden its effects, and it soon evaporates from their constitutions. Sailors and soldiers who are hard wrought also consume enormous quantities without injury: porters and all sorts of labourers do the same. With these men exercise is a corrective; but in towns, where no counteracting agency is employed, it acts with irresistible power upon the frame, and soon proves destructive.

The mind exercises a considerable effect upon drunkenness, and may often control it powerfully. When in the company of a superior whom we respect, or of a female in whose presence it would be indelicate to get intoxicated, a much greater portion of liquor may be withstood than in societies where no such restraints operate.

Some drunkards retain their senses after the physical powers are quite exhausted. Others, even when the mind is wrought to a pitch leading to the most absurd actions, preserve a degree of cunning and observation which enables them to elude the tricks which their companions are preparing to play upon them. In such cases they display great address, and take the first opportunity of retaliating; or, if such does not occur, of slipping out of the room unobserved and getting away. Some, while the whole mind seems locked up in the stupor of forgetfulness, hear all that is going on. No one should ever presume on the intoxicated state of another to talk of him detractingly in his presence. While apparently deprived of all sensation, he may be an attentive listener; and whatever is said, though unheeded at the moment, is not forgotten afterwards, but treasured carefully up in the memory. Much discord and ill-will frequently arise from such imprudence.

There are persons who are exceedingly profuse, and fond of giving away their money, watches, rings, &c. to the company. This peculiarity will never, I believe, be found in a miser: avarice is a passion strong under every circumstance. Drinking does not loosen the grasp of the covetous man, or open his heart. He is for ever the same.

The generality of people are apt to talk of their private affairs when intoxicated. They then reveal the most deeply hidden secrets to their companions. Others have their minds so happily constituted that nothing escapes them. They are, even in their most unguarded moments, secret and close as the grave.

The natural disposition may be better discovered in drunkenness than at any other time. In modern society, life is all a disguise. Every man walks in masquerade, and his most intimate friend very often does not know his real character. Many wear smiles constantly upon their cheeks whose hearts are unprincipled and treacherous. Many with violent tempers have all the external calm and softness of charity itself. Some speak always with sympathy, who, at soul, are full of gall and bitterness. Intoxication tears off the veil, and sets each in its true light, whatever that may be. The combative man will quarrel, the sensualist will love, the detractor will abuse his neighbour. I have known exceptions, but they are few in number. At one time they seemed more numerous, but closer observation convinced me that most of those whom I thought drunkenness had libelled, inherited, at bottom, the genuine dispositions which it brought forth.

<hr />

Drunkenness modified by temperament

UNDER the last head I have described the usual phenomena of intoxication; but it is necessary to remark, that these are apt to be modified by the physical and moral frame of the drinker. Great diversity of opinion exists with regard to the doctrine of the temperaments: the ancients, and Richerand* and others among the moderns, affirming, and Spurzheim† denying their existence. Into this controversy it is needless to enter. All I contend for is, that the bodily and mental constitution of every man is not alike, and that on these peculiarities depend certain differences during a paroxysm of drunkenness.

* Nouveaux Elemens de Physiologie.
† Observations sur la Phrœnologie.

I. *Sanguineous Drunkard.*—The sanguine temperament seems to feel most intensely the excitement of the bottle. Persons of this stamp have usually a ruddy complexion, thick neck, small head, and strong muscular fibre. Their intellect is in general *mediocre*, for great bodily strength and corresponding mental powers are rarely united together. In such people, the animal propensities prevail over the moral and intellectual ones. They are prone to combativeness and sensuality; are either very good-natured or extremely quarrelsome. All their passions are keen: they will fight for their friends or with them as occasion requires. They are talkative from the beginning, and, during confirmed intoxication, perfectly obstreperous. It is men of this class who are the heroes of all drunken companies, the patrons of masonic lodges, the presidents and getters-up of jovial meetings. With them, eating and drinking are the grand ends of human life. Look at their eyes, how they sparkle at the sight of wine, and how their lips smack and their teeth water in the neighbourhood of a good dinner: they would scent out a banquet in Siberia. When intoxicated, their passions are highly excited: the energies of a hundred minds then seem concentrated into one focus. Their mirth, their anger, their love, their folly, are all equally intense and unquenchable. Such men cannot conceal their feelings. In drunkenness, the veil is removed from them, and their characters stand revealed, as in a glass, to the eye of the beholder. The Roderic Random of Smollett had much of this temperament, blended, however, with more intellect than usually belongs to it.

II. *Melancholy Drunkard.*—Melancholy, in drunkards, sometimes arises from temperament, but more frequently from habitual intoxication or misfortune. Some men are melancholy by nature, but become highly mirthful when they have drunk a considerable quantity. Men of this tone of mind seem to enjoy the bottle more exquisitely than even the sanguineous class. The joyousness which it excites breaks in upon their gloom like sunshine upon darkness. Above all, the sensations, at the moment when mirth begins with its magic to charm away care, are inexpressible. Pleasure falls in showers of fragrance upon their souls; they are at peace with themselves and all mankind, and enjoy, as it were, a foretaste of paradise. Robert Burns was an example of this variety. His melancholy was constitutional, but heightened by misfortune. The bottle commonly dispelled it, and gave rise to the most delightful images; sometimes, however, it only aggravated the gloom.

III. *Surly Drunkard.*—Some men are not excited to mirth by intoxication. On the contrary, it renders them gloomy and discontented. Even those who in the sober state are sufficiently gay, become occasionally thus altered. A great propensity to take offence is a characteristic among persons of this temperament. They are suspicious, and very often mischievous. If at some former period they have had a difference with any of the company, they are sure to revive it, although, probably, it has been long ago cemented on both sides, and even forgotten by the other party. People of this description are very unpleasant companions. They are in general so foul-tongued, quarrelsome, and indecent in conversation, that established clubs of drinkers have made it a practice to exclude them from their society.

IV. *Phlegmatic Drunkard.*—Persons of this temperament are heavy-rolling machines, and, like the above, are not roused to mirth by liquor. Their vital actions are dull and spiritless—the blood in their veins as sluggish as the river Jordan, and their energies stagnant as the Dead Sea. They are altogether a negative sort of beings, with passions too inert to lead them to any thing very good or very bad. They are a species of animated clods, but not thoroughly animated—for the vital fire of feeling has got cooled in penetrating their frozen frames. A new Prometheus would require to breathe into their nostrils, to give them the ordinary glow and warmth of humanity. Look at a phlegmatic man—how dead, passionless, and uninspired, is the expression of his clammy lips and vacant eye! Speak to him—how cold, slow, and tame is his conversation! The words come forth as if they were drawn from his mouth with a pair of pincers; and the ideas are as frozen as if concocted in the bowels of Lapland. Liquor produces no effect upon his mental powers, or if it does, it is a smothering one. The whole energies of the drink fall on his almost impassive frame. From the first, his drunkenness is stupifying; he is seized with a kind of lethargy, the white of his eyes turn up, he breathes loud and harshly, and sinks into an apoplectic stupor. Yet all this is perfectly harmless, and wears away without leaving any mark behind it. Such persons are very apt to be played upon by their companions. There are few men who, in their younger days, have not assisted in shaving the heads and painting the faces of these lethargic drunkards.

V. *Nervous Drunkard.*—This is a very harmless and very tiresome personage. Generally of a weak mind and irritable constitution, he does not become boisterous with mirth, and rarely shows the least glimmering of wit or mental energy. He is talkative and fond of long-winded stories, which he tells in a drivelling, silly manner. Never warmed into enthusiasm by liquor, he keeps chatting at some ridiculous tale, very much in the way of a garrulous old man in his dotage.

VI. *Choleric Drunkard.*—There are a variety of drunkards whom I can only class under the above title. They seem to possess few of the qualities of the other races, and are chiefly distinguished by an uncommon testiness of disposition. They are quick, irritable, and impatient, but withal good at heart, and, when in humour, very pleasant and generous. They are easily put out of temper, but it returns almost immediately. This disposition is very prevalent among Welshmen and Highland lairds. Mountaineers are usually quick-tempered; but such men are not the worst or most unpleasant. Sterne is undoubtedly right when he says that more virtue is to be found in warm than in cold dispositions. Commodore Trunnion is a marked example of this temperament; and Captain Fluellen, who compelled the *heroic* Pistol to eat the leek, is another.

These different varieties are sometimes found strongly marked; at other times so blended together that it is not easy to say which predominates. The most agreeable drunkard is he whose temperament lies between the sanguineous and the melancholic. The genuine sanguineous is a sad noisy dog, and so common, that every person must have met with him. The naval service furnishes a great many gentlemen of this description. The phlegmatic, I think, is rarer, but both the nervous and the surly are not unusual.

Drunkenness modified by the inebriating agent

INTOXICATION is not only influenced by temperament, but by the nature of the agent which produces it. Thus, ebriety from ardent spirits differs in some particulars from that brought on by opium or malt liquors, such as porter and ale.

Alcohol is the principle of intoxication in all liquors. It is this which gives to wine, ale, and spirits, their characteristic properties. In the natural state, however, it is so pungent, that it could not be received into the stomach, even in a moderate quantity, without producing death. It can, therefore, only be used in dilution; and in this state we have it from the strongest ardent spirits, to simple small beer. The first (ardent spirits) being the most concentrated of its combinations, act most rapidly upon the constitution. They are more inflammatory, and intoxicate sooner than any of the others. Swallowed in an overdose, they act almost instantaneously—extinguishing the senses and overcoming the whole body with a sudden stupor. When spirits are swallowed raw, as in the form of a dram, they excite a glow of heat in the throat and stomach, succeeded, in those who are not much accustomed to their use, by a flushing of the countenance, and a copious discharge of tears. They are strongly diuretic.

The principal varieties of spirits are rum, brandy, whisky, and gin. It is needless to enter into any detail of the history of these fluids. Brandy kills soonest: it takes most rapidly to the head, and tinges the face to a crimson or livid hue. Rum is probably the next in point of fatality; and, after that, gin and whisky. The superior diuretic qualities of the two latter, and the less luscious sources from which they are procured, may possibly account for these differences.

Drunkenness from wine closely resembles that from ardent spirits. It is equally airy and volatile, more especially if the light wines, such as champaign, claret, chambertin, or volnay, be drunk. On the former, a person may get tipsy several times of a night. The fixed air evolved from it produces a feeling analogous to ebriety, independent of the spirit it contains. Port, sherry, and madeira are heavier wines, and have a stronger tendency to excite headach and fever.

The wine-bibber has usually an ominous rotundity of face, and, not unfrequently, of corporation. His nose is well studded over with carbuncles of the claret complexion; and the red of his cheeks resembles very closely the peculiar hue of that wine. The drunkard from ardent spirits is apt to be a poor, miserable, emaciated figure, broken in mind and in fortune; but the votary of the juice of the grape may usually boast the "paunch well-lined with capon," and recalls to recollection the bluff figure of Sir John Falstaff over his potations of sack.

Malt liquors, under which title we include all kinds of porter and ales, produce the worst species of drunkenness; as, in addition to the intoxicating principle, some noxious ingredients are usually added, for the purpose of preserving them and giving them their bitter. The hop of these fluids is highly narcotic, and brewers often add other substances, to heighten its effect, such as opium, coculus indicus, &c. Malt liquors, therefore, act in two ways upon the body, partly by the alcohol they contain, and partly by the narcotic principle. In addition to this, the fermentation which they undergo is much less perfect than that of spirits or wine. After being swallowed, this process is carried on in the stomach, by which fixed air is copiously liberated, and the digestion of delicate stomachs materially impaired. Cider, spruce, ginger, and table beers, though purposely impregnated with this air for the sake of briskness, produce the same bad effect, even when their briskness has vanished. The cause of all this is the want of due fermentation.

Persons addicted to malt liquors increase enormously in bulk. They become loaded with fat: their chin gets double or triple, the eye prominent, and the whole face bloated and stupid. Their circulation is clogged, while the pulse feels like a cord, and is full and labouring, but not quick. During sleep the breathing is sterterous. Every thing indicates an excess of blood; and when a pound or two is taken away, immense relief is obtained. The blood in such cases is more dark and sizy than in the others. In seven cases out of ten, malt liquor drunkards die of apoplexy or palsy. If they escape this hazard, swelled liver or dropsy carries them off. The abdomen seldom loses its prominency, but the lower extremities get ultimately emaciated. Profuse bleedings frequently ensue from the nose, and save life, by emptying the blood-vessels of the brain.

The drunkenness in question is peculiarly of British growth. The most noted examples of it are to be found in innkeepers and their wives, recruiting serjeants, guards of stage-coaches, &c.

The effects of malt liquors on the body, if not so immediately rapid as those of ardent spirits, are more stupifying, more lasting, and less easily removed. The last are particularly prone to produce levity and mirth, but the first have a stunning influence upon the brain, and, in a short time, render dull and sluggish the gayest disposition. They also produce sickness and vomiting more readily than either spirits or wine.

Both wine and malt liquors have a greater tendency to swell the body than ardent spirits. They form blood with greater rapidity, and are altogether more nourishing. The most dreadful effects, upon the whole, are brought on by spirits, but drunkenness by malt liquors is the most speedily fatal. The former break down the body by degrees; the latter operate by some instantaneous apoplexy or rapid inflammation.

Persons who indulge too much in spirits rarely get corpulent, unless their indulgence be coupled with good living. Their bodies become emaciated; they get spindle-shanked; their eyes are glazed and hollow; their cheeks fall in; and a premature old age overtakes them. They do not eat so well as their brother drunkards. An insatiable desire for a morning dram makes them early risers, and their breakfast amounts to almost nothing.

Opium.—The drunkenness produced by opium has also some characteristics which it is necessary to mention. This drug is principally employed by the Mahommetans. By their religion these people are forbidden the use of wine, and use opium as a substitute. And a delightful substitute it is while the first excitation continues; for the images it occasions in the mind are more exquisite than any produced even by wine.

There is reason to believe that the use of this medicine has, of late years, gained ground in Great Britain. We are told by the "English Opium-Eater,"* whose powerful and interesting "Confessions" have excited so deep an interest, that the practice exists among the work people at Manchester. Many of our fashionable ladies have recourse to it when troubled with vapours, or low spirits: some of them carry it even about with them for the purpose. This practice is most pernicious, and no way different from that of drunkards, who swallow wine and other liquors to drive away care. While the first effects continue, the intended purpose is sufficiently gained, but the melancholy which follows is infinitely greater than can be compensated by the previous exhileration.

Opium acts differently on different constitutions. While it disposes some to calm, it arouses others to fury. Whatever passion predominates at the time, it increases; whether it be love, or hatred, or revenge, or benevolence. Lord Kames, in his Sketches of Man, speaks of the fanatical Faquirs who, when excited by this drug, have been known, with poisoned daggers, to assail and butcher every European whom they could overcome. In the century before last, one of this nation attacked a body of Dutch sailors, and murdered seventeen of them in one minute. The Malays are strongly addicted to opium. When violently aroused by it, they sometimes perform what is called *Running-a-Muck*, which consists in rushing out in a state of phrenzied excitement, heightened by fanaticism, and murdering every one who comes in their way. The Turkish commanders are well aware of the powers of this drug in inspiring an artificial courage; and frequently give it to their men when they put them on any enterprise of great danger.

Some minds are rendered melancholy by opium. Its usual effect, however, is to give rise to lively and happy sensations. The late Duchess of Gordon is said to have used it freely, previous to appearing in great parties, where she wished to shine by the gaiety of her conversation and brilliancy of her wit. A celebrated pleader at the Scotch bar is reported to do the same thing, and always with a happy effect.

* London Magazine, Vols. IV. and VI.

In this country opium is much used, but seldom with the view of producing intoxication. Some, indeed, deny that it can do so, strictly speaking. If by intoxication is meant a state precisely similar to that from over-indulgence in vinous or spirituous liquors, they are undoubtedly right; but drunkenness merits a wider latitude of signification. The ecstacies of opium are much more entrancing than those of wine. There is more poetry in its visions, more mental aggrandisement, more range of imagination. Wine invigorates the animal powers and propensities chiefly, but opium strengthens those peculiar to man, and gives for a period, amounting to hours, a higher tone to the thinking faculties. Then the dreams of the opium-eater—they are the creations of a highly excited fancy, rich and unspeakably delightful. But when the medicine has been continued too long, or operates on a diseased constitution, these feelings wear away. The sleep is no longer cheered with its former visions of happiness. Frightful dreams usurp their place, and the person becomes the victim of an almost perpetual misery.

Opium resembles the other agents of intoxication in this, that the fondness for it increases with use, and that, at last, it becomes nearly essential for bodily comfort and peace of mind. Some will take to the extent of from one to two drachms daily. There are many persons who make a practice of swallowing half an ounce of laudanum night and morning. The "English Opium-Eater" himself, furnishes the most extraordinary instance on record of the power of habit in bringing the body to withstand this drug. He took daily *eight thousand drops* of laudanum, containing *three hundred and twenty grains* of opium. This enormous quantity he reduced suddenly, and without any considerable effort, to *one thousand drops*, or *forty grains*. "Instantaneously," says he, "and as if by magic, the cloud of profoundest melancholy which rested upon my brain, like some black vapours which I have seen roll away from the summits of the mountains, drew off in one day; passed off with its murky banners, as simultaneously as a ship that has been stranded, and is floated off by the spring-tide."

Opium resembles wine, spirits, and ales, in affecting the brain, and disposing to apoplexy. Taken in an overdose, it is fatal in three or four hours. The person is seized with giddiness, and then falls into a stupor, from which it is almost impossible to arouse him. His eyes are closed; his face at first flushed and turgid, afterwards pale and clammy; his pulse slow; his breathing sterterous, and his body convulsed.

I extract the following interesting case of opium-eating from a London paper:

"An inquest was held at Walpole lately, on the body of Rebecca Eason, aged five years, who had been diseased from her birth, was unable to walk or articulate, and, from her size, did not appear to be more than *five weeks* old. The mother had for many years been in the habit of taking opium in large quantities, (nearly a quarter of an ounce a-day;)* and, it is supposed, had entailed a disease on her child which caused its death: it was reduced to a mere skeleton, and had been in

---

* Equal to nearly three thousand drops of laudanum.

that state from birth. Verdict; 'Died by the visitation of God; but from the great quantity of opium taken by the mother during her pregnancy of the said child, and of suckling it, she had greatly injured its health.' It appeared that the mother of the deceased had had five children; that she began to take opium after the birth and weaning of her first child, which was and is remarkably healthy; and that the other children have all lingered and died in the same emaciated state as the child who was the subject of this investigation. The mother is under thirty: she was severely censured by the Coroner for indulging in so pernicious a practice."

Tobacco.—Tobacco, when used to excess, may produce a species of intoxication. It does not give rise to pleasurable ideas. Its effect is principally upon the body, and differs widely from that of any other inebriating agent. Instead of quickening, it lowers the pulse, and produces a general langour and depression of the whole system. Persons often reel and become giddy, as in liquor, from smoking and chewing, and even from snuffing to excess. Excessive sickness and vomiting are consequences of an over-indulgence in tobacco.

Nitrous Oxide.—The drunkenness, if it merit that name, from inhaling nitrous oxide, is likewise of a character widely differing from intoxication in general. This gas was discovered by Dr. Priestley, but its peculiar effects upon the human body were first perceived in 1799, by Sir Humphry Davy, who, in the following year, published a very elaborate account of its nature and properties, interspersed with details by some of the most eminent literary and scientific characters, of the sensations they experienced on receiving it into their lungs.

According to these statements, on breathing the gas the pulse is accelerated, and a feeling of heat and expansion pervades the chest. The most vivid and highly pleasurable ideas pass, at the same time, through the mind; and the imagination is exalted to a pitch of entrancing ecstacy. The hearing is rendered more acute, the face is flushed, and the body seems so light that the person conceives himself capable of rising up and mounting into the air. Some assume theatrical attitudes; others laugh immoderately, and stamp upon the ground. There is an universal increase of muscular power, attended with the most exquisite delight. In a few cases there are melancholy, giddiness, and indistinct vision; but generally the feelings are those of perfect pleasure. After these strange effects have ceased, no debility ensues, like that which commonly follows high excitement. On the contrary, the mind is strong and collected, and the body unusually vigorous for some hours after the operation.

At the time of the discovery of the effects of nitrous oxide, strong hopes were excited that it might prove useful in various diseases. These, unfortunately, have not been realized. Even the alleged properties of the gas have now fallen into some discredit. That it has produced remarkable effects, cannot be denied, but there is much reason for thinking that, in many cases, these were principally brought about by the influence of imagination. Philosophers seem to be divided on this point, and their conflicting testimonies I do not pretend to reconcile. My own opinion is, that there must be some truth in its reported attributes; but that by the power of fancy these attributes have been grossly, though unintentionally, exaggerated. If the statements first published concerning it be true, the intoxication it produces is entirely one *sui generis*, and differs so much from that produced by other agents, that it can hardly be looked upon as the same thing.

Differences in the action of opium & spirits

THE *modus operandi* of opium upon the body is considerably different from that of alcohol. The last acts principally upon the nerves; the first principally by absorption. This is easily proved by injecting a quantity of each into the cellular tissue of any animal, and comparing the effects with those produced when either is received into the stomach. M. Orfila* details some interesting experiments which he made upon dogs. In applying the watery extract of opium to them in the first manner, (by injection into the cellular tissue,) immediate stupor, convulsions, and debility ensued, and proved fatal in an hour or two. When, on the contrary, even a larger quantity was introduced into the stomach of the animal, it survived ten, twelve, or eighteen hours, although the œsophagus was purposely tied to prevent vomiting. The operation of alcohol was the reverse of this; for, when injected into the cellular substance, the effects were slight; but when carried into the stomach, they were powerful and almost instantaneous. This proves that opium acts chiefly by being taken up by the absorbents, as this is done much more rapidly by the drug being directly applied to a raw surface than in the stomach, where the various secretions and processes of digestion retard its agency. Besides, alcohol taken in quantity produces instant stupefaction. It is no sooner swallowed than the person drops down insensible. Here is no time for absorption: the whole energies of the spirit are exerted against the nervous system. The same rapid privation of power never occurs after swallowing opium. There is always an interval, and generally one of some extent, between the swallowing and the stupor which succeeds. Another proof that opium acts in this manner is the circumstance of its being much more speedily fatal than the other, when injected into the blood-vessels. Three or four grains in solution, forced into the carotid artery of a dog, will kill him in a few minutes. Alcohol, used in the same manner, would not bring on death for several hours.

In addition, it may be stated that a species of drunkenness is produced by inhaling the gas of intoxicating liquors. Those employed in bottling spirits from the cask, feel it frequently with great severity. This proves that there is a close sympathy between the nerves of the nose and lungs, and those of the stomach. From all

---

* Toxicologie Générale.

ANATOMY OF DRUNKENNESS: AN INAUGURAL ESSAY

these circumstances it is pretty evident that intoxication from spirits is produced more by the action of the fluid upon the nerves of the latter organ, than by absorption; an additional proof of which is afforded in the fact, that vomiting does not cure drunkenness, even when had recourse to at an early period; its only effect is to prevent it from getting worse.

Dr. Brodie supposes that there is no absorption whatever, and supports his views with a number of striking facts. His arguments, however, are opposed to the general laws of the animal economy, and can hardly be admitted. There can be little doubt that absorption to a considerable extent does take place. Not only the breath, but the blood of a drunkard is different from that of another man. The former, Dr. Trotter* supposes, is influenced by some chemical change. Alcohol is supposed to de-oxygenize the blood, by which means the latter gives out in respiration an unusual quantity of hydrogen gas. The quantity of this gas in the body of drunkards is so great, that many have attempted to explain from it the phenomena of *spontaneous combustion*, by which, it is alleged, the body has been sometimes destroyed and burned to ashes.

---

* Essay on Drunkenness.

Part 5

THE VIRTUES OF DRINK

15

ERASMUS DARWIN, 'ON DRUNKENNESS', *ZOONOMIA; OR THE LAWS OF ORGANIC LIFE* (FOURTH AMERICAN EDITION, 1818), PP. 191–197

1. *Sleep from satiety of hunger. From rocking children. From uniform sounds. 2. Intoxication from common food after fatigue and inanition. 3. From wine or opium. Chilness after meals. Vertigo. Why pleasure is produced by intoxication, and by swinging and rocking children. And why pain is relieved by it. 4. Why drunkards stagger and stammer, and are liable to weep. 5. And become delirious, sleepy, and stupid. 6. Or make pale urine and vomit. 7. Objects are seen double. 8. Attention of the mind diminishes drunkenness. 9. Disordered irritative motions of all the senses. 10. Diseases from drunkenness. 11. Definition of drunkenness.*

1. In the state of nature when the sense of hunger is appeased by the stimulus of agreeable food, the business of the day is over, and the human savage is at peace with the world, he then exerts little attention to external objects, pleasing reveries of imagination succeed, and at length sleep is the result: till the nourishment which he has procured, is carried over every part of the system to repair the injuries of action, and he awakens with fresh vigour, and feels a renewal of his sense of hunger.

The juices of some bitter vegetables, as of the poppy and the laurocerasus, and the ardent spirit produced in the fermentation of the sugar found in vegetable juices, are so agreeable to the nerves of the stomach, that, taken in a small quantity, they instantly pacify the sense of hunger; and the inattention to external stimuli with the reveries of imagination, and sleep succeeds, in the same manner as when the stomach is filled with other less intoxicating food.

This inattention to the irritative motions occasioned by external stimuli is a very important circumstance in the approach of sleep, and is produced in young children by rocking their cradles; during which all visible objects become indistinct to them. An uniform soft repeated sound, as the murmurs of a gentle current,

THE VIRTUES OF DRINK

or of bees, are said to produce the same effect, by presenting indistinct ideas of inconsequential sounds, and by thus stealing our attention from other objects; whilst by their continued reiterations they become familiar themselves, and we cease gradually to attend to any thing, and sleep ensues.

2. After great fatigue or inanition, when the stomach is suddenly filled with flesh and vegetable food, the inattention to external stimuli, and the reveries of imagination, become so conspicuous as to amount to a degree of intoxication. The same is at any time produced by superadding a little wine or opium to our common meals; or by taking these separately in considerable quantity; and this more efficaciously after fatigue or inanition; because a less quantity of any stimulating material will excite an organ into energetic action, after it has lately been torpid from defect of stimulus; as objects appear more luminous, after we have been in the dark; and because the suspension of volition, which is the immediate cause of sleep, is sooner induced, after a cotinued voluntary exertion has in part exhausted the sensorial power of volition; in the same manner as we cannot contract a single muscle long together without intervals of inaction.

3. In the beginning of intoxication we are inclined to sleep, as mentioned above, but by the excitement of external circumstances, as of noise, light, business, or by the exertion of volition, we prevent the approaches of it, and continue to take into our stomach greater quantities of the inebriating materials. By these means the irritative movements of the stomach are excited into greater action than is natural; and in consequence all the irritative tribes and trains of motion, which are catenated with them, become susceptible of stronger action from their accustomed stimuli; because these motions are excited both by their usual irritation, and by their association with the increased actions of the stomach and lacteals. Hence the skin glows, and the heat of the body is increased, by the more energetic action of the whole glandular system; and pleasure is introduced in consequence of these increased motions from internal stimulus. According to Law 5. Sect. IV. on Animal Causation.

From this great increase of irritative motions from internal stimulus, and the increased sensation introduced into the system in consequence; and secondly, from the increased sensitive motions in consequence of this additional quantity of sensation, so much sensorial power is expended, that the voluntary power becomes feebly exerted, and the irritation from the stimulus of external objects is less forcible; the external parts of the eye are not therefore voluntarily adapted to the distances of objects, whence the apparent motions of those objects either are seen double, or become too indistinct for the purpose of balancing the body, and vertigo is induced.

Hence we become acquainted with that very curious circumstance, why the drunken vertigo is attended with an increase of pleasure; for the irritative ideas and motions occasioned by internal stimulus, that were not attended to in our sober hours, are now just so much increased as to be succeeded by pleasurable sensation, in the same manner as the more violent motions of our organs are succeeded by painful sensation. And hence a greater quantity of pleasurable sensation is introduced into the constitution; which is attended in some people with an increase of benevolence and good humour.

If the apparent motions of objects is much increased, as when we revolve on one foot, or are swung on a rope, the ideas of these apparent motions are also attended to, and are succeeded with pleasurable sensation, till they become familiar to us by frequent use. Hence children are at first delighted with these kinds of exercise, and with riding, and sailing, and hence rocking young children inclines them to sleep. For though in the vertigo from intoxication the irritative ideas of the apparent motions of objects are indistinct from their decrease of energy; yet in the vertigo occasioned by rocking or swinging, the irritative ideas of the apparent motions of objects are increased in energy, and hence they induce pleasure into the system, but are equally indistinct, and in consequence equally unfit to balance ourselves by. This addition of pleasure precludes desire or aversion, and in consequence the voluntary power is feebly exerted, and on this account, rocking young children inclines them to sleep.

In what manner opium and wine act in relieving pain is another article, that well deserves our attention. There are many pains that originate from defect as well as from excess of stimulus; of these are those of the six appetites of hunger, thirst, lust, the want of heat, of distention, and of fresh air. Thus if our cutaneous capillaries cease to act from the diminished stimulus of heat, when we are exposed to cold weather, or our stomach is uneasy for want of food; these are both pains from defect of stimulus, and in consequence, opium, which stimulates all the moving system into increased action, must relieve them. But this is not the case in those pains which arise from excess of stimulus, as in violent inflammations: in these the exhibition of opium is frequently injurious by increasing the action of the system already too great, as in inflammations of the bowels mortification is often produced by the stimulus of opium. Where, however, no such bad consequences follow, the stimulus of opium, by increasing all the motions of the system, expends so much of the sensorial power, that the actions of the whole system soon become feebler, and in consequence those which produced the pain and inflammation.

4. When intoxication proceeds a little further, the quantity of pleasurable sensation is so far increased, that all desire ceases, for there is no pain in the system to excite it. Hence the voluntary exertions are diminished, staggering and stammering succeed; and the trains of ideas become more and more inconsistent from this defect of voluntary exertion, as explained in the sections on sleep and reverie, whilst those passions which are unmixed with volition are more vividly felt, and shewn with less reserve; hence pining love, or superstitious fear, and the maudling tear dropped on the remembrance of the most trifling distress.

5. At length all these circumstances are increased; the quantity of pleasure introduced into the system by the increased irritative muscular motion of the whole sanguiferous, and glandular, and absorbent systems, becomes so great, that the organs of sense are more forcibly excited into action by this internal

THE VIRTUES OF DRINK

pleasurable sensation, than by the irritation from the stimulus of external objects. Hence the drunkard ceases to attend to external stimuli, and as volition is now also suspended, the trains of his ideas become totally inconsistent as in dreams, or delirium: and at length a stupor succeeds from the great exhaustion of sensorial power, which probably does not even admit of dreams, and in which, as in apoplexy, no motions continue but those from internal stimuli, from sensation, and from association.

6. In other people a paroxysm of drunkenness has another termination; the inebriate, as soon as he begins to be vertiginous, makes pale urine in great quantities and very frequently, and at length becomes sick, vomits repeatedly, or purges, or has profuse sweats, and a temporary fever ensues with a quick strong pulse. This in some hours is succeeded by sleep; but the unfortunate bacchanalian does not perfectly recover himself till about the same time of the succeeding day, when his course of inebriation began. As shewn in Sect. XVII. 1. 7. on Catenation. The temporary fever with strong pulse is owing to the same cause as the glow on the skin mentioned in the third paragraph of this Section: the flow of urine and sickness arises from the whole system of irritative motions being thrown into confusion by their associations with each other as in sea-sickness, mentioned in Sect. XX. 4. on Vertigo; and which is more fully explained in Section XXIX. on Diabetes.

7. In this vertigo from internal causes we see objects double, as two candles instead of one, which is thus explained. Two lines drawn through the axis of our two eyes meet at the object we attend to: this angle of the optic axis increases or diminishes with the less or greater distances of objects. All objects before or behind the place where this angle is formed, appear double; as any one may observe by holding up a pen between his eyes and the candle; when he looks attentively at a spot on the pen, and carelessly at the candle, it will appear double; and the reverse when he looks attentively at the candle and carelessly at the pen; so that in this case the muscles of the eye, like those of the limbs, stagger, and are disobedient to the expiring efforts of volition. Numerous objects are indeed sometimes seen by the inebriate, occasioned by the refractions made by the tears, which stand upon his eye-lids.

8. This vertigo also continues, when the inebriate lies in his bed, in the dark, or with his eyes closed; and this more powerfully than when he is erect, and in the light. For the irritative ideas of the apparent motions of objects are now excited by irritation from internal stimulus, or by association with other irritative motions; and the inebriate, like one in a dream, believes the objects of these irritative motions to be present, and feels himself vertiginous. I have observed in this situation, so long as my eyes and mind were intent upon a book, the sickness and vertigo ceased, and were renewed again the moment I discontinued this attention; as was explained in the preceding account of sea-sickness. Some drunken people have been known to become sober instantly from some accident, that has strongly excited their attention, as the pain of a broken bone, or the news of their house being on fire.

9. Sometimes the vertigo from internal causes, as from intoxication, or at the beginning of some fevers, becomes so universal, that the irritative motions which

belong to other organs of sense are succeeded by sensation or attention, as well as those of the eye. The vertiginous noise in the ears has been explained in Section XX on Vertigo. The taste of the saliva which in general is not attended to, becomes perceptible, and the patients complain of a bad taste in their mouth.

The common smells of the surrounding air sometimes excite the attention of these patients, and bad smells are complained of, which to other people are imperceptible. The irritative motions that belong to the sense of pressure, or of touch, are attended to, and the patient conceives the bed to librate, and is fearful of falling out of it. The irritative motions belonging to the senses of distention, and of heat, like those above mentioned, become attended to at this time; hence we feel the pulsation of our arteries all over us, and complain of heat, or of cold, in parts of the body where there is no accumulation or diminution of actual heat. All which are to be explained, as in the last paragraph, by the irritative ideas belonging to the various senses being now excited by internal stimuli, or by their associations with other irritative motions. And that the inebriate, like one in a dream, believes the external objects, which usually caused these irritative ideas, to be now present.

10. The diseases in consequence of frequent inebriety, or of daily taking much vinous spirit without inebriety, consist in the paralysis, which is liable to succeed violent stimulation. Organs, whose actions are associated with others, are frequently more affected than the organ which is stimulated into too violent action. See Sect. XXIV. 2. 8. Hence in drunken people it generally happens, that the secretory vessels of the liver become first paralytic, and a torpor with consequent gall-stones or scirrhus of this viscus is induced with concomitant jaundice; otherwise it becomes inflamed in consequence of previous torpor, and this inflammation is frequently transferred to a more sensible part, which is associated with it, and produces the gout, or the rosy eruption of the face, or some other leprous eruption on the head, or arms, or legs. Sometimes the stomach is first affected, and paralysis of the lacteal system is induced: whence a total abhorrence from flesh-food, and general emaciation. In others the lymphatic system is affected with paralysis, and dropsy is the consequence. In some inebriates the torpor of the liver produces pain without apparent scirrhus, or gall-stones, or inflammation, or consequent gout, and in these epilepsy or insanity is often the consequence. All which will be more fully treated of in the course of the work.

I am well aware that it is a common opinion, that the gout is as frequently owing to gluttony in eating, as to intemperance in drinking fermented or spirituous liquors. To this I answer, that I have seen no person afflicted with the gout, who has not drunk freely of fermented liquor, as wine and water, or small beer; though as the disposition to all the diseases, which have originated from intoxication, is in some degree hereditary, a less quantity of spirituous potation will induce the gout in these, who inherit the disposition from their parents. To which I must add, that in young people the rheumatism is frequently mistaken for the gout.

Spice is seldom taken in such quantity as to do any material injury to the system; flesh-meats as well as vegetables are the natural diet of mankind; with these a glutton may be crammed up to the throat, and fed fat like a stalled ox; but he

THE VIRTUES OF DRINK

will not be diseased, unless he adds spirituous or fermented liquor to his food. This is well known in the distilleries, where the swine, which are fattened by the spirituous sediments of barrels, acquire diseased livers. But mark what happens to a man, who drinks a quart of wine or of ale, if he has not been habituated to it. He loses the use of both his limbs and of his understanding! He becomes a temporary idiot, and has a temporary stroke of the palsy! And though he slowly recovers after some hours, is it not reasonable to conclude, that a perpetual repetition of so powerful a poison must at length permanently affect him?—If a person accidentally becomes intoxicated by eating a few mushrooms of a peculiar kind, a general alarm is excited, and he is said to be poisoned, and emetics are exhibited; but so familiarised are we to the intoxication from vinous spirit, that it occasions laughter rather than alarm.

There is however considerable danger in too hastily discontinuing the use of so strong a stimulus, lest the torpor of the system, or paralysis, should sooner be induced by the omission than by the continuance of this habit, when unfortunately acquired. A golden rule for determining the quantity, which may with safety be discontinued, is delivered in Sect. XII. 7. 8.

1. Definition of drunkenness. Many of the irritative motions are much increased in energy by internal stimulation.

2. A great additional quantity of pleasurable sensation is occasioned by this increased exertion of the irritative motions. And many sensitive motions are produced in consequence of this increased sensation.

3. The associated trains and tribes of motions, catenated with the increased irritative and sensitive motions, are disturbed, and proceed in confusion.

4. The faculty of volition is gradually impaired, whence proceed the instability of locomotion, inaccuracy of perception, and inconsistency of ideas; and is at length totally suspended, and a temporary apoplexy succeeds.

16

EDWARD CUTBUSH, *OBSERVATIONS ON THE MEANS OF PRESERVING THE HEALTH OF SOLDIERS AND SAILORS* (PHILADELPHIA: THOMAS DOBSON, 1808), PP. 22–30

On the subsistence of troops

Drinks

WATER is generally the principal drink of soldiers, serving likewise for the preparation of their food and other purposes; that which is lively and agreeable, transparent and without odour, which boils beans or peas readily and dissolves soap without curdling, should be preferred. Water that is most pure and healthy is that which has been agitated and combined with the air of the atmosphere; water from dissolved snow is not considered healthful. Of the different waters those from rivers, or from sources, which are limpid and running, are the most salutary and agreeable. Care should be taken to use those only that are perfectly free from impurities. Limpid waters issuing from mountains, rocks or high lands, composed of clean earth and gravel, are very proper for *common use* provided they be not impregnated with any *mineral substances*. Waters of lakes and ponds* have long been considered prejudicial to health, unless they are frequently renewed from their source. Marshy and stagnant waters are extremely pernicious and should never be used unless necessity absolutely require it, and then some mode of purifying them should be adopted; in fact the same should be practised when river water is muddy or otherwise filled with impurities. Muddy water may be cleansed by adding two or three grains of alum to each pint; if hard, it may be rendered soft by adding ten grains of alcali to every pint. Chalk may also be used for the same purpose. There have been various means adopted for the correction of the pernicious effects of impure water. Some recommend frequent agitation in a trough with the bough of a tree, and then suffering it to settle; others propose filtering it through a sponge placed in the bottom of a cask. Portius proposes

---

* Nec perniciosis vel paludosis aquis utatur exercitus. Vigetius.

233

THE VIRTUES OF DRINK

straining it through sand. Dr. Lind's plan is very simple: he directs a cask of a large diameter to be procured with one head out, in which, another of less diameter, but longer and with both heads taken out, is to be fixed; about one half of the inner cask is to be filled up with clean sand and the *space* between the casks is also to be filled one third of its height, with sand; the casks are then prepared for filtering. Fill the cavity of the *inner cask* with the impure water, it will filter through the sand and rise in the space between the inner and outer casks; from whence it may be drawn off into vessels placed to receive it, by means of a cock put into the side of the outer cask about fifteen or twenty inches above the level of the sand. The water may be permitted to run into a fosse about three or four feet in depth, the bottom and sides of which should be covered with stones and gravel. Each man who carries water from the fosse should be obliged to fill up the filtering cask from the lake or pond, by this plan there will be a continual supply of water *to drink*. As casks cannot always be procured, a large box or trunk may be constructed by the artificers in camp. But if circumstances absolutely oblige troops to use stagnant water, it may be rendered less noxious by pouring it frequently from one vessel into another, or by infusing a small quantity of calamus aromaticus in it, which may be found in most swampy situations; it will give a bitter taste to the water but will make it more healthful. Water from marshy situations ought to be boiled, to kill the animalcula which it contains, and then strained and passed through a cullender or camp kettle pierced with a number of small holes to render it brisker by its union with the air of the atmosphere. Vinegar may sometimes be added with advantage. Though ill effects are produced by an excess in the use of water, yet, if drunk in moderation, it assists digestion, quenches thirst and is almost a universal vehicle for solid food; it dilutes the fluids, corrects acrimony, promotes perspiration and the secretions. It is consequently an article of primary importance.

Although we have said that water is the principal drink of soldiers, yet we do not find that they use it when other articles can be procured. Their choice of drink depending very much on the country where they serve; the ration of spirits is seldom sufficient to gratify their appetites; which are too often governed by the price of the article, consequently they frequently purchase pernicious whiskey or rum, fresh from the still, because it is cheap, to the great injury of their constitutions. As I do not, in these instructions, contemplate the employment of troops out of the United States, I shall confine my remarks to such articles as soldiers readily procure, viz. whiskey, beer, cider and the compound called cider-royal.

Whiskey is made from grain of different kinds, such as barley, wheat, rye, oats, buck-wheat and Indian corn; also from apples, peaches and many other articles. Rye, wheat, apples and peaches are more commonly used for distillation in the United States; all of which give to the spirit more or less of their odour, owing to the phlegm and essential oil which come over during the distillation. That spirit which possesses the flavour of the apple and peach has a great many admirers,

234

when it is old. But that which is drawn from grain, when new, is extremely nauseous to those, who are unaccustomed to its use. Like all other ardent spirits, when used to excess, it is attended by a train of consequences highly pernicious to the constitution. It is true that the stomach will, by degrees, become accustomed to the use of ardent spirits, and will at length bear the most pungent or fiery, without feeling immediately their effects; but they operate like a secret enemy, the stomach will be deprived of its natural functions, the appetite for solid food impaired, the nervous system and intellectual faculties will be assailed. Obstructions of the liver and viscera, swelled legs with ulcers, dropsy and convulsions will too frequently be the fatal consequences of a liberal use of this *"liquid fire."* Whoever has attended to the effects of spirituous liquors, when used to excess, especially among those, who use the worst quality, must have witnessed the whole or part of these baneful consequences. Within a few days past, I have seen a case of hæmorrhagy from the intestines brought on I am confident by the free use of *new whiskey.*

The practice of issuing whiskey in an undiluted state to soldiers in garrisons ought to be abolished; few men take the trouble to preserve it to use at their meals; the allowance is swallowed, though they are apprised of the pernicious consequences. Soldiers are like children in many respects; it therefore becomes the duty of their commanders to see that they do not abuse their constitutions by excesses. Were I to indulge myself in enumerating all the pernicious consequences of new rum or whiskey, on the constitutions and *morals* of soldiers, I should enlarge this part of the subject beyond the limits I have proposed; I will therefore conclude by observing that the effects which have already been noticed ought to point out the necessity of enforcing the penalties attached to drunkenness by the acts of congress for the government of the army.

Cider

Cider furnishes an agreeable and healthy beverage, nourishing and refreshing; it excites a pleasant warmth in the stomach and is free from the pernicious effects we have noticed above. It should be perfectly sound and well refined. But when recently made and used in immoderate quantities, it occasions flatulence, colic, or diarrhœa. To remedy these a teaspoonful of powdered ginger may be added occasionally to every quart, or a heated iron may be plunged into it; this is a common practice in the northern parts of the United States.

Cider-royal

This is an article of which I have very little knowledge; but am informed that it is cider boiled with ardent spirits; it is a very insidious drink, which quickly produces intoxication; and therefore improper to use without being diluted with water. Its use is common in most of the German settlements of Pennsylvania.

THE VIRTUES OF DRINK

Beer

It were to be wished, that beer was more commonly used among soldiers in garrisons. I am aware of the difficulty of transporting a sufficient quantity for an army, but in all garrisons on the sea board or in the interior where beer can be procured, it should be issued in lieu of ardent spirits. The beer that I would recommend is not that, which becomes *sour in ten or fifteen* days; it should be made with the proper quantity of *malt* and *hops*, but not with disagreeable bitter herbs; which, though useful as medicines, will be disgusting to soldiers in health; neither should it contain any article to make it "*heady*," (Cocculus Indicus for example.) It should be sound and well depurated from feculent matter, and have a sufficient quantity of hops to preserve it.

An extract might be made from malt and hops, which would facilitate the brewing of beer, would be very proper for garrisons, and might be conveniently transported to all parts of the United States. Care should be taken in evaporating the infusion of these articles that the extract may not be burnt; a *water bath* should therefore be used for this purpose. The extract from six bushels of barley malted and two or three pounds of hops would be sufficient for two hogsheads of beer. The yeast for fermenting may be preserved by drying it on a board, layer after layer, until it be an inch thick, when it may be cut into squares and preserved in a tight vessel for use.

Beer when properly made is very healthful and nourishing, but when *too new* it is apt to produce flatulency and colic. Should it become tart in the summer season (which will seldom be the case when there is a proper quantity of hops used) the addition of an alcalic or chalk will correct it; the former I have seen used frequently in the West Indies, among porter drinkers.*

---

* "Heureux les régimens qui tombent dans un pays à bière."

17

FRANCIS E. ANSTIE, *ON THE USES OF WINES IN HEALTH AND DISEASE* (NEW YORK: J. S. REDFIELD, 1870), PP. 7–48

Part I

On the place of wines in the diet of ordinary life

In approaching the subject of the uses of Wines in health and in disease, we must briefly define the intended scope of our inquiry, in order to avoid misunderstandings. In the first place, it is no part of our object to discuss the question of the lawfulness or the advisability of using alcoholic liquors in general, either as food or as medicine; we shall take it as established, both by wide-spread custom and by the most recent physiological research, that alcohol, as such, has its legitimate place in the sustentation both of the healthy and of the diseased organism. Nor shall we occupy space with the re-assertion of the doctrine, already repeatedly laid down in the pages of this journal,* of the absolutely different effects respectively produced by the moderate and by the excessive use of this class of drinks.

It is our intention to deal specially with Wines as such; to show that the whole group of these beverages has common properties and uses that separate it from other alcoholic liquids, and further, that among wines themselves there are very numerous differences, of which many are probably not yet understood either by the public or even by the majority of medical men. We can hardly be mistaken in the latter assertion, sweeping though it seems; since not only is it common to meet with invalids and others who have received diametrically opposite directions as to the choice of beverages from different practitioners of equal standing, but we have observed after a pretty close study of this subject, extending over more than thirteen years, that hasty generalizations, which will not bear sifting, are almost as common in the pages of recent as of older writers on this topic.

---

* The Practitioner—London and New York.—Macmillan.

THE VIRTUES OF DRINK

One part of our knowledge has, indeed, of late made solid, though limited advances—viz., the chemistry of wines. But the far wider question of their choice and practical uses is still in the most uncertain state; and it must be confessed that recent literature on the subject, though it may have cleared away some gross misconceptions, has almost neutralized this benefit by fostering the growth of new prejudices which are scarcely less unfounded than the old ones. And there is one aspect of the new discussions upon which, though we would willingly ignore it, our duty compels us to animadvert with plainness; we mean the influence of commercial motives. We are not imputing conscious dishonesty to the writers even of the most objectionable of the many trade circulars which have been published under the guise of scientific pamphlets on wine; but it is only too obvious to those who are at all behind the scenes that commercial bias has in several instances assisted powerfully in the development of exclusive dogmas which, from a scientific standpoint, must be regarded as capricious and absurd.

It may perhaps be necessary, hereafter, to illustrate this with some particularity; at present it will be enough to adduce an instance which is so common that our criticism of it can scarcely inflict the sting of personal reproach; we refer to the clamor for the exclusive use of particular "natural" or "unfortified" wines. Doubtless this cry represents a natural, and on the whole a wise, reaction from certain stupid and pernicious routine habits of English life; but it has been largely fostered and exaggerated by traders and by a certain class of scientific men, in a manner which scarcely corresponds with the idea of disinterestedness, unless we are to suppose that their enthusiasm is strongly leavened with ignorance.

To a medical writer on wines there are several inducements to attack the subject first from the side of the medicinal uses of these drinks; the strongest reason being that, from the nature of his daily experience, he is most familiar with this aspect of the question. We prefer, however, to start from the view of wine as a beverage of ordinary life; being persuaded that the subject can only be fairly examined in this way. It is no doubt true, on the one hand, that a complete statement of the physiological action of wines cannot, in the present state of science, be given; and, on the other hand, it may be urged that if empirical experience is to be our guide, the circumstances of sickness offer a guarantee for closer and more accurate observation of the phenomena than can be expected when wines are used as a mere beverage of the healthy. To this argument we believe there is one conclusive reply—that there is no such clear line between health and disease as is assumed in common speech; that the foreshadowings and faint images of disease are to be seen in sundry incidents of the life of those who are conventionally regarded as healthy; and that it is in the study of these "natural diseases" (if we may use such a phrase), and their relations to the dietary remedies which general custom, independently of medical authority, has prescribed for them, that we are most likely to discover a reasonable basis for the use of these remedies in diseases which involve extensive and obvious departures from the standard of health. It need scarcely be said that alcoholic drinks, rightly or wrongly, are the commonest of all household remedies for a large number of paltry ailments; and one of the first things which we wish

238

to demonstrate is the prominent fitness of wines, above other alcoholic drinks, for all legitimate purposes of this kind. Accordingly, we shall in the first place very simply sum up the composition of wines, as a class; and also the main distinctions between the principal kinds.

I. In the first place, we have to consider wines as alcoholic fluids; and we must remind our readers of the elementary facts as to their relative strengths as compared with each other, and with other kinds of alcoholic drinks. It will be enough for the present to say that the *strong* wines, including port, sherry, Madeira, Marsala, and all that genus, contain on the average something like 17 per cent. of absolute alcohol (the strongest ports ranging as high as 23 per cent. or more), and that the *light* wines, including claret, burgundy, champagne, Rhine and Moselle wines, Hungarian wines, &c., average between 10 and 11 per cent. of absolute alcohol (the lightest champagnes not containing more than 5 or 6 per cent.). Comparing wines with beers, we may note that the poorest sorts of beer contain about 2 per cent. of absolute alcohol; ordinary table ale, as drunk in most middle-class households, about 3 per cent.; ordinary porter between 3 and 4 per cent.; stout from 5 to 6 per cent.; while the strongest kinds of malt liquors range through various degrees up to even 10 per cent.; and a common strength for good bottled ale or stout is about 7 per cent. of absolute alcohol. On the other hand, good brandies and rum average between 45 and 50 per cent.

The above rough averages are only drawn with a view to place before the reader a standard of comparison by the help of which he may realize somewhat more accurately than is usually done, even by medical men, the comparative alcoholic potency of beverages which are so commonly recommended in an off-hand and careless fashion. For instance, let us take the very common case of a lady, not exactly ill, but delicate, and "needing generous living," who takes "three or four glasses of port wine a day." Now, it need hardly be said that wine-glasses vary greatly in size, and that of late years there has been a marked tendency to make them larger than formerly; but we will take the moderate average of two ounces for a port glass: then four of these will contain 8 ounces of wine, which, on the supposition that the liquor is of a fair age and quality, will represent 1½ ounces of absolute alcohol, or the alcoholic equivalent of 50 ounces (five large tumblers) of table-beer, or three ounces of good brandy, or two-thirds of a bottle of a generous claret or Rhine wine. Or to put the comparison in another practical form (still avoiding the nuisance of a dry tabular statement) we may say that a bottle of twelve glasses of average port is equal, in alcoholic strength, to rather less than half a bottle of brandy, or two bottles of good claret or hock, or nearly a gallon of table-beer or of light champagne.

Now, it would be easy to make a somewhat sensational point, by showing that the by no means unusual allowance for ladies who are at all "delicate" of two glasses of port or sherry at lunch, and the same quantity at dinner daily, makes up the alcoholic equivalent of a bottle of brandy every week, which looks rather shocking on paper. But apart from the question whether such an allowance is excessive or not, we would insist on the value of this kind of comparison, as

THE VIRTUES OF DRINK

tending to show very distinctly that the place of the stronger wines is rather among the cordials, to be used under express and careful medical sanction, than among the beverages of common life, since it is plain that a very little carelessness in their use may lead to actual excess. The daily allowance above mentioned includes an amount of absolute alcohol which our own experimental researches have shown to be about the limit of what can be habitually taken by persons leading a not very active life, without provoking symptoms of chronic malaise indicative of actual alcoholic poisoning.

It is otherwise with the class of light wines, speaking in the broadest sense; wines, namely, that average no more than ten per cent. of alcoholic strength. So far as alcoholic strength is concerned it may be said in general terms, that half a bottle a day of such wine for a sedentary, and a bottle a day for a vigorous and actively employed adult, affords a reasonable and prudent allowance of alcohol; and this quantity of wine, either alone or with water, will be enough to satisfy the needs of moderate persons for a beverage at lunch and dinner, the only two meals at which alcohol should, as a rule, be taken.

We have put this question of the absolute alcoholic allowance for healthy adults in a somewhat crude and abstract form, not undesignedly; for we wish to compel the upper and middle classes, and their medical advisers, to look the facts of alcoholic consumption honestly in the face. No one who is at all conversant with the habits of the wine-drinking classes will deny that such a daily allowance of alcohol as we have above mentioned is distinctly within the average consumption of persons of moderate habits as the ways of society go; and indeed we fear that a good many persons will characterize it as utopian in its standard of temperance. It is therefore well to remember, that the same quantity of alcohol, represented in beer, makes up between two and three pints; and that a laboring man who exceeded this daily allowance would certainly fall under the ban of conventional moralists as "intemperate."

It would probably be a surprise to many worthy philanthropists, if they chance to read this paper, to find themselves placed so nearly on a level with Hodge the carter, who reprehensibly fuddles himself with "t' other pint." But in fact the matter is stronger than this: and for once we must beg leave to drop the conventional theory of educated manners, and describe plain facts. It is true that there has been a real advance towards temperance of late years, and that intoxication has become a monstrous exception among the cultivated classes. But we may appeal to any medical man with a knowledge either of metropolitan or of provincial society as to the accuracy of the following computation. We shall admit, in the first place, that there are many men, and very many women, who drink almost no alcohol. But the greater number of men, and a large number of women, of the middle and upper ranks habitually take a daily allowance of alcohol far larger than that above indicated. We purposely leave out of sight the reckless "fast" men who are perpetually "nipping" at bitters or absinthe, or "setting themselves right" with just another "brandy and soda," and also the miserable women—whose numbers none but the doctors even faintly suspect—who indulge in secret dram-drinking.

ON THE USES OF WINES IN HEALTH AND DISEASE

Excluding all such persons from our reckoning, let us merely consider the case of the moderate diners-out, and the virtuous dancing young ladies. The former will certainly take on the average eight ounces of strong wines, and twelve to sixteen of light wines, daily; or he will make up the equivalent of this with beer or with spirits: in fact, he will take about three ounces of absolute alcohol, or the equivalent of about a gallon of the puddle-beer that laborers drink. And the young lady will not take less than three-fourths of this quantity, by the time she has finished her last champagne-cup at the ball or rout. If any one thinks this estimate excessive, we assure him that, were it discreet, we could produce accurate notes of the performances of sundry terpsichorean and otherwise athletic young ladies, of irreproachable character, to which the foregoing facts are a trifle.

It is, in fact, a considerable puzzle to understand, at first, how our respectable classes manage to consume so much more alcohol, without reproach, than the unfortunate Wiltshire clodhopper, for example, can do. No doubt one reason is that their drinks are not muddled with Cocculus indicus, &c., as his is. But no doubt the truth is that the intoxicative, that is the *visibly* poisonous, effects of alcohol are mainly kept at bay by powerful exertion either of the muscular or nervous system: and the wealthy classes to a large extent do task either one or both of these systems far more heavily than laborers, except those employed in some specially fatiguing callings. Nevertheless there is grave danger of excess, were it merely from the multiplication of alcoholic drinks which are taken by the richer classes: and we propose hereafter to show that adherence to one drink, and generally one *wine*, is almost a necessity for the purposes of health.

We have already shown that there is a great tendency in the customs of modern middle and upper-class society to introduce modes of wine-drinking which would easily involve people in habits of alcoholic excess, though such an idea might be far enough from their wishes or intentions.

It is very obvious that the multiplication of alcoholic drinks, with different flavors, each tempting in its turn, must lead the sharer in convivial feasts to forget how much he has already drunk; more especially if (as is usually the case) he has no accurate knowledge of the alcoholic strength of the liquors which he takes. And even in every-day life, it cannot be easy for those who adopt the common plan of drinking at least two, and generally three, separate alcoholic liquors in the course of the day, to regulate their allowance of alcohol with anything like nicety. It is therefore much to be desired that people may be educated in the direction of using only one alcoholic drink; at least for every-day consumption. The choice of this one drink must in each individual case depend upon a number of other considerations besides mere alcoholic strength, and these will be discussed further on; at present we have to point out those drinks which are suitable, in the single matter of strength, to be selected as the only alcoholic beverage.

What we have practically to consider is the possibility of selecting some alcoholic fluid which shall be weak enough—either when taken neat, or with only so much water as will not make it distasteful—to enable us to drink so much of it as will satisfy all needs for fluid at lunch and dinner (or dinner and supper with folk

THE VIRTUES OF DRINK

of early habits), without producing any of the injurious effects of alcohol. Weak beers would, of course, very well fulfil these requirements; for instance, a sound, light table-beer, containing about 3 per cent. of absolute alcohol. But to a large number of persons the quantity of such beer that would satisfy thirst, and also prove sufficiently stimulant, would not be readily digestible; or, if it did not disorder primary digestion, would cause disagreeable after-consequences. Especially to persons of a gouty constitution, such a regimen would be most unwholesome; also to many persons with rheumatic tendencies, on account of the sugar and dextrine which some light beers contain. Beers, again, cannot be mixed with water and retain their agreeable flavor.

It is among the class of natural wines, averaging not more than 10 per cent. of absolute alcohol, that we must seek the type of a universal alcoholic beverage for every-day life. If we turn to the most recent analyses (the very careful work of Dr. A. Dupré, of the Westminster Hospital), we find two kinds of wine which, as far as alcoholic strength is concerned, meet the ideal want—viz., a Rhine wine at 9½ per cent. alcohol, and a claret at 8½ per cent. Such wines are easily procurable, and we may say that we have, in either of them, a beverage which, alone or diluted with a certain amount of water would at once satisfy all needs for liquid with the principal meals, and all needs for alcohol, in the most convenient and agreeable way. A bottle a day of either of these wines for an actively employed adult, and a proportionately less quantity for one whose life is more sedentary, would very well represent the allowance of alcohol which may be said to suit best the standard of ordinary health.

It is quite possible (*experto crede*) to procure in London an admirably sound, ordinary Bordeaux for 12s. a dozen (alcoholic strength 8 to 9 per cent.); but a German wine of anything like equal merit would cost 18s., and the same may be said respecting Hungarian, Burgundian, and Greek wines; other objections will be noticed hereafter.

Practically, then, those who wish to adopt the plan of drinking all their alcohol in the shape of one wine, will probably do best with Bordeaux, which is also, *par excellence*, the wine which may be mixed with water (of course we speak of the humbler growths) without spoiling. We maintain that for the hard-working student,*

---

* We do not intend, when recommending the "hard-working *student*" to allow himself a bottle per diem of weak Bordeaux wine, to give that recommendation to young lads. We are thinking of "hard-working students" of middle age; and we would state our very firm conviction, that for youths (say under 25) whose bodily frame is as yet not fully consolidated, the proper rule is, *either no alcohol or very little indeed.*

From the time of puberty onwards, there arises a much greater susceptibility to the injurious influences of alcohol upon the emotions and the character; and between the date of puberty and the age of 25, or even 30, it would be better in ordinary cases, either to abstain altogether, or to limit the allowance to one-third or one-half the amount above named. Still, there can be no question that to many rapidly-growing lads an amount of alcohol (preferably as beer) strictly limited to these latter qualities is not only harmless but most actively useful.

politician, professional man, or busy merchant, there is no better arrangement possible than that of taking, as the regular daily allowance, a bottle of sound ordinary wine of Bordeaux; and that the number of persons with whom such a diet really disagrees is very limited; but on the latter point we shall have more to say hereafter, in discussing the other ingredients of wines. It may be added that no other wines which the world produces are capable of yielding, day after day, such unwearied pleasure to the palate, as the sound ordinary wines of Bordeaux and of the Rhine.

While, however, we vindicate, for the light, natural wines, the position of the best common alcoholic drink for healthy adults, we have some remarks to make on certain more limited and occasional uses of wines, which embody ideas not commonly received by the profession. We refer to the employment of the stronger wines, such as port, sherry, madeira, or marsala, all of which are fortified by the addition of alcohol over and above that produced by their own fermentation.

It is a common idea that the stronger wines are particularly suited to healthy adult life, and especially to middle age; but we believe that this is a complete mistake. The vigorous frame and perfect digestion of a healthy young or middle-aged person requires but a moderate daily allowance of alcohol to assist functional activity; and as, nevertheless, the temptation to free indulgence in the pleasures of the table is most influential in the middle period of life, it is of the greatest consequence that the alcohol should be taken in the most diluted forms: and we may add that this is especially necessary for persons (particularly women) who possess a nervous temperament, and are, therefore, highly sensitive to strong and pleasing impressions on the nervous system. It is otherwise with the two extremes of life—infancy and old age; in both these periods there are tendencies to a variety of afflictions which scarcely appear to deserve the name of positive disease, but which demand serious modifications of the diet; these conditions may, we affirm, be far more advantageously treated by the administration of the *stronger wines* than by any other means whatever. We shall defer the full consideration of this subject till we come to speak of the ethereal constituents of wine, which count for at least an equal, if not a greater, value than that of the alcohol in this particular use of the stronger wines, more especially of sherry.

II. Sugar is the next ingredient of wines which we have to consider in the selection of appropriate beverages for persons in ordinary health; and here we get a forcible illustration of the maxim laid down in a former page, that "health" is not a constant and uniform thing, capable of being separated by a sharp line from "disease:" for there are the greatest possible differences between the respective capability of different persons, equally healthy in appearance, to digest saccharine wines.

The respective proportions in which the various classes of wines contain sugar cannot, of course, be stated in a summary manner, sugar being precisely the most varying element. Given a wine made from a certain grape, and under certain climatic conditions, then, of course, the amount of sugar which it actually contains when drunk will depend, (1) on the degree of completeness to

THE VIRTUES OF DRINK

which fermentation was allowed to proceed in the wine-making; and (2) on the age of the wine. Taking the matter broadly, it may be said that the natural wines are the non-saccharine, and the fortified wines are saccharine; though there are important exceptions to this which must be specially mentioned. Here are the results of Dr. Dupré's analyses of four clarets (red Bordeaux), of the respective prices of 12*s*., 15*s*., 30*s*., and 66*s*. per doz.: the first contained 13·56 grains of sugar in the bottle, the second 51·62 grains, the third 18·48 grains, and the fourth (an old bottled wine) 11·40 grains. Contrast with this the same chemist's analyses of four sherries, prices respectively 22*s*., 36*s*., "high" and "high," the two last being wines of good vintage, and some years in bottle: the quantities of sugar are, 307·8 grains, 217·2 grains, 356·4 grains, and 421·2 grains per bottle, respectively. Take also the analyses of four ports (vintages 1864, 1851, 1851, and 1842): the quantities of sugar per bottle are 519·72 grains, 460·80 grains, 190·20 grains, and 121·20 grains. Two samples of marsala (old and good) contained 388·8 and 451·2 grains of sugar per bottle, respectively. The natural wines of the Rhine, on the other hand, contain even less sugar than clarets: thus, in four samples examined by Dr. Dupré (prices 15*s*., 20*s*., 36*s*., and 72*s*. per doz.), the sugar per bottle amounted to 1·44 grains and 8·64 grains, respectively, in the two cheapest, and to a mere "trace" in the two others. Champagne stands in a peculiar position, as it is intentionally sweetened: according to Bence Jones's analysis there are about 500 grains of sugar per bottle in such varieties as find most favor in this country (*e. g.* Moet and Chandon, *premier qualité*); but some champagnes are sweetened to a much higher pitch, while, on the contrary, some English connoisseurs demand a champagne which scarcely contains half this amount of sugar. Hungarian natural wines contain but a small amount of sugar; they stand somewhat intermediate, as regards this element, between Rhine wines and red Bordeaux.

One of the richest in sugar of all the natural wines is Bordeaux-Sauterne, a white wine of great popularity, from its fragrant bouquet and flavor. Bence Jones's analysis of a sample of a fine Sauterne (72*s*. per doz.) gives 125 grains of sugar to the bottle; and the taste of this wine, until it has been many years in bottle, is distinctly sweet, too much so, indeed, for the taste of many wine-drinkers. On the other hand, among the fortified wines we occasionally meet with sherries of extreme "dryness," containing, in fact, almost no sugar at all: such, for instance, as an amontillado (marked "very good" in Bence Jones's tables). But such wines, *when genuine*, are too expensive for common use.

The above brief summary of the proportion of sugar in the principal varieties of wine will be sufficient for the purposes of those who merely require some guidance in the choice of an every-day beverage. It is clear that for those who wish to employ wine as a beverage, and to avoid the use of a highly saccharine liquor, the safest choice, in this respect, lies between the sound ordinary wines of Bordeaux, the Rhine, and Hungary. It now remains for us to inquire what are the facts as to the wholesomeness or unwholesomeness of saccharine wines, as such, to persons in ordinary health.

It must be remembered, in the first place, that we are not dealing with the possible effects of *very large* quantities of sugar in wine. The "dietetic use of wines" does not practically include the employment of any wine which would contain more than one ounce to the bottle, and the facts already detailed as to alcoholic strength will show that the wines (except champagne) that contain anything like this percentage of sugar—port, sherry, madeira, marsala—cannot (on the ground of alcoholic strength) be safely taken in larger daily quantities than one-third to one-half of a bottle. The question then arises, whether—and if so in what circumstances—the ingestion of from one-third to half an ounce of sugar in their wine has a deleterious influence upon persons in what would ordinarily be called "health."

There are three classes of individuals enjoying fairly good general health respecting whom there is a certain amount of evidence that saccharine wines are apt to unfavorably influence their bodily condition.

(1.) A considerable number of persons possess a marked proclivity to excessive deposit of *fat* in the cellular tissues; and a good deal of evidence has been adduced by various writers—from Brillat-Savarin to Banting—to show that the saccharine and sugar-making ingredients of food aggravate this tendency. It is not necessary, however, to dwell on this subject, as the amount of sugar introduced into the body by anything like a temperate consumption of saccharine wines would obviously be trifling as compared with the supplies furnished by ordinary food.

(2.) The tendency to *gouty* affections, which is hereditary, is widely diffused among persons otherwise healthy, and a certain amount of evidence exists to show that a considerable saccharine ingredient perceptibly increases the well-known tendency of alcoholic drinks to evoke the tendency to gout, which is latent in such constitutions. Our own investigations lead us to entire concurrence with the opinion of Garrod—the greatest living authority on gout—that the saccharine element of alcoholic liquors has never yet been proved to be the *only* effective element in provoking the disease. Nevertheless, the fact that the one common feature in all those classes of drinks which really do seem convicted of a strong gout-producing tendency—malt liquors, strong wines, champagnes, and sweet cider—is their saccharine or sugar-producing quality, does suggest an almost necessary connection between saccharine beverages and gout.

If it be true, as Dr. Garrod maintains, that even the "driest" sherry will often appear to excite gout in a predisposed individual, we cannot believe that the saccharine element of wines has not a powerful influence in developing gouty manifestations. In truth, however, we question the accuracy of this assertion; at least we greatly doubt whether really non-saccharine sherry ever produced a *first attack* of gout; but when the tendency to the attacks has become very strong, a trifling disturbance of digestion might be sufficient to bring on a fit of gout, and even so innocent a fluid as dry sherry might suffice for this purpose. Still, there can be no question that for persons who are born of gouty families, especially if they have themselves experienced warnings of gout, the safest course is to avoid the whole

THE VIRTUES OF DRINK

class of fortified wines, and confine themselves to sound light claret, or, in the rare cases where this disagrees, to very weak cold spirits and water, carefully bearing in mind that though, when used in moderation, alcohol itself does not appear to be a gout-producer, yet the depression of the nervous system which inevitably follows excesses, even with plain gin, is perfectly competent to induce gout in predisposed persons.

(3.) Even more than to those persons who are liable to well-pronounced gout, saccharine wines are a danger for that class of dyspeptic patients who are the victims of a latent, gouty disposition. In subjects of this temperament the effects of even a small indulgence in this kind of liquor are often extremely disastrous. We are acquainted with one lady whose sensitiveness in this regard makes her stomach an extraordinary delicate tester of the sweetness of wines. The least approach to high saccharine quality makes wine, to her, a poison which infallibly provokes severe vomiting or bilions diarrhœa, or both. It is a curious circumstance, however, that this particular lady only showed the tendency in question rather late in life, previously to which period she had habitually, though very moderately, taken port wine of a decidedly saccharine type; and it was soon after her first development of an incapacity to bear this wine that her first (very slight) symptoms of articular gout appeared. The same lady drinks very dry sherry with perfect impunity.

The peculiar form of dyspepsia which is found in persons of gouty habit is, however, by no means the only dyspepsia with which the saccharine wines disagree. It is one of the commonest medical observations that a considerable number of persons can only maintain a good and active state of the digestive powers by means of a very strict limitation of their allowance of sugar, and also of the starch-containing foods, which undergo conversion into sugar at an early stage of the digestion. Such persons are obliged to be extremely moderate, for instance, in their consumption, not merely of pastry and sweets, but even of bread and potatoes, under penalty of severe dyspepsia if they transgress this rule. To such individuals the saccharine wines are commonly very unsuitable and disturbing. For some reason, not clearly apparent, in the present state of our knowledge of the chemistry of digestion, the tendency of sugar to "turn acid" on the stomach is very much heightened when that substance is given in combination with alcohol. This is the case even when it is taken with a plain spirit like gin. But the mischief is still further heightened in the case of wines, since all wines contain a considerable proportion both of fixed and volatile acids, as will be presently seen. The tendency of the sugary wines to produce sour dyspepsia is, however, altogether out of proportion to their chemical degree of acidity. For instance, such a wine as one of the ports analyzed by Dr. Dupré (vintage 1864), which contained 43·31 grains per 1,000 of sugar, and only 4·13 per 1,000 of total free acids, is far more likely to be mischievous in this direction than a light natural wine like claret of good quality, which may contain as much as six grains of free acid per 1000.

III. The natural *acidity* of wines is the next item which needs consideration in reference to their use as beverages. A more general diffusion of accurate

246

knowledge on this subject is highly desirable, since the taste of wines, by which people ordinarily judge of their acidity, is often highly misleading. The following are the figures given by Dr. Dupré for the principal wines: In four red Bordeaux (prices 12*s*., 15*s*., 30*s*., and 66*s*. per doz.) the total quantities of free acid were 77·40 grs., 72·96 grs., 74·28 grs., and 65·76 grs. per bottle respectively. In four samples of hock (prices 15*s*., 20*s*., 36*s*., and 72*s*. per doz.) the total free acids were, 67·44 grs., 57·60 grs., 70·32 grs., and 69·24 grs. per bottle. In three samples of Hungarian wine (prices 21*s*., 34*s*., and 42*s*. per doz.) the total free acids were, 80·16 grs., 85·92 grs., and 83·88 grs. per bottle. In four sherries (prices 22*s*., 36*s*., "high" and "high") the total free acids were, 55·32 grs., 54·48 grs., 61·16 grs., and 58·08 grs. per bottle. In four ports (prices 32*s*., 50*s*., "high" and "high") the total free acids were, 49·56 grs., 49·56 grs., 62·16 grs., and 58·08 grs. per bottle. In two marsalas ("old" and "very old") the total free acids were 39·12 grs., and 47·76 grs. per bottle.

When we analyze further the free acid constituents of wine, we find that they are made up of three principal ingredients, malic, tartaric, and acetic acids, and a small proportion of several volatile acids closely akin to the latter, which, however, have but a trifling influence on the acidity of wines, though they are important ingredients in flavor and bouquet.

Of the three principal acids, malic and tartaric are the direct product of the grape-juice, the former preponderating; they are fixed, or non-volatile. The acetic, and other volatile acids, are the consequence of fermentation, and of the slower oxidizing processes which go on after fermentation. Supposing the total amount of free acids to range (as it does in sound wines) between 4 and 6 per 1,000, the volatile acids should not exceed one-fourth of this amount in the case of white, or one-third in that of red wines. More than this indicates that the wine is losing its vinous character and turning to vinegar.

Now as regards the acidity of wines, it need hardly be said here that a very popular prejudice in this country regards the light, natural wines as essentially sour, and consequently, in that respect at least, inferior in wholesomeness to the port and sherry which are consecrated by English drinking traditions. Of course if we judge by mere taste this idea is correct; a light claret, or still more, a light hock, will appear strikingly sour as compared with a sherry of fair soundness: one would judge that there was five or six times as much free acid in the light wine as there is in the stronger. In truth, however, if we turn to the analyses of Dr. Dupré, we find that a light claret of 1865, costing only 15*s*. a dozen, contains but 6·08 per thousand of total free acids, as against 5·18 per thousand in an expensive old bottled sherry of 1860 vintage; and that the proportion of acetic to total free acid is much greater in the case of the sherry than of the claret. There is, perhaps, even a more settled prejudice against hock than against claret on the score of supposed acidity; yet if we turn again to the tables we find hock at 15*s*. per dozen, containing no more than 5·62 per thousand of free acids, of which, again, a less proportion than in the case of the sherry above mentioned is volatile acid. The explanation of the common mistake is, of course, to be found in the large quantity

THE VIRTUES OF DRINK

of sugar (29·70 per 1,000) which the sherry contains, and which *masks* the acid; and it therefore becomes an important question, whether the mere masking of an acid taste in this way really renders the wine more digestible.

For our own part we arc totally opposed to such a view, and indeed are strongly inclined to believe that, as applied to wines, it is actually the reverse of the truth. We believe that in reality the maximum of injurious quality is reached when a wine of tolerably high natural acidity contains also a considerable amount of sugar. For (1) the dyspepsia, gout, and other symptoms which (putting aside *alcoholism*) are supposed to be *the special* results of indulgence in wine, arc comparatively uncommon among the European nations, who habitually consume the natural acid-tasting light wines in large quantities. (2) We have personally sought in vain for any instance where the moderate use of a really non-saccharine sherry has produced gout; and we strongly suspect that those persons who have fancied that gout was provoked in them by the use of a "dry" sherry were merely judging of the quality of the liquor from its taste, and had really been drinking a sherry, the composition of which resembled that mentioned above. (3) Whatever may be ultimately shown to be the true origin of the gouty and other allied forms of dyspepsia, it can scarcely be doubted that one of their most important phenomena is an interference with the normally rapid rate of absorption of saccharine matters from the stomach, or that the presence of alcohol (especially alcohol of some strength) would increase this delay of the sugar-absorption. That under these circumstances fermentative changes, with abnormal formation of acid and irritant matters, would occur in the stomach, seems highly probable. (4) It is very difficult to believe that the trifling proportion of fixed and volatile acids present in any drinkable wine, would be sufficient to disturb digestion save in persons of exceptional sensitiveness; one has only to remember the quantities of malic and tartaric acid which every one swallows during the fruit season, and the quantities of acetic acid which even the most modest consumer of pickles, sauces, and salads habitually takes, to perceive how extremely improbable it is that a wine containing not more than 6 per 1,000 total free acids should (from *that* cause) disturb the digestion of any moderate drinker of it.

It is needless to say that throughout the above remarks we are dealing with the case of wines which are fair specimens of their respective classes, and not with those which, whether from careless manufacture, or fraudulent manipulation, depart widely from the standard of sound wines. The latter is a subject to which we shall devote another chapter when we have completed our survey of the principal normal ingredients of wines, and their several relations to the diet of ordinary life.

We have been speaking of the natural *acidity* of wines chiefly from the point of view of indicating the limits within which the presence of this quality is not a mark of unwholesomeness in a beverage intended for healthy adults. It would be a serious omission, however, did we not show that the free acids, provided that they are present only in the several proportions which have been already indicated, are far more than merely harmless in their action.

It is a singular thing that while the tonic powers of mineral acids, as used in medicine, have obtained universal recognition, the no less remarkable tonic qualities of the vegetable acids which are essential ingredients of a variety of foods which we consume in ordinary life should have been so slightly dwelt upon: one can only ascribe the fact to the vicious conventional tradition which habitually separates the action of foods from that of medicines. The value of acetic acid has, indeed, been practically confessed in the popular use of vinegar as a so-called condiment; in plain language, a tonic to the function of primary digestion; and a more profound and important action of this substance on the organism is indicated by the empirical observation of numerous physicians and travelers, that vinegar is an antidote of no mean power to scurvy. An equally decided instinct to that which makes men crave for sour pickles, makes them crave also for sour fruits; and it is certain that a moderate use of these things powerfully aids primary digestion, more especially in the condition of digestive languor which is apt to prevail during the height of summer weather.

Moreover it is probable that malic and tartaric acids, which are the principal representatives of vegetable acid in natural wines, are able to exert a real influence on secondary assimilative processes, since, like acetic and most other vegetable acids, they are converted into carbonic acid in their transit through the body; and the same holds good of that further proportion of these acids which exists in wines under the form of *salts*. On the whole, however, it may be presumed that the useful functions of such quantities of free acids as are found in natural wines are limited to their tonic stimulant action upon stomach-digestion. And that this must be a powerful action no one will doubt who has systematically observed the effects of acid (but otherwise sound) wine in restoring appetite and digestion from the state of prostration in which they are often left after an acute illness.

IV. Closely connected in the minds of most persons with *acidity* is the quality of *astringency;* and indeed the latter might be plausibly regarded as a branch of the former subject, since a vegetable acid, the *tannic*, is its chief cause. But, in the first place, the astringency of wines is essentially different from their mere acidity in its effects upon primary digestion; and secondly, there is the important physiological distinction between tannic and the other vegetable acids of wine, that it does not undergo conversion to carbonic acid within the body.

To say the truth, tannic acid, with its peculiar, so-called astringency, is the real culprit in many cases where a natural red wine of low alcoholic strength is accused of "acidity." The impression of *roughness* on the tongue is easily confounded with actual sourness. Tannic acid in wines is almost exclusively the product of grape-skins and stones, not of grape-juce. And hence it is only in red wines that it exists in any high proportion; the maximum is found in *young* dark-colored wines, for in process of time the tannin precipitates along with an albuminoid matter, which is a notable constituent of such wines, especially when they have been only partially fermented. The coloring matter also precipitates with the tannin, and hence an old port wine becomes "tawny." If any one wants to know what the astringent element of wine is, at its worst, he must taste some of the dark purple wines of the Valais,

THE VIRTUES OF DRINK

or of North Italy, quite new. Generally speaking, the tannin element of wine may be said to be neutral as regards its influence on persons in ordinary health. But there are wines to be met with, here and there, which when young contain enough tannin to set any ordinary teeth on edge, and to upset any ordinary digestion. We remember with horror such a liquor which we once drank at a roadside station in crossing the Simplon, and which produced the most violent diarrhœa. This wine, which was a very cheap sort, of a dark purple tint, rough-tasting, but not sour, had probably been fermented not only with the grape-skins and stones, but also with the fruit-stalks; and as it was very new there had been no time for the tannin to deposit.

On the other hand, the astringent qualities of red wines may become very valuable in certain morbid conditions. But this consideration does not come under our present subject; and we may take the opportunity, here, of remarking that a great many erroneous statements have been made in recommendation of the highly tannic wines for a daily drink, on account of their "bracing" qualities. It is only in certain limited conditions of *disease* that the tannic element of wine possesses any value: and it may be feared that doctors have inflicted much useless misery on unoffending persons, who were not ill, but merely delicate, by recommending them to drink repulsive liquids, which turn the tongue to leather, on account of an imaginary "robustness" of the latter. There is no need of this.

V. We now pass to the consideration of the *salts* of wines. The importance of the saline constituents of wine was recognized very early in the history of chemistry; in fact, the "tartar" of wine was regarded with almost mystic reverence by physicians and chemists from Paracelsus onward, and we see traces of this feeling even in the pages of a sceptical, and, for the times, enlightened pamphlet published by "A Fellow of the College," in 1724, and entitled "The Juice of the Grape, or Wine preferable to Water." Modern physiological chemistry assures us that there is a sound basis for this belief in the importance of wine-salts. The combinations of alkalies (more especially of potash) with vegetable acids, which every natural wine contains, are of a dietetic value not to be easily overrated; and in the particular function of warding off *scurvy* and some allied diseases of mal-nutrition, they rise to the highest importance.

It has been already said that tartaric acid is a prominent ingredient in the majority of natural wines; but it is not only present as a *free* acid, but largely also in combination, as acid tartrate of potash (cream of tartar), and to a smaller amount, as tartrate of lime. There are also chlorides of potassium and sodium, phosphate of lime, and traces of silica and magnesia, besides other occasional salts. The above is a list of the characteristic saline ingredients of wines.

Among these various saline ingredients there is none other so characteristic of natural and unadulterated wine as the acid tartrate of potash; this is especially the case with the wines of Bordeaux. For instance, of four samples of Bordeaux wine already referred to, we find the total *ash* (left after evaporation, and incineration of the residue) amounted to 2·35, 2·08, 2·23, and 2·00 parts per thousand respectively; of this total, 0·45, 0·66, 0·41, and 0·38 respectively, consisted of *carbonate*

250

of potash, the representative of the *tartrate* in the wine. In Rhenish wines there is also much tartaric acid, but a larger proportion of it is in combination with lime than with potash. In port wines, when new, there is a high proportion of tartrates, which tend to deposit with age. But in sherries as sold, even when new, there is a remarkable deficiency of tartrates, which require special comment, because it is not a natural feature of the wine, but a result of a special process of adulteration which is, unfortunately, universal. Sulphate of lime (in the shape of plaster of Paris) is employed in the manufacture of these wines, with a view to precipitate the tartaric acid and the albuminoid matters; the result is strikingly manifest in the character of the ash left by the wine after evaporation and incineration. Of four sherries analyzed the total ash was found to be as much as $4\cdot50$, $5\cdot15$, $5\cdot50$, and $5\cdot13$ per thousand parts respectively; but of this large ash only $0\cdot07$, $0\cdot10$, $0\cdot14$, and $0\cdot07$ consisted of carbonate of potash, the representative of tartrate in the wine. That means, that the wine is by the "plastering" strongly impregnated with sulphate of potash, a serious evil, for sulphate of potash is a very depressing salt, and its effects might materially interfere with the stimulant action of the wine, and doubtless does so, except in the case of the old bottled sherries, which have counterbalancing virtues of their own, to be presently noticed. It may be said, also, in general terms, that any attempt to rob a young wine of its tartaric acid and tartrates is a mistake of the most serious kind; for the presence of these substances really tends to keep the wine in good condition, and their premature removal decreases the chance of the liquor keeping well, not to mention that it abstracts a valuable nutritious ingredient for which, in its youth, the wine possesses no compensating advantage. It is to be feared that the same objectionable process of "plastering" is also followed in the case of several Greek wines, since it is difficult, otherwise, to account for the high percentage of sulphate of potash in the ash of these wines, and the low percentage of carbonates.

On the whole, we are inclined to believe that of all the saline ingredients of wine, the only ones which seriously influence the organism, and possess a real dietetic value are the tartrates of potash and of lime, and possibly the phosphates of lime. In regard to the phosphates generally, there is one popular delusion much fostered by certain wine-dealers, and unfortunately abetted by some hasty and ill-considered statements of a chemist of European celebrity, that the presence of these salts gives to wine an exceptional value as a nervine tonic. In reality there is not the least support, in the facts either of physiological chemistry or of clinical medicine, for the theory that salts of phosphoric acid influence the nervous system except in the most indirect manner. It is true that phosphorus is a constituent of the nervous system, and it is probable that phosphates in the excretions are partly due to disintegration of nervous tissue, but there is no proof that phosphates, administered as such, will nourish the nervous tissues; and, on the other hand, there is a great deal of evidence tending to show that their action is limited to certain changes in the relative proportion of the alkaline constituents of the blood, and in the alkaline constituents of the wine. The phosphate of *lime* stands on a different footing from the other phosphates; and although the question of its functions

THE VIRTUES OF DRINK

within the body is far too elaborate to be discussed here, there is some reason to think that even in small quantities, such as are present in lime, it may prove a valuable agent in assisting the processes of cell-growth in young tissues or in tissues that are undergoing rapid repair after disease or injury.

Upon a general review of the question of saline constituents of the various wines, there can be little doubt that, in this respect, the varieties which possess the highest merits are, successively, the wines of Bordeaux, Burgundy, the Rhine, and Hungary; that is to say, among natural wines, which must be the principal subject of our consideration in regard to the use of wines as a daily beverage.

VI. We come now to what is by far the most difficult and obscure part of the discussion upon wines; the estimate, namely, of the value of their highly characteristic secondary elements, which are formed during the period of storage. The chemistry of the subject is only in its infancy, and so much of it as is already made out is by no means easy to explain in brief outline. But the difficulty of application of such chemical facts as are known to the practical selection of wines for dietetic purposes, is aggravated by the fact that the question becomes immediately complicated by secondary considerations. In dealing with those elements of wine which have already been discussed, the task was simple, for the very first of these topics—that of alcoholic strength—introduced considerations which showed that if wine is to be used as a beverage, both temperance and economy most strongly argue that the bulk of the community should limit themselves to the class of natural wines produced under such conditions as enable the cheaper varieties to be relied on as sound, wholesome, and palatable.

We have now to deal with properties of wine which can only be legitimately developed by age and careful handling, and must, therefore, involve increased costliness; but which, when developed, have the most valuable effects, not merely in increasing delicacy of flavor, but in fitting the wine to supply, in a very important manner, certain special needs of life. We must, therefore, comparatively disregard questions of economy, and deal with wines from the point of view of a refined, yet not unwholesome luxury on the one hand, and of a cordial, for special emergencies, on the other. This greatly widens the field which we have to survey, for without meddling with the strictly medicinal uses of wines at all, we are bound to examine the properties of a variety of wines (especially the *fortified* kinds), which, as beverages of daily life for healthy adults, we deliberately disapprove of, or set aside as too expensive for consumers whose income is but moderate.

These substances of secondary formation are the *compound ethers*, to which wine of a certain age owes the greater part of its flavor and bouquet, and which have a scarcely less important influence in heightening the quality of the liquor as a stimulant of vital functions. The first of these results is well recognized by connoisseurs, though the most accomplished amateurs are often singularly ignorant of some important features of wine flavor; the second is most perversely ignored or misunderstood by the majority of medical men in their capacity of instructors of the public.

When the primary process of fermentation of wine has been brought to a standstill, whether because there is no more sugar to be destroyed, or because there is no more available* ferment to carry on the process, there remain in the liquid, two kinds of substances—alcohol and acid, or rather several alcohols and several acids, which must react upon each other, producing, more or less rapidly and completely, a substitution of compound ethers for the alcohol generated by the primary fermentation. The compound ethers are of two kinds, fixed and volatile, and there is a great difference between the importance of the two classes; according to Dr. Dupré, the fixed ethers have probably scarcely any value beyond the indirect one of neutralizing a part of the acid and facilitating the formation of volatile ethers.[†]

It is the great merit of Dr. Dupré's investigations into the constitution of wines, that he has enabled us to take the first important steps in the appreciation of the relative proportions, as well as the relative merits, of these two classes of compound ethers, and has opened the way for a large amount of promising inquiry into the more obscure questions as to the physiological action of wines.

If we glance down the tables already referred to, bearing in mind the explanatory directions which accompany them, we note the following capital facts as regards the ethers of the principal European wines. Among the natural wines we find the Hungarian predominant, on the average, in the important merit of excess of volatile over fixed ethers; but inferior to Rhine and Bordeaux wines in the total amount of ethers. Bordeaux comes next, on the average, in the excess of volatile over fixed ethers, but is somewhat inferior on the average, to Rhine wine, in total ethers. One specimen of expensive hock (72*s.* per doz., vintage 1862) exceeds any single Bordeaux or Hungarian wine quoted, both in total ethers and in the excess of the volatile over the fixed; the general composition of this wine is typical of a high-class natural white wine, thoroughly fermented, and possessing all the best qualities of a bottled wine.

It is interesting to contrast Greek wine with Hungarian in respect of the ethers; *e. g.*, in a white Hungarian at 34*s.* and a Greek at 36*s.* per dozen, from Dr. Dupré's tables, we observe that the total ethers are about equal, but that whereas in the Hungarian the volatile ethers are largely in excess of the fixed, in the Greek the relative proportions are reversed. The low proportion of volatile ethers in the three samples of Greek wine quoted in these tables must be considered a not unimportant defect; and we must here mention another fault of these wines which should have been referred to in our last paper, viz. the high proportion of volatile to fixed acids. We will also notify a further indictment of Dr. Dupré's against Greek wines, viz. that they frequently contain an appreciable

---

* We say *available,* because the albuminoid substance may be only temporarily locked up by other natural constituents of the wine, or by alcohol artificially added.

† This is probably true from a chemical point of view, but is too absolute a statement, I think, if it be applied to physiological action.

THE VIRTUES OF DRINK

amount of *aldehyde*, an oxide of alcohol, which, so far as known, is rarely or never present in any wine except when it is about to turn into vinegar. On the other hand, we are bound in fairness to mention that a very distinguished chemist, Dr. Williamson, has recently referred to the presence of aldehyde in these wines as a positive merit. Personally, we must disagree with this verdict, on the double ground that the flavor of aldehyde is, we think, extremely disagreeable, and that this substance is more likely, from what we know, to be injurious than useful as a physiological agent.

Without pretending to give a final judgment, or one intended to be universally applicable to Greek wines, we may certainly say, that supposing the analyses given in Dr. Dupré's tables to represent at all fairly the average composition of these wines, it would appear that, as a class, they are rich in promise rather than in performance, as yet achieved; since the concurrence of the several peculiarities which have now been named points with much force to the conclusion that, from some reason, the capacity for keeping sound in bottle is defective. On the other hand, we must say that from a recent careful tasting of a number of these wines, we have recognized unmistakable natural vinous quality of a high order in several which are quoted at moderate prices, and we are inclined to believe that, as *medicinal* agents, they will be found very valuable. We also rather believe that the defects in keeping power which seem to be indicated by the peculiarities above mentioned depend solely on imperfections in the present mode of manufacture, and we venture to doubt whether Dr. Dupré's anticipation that the climate of Greece will not admit of the perfection of wine-making is just. It would be a thousand pities if a country so rich in capacity for the production of full-bodied and rich-flavored natural wines, with an alcoholic strength conveniently intermediate between the wines of France and Germany and the fortified liquors of Spain and Portugal, should prove unable to bring its products into the European markets in a state of perfect soundness. At any rate, there is no reason to believe that the experiment has been fairly tried as yet, and we may all hope that the same energy which has done so much to introduce Greek wines to general notice, will be successful in perfecting their preparation.

We turn now to the ethereal constituents of the fortified wines, taking port, sherry, madeira, and marsala as sufficient examples for practical purposes. We at once notice the fact that these wines, as a rule, only very slowly develop any considerable quantity of volatile ethers. From the quantity of alcohol and of acids present in the wine from the first, one would suppose that a large quantity both of fixed and volatile ethers must be formed, but, as a matter of fact, one finds in a port two years in bottle (price 32*s*.) only 0·430 per thousand total ethers as against 0·415 per thousand in a thin 12*s*. claret of the same age; and, on the other hand, the claret has altogether the advantage as regards *volatile* ethers, which it contains in the proportion of 0·235 to 0·180 fixed, while the port has 0·302 fixed and only 0·128 volatile per thousand.

The dosing with alcohol which port undergoes, not merely arrests the primary fermentation processes, but delays indefinitely the vitally important processes of

254

etherification. Even so old and, in many respects, splendid a wine as the port of 1851 does not contain quite so much volatile as fixed ether, though the total amount of ethers is high. The wine of 1842, on the other hand, yields a very high total percentage of ethers, of which a rather larger part is volatile than fixed. This is a magnificent wine as regards every item of its composition, and where it has been judiciously kept is still in first-rate order. The alcoholic strength is only 18 per cent., and there are but 130 grains of sugar to the bottle; the wine also still contains a high proportion of tartrates, as is evident from the ash. The wine of 1851 is yet more moderate in alcoholic strength (15 per cent.), contains also a high proportion of tartrates, but has the advantage, or disadvantage, according as we take it, of containing more sugar, viz., 235 grains to the bottle; quite enough to make this delicious drink a gout-provoker for predisposed persons; indeed, even the '42 wine will sometimes act in that way.

One has been accustomed, of late years, to hear port wine abused with indiscriminate vehemence, and there can be little doubt that in its young and rough state it is a barbarous drink, however much its most objectionable features may be disguised by the presence of sugar and spirit. Put aside the question of expense, however, and it is simply dishonest to deny that port wine can be procured which represents nearly all the elements of a fine wine at their best; and for certain special purposes to be named presently it is as singularly useful, as it is undoubtedly agreeable to a refined palate.

Marsala, which is easily and cheaply procured in sound condition, is a really fine wine in many ways. A very old wine of this sort was found to contain a high total percentage of ethers, of which, however, the fixed were still in excess of the volatile. Marsala is free from the defects of "plastered" wines.

The case of sherry is singular among fortified wines, and affords a good instance of the way in which a popular cry confounds things which are utterly distinct in one condemnation. At the present moment there are hundreds of persons who imagine that all sherry is, from first to last, a coarse sophisticated drink, of the same general character and strength as port, and like it to be utterly repudiated by reformers in wine. Doubtless sherry has the fault of being universally fortified; and it is already mischievously affected by the "plastering" already mentioned. But on the other hand, it is remarkable that in sherries, from an early period, a high proportion of volatile ethers is developed; and an expensive bottled sherry of the 1857 vintage mentioned in Dupré's tables presents about the highest development of this quality which it is possible to find in any wine. There is no reason, then, that even a young sherry (two years in bottle), if genuine, should not present the most important characteristics of a well-made wine; while, as regards the older specimens, analysis fully confirms the opinion which, personally, we have long entertained—that of all the strong wines there is none to compare, either in generous character, or in delicacy of flavor, with a really fine, old bottled sherry. We shall revert to this point when we speak of the employment of the stronger wines in the treatment of disease; at present we must introduce some remarks on the special dietetic uses to which the more potent wines are particularly adapted.

THE VIRTUES OF DRINK

And first, as regards the infancy of delicate children. Of all the subjects on which conventional morality has talked pernicious nonsense, there is none upon which, in a small way, it has done more decided mischief. The worthy teetotallers have easily enlisted the sympathies of persons whose experience of the management of children was limited, when they have declaimed against the practice of "rearing drunkards from the cradle," &c. &c.; and it is, of course, quite possible to do even so dreadful a thing as this. But the judicious use of wine as a part of the diet even of quite young children (of course always under medical sanction) is entirely free from such dangers, and, on the other hand, may do positive good of a visible kind.

The cases in which it is useful (we are now talking of children not absolutely diseased) are, (1) those where a tendency to wasting is very marked; *i. e.* where children are very apt, without positively seeming ill, to run down suddenly in flesh, with or without simultaneous failure of appetite; and (2) those where trifling catarrhal affections are very easily caught, and very slowly shaken off. We are firmly convinced that multitudes of such children have been allowed to slide into confirmed ill-health, and then into organic disease, who would have done perfectly well had such symptoms as the above been attended to by the administration of wine. Now the right way to deal with children about wine is precisely the reverse of the plan which is appropriate for adults. The latter should be advised to take wine only with their meals, and the problem, therefore, is to find for them a light, natural wine which may safely be used as a beverage. With children, on the contrary, it is much better to give wine at separate hours, as if it were strictly a medicine; and the potent wines, disguised and made somewhat disagreeable by the addition of bitters, are much the best; for example, a teaspoonful of sherry or port made up to a tablespoonful with strong infusion of gentian, which might be given three times a day to a child of three or four years old; or even double this quantity may sometimes be advantageously given.

But the point which we wish to dwell on more particularly here, is the superiority of sherries to all except the most *recherché* kinds of port for this purpose. The improvement of appetite and nutrition, which is sometimes marvelous in young children who have been put on an allowance of wine, is never observed in so striking a degree as after the administration of wine containing a high proportion of volatile ethers. Even a common 30*s.* sherry, such as any respectable wine merchant will supply, is more highly gifted in this particular respect than any port which is within the reach of ordinary purchasers. It is therefore a point of much consequence that in prescribing wine as supplementary food for children whose parents are not wealthy we should recommend sherry rather than port. Sherry is also markedly superior to marsala for this purpose.

Used under the precautions above given, not merely is there no danger of wine corrupting children's tastes, but the services it renders to health are more important than those of any medicine with which we are acquainted; indeed, it is just in the cases where medicines would disorder the stomach and aggravate the child's *malaise* that wine plays the most remarkable dietetic *rôle*.

256

As a dietetic aid in the debility of old age the more potent wines are even more remarkably useful than in infancy and childhood. More particularly in the condition of sleeplessness, attended often with slow and inefficient digestion, and a tendency to stomach cramps, a generous and potent wine is often of great value. It is not desirable for such persons to include a large allowance of fluid in their daily diet, and their alcohol may well be taken in the more concentrated forms. Moreover the fine volatile ethers which develop in well-kept, old bottled port and sherry have an extraordinary influence in heightening the stimulant and tonic influence of alcohol. But in this category sherry is to be reckoned as a much more convenient agent than port, because we are able to get the specific effects of the volatile ethers at a much more reasonable price in the case of the former than of the latter wine.

One very important effect of the highly etherized wines, which are at the same time of rather high alcoholic strength, is their power to produce tranquil and prolonged sleep in aged persons. Supposing that we allow an aged person eight ounces (four glasses) of sound sherry for total daily alcoholic allowance, then we shall afford him the maximum of comfort by ordering that half this quantity shall be taken, with some light food, at his supper hour. Considering how simple a prescription this is, it is surprising how often its value is ignored by medical men, though the popular custom of a "night-cap" of toddy for old people, even when they have been little accustomed to alcohol in their younger days, shows the existence of a need for some agent of this kind. Plain alcohol is, however, a much less efficient hypnotic, unless taken in objectionable quantities, than the highly etherized wines; and no spirit, except the finest and most expensive old cognac or rum, approaches good sherry in this kind of value. In all probability it is precisely the ethereal constituents of such old bottled spirits which give them their hypnotic and calmative power over the nervous systems of the aged.

We here conclude what we had to say about the dietetic use of wines by healthy persons. It was never our intention to dwell in detail upon the merits and demerits of individual wines, except as they fall into main groups which illustrate leading dietetic rules. It was our object to lay down certain great principles which ought to govern the selection of wines for daily use, and especially to show how wine might be made the wholesome beverage of ordinary life, rather than a dangerously seductive luxury, leading easily to mischievous excess. We have purposely abstained from dwelling upon such wines as fall merely within the category of luxuries for occasional indulgence; but some of them, which are either too expensive, or in other ways objectionable for daily consumption, will find an important place in the remarks which we shall have to make hereafter, on the use of wines in disease. For the present we may be content with the following summary of the points we desire to insist upon:

1. Wines for daily use by healthy adults should not, on the average, contain more than 10 per cent. absolute alcohol; 8 or 9 per cent. is better.

2. If wine be used as the daily drink, it is best, as far as may be, to use only one kind at a time, and no other form of alcoholic liquid.

THE VIRTUES OF DRINK

3. Sound, natural wines are to be obtained at the best economic advantage from the Bordeaux district; the red wines are to be preferred.

4. Rhine wines (white) are equally excellent, but more expensive.

5. Hungarian wines are also, in many instances, excellent, but are at present too dear for daily use except by the rich. They are also unequal in quality, owing to defects of manufacture.

6. Greek wines labor under the same defects; the latter, especially, in an aggravated degree.

7. The fortified wines, as a class, develop no proper vinous qualities till they have been some years in bottle. Sherry, however, is greatly superior to the other wines of this class, in the rapidity with which it develops the volatile ethers.

8. Fortified wines in small quantities, especially sherry, for the reason just named, are the appropriate stimuli of certain kinds of infantile and youthful debility, and of the enfeebled nervous system of old persons.

18

G. G. GERVINUS, *ART OF DRINKING: A HISTORICAL SKETCH* (NEW YORK: UNITED STATES BREWERS' ASSOCIATION, 1890), PP. 5–23

A sketch of the art of drinking might seem to announce a subject unworthy of a man whose energies have been devoted to earnest purposes and serious aims in life. But it is not my intention to make the sketch a mere treasure-box of all sorts of curiosities, nor to gratify thereby the curiosity of idle readers. When it is approached from a scientific standpoint, the dignity of science must necessarily exclude all frivolous treatment, as well as all shallow and superficial purpose. Many would be satisfied if an insignificant sketch of this kind simply bore some pathetic motto, as these words of Seneca's: *Animum aliquando debemus relaxare et quibusdam oblectamentis reficere; sed ipsa oblectamenta opera sint.* I, however, would scorn a justification of this kind, for I hold that recreation ought to be recreation, and not work, and should consider it far better if our labors were pleasures, rather than our pleasures, labors.

I wish in this sketch to point out the importance and serious significance of a work of this sort, and shall have, above all, to prove that the apparently somewhat jocular subject has a very serious side, and may be contemplated from a grave standpoint.

If I succeed from the very first in inducing the reader to adopt the same historical view of the matter that I take myself, I shall have gained a great point, for he will then lay aside all prejudice and preconceived opinion. The real historian must be a stranger to all prejudice and preconceived opinion; he cannot treat of any subject separately, but is attracted by everything in a certain order and connection. He must not choose any subject from personal inclination, but according to the needs and demands of his time and of human society; nor must he treat the chosen subject with that pathological interest and sympathy so common among the writers of the New World. He must understand and know, from historical experience, that in times like ours, which have outgrown the activity of imagination—that is to say, *Art*—and, on the other hand, are not yet ripe for speculation—that is to say, *Philosophy*,—universal observation, which includes all departments of human activity, is the only thing that in these very times and for this generation can

THE VIRTUES OF DRINK

furnish positive information and prove a certain gain. The real historian, whose profession it is to be equally interested in everything, thus becomes an image of impartiality. The impartial observer is attracted by all phenomena, and to him nothing appears small, insignificant or unimportant, as soon as he begins to draw conclusions from his observations and to discover laws in the physical as well as the moral world. In the world of reason there exists nothing small, accidental or unimportant. If the same laws of chemical combination govern immense masses of matter as well as the smallest atom, if the march and development of mankind are the same as those of the most insignificant individual, the observation of the smallest as well as the greatest is of equal importance, and man may well feel comfort in the fact that each hair upon his head is, indeed, numbered. This alone might refute any serious objection to my theme.

A history of oinology or potology would be able to show that man, in satisfying a partly physical and partly intellectual desire, is bound by the same laws that govern him in the satisfaction of the highest needs of his striving mind. And if this be the case, the theme might be considered worthy of being chosen by the most severe scientific moralist; and matters of this kind are apt to be overlooked only because other things appear comparatively more important. There is a history of wine and wine-drinking (for of these alone I speak), because it is connected with our spiritual development. Wine itself shows a certain element of development and perfectibility—a relation to organic life in its fermentation, and a sympathetic feeling, as it were, in its movement during the period of the blooming of the vine, while in the plant itself it shows an inner development. I have just called wine-drinking a partly physical, partly intellectual enjoyment, and it is almost impossible to call up the image of any social gathering or entertainment without it. And since all human culture proceeds from the manners and forms of society and social intercourse, we would plainly see in such a history—what has often been divined and pointed out, but also frequently smiled at—that wine is most closely connected with the civilization of States and with the development of free human culture, and that the art of drinking at all times keeps step with this culture and development, and sinks or rises with them. For not at all times have men practiced this art with equal wisdom, nor yet even practiced it in like manner; and there is spiritual progress from the blood-thirsty revels of Ægisthe to those of the philosophers with Plato; from the cup-bearer Hephæstos to Hebe and Ganymede; from the heavy, dull metal cup to the transparent, rounded crystal glass, in Lucian's time, or our own, which shows the color, retains the perfume and promotes sound. *As the culture of the grape is only found where a higher human civilization has begun to develop, it also shows itself at once where a new civilization appears; it may be even in regions unfavorable to it, where it is only cultivated till wine has become so great a want that it can no longer be dispensed with, despite the lack of sufficient native production.* The first cultivators of the vine, history praises as benefactors of mankind and propagators of civilization. Noah was the elect of God, in spite of the improprieties produced by his wine; old

260

Dionysos, for all the ravings of his service, a kindly god; and Urban, of the Middle Ages, a saint, although he committed the greatest misdeeds under the influence of wine. And wherever, on the other hand, in more enlightened history, a man took an active part in the development of human civilization, he did so also instinctively, it would seem, for that of wine—be it a Heracles Ipoctonos among the Erythræans; or an Alexander, who, with his Greek culture, brought the grape-vine back to hot Babylon; or a Charles IV., who, with his Italian education, wished to force it upon cold Bohemia. We shall see that wherever hierarchical constitutions deprived the people of the advantages of education, the wisdom of the priests was subtle enough to forbid wine too, and the course of the Mohammedan hierarchy will show us most plainly how the art of drinking brought with it bold reformatory deviations from the laws. We shall observe, even with Christian nations, how, among certain races where the use of wine was confined to the Communion table, civilization also came to a stand-still. We can then point to a patriarchal and heroic period of the art of drinking, where wine, as was formerly done by the Gauls, and even by our own Suabian ancestors, was despised, and afterwards, by all sorts of artificial means, made more substantial than it is by nature—more like mead or beer, which is at such periods the natural drink of the people. At an aristocratic and knightly epoch, in which society is unnaturally sublimated, it is sought to increase and make more spiritual still the effect of wine also, by the addition of spicy herbs. With the first civil development of nations they return to simple nature; a number of corporations and brotherhoods make it their business to watch over the art of drinking, over the purity of the wine itself, and its lawful use; from king to beggar, all cultivate the cheering art, just as all are anxious, also, for spiritual enlightenment. We see, then, in the last centuries the pedantic return to tea and coffee, and among those nations who have shared but in very small measure in the intellectual progress of Europe, we find that the coffee-house (café)—an institution which is scarcely a century and a half old—almost crowded out the wine-saloons.

I have alluded to wine-drinking as a partly intellectual and partly physical enjoyment. Among material enjoyments, it is one of the most spiritual; among spiritual ones, one of the most material, keeping about the right middle course. A history of the art of drinking would prove this. Everywhere in the history of nations we shall come upon times where amid a fulness of physical power, the desire for more refinement in outward life, as well as a striving for greater inner perfection, began to manifest itself. In Germany, the time of the Reformation was such a period. And at such times, when outer and inner powers begin to stir with wonderful energy—times as yet divided between old roughness and new humanity; between the coarse, ordinary fare of every day for mind and imagination, and the new hope of some finer nourishment—at such times the genial enjoyment of wine, and the delights of regular social pleasures, have always struck deepest root and had freest play. Such images as those, this history would most willingly depict; nor would it be superfluous to present them in our day, when society seems

THE VIRTUES OF DRINK

more and more to forget that its aim is to be simply pleasure and recreation. The future seems to offer nothing that could take the place of the great simplicity of past manners; of those feasts of youth which asked nothing but uncontrolled enjoyment; of those evening entertainments of the citizens, which were devoted to their immediate surroundings in house or community; of the frank and manly rectitude of that race which seemed, indeed, to find truth and constancy in wine, and its best pleasures in an afternoon spent in the "wine-garden," surrounded by wife and children, relatives and friends. All public pleasure has disappeared from among us, and we arrange parties and receptions that only tire ourselves and others. Ceremonious etiquette gives us work and trouble when we should find recreation, and fatigues our minds when imagination should have free play. Only where men, here and there, permit themselves to meet about the bottle, according to the good old custom, and where no committee is necessary to approve of the toasts, pure, genuine pleasure revives once more, together with the pure, genuine art of drinking. For there is no intellectual power that is so directly quickened and strengthened by any nourishment as imagination is by wine. Tea keeps conversation within the bounds of pedantic propriety, and beer soothes but checks quick repartee; but wine sharpens the sting of wit, stimulates spirited conversation, and brightens the whole social atmosphere. The poet, who lives in imagination, and turns his back upon reality, was always a lover of wine—the beverage which intensifies reality, and, at the same time, lifts him above it. The drinking-song, from Anacreon down to all his imitators in Germany, occupies a special and very prominent place in literature. To wine are dedicated the first productions of the tragic art; and to it has been assigned a particular dithyrambic measure, which a poet who should set water above wine could never soar high enough to make his own. And whosoever has any cause to turn away from the real world, and longs for the freedom of living in an ideal one, is fond of wine. If I wished to spoil my idyllic picture by satire, I should here name the converts and the monks; but I should rather call up the wandering beggar, whom want and hardship have made weary of the world. Sleep has been praised as the friend of poverty; but there were times when wine also was called its friend, which, even in waking hours, calls up dreams that charm away the burden of a miserable existence. For wine tempts even the beggar to extravagance, that vice which has often been set down to the account of wine; although, if there be such a thing as degrees in vice, it may be called one of the nobler ones. And this genial pleasure in spending helps the poor man in his misery; consoles him for his destitution; offers him who is homeless a spot where he may feel comfortable, and teaches him to forget all that oppresses him. Wine makes man liberal and generous; the offered cup was formerly the symbol of hospitality granted, and even the miser is more ready to share tobacco and wine than any of his other possessions. For it makes us communicative and confidential in social intercourse; it founds friendships, and is still the symbol of brotherhood. If it sometimes stirs up heat and dissension, it also smooths the way to union again; and, formerly, no reconciliation could take place without having a seal set upon it by a common cup of wine. At your cup you find the freest and most enlightened spot in the world, where you may not only think what you please, and say what you think, but where your thoughts themselves take the highest flight man is capable of. I do not know whether it is due to jealous gods that the excessive enjoyment of wine proves its own penalty. Without this depressing fire in the wine itself, it seems to me heaven and its secrets would be far more endangered by the spiritual flight of the drinker than by the towering rocks of the Titans. Thus, wherever despots and hierarchs intended to keep nations in drowsy stupidity, they forbade wine. Only at times, when liberty and enlightenment were common property, when no castes possessed an exclusive monoply of wisdom, right or might, was it possible to introduce political discussion at the cup. For only at such times of universal public spirit and feeling could one take counsel of the imagination in practical affairs and matters of State, and hope for such results of the evening discussion at the cup as would bear the test of the sober next day's light. For only such heroic conditions as are represented by the Germans and Persians of ancient times can really show the virtues of truth and faithfulness, and in the most public concerns could hear the voice that always speaks in wine; and, in those days, no one needed to fear that wine would impel him to speak truth too freely. Only nations of really active nature, who called manliness and war-power by the name of virtue, could do full honor to wine, and it could only be a Greek who asked, as did Aristophanes:—

> "Dost thou boldly venture to say wine is not good for our reason?
> What more than wine impels us to deeds and to action?
> Why, look you, as soon as men are drinkers of wine, then
> Rich are they all and active, victorious in law-courts;
> Aye, very happy too, and to their friends useful."

Among the Germans, too, it has long been customary to settle all business with a drink, and there was no betrothal, no bargain, and no compact that was not accompanied by the purchase of wine. All German history is filled with the love of wine. When the German border-line was first drawn, the Germans insisted on keeping the left bank of the Rhine, on account of its richness in grapes. They wrote books about the national disposition to drink; they divided their history according to drinking periods, and old proverbs call the love of drink the German national vice, as theft is that of the Spaniards, deceit that of the Italians, and vanity that of the French. Nowhere exist wines so capable of purity as the German wines, and no real German will ever compare with their genuine wine-qualities those of the tricky southern wines; and nowhere have mixtures been so carefully avoided, as well as the purity of the art of drinking, and the old drinking customs so scrupulously preserved, as in Germany. Only in Germany could be conceived the idea of a history of the art of drinking. Perhaps the fates have ordained me to be the historian of wine, in the very meaning of my name—ger-wîn, not gêr-wîn. And perhaps some readers may be found for it in Germany who do not consider it too indelicate to speak or to read of the natural needs of man. Let man never, in foolish pride, think himself above his own natural wishes and enjoyments, for it is the reasonable care given to these which keeps him close to human nature. As long as a people cannot live on newspaper reading and on staring about in public places, as do Frenchmen and Italians, it keeps its hands busy, its powers actively employed, and its eyes open, and wherever active powers are astir, no nation is in so very bad a condition. I should be well content if I could bring before active and manly minds a cheerful picture of those manly enjoyments, and induce them to taste of this somewhat coarser fare, in addition to the delicate dishes of our literature.

I

The fatherland of wine

I would only here and there touch upon the botanical and industrial culture of the grape, as many very valuable works on the subject already exist (among others, Henderson's "History of Ancient and Modern Wines"), which make almost a complete literature of wine. I shall also speak of the home of the grape only for the sake of preserving the natural order of things, and shall touch later upon the mythical origin of wine, or the preparation of wine. If we look for the original country of the grape, we shall find that here, too, as in almost every other branch of culture, the western highlands of Asia are pointed out to us, whether we follow the fable of Father Noah, the Nysæan Bacchus, or the researches of the naturalists. The latter teach us that on the Canary Isles and in America the grape grows not so much wild as in a degenerate condition; but in the southwest of Europe, for instance the Italian woods, it is here and there found growing really wild; that in the southeast this is still more common, and in Asia ever on the increase. It is singular that at the Ararat, to which Jewish tradition also points, Tournefort, in his "Journey to the Levant," discovered a regular workshop of the European plant, and on the borders of transcaucasian Georgia he saw the land covered with wild grape-vines and fruit-trees. In the Caucasus, Marshall found the grape flourishing independently in the forest and covering whole trees, and we see in the rough and indifferent manner in which the inhabitants of these countries harvest and treat the grape that they consider it a very common product. The manner in which they preserve the wine, and the quantity they daily consume, prove the same, and this entirely agrees with what Xenophon tells of the preservation of the wine in cisterns. Elphinstone, in his report on Cabul, relates that the Sultan presented him with grapes that grew without cultivation in his country. And not only the quantities of the wild grapes in those countries induce us to regard them as their native soil, it is also the excellent quality of the cultivated grape in Persia. The quantity and quality of the Persian wine opposed in this respect an effective barrier to the laws of the Koran, which enjoined against the enjoyment of the beverage, even in the Orient, which is so set in its religious rites and ceremonies. Olivier preferred the grapes about Ispahan to all he had tasted in Greece, on the islands of the

Mediterranean, and in Syria. None, he says, equals the *Kismish*, which bears a berry of middling size, without seeds and with a thin skin. Shiraz, rich in poets, is celebrated on account of the excellence and plenty of its wine and its fine air, and Morier, in his "Journey through Persia," places the wine of Kazwin even above that of Shiraz, and the former city is so beautifully situated in so mild a climate that the Persians have given it the name of "Paradise." In regard to the fruitfulness of the vine, Strabo tells us that in Hyrcania *one* vine was apt to yield about thirty-three quarts of wine. In Margiana were said to be vines measuring at the base of the stem two fathoms in circumference and bearing grapes two yards long. In Asia the fruitfulness is said to be still greater, and there the wine keeps, in unpitched vessels, through three generations.

II

Wine is not domesticated among the negroes

The course from east to west, marked by the higher culture of the human race, has been also closely followed by the culture of the grape. Other regions, north and south from the boundary marked out, may have had a certain share in that civilization; but it seems now to be proved that the negro races, the original inhabitants of Africa, have not in any way been connected with it. In those regions of Africa always inhabited by these races, no grape-culture is, up to the present day, to be found; and, both in ancient and modern times, the grape has been a stranger in Africa, and a stranger scarcely to be called naturalized anywhere. To that king of the long-lived Ethiopians in Herodotus, to whom Cambyses sent his gifts, wine, therefore, seemed the only desirable thing they possessed, and to it he ascribed the brief old age which, in the best case, it was given the Persians to attain. His negroes, therefore, were not acquainted with wine, and in this they were like all uncivilized people, as we shall frequently see; nor did they ever accept it, any more than they accepted any other part of civilization; they never advanced any further than to their *Towak*, the palm-wine made of flower-stems; even the lotus-wine, of the preparation of which Herodotus knew, seems to belong only to the Libyans. Only emigrants, in the most ancient as well as most recent times, have introduced the grape-vine at different times into Africa, and we will briefly glance at this. First, the Egyptians must be named, Caucasian races not autochthonically at home in Libya. The ancient culture of the grape in Egypt is proved not only by historical documents, but even by the ruins of old buildings, and I shall return to the paintings in the vaults near El Kab, which represent, among other things, the manner of gathering the grapes, and of preserving and cooling the wine. Several regions are specially mentioned as celebrated for their wine. Eleithya had grape-culture; the lakes of Mareos and Taenia, where all is now a barren desert, were commended for their wine; Alexandria exported wine to Rome, and Horace is acquainted with that of Mareos. To the Epicureans, however, the Falernian

THE VIRTUES OF DRINK

wine seemed better when treated in the Egyptian manner; and the wine of Taenia was considered stronger and spicier than the Alexandrian. But even in the time of Ahenæos this culture had almost disappeared, and only that of Antylla still had a good name in those days. And even in better times, the native wine does not seem to have sufficed for home consumption, for Herodotus speaks at length of imported wine from Hellas and Phœnicia. The Libyans and Berbers probably never knew a grape-culture of their own without foreign aid. It is certain that in old times the colonies of the Greeks and Carthagenians in the north of Africa were full of the grape; and we shall find further on that the cult of Bacchus was widespread in Cyrenaica, and that traces of it still remain in the ruins. Pliny speaks of vineyards as traces of ancient civilization in the mountains of Dyris (Atlas); and there are still, more for the sake of the grapes than the wine, vineyards near Tunis, in the rich district of Derna, as well as the poor one of Mafa, in Fezzan. In Mauritania, as Strabo reports, were found grapes a yard in circumference. In the oases, Belzoni saw grapes, and in that of Siwah they are excellent, as other southern fruit also. In recent times the Portuguese brought the grape, with other fruit, as well to Madeira and the Canary Isles as to Abyssinia. There the poorness of the plant itself, no less than the peculiar use of it, shows plainly what a stranger it is. Thus, also, among the Griquas it is cultivated by the missionaries only, who, confining, as they are wont, all civilization which they offer to the elements of Christian religion, give to grape-culture also only a Christian significance, planting the vine merely for its use at the Communion table. The celebrated Cape wine is a different matter. Enlightened French emigrants, Protestants driven from home by the Edict of Nantes, first planted the grape there; but it is not certain whether the vines came both from Persia and from the Rhine, or only from Shiraz. The climate seems there to favor the culture of the grape extremely; the soil, however, appears most unfavorable, and Colebrooke, in his work on the condition of the Cape of Good Hope, ascribes the earthy taste, which makes the Cape wines unpleasant, to a substratum of the soil, otherwise rather good, consisting in many places of layers of clay and sand that has been washed up. And what is not spoiled by the soil, seems to have been spoiled by the indolence of the Dutchmen, or some other disadvantage with which the African country is cursed. A sort of fairy-tale is told of the totally wrong manner of planting the first vineyard; and still not even the example of the far better Constantia wine has induced men to make vineyards in rockier spots.

III

The degenerate culture of the grape and the art of drinking in China

If the learned men of China can be trusted, the grapevine must have been known in their country more than a thousand years B. C. They refer to this in old books, the "Tshu-ly" and the "Shi-King;" but as to the latter, that seems everywhere to

ART OF DRINKING: A HISTORICAL SKETCH

refer to the wine made of various grains, which is almost exclusively used in China.

At all events, it seems to be proved by the most trustworthy witnesses that rice-wine is older in China than the wine of grapes; for while the highest age that can be assigned to wine is only given by the doubtful testimony of the supposed author of the "Tshu-ly," Tshu-Kang, who mounted the throne 1122 B. C., the invention of rice-wine is set down to the Dynasty Hia, 2209 (1716 B. C.). This also accords with experience elsewhere, for beer of various kinds (and the grain-wines of the Chinese are nothing else, except that they frequently mix them with all sorts of fruit, including grapes) everywhere became the national drink in advance of wine, as brandy and other liquors follow wine. Grape-brandy has, it appears, been known in China only since the seventh century of our era, but is now a favorite beverage with the common Chinamen, and is drunk by them warm and almost as strong as alcohol in large quantities, in spite of its very unpleasant taste. For only a comparatively short time the grape-culture seems to have flourished in China. The Chinese always have had their grain-wines and their brandy more at heart. The inventor of the rice-wine was, it is true, banished by the Emperor Yu-te, because he well foresaw the sad consequences of its use, and yet the beverage has kept its place to the present day as an ornament of the Chinese table. It is like this people, who live on nothing but that water-plant, rice, and tea, to cling with the same obstinacy as they do to all old orders and customs, to this beverage, which is something between brandy and water, and taken neither hot nor cold. These wines are said to have a very bad effect; they fatten at first, but then bring on consumption, entire loss of appetite, and at last complete emaciation and death. It was natural, therefore, that the paternal Emperors, who looked after their subjects as after real children, and in whose laws dietetics always played a great part, should forbid these injurious beverages, and several of the Emperors set the good example. The third Emperor of the Dynasty Mant-shu, Yong-Tsheng, devoted one of his ten commandments to this subject, and the great Kanghi says in his writings that, despite his pleasure in them, he never became accustomed to wine and spirits. At feasts and banquets he only touched it with his lips, and so might well boast of not drinking any at all. Moreover, this wine consumes a great deal of grain, which in a densely peopled country, whose very existence depends upon its supplies of grain, is a matter of some importance, so that perhaps from this higher standpoint also there was good reason for the prohibition. But the most important reason lies deeper still, and was still more carefully considered; and as this chiefly concerns the wine from grapes, we must first cast another glance at grape-culture.

We have seen above that grapes existed of old in China. The just-mentioned learned, philosophical and humane Kanghi himself shows, in his remarks on natural history in China, that grapes came to China from the West, and that before his time but few kinds had existed in China, and boasts that he had sent for three new varieties to Ha-mi, as he would rather introduce a new fruit into his country than build a hundred porcelain towers. He observes, also, that these

THE VIRTUES OF DRINK

grapes degenerate in the south, but do well in the north in dry and stony soil. The experiences of the missionaries in Pekin, however, were unfavorable; the soil was against them, as well as the remarkably rough climate, and possibly they went to work awkwardly in other respects also. For it is certain that these very southern provinces once had many grape-vines, and the wine made in Shan-si, Shen-si, Petshe-ly, Shantong, Honan and Hu-Kuang, put into well-closed vessels and buried in the ground, could be preserved for years. This goes to prove an observation we shall often find repeated, that after a time the most favorable soil no longer suffices for the grape, which demands a certain youthful power in the soil in which it is to flourish most luxuriantly. In the older and middle ages of China we therefore find the grape-wine mentioned in all their songs, and that of the river Kiang is specially praised. It is known that at different periods vines were introduced from Samarcand, Persia, Thibet, Kashgar, Turfu and Ha-mi, and the annals themselves plainly mention wine under the reign of Emperor Wu-ty, Dynasty Han, 140 B. C. From there we can follow up its use almost from reign to reign, and after the already-mentioned Kanghi, the last dynasty shows still more rulers who introduced new grapes from distant countries, so that the southern provinces begin to restore their old grape-culture again. But the grapes in Ha-mi and Shan-si seem mostly to be used for raisins, and what we occasionally hear of their condition in Hoai-lai-hien—that their berries are of gigantic size, like plums, with a thick skin, and that their size is not so much due to the climate as to the fact that the vines are grafted on mulberry-trees, and that they ripen as early as April, May and June—all this seems highly characteristic of a degenerate culture, and gives us the poorest possible opinion of the wine that might be made there. Highly, therefore, as the Jesuits attempt to praise grape-culture in China, we can yet have but little belief in it; but in the Middle Ages it must have been all the more brilliant. The reports concerning it are, however, wrapped in a certain obscurity, from which no fact stands out clearly. The grape, it is said, flourished only too well in China—it caused various revolutions. As often as the Government had ordered the destruction of such trees as obstructed the grain-fields, the useless grape-vine was also included, and, if memory served the reporters, that plant was several times specially mentioned. It is certain that the destruction of the vine in most of the provinces, under various reigns, was carried so far that even the recollection of it was lost, and this induced the belief that the grape had been brought to China but recently from the Occident. It is plain that there was always a pretense put forward that the grape-wine detracted from the culture of the grain, although, with some care, the same area might probably have yielded a nobler beverage than was made of the rice and barley, grown where the grape had been rooted out. But the intellectual effect of it was evidently feared. In so regular a clock-work as the Chinese State, what might be more dangerous than irregular movements so very easily produced by wine in the heads of people? Even the making of the grape-wine was often prohibited. When that did not avail, its use was limited to feasts, banquets and sacrifices, and to guests and infirm old age. Not enough with this, at such feasts a special Mandarin was set over even the princes of the blood to keep watch over and not permit them to drink more than three glasses. And still more, certain ceremonies were prescribed, long healths and salutations, circumstantial rites, at which a free-thinker, as the Jesuits say, may laugh, but in in which a philosopher must admire the wisdom of the lawgiver, and the subtlety with which he banished intemperance, and that injudicious freedom of speech which is its inseparable companion, from among the people! We have seen the effects of grain-wine in China. The wise Emperor Kanghi complains that it makes one stupid and dull and confuses the brain. And how much more terrible still must have been the effect of the grape-wine! This is probably meant in a certain book of the Dynasty Tshu, where it is said in warning explanation of the well-founded apprehensions of the Chinese Government, that if a spirit of rebellion and insurrection was then rife among the people of China, if they had lost much of their old virtues and principles, the cause of it must be sought solely in the effects of wine. Away, therefore, with that cursed boldness which betrays a tongue set free by wine; that noisy action and damnable confidence in one's own strength; that rising of the spirit, which must have appeared to the learned Emperor as synonymous with confusion; the impudent overstepping of the good old laws of etiquette; the wild breaking away from the good old ruts! How should not all this, which was inseparably connected with wine, seem to the philosophical head of the State in his immovable peace and calmness, and to the council of his ministerial pedants, extremely dangerous to the State, and worthy of being annihilated to the last trace? Need we be surprised, therefore, at the stories of abstinence told of the Emperors? It was their duty to give a good example to the people. Had not their prophet, Confucius, left these words of moderation—that coarse rice for food, and water for drink, and the curved arm for a pillow, were enough for happiness!

And thus the Governments of China succeeded in establishing, even in very early times, a condition of submissive decency everywhere. They confined wine to festive occasions, and we learn from the "Shi-King" that to the guest was granted the honor of the cup; even to him, however, in but the spare measure that chimes with the sordid miserliness of the Chinaman, who could never have understood the art of drinking, if for no other reason than because he has nothing of the liberality which the Orient calls the "flowing hand." They say in a guest-song:—

> "A noble guest has come beneath our roof;
> For him melodious tunes were played,
> So long as thus it pleased our guest,
> And with the cup I sought to cheer him.

> "The sound of music rang incessantly,
> And ever was the cup kept full;
> And in our honor did he empty it;
> The wine was light and pure, and harmed him not."

THE VIRTUES OF DRINK

And in another place:—

> "A hare is roasting on the spit;
> A pumpkin leaf we go to pick;
> A banquet we prepare our guest,
> And fill his cup with wine the best."

We have seen from other authorities that wine was chiefly reserved to old age, and here it is confirmed:—

> "Serve round the circle the wine-cup, ye bearers;
> With the spiced wine the aged refresh them;
> In it their youth and their vigor reviving,
> But your own youth surely needs no concoction."

Even at the feasts where wine was permitted, its use was limited by cautions restrictions. All meals and banquets were subjected to rules of etiquette almost as rigorous as those which the Court is accustomed to give its ambassadors. The careful law is extended to the very preparation and serving of the viands, and everywhere clips the wings of the art of cooking and of drinking. If the Emperor U-tse gave his warriors a banquet to gain their favor, he still preserved the most rigid order of rank in the seating, and the food and the drink; and the Emperor Tsi-she-hoang is praised for restoring the old invitations and banquets, where every single ceremony took its due course in beginning and end, so that a modest and decent joy beamed in all eyes. To give a model for domestic feasts, they order public ceremonies in all the cities; Mandarins preside at them; the law invites scholars and distinguished citizens to them; and here, too, the rites are prescribed down to the minutest detail. The chief object of these feasts is to signalize merit, to preserve morality, and the friendly as well as conventional proprieties. The President reads aloud for that purpose, in the name of the Emperor, certain paragraphs of the law, the introduction to which specially calls to mind that the gathering is not really made for the sake of the enjoyment of meat and drink, but to revive loyalty to the Prince, and more to the same effect; and all their songs and pieces of music have reference to that. A single drinking-song, of somewhat more liberal spirit, I found in the "Shi-King," but in that the translator may possibly have had a large share, especially in regard to the form. The contents are very characteristic of Chinese poetry in general, whose bare realism offers a remarkable contrast to that of the Orientals:—

> "Water, the fresh,
> Is drunk by the fish—
> The carps and the pikes;
> And each noble knight
> At the board
> Drinks water pure and bright.

> "Water, the fresh,
>   Is drunk by the fish—
>   The eels and the salmon;
>   You sad fellows all
>   At the board,
>   Drink, till for more ye shall call.
>
> "Water, the fresh,
>   Is drunk by the fish—
>   The perch and the barbel;
>   Ye good chums of mine
>   At the board,
>   Now drain ye the pearl of the wine.
>
> "Water, the fresh,
>   Is drunk by the fish—
>   The trout and the merlin;
>   But we boys gay and bold
>   At the board
>   Drain waves of the wine untold."

But, even in their highest ecstasy, the brave drinkers still preserve a sort of calmness; and if there is anything that can be called a sober intoxication, this seems to be excellently expressed in the following very characteristic song:—

> "Now our guests are growing tipsy;
>   Decency is at an end;
>   Sparks from out their eyes are darting,
>   And the babbling tongues unbend.
>
> "Crooked caps shake back and forward,
>   Hung but by a single hair;
>   Stiff old legs the dance are trying,
>   Hoarse old voices sing out fair.
>
> "At the first cup which thou drainest,
>   Didst thou seem transformed to me;
>   If another now thou'dst empty,
>   Wholly tipsy wouldst thou be.
>
> "Truly thou dost shame me sorely;
>   Sober quite you see I stay;
>   But if thou wilt take me homeward,
>   Lead me gently on the way.

THE VIRTUES OF DRINK

"True, thou lead'st me into ditches,
But my own head reels at last.;
Hold me by thy arm supported,
By thy pig-tail hanging fast."

With this extreme point of drinking I will close. This dull intoxication is about what a warm grain-wine would produce, and fits the disagreeable character of the Chinese as well as the anecdote occurring in another song, where one whose invited guests do not appear at the right time, is actually rejoiced to think he may now drink up his wine alone. The value of wine for social enjoyment can scarcely be known there, where conventionality ties the tongues, where there is a tribunal of ceremonies, and where the tea-kettle is forever on the fire, which among us, too, fosters only embroidery, gossip and nervous debility. And then the greedy desire for physical enjoyment is the one thing which makes the Chinaman love his wine and his spicy concoctions, and which in this point has ever driven him into a never-before-heard-of opposition against his Government. How dreadful it is, however, to see these crude and childish remnants of antiquated customs most closely knit now with the most refined and elaborate tastes, wants and habits thus in vogue among the people, together with secret and most pernicious vices, and yet to find that not a single voice can be raised against it, because, with the most subtle cunning, down to the very limits of physical needs, every expression of indignation or of joy has been forbidden by law!

Part 6

PLACES AND SPACES

19

CHARLES DICKENS, *BARNABY RUDGE: A TALE OF THE RIOTS OF EIGHTY* (LONDON: GEORGE ROUTLEDGE AND SONS, 1884 [1841]), PP. 172–73

ONE wintry evening, early in the year of our Lord one thousand seven hundred and eighty, a keen north wind arose as it grew dark, and night came on with black and dismal looks. A bitter storm of sleet, sharp, dense, and icy cold, swept the wet streets, and rattled on the trembling windows. Signboards, shaken past endurance in their creaking frames, fell crashing on the pavement; old tottering chimneys reeled and staggered in the blast; and many a steeple rocked again that night, as though the earth were troubled.

It was not a time for those who could by any means get light and warmth, to brave the fury of the weather. In coffee-houses of the better sort, guests crowded round the fire, forgot to be political, and told each other with a secret gladness that the blast grew fiercer every minute. Each humble tavern by the waterside had its group of uncouth figures round the hearth, who talked of vessels foundering at sea, and all hands lost; related many a dismal tale of shipwreck and drowned men, and hoped that some they knew were safe, and shook their heads in doubt. In private dwellings, children clustered near the blaze; listening with timid pleasure to tales of ghosts and goblins, and tall figures clad in white standing by bedsides, and people who had gone to sleep in old churches and being overlooked had found themselves alone there at the dead hour of the night: until they shuddered at the thought of the dark rooms upstairs, yet loved to hear the wind moan too, and hoped it would continue bravely. From time to time these happy indoor people stopped to listen, or one held up his finger and cried "Hark!" and then above the rumbling in the chimney, and the fast pattering on the glass, was heard a wailing, rushing sound, which shook the walls as though a giant's hand were on them; then a hoarse roar as if the sea had risen; then such a whirl and tumult that the air seemed mad; and then, with a lengthened howl, the waves of wind swept on, and left a moment's interval of rest.

Cheerily, though there were none abroad to see it, shone the Maypole light that evening. Blessings on the red—deep, ruby-glowing red—old curtain of the

PLACES AND SPACES

window; bending into one rich stream of brightness, fire and candle, meat, drink, and company, and gleaming like a jovial eye upon the bleak waste out of doors! Within, what carpet like its crunching sand, what music merry as its crackling logs, what perfume like its kitchen's dainty breath, what weather genial as its hearty warmth! Blessings on the old house, how sturdily it stood! How did the vexed wind chafe and roar about its stalwart roof; how did it pant and strive with its wide chimneys, which still poured forth from their hospitable throats, great clouds of smoke, and puffed defiance in its face; how, above all, did it drive and rattle at the casement, emulous to extinguish that cheerful glow, which would not be put down, and seemed the brighter for the conflict.

The profusion, too, the rich and lavish bounty, of that goodly tavern! It was not enough that one fire roared and sparkled on its spacious hearth; in the tiles which paved and compassed it, five hundred flickering fires burnt brightly also. It was not enough that one red curtain shut the wild night out, and shed its cheerful influence on the room. In every saucepan-lid, and candlestick, and vessel of copper, brass, or tin that hung upon the walls, were countless ruddy hangings, flashing and gleaming with every motion of the blaze, and offering, let the eye wander where it might, interminable vistas of the same rich colour. The old oak wainscoting, the beams, the chairs, the seats, reflected it in a deep dull glimmer. There were fires and red curtains in the very eyes of the drinkers, in their buttons, in their liquor, in the pipes they smoked.

Mr. Willet sat in what had been his accustomed place five years before, with his eyes on the eternal boiler; and had sat there since the clock struck eight, giving no other signs of life than breathing with a loud and constant snore (though he was wide awake), and from time to time putting his glass to his lips, or knocking the ashes out of his pipe, and filling it anew. It was now half-past ten. Mr. Cobb and long Phil Parkes were his companions, as of old, and for two mortal hours and a half, none of the company had pronounced one word.

Whether people, by dint of sitting together in the same place and the same relative positions, and doing exactly the same things for a great many years, acquire a sixth sense, or some unknown power of influencing each other which serves them in its stead, is a question for a philosopher to settle. But certain it is that old John Willet, Mr. Parkes, and Mr. Cobb, were one and all firmly of opinion that they were very jolly companions—rather choice spirits than otherwise; that they looked at each other every now and then as if there were a perpetual interchange of ideas going on among them; that no man considered himself or his neighbour by any means silent; and that each of them nodded occasionally when he caught the eye of another, as if he would say, "You have expressed yourself extremely well, sir, in relation to that sentiment, and I quite agree with you."

The room was so very warm, the tobacco so very good, and the fire so very soothing, that Mr. Willet by degrees began to doze; but as he had perfectly acquired, by dint of long habit, the art of smoking in his sleep, and as his breathing was pretty much the same, awake or asleep, saving that in the latter case he sometimes experienced a slight difficulty in respiration (such as the carpenter meets with when he is planing and comes to a knot), neither of his companions was aware of the circumstance, until he met with one of these impediments, and was obliged to try again.

"Johnny's dropped off," said Mr. Parkes in a whisper.

"Fast as a top," said Mr. Cobb.

Neither of them said any more until Mr. Willet came to another knot—one of surpassing obduracy—which bade fair to throw him into convulsions, but which he got over at last without waking, by an effort quite superhuman.

"He sleeps uncommon hard," said Mr. Cobb.

20

CHARLES DICKENS, 'THE DAWN', IN *THE MYSTERY OF EDWIN DROOD* (LONDON: CHAPMAN AND HALL, 1870), PP. 1–3

The mystery of Edwin Drood

The dawn

AN ancient English Cathedral Tower? How can the ancient English Cathedral tower be here! The well-known massive grey square tower of its old Cathedral? How can that be here! There is no spike of rusty iron in the air, between the eye and it, from any point of the real prospect. What is the spike that intervenes, and who has set it up? Maybe, it is set up by the Sultan's orders for the impaling of a horde of Turkish robbers, one by one. It is so, for cymbals clash, and the Sultan goes by to his palace in long procession. Ten thousand scimitars flash in the sunlight, and thrice ten thousand dancing-girls strew flowers. Then, follow white elephants caparisoned in countless gorgeous colors, and infinite in number and attendants. Still, the Cathedral Tower rises in the background, where it cannot be, and still no writhing figure is on the grim spike. Stay! Is the spike so low a thing as the rusty spike on the top of a post of an old bedstead that has tumbled all awry? Some vague period of drowsy laughter must be devoted to the consideration of this possibility.

Shaking from head to foot, the man whose scattered consciousness has thus fantastically pieced itself together, at length rises, supports his trembling frame upon his arms, and looks around. He is in the meanest and closest of small rooms. Through the ragged window-curtain, the light of early day steals in from a miserable court. He lies, dressed, across a large unseemly bed, upon a bedstead that has indeed given way under the weight upon it. Lying, also dressed and also across the bed, not longwise, are a Chinaman, a Lascar, and a haggard woman. The two first are in a sleep or stupor; the last is blowing at a kind of pipe, to kindle it. And as she blows, and shading it with her lean hand, concentrates its red spark of light, it serves in the dim morning as a lamp to show him what he sees of her.

"Another?" says this woman, in a querulous, rattling whisper. "Have another?"

He looks about him, with his hand to his forehead.

"Ye've smoked as many as five since ye come in at midnight," the woman goes on, as she chronically complains. "Poor me, poor me, my head is so bad! Them two come in after ye. Ah, poor me, the business is slack, is slack! Few Chinamen about the Docks, and fewer Lascars, and no ships coming in, these say! Here's another ready for ye, deary. Ye'll remember like a good soul, won't ye, that the market price is dreffle high just now? More nor three shillings and sixpence for a thimbleful! And ye'll remember that nobody but me (and Jack Chinaman t'other side the court; but he can't do it as well as me) has the true secret of mixing it? Ye'll pay up according, deary, won't ye?"

She blows at the pipe as she speaks, and, occasionally bubbling at it, inhales much of its contents.

"O me, O me, my lungs is weak, my lungs is bad! It's nearly ready for ye, deary. Ah poor me, poor me, my poor hand shakes like to drop off! I see ye coming-to, and I ses to my poor self, 'I'll have another ready for him, and he'll bear in mind the market price of opium, and pay according.' O my poor head! I makes my pipes of old penny ink-bottles, ye see, deary—this is one—and I fits in a mouthpiece, this way, and I takes my mixter out of this thimble with this little horn spoon; and so I fills, deary. Ah, my poor nerves! I got Heavens-hard drunk for sixteen year afore I took to this; but this don't hurt me, not to speak of. And it takes away the hunger as well as wittles, deary."

She hands him the nearly-emptied pipe, and sinks back, turning over on her face.

He rises unsteadily from the bed, lays the pipe upon the hearth-stone, draws back the ragged curtain, and looks with repugnance at his three companions. He notices that the woman has opium-smoked herself into a strange likeness of the Chinaman. His form of cheek, eye, and temple, and his color, are repeated in her. Said Chinaman convulsively wrestles with one of his many Gods, or Devils, perhaps, and snarls horribly. The Lascar laughs and dribbles at the mouth. The hostess is still.

"What visions can *she* have?" the waking man muses, as he turns her face towards him, and stands looking down at it. "Visions of many butchers' shops, and public-houses, and much credit? Of an increase of hideous customers, and this horrible bedstead set upright again, and this horrible court swept clean? What can she rise to, under any quantity of opium, higher than that!—Eh?"

He bends down his ear, to listen to her mutterings.

"Unintelligible!"

As he watches the spasmodic shoots and darts that break out of her face and limbs, like fitful lightning out of a dark sky, some contagion in them seizes upon him: insomuch that he has to withdraw himself to a lean arm-chair by the hearth— placed there, perhaps, for such emergencies—and to sit in it, holding tight, until he has got the better of this unclean spirit of imitation.

Then he comes back, pounces on the Chinaman, and, seizing him with both hands by the throat, turns him violently on the bed. The Chinaman clutches the aggressive hands, resists, gasps, and protests.

"What do you say?"

A watchful pause.

"Unintelligible!"

PLACES AND SPACES

Slowly loosening his grasp as he listens to the incoherent jargon with an attentive frown, he turns to the Lascar and fairly drags him forth upon the floor. As he falls, the Lascar starts into a half-risen attitude, glares with his eyes, lashes about him fiercely with his arms, and draws a phantom knife. It then becomes apparent that the woman has taken possession of his knife, for safety's sake; for, she too starting up, and restraining and expostulating with him, the knife is visible in her dress, not in his, when they drowsily drop back, side by side.

There has been chattering and clattering enough between them, but to no purpose. When any distinct word has been flung into the air, it has had no sense or sequence. Wherefore "unintelligible!" is again the comment of the watcher, made with some reassured nodding of his head, and a gloomy smile. He then lays certain silver money on the table, finds his hat, gropes his way down the broken stairs, gives a good morning to some rat-ridden doorkeeper, in bed in a black hutch beneath the stairs, and passes out.

That same afternoon, the massive grey square tower of an old Cathedral rises before the sight of a jaded traveller. The bells are going for daily vesper service, and he must needs attend it, one would say, from his haste to reach the open cathedral door. The choir are getting on their sullied white robes, in a hurry, when he arrives among them, gets on his own robe, and falls into the procession filing in to service. Then, the Sacristan locks the iron-barred gates that divide the sanctuary from the chancel, and all of the procession having scuttled into their places, hide their faces; and then the intoned words, "WHEN THE WICKED MAN—" rise among groins of arches and beams of roof, awakening muttered thunder.

21

ANON, 'EAST LONDON OPIUM SMOKERS', *LONDON SOCIETY*, 14, 1868, 68–72

OF all carnal delights that over which opium rules as the presiding genius is most shrouded in mystery. It is invested with a weird and fantastic interest (for which its Oriental origin is doubtless in some degree accountable), and there hovers about it a vague fascination, such as is felt towards ghostly legend and the lore of fairy land. There exists a strange yearning to make more intimate acquaintance with the miraculous drug concerning which there is so much whispering, and at the same time a superstitious dread of approaching it, such as, when it comes to the pinch, possesses the rustic believer in the efficacy of repeating a prayer backwards as a means of raising the devil. It is the vulgar supposition that the one occupation of the lives of eastern grandees is to recline on soft cushions and indulge in the charming narcotic; that the thousand and one seductive stories contained in the 'Arabian Nights' were composed by writers whose senses were steeped in it, and that our Poet Laureate and his brethren constantly draw inspiration from it, either through a pipe-stem or by means of mastication. Furthermore, it is largely believed that any man might become a poet, or at least a writer of flowing and flowery prose, if he only possessed courage sufficient to avail himself of this convenient picklock of the gates of paradise.

And who shall tell of the multitude of youthful aspirants for poetic fame who have daringly grasped the magic key and essayed to apply it? Also, and alas! who shall make known to an unkind world the many who have bungled over the gentle burglary, who have failed at the gate, and come away with no more delightful sensation than that which might arise through butting their unlucky heads against the bars of it? That is the most tantalising part of the business. Opium may be procured—any chemist will sell you an ounce of it for eighteen pence—but possessed of it and not of the secret of its use, the novico is no better off than he would be if he set up as a painter on the strength of a colour-box and a few brushes. It is this secret that constitutes the rarity of the luxury. To be enjoyed, the opium must be prepared by a competent hand. There are few such in London, few, that is, who are willing to receive pupils and give lessons. How limited their number is determined by the fact that when an 'opium master' is discovered, even though his den is situate in, without exception, the most vile and villainous part

PLACES AND SPACES

of the metropolis, he is regarded as a person worth visiting by lords and dukes and even princes and kings. The writer hereof, taking it for granted that a sight that could draw earls and princes to Bluegate Fields could not be otherwise than highly curious and interesting, ventured a journey thither recently.

Only such of the public as are accustomed to read the police news in the daily papers can form any idea as to the kind of place Bluegate Fields is. Commonly it is known as 'Tiger Bay,' on account of the number of ferocious she creatures in petticoats that lurk and lair there. It is a narrow lane opening on to High Street, Shadwell, at one end, and St. George's Street at the other. To the left and right of the narrow lane are many villainous courts and alleys, consisting of one-story high hovels, each one accommodating as many lodgers as might reasonably occupy an eight-roomed house. The inhabitants of Bluegate Fields are the worst in England, consisting of man-trappers for the shipping lying in the river just below, and the tigresses before mentioned, who inveigle tipsy sailors from the many surrounding abominable dens 'licensed for dancing and music,' and drug them and strip and rob and ill use them, and pickpockets and coiners and robbers of every degree. The mere blacking of an eye or extraction of human hair by the violent process of dragging it from the head is not regarded in the light of an assault in Bluegate Fields, but rather as a pleasant pastime to beguile the lazy hours of daylight. Judging from the reports of the Thames Police Court, nothing of less importance than the biting off of a nose or an ear, or the fracture of a skull with a poker, calls for the interference of the police. It is a fact that while I was inquiring at a public-house for the address of Chi Ki, the Chinaman, I overheard two women at the bar discussing a murderous assault that had happened in the 'Fields' that morning. 'What I say is,' remarked the elder woman of the two, who was a fat woman with a horribly dirty face and a blue seam across her nose that was curiously suggestive of the rim of a pewter pot, 'what I say is, if I wants it, punch me. Punch me in the face and black my eyes, or punch me about the head. Kick me if you like; I don't so much mind that; but when it comes to pokers and shovels, it's a little *too* hot.'

I was lucky in calling at the public-house where the two women were, since on inquiry I discovered that it was to this place that Chi Ki had directed all letters from his numerous friends. I was glad to find that the barmaid spoke of the opium master in a very respectful manner, calling him Mr. Chi Ki. She happened to know, moreover, that the distinguished Chinaman was from home; so I left with her a message for him to the effect that if it accorded with Mr. Chi Ki's convenience, a gentleman would be glad to meet him on business at that hostelry at six o'clock the following evening.

He was punctual. Precisely as the clock marked six he put his head in at the door. 'Mr. Chi Ki, here's your gentleman,' called out the obliging barmaid, and the Chinaman's body followed his head, and he came towards me bowing low and rubbing his hands. I must confess that I was disappointed at Chi Ki's appearance. Being so celebrated a character, with lords and marquises for his patrons and customers, I expected to see a man able and willing to demonstrate in his attire his

282

native ideas of splendour. It would not have surprised me if so exalted a personage as an opium master had appeared dressed in a gown of gold-embroidered crimson silk, and with a sash and curly-toed slippers; but poor Chi Ki was very poorly clad indeed. He is a man of ostlerish cut, wearing a long jacket and a comforter wisped round his neck, and tight trousers, and an old cloth cap on his head. He is lame of a leg, too, as many ostlers are. In a few words I explained my business, and without betraying the least astonishment at its nature he expressed his readiness to conduct me to his house there and then.

We went a little way into Bluegate Fields and then turned into the arched way of an alley, a trifle higher, may be, but not nearly so wide as an ordinary coal-cellar doorway. It was as dark as any coal-cellar. 'Come along, sir,' said Chi Ki encouragingly, in his 'pigeon English.' 'It is down at the bottom and turn round the corner; come along.'

We arrived at the bottom, and came on a tiny square of ill-looking little houses and an appalling odour of bad drainage, and Chi Ki guided me to a house in a corner as his. It was no larger than the rest and scarcely as good looking, on account of its many fractured window-panes and the rough-and-ready measures that had been resorted to to block out the wind. Pushing open the outer door, Chi Ki called at the foot of the stairs for a light. While we waited for it I peeped into the parlour, which was dark except for a little blinking fire in an iron skillet, crouching over which was a Chinaman, looking the picture of despair, with his knees supporting his arms and his head resting on his hands, and his pigtail slewed to the fore and projecting over his forehead as a unicorn wears his horn. I observed, too, that there was in the room a large bedstead, with a bed made the wrong way on it.

It was an English voice that responded to Chi Ki's demand for a light; and presently a youngish woman, very thin and pale-looking, and scarcely as tidy as she might have been, made her appearance above with a tallow candle in her hand, and politely invited me to walk up. We walked up, and at once came in full view of the renowned opium master's public smoking-room, which served likewise for his private sitting-room and his private bedroom, and, judging from the handle of a saucepan and a suspicion of dirty plates under the bed, for his kitchen as well.

It was an extremely mean and miserable little room. The fireplace was very narrow, and the stove of the ancient narrow-waisted pattern. There was no fender. In the centre of the room was a small round table, and there were three wooden chairs. The chief and most conspicuous article of furniture the room contained was a large four-post bedstead, and a bed like the one downstairs. The bed was not arranged according to the English fashion. It was rolled up bolsterwise all along the length of the bedstead, leaving the mattress bare except for a large mat of Chinese grass. The bed-hangings were of some light Chinese gauze, but very dirty, and hitched up slatternly on the hanging-rails. The walls of the room were hung with a few tawdry pictures highly coloured, and contrasting grimly with the blackened walls, all stained above with rain-leakage, and below with the filthy saliva with which the smokers had besprinkled them. The ceiling was as black as the walls, and just over the window there had been an extensive fall of plaster, showing the laths, like grinning teeth in an ugly mouth.

There was a customer waiting, which at once gave Chi Ki an opportunity for displaying the mysteries of his craft. The preparations for enjoying the luxury of opium smoking were curious enough. Chi Ki's first move was to spread a piece of cloth on the mat that covered the mattress. Then he brought out a small common oil lamp and lit it and placed it in the centre of the piece of cloth. Next he produced a small box containing his smoking tools, and finally a little gallipot and an instrument like a flute, with a wooden cup with a lid to it screwed on at a distance of about three inches from the end. It was not a flute, however, but a pipe,—*the* pipe. As the customer caught sight of the odd-looking implement (he was quite a young man and more respectable-looking than Chi Ki himself) he licked his lips, and his eyes glistened like those of the domestic feline creature when it hears the welcome cry that announces its dinner. I asked permission to examine the pipe. It was simply an eighteen-inch length of yellow bamboo with the cup of dark-coloured baked clay before mentioned fitted into a sort of spiggot hole near the end. Had I been asked to appraise its value, I could not conscientiously have gone beyond fourpence.

'He's been offered five pound for that pipe,' remarked English Mrs. Chi Ki, who appeared to be almost as proud of it as was her husband. 'A gentleman offered him five pound for it last autumn.'

'Why didn't he sell it, and buy another?' was my natural question; but at this old Chi Ki chuckled, and hugging the pipe chafed its bowl tenderly with his jacket cuff.

'It's worth ten pounds,' said his wife; 'it has had nothing but the best opium smoked in it these fourteen years.'

And she then went on further to enumerate the many excellences of the pipe; from which I gathered that its value was not after all so fanciful as at first appeared: since half a given quantity of opium would yield more satisfaction when smoked in a ripe, well-saturated old pipe than the whole quantity in a comparatively new one.

Chi Ki, having made all necessary preparations, got up on to the mattress on the bed, and, reclining at his ease, proceeded to load the pipe for his customer. I was curious to see how this was managed. The stuff in the gallipot looked exactly like thin treacle, and smelt like burnt sugar and laudanum. Decidedly it seemed queer stuff to load a pipe with. But it had yet to be cooked—grilled. Taking an iron bodkin from his little tool-chest, Chi Ki dipped the tip of it into the semi-liquid stuff, and withdrawing a little drop of it, held it in the flame of the lamp until it hardened somewhat. Keeping this still on the point of the bodkin, he dipped it again into the gallipot and again held it in the lamp flame, and repeated the process until a piece of the size of a large pea was accumulated and properly toasted. This was placed in the pipe-bowl, and the hungry customer sprang up on to the bed to enjoy it.

It was lit at the little lamp, and then the young Chinaman reclining at his ease, laid his head comfortably on the dirty counterpane that covered the rolled-up bed, and took the pipe-stem in his mouth. There is no mouthpiece to the pipe; the stem is cut sheer off, leaving something as thick as an office ruler to suck at. And suck the Chinaman did. He took the bamboo fairly into his mouth, and there was at once emitted from the pipe a gurgling sound—the spirits of ten thousand previously smoked pipe-loads stirred to life. As the smoker heard the delicious sound, the lids of his elongated eyes quivered in ecstasy, and he sucked harder, swallowing all the black smoke except just so little as he was bound to waste in the process of breathing. He was as economical as could be, however, and expelled but the merest thread of the precious smoke through his nostrils and none by means of his mouth. If his sensations induced by the indulgence were heavenly, his countenance grossly belied them. Gradually, as he sucked and swallowed, the veins of his forehead thickened, his cheeks flushed, and his half-closed eyes gleamed like those of a satisfied pig. Still he sucked, and the nostril wreaths came quicker and finer, and he grew more and more like an enraptured hog: when suddenly the gurgling in the throat of the pipe-stem terminated in a brief rattle, and all was over. While the opium in the pipe was waning to extremity, Chi Ki had busied himself in the manufacture of a little cigarette composed of paper and common tobacco, and as the pipe-stem dropped from the mouth of the young Chinaman, Chi Ki promptly handed him the cigarette, which he proceeded to light and consume, with a languid relish edifying to behold. I inquired why this was, but beyond the assertion that it was always done, Chi Ki had no explanation to offer.

'Was the lingering flavour of opium in the mouth objectionable?' I asked.

'No, indeed,' replied Chi Ki, with a grin; 'oh, no, no; it's always done; I don't know why, not in the least, but they will have the cigar afterwards.'

I can't help thinking, however, that this taking tobacco after opium must be something more than a meaningless 'custom.' Perhaps an abrupt and sudden descent from paradise to earth would be too much for a Chinaman's nerves, and so he applies himself to the milder narcotic by way of a gentle letting down.

What chiefly surprised me was the short time it took to consume the charging of a pipe. From the time of the young Chinaman's taking the stem in his mouth till the opium was exhausted, not more than a minute and a half was occupied. In five minutes the cigarette was smoked and the customer took his departure. He paid no money, so I suppose he went 'tick' with Chi Ki; but as far as I could make out, his treat would cost about three halfpence. Evidently opium smoking is a more expensive enjoyment than dram drinking. Chi Ki showed me his 'measures.' They were three little ivory cups, the smallest the size of a lady's thimble. For this full of the treacle-like opium, fourpence was charged; the next-sized cup was sixpence, and the largest a shilling. This, it seemed, included the loan of Chi Ki's pipe as well as of the bed to lie on and the cigarette for after smoking, and the trouble of frizzling and preparing the drug.

Chi Ki keeps open house for opium smokers, and his chief customers are the sailors who arrive at the London ports. Sometimes, I was informed, trade was so slack that not more than two or three customers would apply all day long; while at other times it was as much as Chi Ki could do, distilling and frizzling and frying,

PLACES AND SPACES

to keep the smokers going. The opium has to be put through a peculiar process before it is reduced to the semi-liquid state. It has to be cooked. Chi Ki was good enough to crawl under the bedstead and produce therefrom, for my inspection, his implements of cookery, and to explain their use. I should hardly advise an amateur to essay opium brewing on the strength of my directions; but it seemed to me that the opium of the druggist is shredded into little slices, which are laid on a piece of stout coarse canvas, which is suspended in a small iron pot partly filled with water. In the process of boiling the essence of the opium drains through the canvas and forms a sediment at the bottom of the pot, leaving on the canvas the refuse, looking not unlike tea-leaves.

The cookery was performed at the miserable little fireplace before mentioned. Poor English Mrs. Chi Ki looks as though she is being gradually smoke-dried, and by and by will present the appearance of an Egyptian mummy.

'I can stand a good deal of it,' said she, 'but sometimes it's awful. Sometimes two or three ships come in at once, and then we have a houseful. Upstairs as well as down. We've had as many as fourteen smoking in this room at one time, and them that couldn't find room on the bed lay all about the floor. There are only two pipes, one for the parlour, and one for the best room,—this room. It is hot work I assure you when we are busy. As soon as one has smoked out, another is ready to snatch at it; and it is in lighting the opium that the smoke is wasted so. They are awful hungry after it sometimes when they've gone a long while without and got their pay. They'll smoke as much as a shilling's worth out in half an hour, and there they'll lay like logs. It don't often make me ill; it makes me silly. I am ill sometimes, though. I was ill a-bed when the Prince of Wales and the other gentlemen came up here to see the smokers. There were only three or four of them, and they were friends like. I was sorry that the place was in such a muddle; but the Prince didn't seem to mind.'

'Yas,' observed Chi Ki, suddenly lighting up; 'the Prince, he say, "Come smokee pipe wi' me, and bring you' lady, whens conwenince." '

'Ah, yes; but I don't believe he meant it,' said Mrs. Chi Ki, dubiously.

But the lame old Chinaman grinned and winked to himself knowingly; so that I should not be in the least surprised if, one of these fine days, the porter at Marlborough House is startled by a Celestial apparition.

22

J. PLATT, 'CHINESE LONDON AND ITS OPIUM DENS', *GENTLEMAN'S MAGAZINE*, 279, 1895, 272–82

THE subject to which I invite attention is that of the Chinese colony in the East End of London. I shall make no attempt at what my Chinese friends would call *handsome talkee*. My sole effort will be to explain in the simplest possible manner what I have myself seen and heard, touched, tasted, and smelt. At different times, extending over a long series of years, I have made many "trips to Chinatown." But I have done more than this—I have been animated from the first by a scientific curiosity to understand the inner meaning of everything. I soon found that my ignorance of the Cantonese dialect in which the London Chinese transact their business among themselves, rendered it impossible to advance far without help. On one occasion I took an interpreter with me in the person of a Portuguese friend of mine from Macao. But as a general rule the medium of communication between myself and the Chinese was Pidgin-English. Now, if any of my readers have the least acquaintance with that truly astounding jargon they will readily admit that it does not lend itself to the purposes of scientific investigations. It is fearfully and wonderfully made. Only a very limited range of ideas can be expressed. I think I could do better with the monkey language, or Volapuk. One of the Chinamen who had come from Cuba spoke Spanish, and here I got on better. But the long and the short of it is that I found it necessary to appeal to higher authority for the explanation of some items, which the people themselves could in no way elucidate. Our little community here is as a drop of water to the ocean compared with the vast Chinese settlements which are to be found in the United States. But, like a drop of water, in spite of the difference in volume, Chinese London is composed of the same constituents as Chinese Philadelphia. I accordingly put myself into communication with Mr. Stewart Culin, an American, who had made much the same study of the Chinese element in his own city as I was trying to do in mine. I wish to place it upon record that I received much very courteous help by letter, from this (if I may make bold so to call him) *fellow explorer*. I had, also, more than one interview with Professor Douglas of the British Museum. He, in turn, referred me to Mr. Wilkinson of the treaty port of Swatow in China, who, fortunately for me, happened to be at that precise moment upon a visit to England. Altogether I think I may call myself lucky in my helpers, whom I here severally

PLACES AND SPACES

thank. The results I have attained may, in comparison, seem small, yet they form at any rate the most complete account of the opium dens of London which has ever been made public. The very existence of such places is unknown to many Londoners. As far as I have examined them, none of the hand-books to London invite the tourist to do "China before breakfast." Chinatown is marked upon no map. The Lady Guide Office never personally conducts there. The popular novelist, it is true, is aware of its value as furnishing local colour for his shilling shockers. But judging from what I have read of these works the writers never take the trouble to inspect the dens themselves. They rely upon their imagination for the thrilling pictures they draw of them. Occasionally in the silly season a journalist badly off for *copy* sandwiches a paragraph about the Chinese between the Great Sea Serpent and the Gigantic Gooseberry. But as the reporter appears to consider it necessary to be escorted in his tour of inspection by either a policeman or the Chinese missionary, I need hardly say that he sees little of the genuine article. Chinatown is, above all things, suspicious of the *chiel* that goes among its inhabitants taking notes. Even Charles Dickens attained a very slight degree of its confidence, judging by the confused account of the process of opium smoking which he gave to the world in the last chapter of his last work, "Edwin Drood." A long apprenticeship is needed before the European learns to smoke opium as it should be smoked. In the first place you must always take your smoke lying down, whether on a couch or bed, or the more orthodox shelf in a cupboard, or something similar to the berth of a ship's cabin. Dickens is right so far, when he says of his hero: "he divests himself of his shoes, loosens his cravat, and lies across the foot of the squalid bed with his head resting on his left hand." The opium, which has been imported in slabs as hard as iron, has been rendered, by a long course of subsequent cooking, a thick paste resembling treacle. As for the pipe, it must be seen to be appreciated. The stem is a piece of natural bamboo. The bowl is not open like that of a tobacco pipe, but closed, with the exception of a tiny hole in the top of it. This bowl is very securely fastened to the stem, because the opium pipe is, of necessity, smoked bowl downwards. It would be obviously annoying if bowl and stem parted company. It might lead to celestial profanity. Other accessories to the toilet (generally placed all together upon the so-called opium tray) are a lighted oil lamp, and a long needle. The smoker dips the end of a needle into the opium, and draws out a small pill about the size of a pea. He hardens this into shape by turning and twisting it over the lamp flame at the point of the needle. The pipe is then held so as to bring the bowl over the lamp while the pill, insinuated with the aid of the needle point into the tiny aperture of the bowl, is at one and the same time cooked in the flame, and smoked. One pill does not last long; the Chinaman sucks in such a pipeful without taking breath. When it has disappeared he lays down the pipe, and then, and then only, expels the smoke through his nostrils. He then takes another pill, and goes through the whole process again. I may add that only the ignoramus buys for smoking purposes a nice, clean, new pipe. The aged and apparently done-for pipes are really the most valuable ones. Their price (always high) varies according to the length of time they have been smoked, and

288

the resulting richness of their colour. Every tobacco smoker who has coloured a meerschaum for himself will understand this. A friend of mine has a curiosity in the way of pipes. Some genius, unable to afford a real pipe, has manufactured one for himself out of a brass door-knob and an old flute. He has drilled a small hole in the top of the door-knob, and affixed it by way of bowl to the flute (its holes stopped up), which serves for stem. The result is a most workmanlike and capable pipe. It is, I think, as admirable an example of Oriental ingenuity as I have ever seen or heard of. Not only that, but coming as it does from the Dickens opium den, it must be the very "broken-down flageolet" alluded to in the "Dictionary of London." It may also very well be the pipe Mr. Field saw when the novelist took him with him to the same den. "In a miserable court, at night," Mr. Field tells us, "we found a haggard old woman blowing at a kind of pipe made of an old ink-bottle, and the words that Dickens put into the mouth of this wretched creature in 'Edwin Drood' we heard her croon, as we leaned over the tattered bed on which she was lying."

Besides opium, tobacco is smoked in Chinatown. Their tobacco pipes are of two kinds, the ordinary and the water pipe—the ordinary differs from our own chiefly in the excessive smallness of the bowl, which may be of iron, brass, or silver. It only holds a thimbleful of the fragrant weed. A few whiffs are taken, and then it is refilled. The water-pipe is for inhaling the smoke of tobacco through water, on the principle of the hookah or hubble-bubble. But the Chinese water-pipe differs from these in having no flexible tube.

I was well acquainted with the particular den described by the two Dickenses, which was situated in New Court, Victoria Street. It is now destroyed to make a schoolboard playground, so that no one will ever see it again. It was worth going to, if only to see a Chinaman and an Englishwoman so sincerely attached to one another as were the old couple who kept it. They might without impropriety have been called Darby and Joan. I once took a lady artist to see this interesting pair. She was delighted with them, and they with her. The Chinaman even went the length of allowing her to sketch him in the act of smoking. Those who know the dread this people have of anything that suggests publicity, will appreciate this concession at its full value. The lady never revisited them, but they often spoke of her, and always wished to be kindly remembered to her when they saw me. Another former visitor whom they were never tired of recalling was no less a person than the Prince of Wales.

Upon his departure, it appears, His Royal Highness gave the old man a sovereign. He had never forgotten that coin, although, in the lapse of time, it had acquired something of a mythological halo. Johnny was an epicure, eating very little, but requiring everything to be of the best. He was a literary man, and had quite a small library of Chinese books. He had a taste for art, and displayed conspicuously upon his wall for twenty years an amateur effort (the work of a Chinese sailor), being curiously enough the picture of an English church. It is now in the possession of a friend of mine. It was sold, with other effects, upon his eviction from his old quarters, including his scales for weighing opium, his opiumlamp,

PLACES AND SPACES

his gambling-cards, his dominoes, two photographs, and reading books. The very next place he went to (Angel Gardens), he had no sooner settled in than the street was condemned, and he had to turn out once more. In fact, he never settled down again, but wandered from lodging to lodging. I never lost sight of him till the day of his decease, which took place in Cornwall Street, in his sixty-fourth year, and after that I traced his widow from one address to another, until she was taken in charge by some charitable ladies. Since then I have heard nothing further of her, and know not whether she is living or dead.

Their house, which appears to have been the only one known to Dickens, was really outside the boundary of what I call Chinese London. By this term I understand a single long narrow street with Chinese boarding houses and shops on both sides of the way. This street constitutes the quarter of which I shall sketch the essential features. It exists by and for the Chinese firemen, seamen, stewards, cooks, and carpenters who serve on board the steamers plying between China and the port of London. All the while their vessels are in port these almond-eyed birds of passage lodge on shore in these boarding-houses, and deal at these shops, which also enjoy the custom of the Chinese Ambassador at the other end of London. These Chinese shops are the quaintest places imaginable. Their walls are decorated with red and orange papers, covered with Chinese writing indicating the "chop," or style of the firm, or some such announcement. There is also sure to be a map of China, and a hanging Chinese almanac. There is another kind of Chinese almanac in book form, published in Pekin, which, among other useful information, tells which days are lucky and which unlucky. It is a pity this is no longer done in the almanacs of Europe. It is obviously of the utmost importance to anyone who contemplates getting born, or dying, or being married, to know the luckiest days for doing it. The atmosphere of the Chinese shop is indescribable. The smell of tobacco I like, and the smell of opium I like, and the smell of joss-sticks I like, but there are others such as the smell of Chinese cooking. The visitor to Chinatown finds cooking going on at all hours. This quite contradicts the common notion that the opium smoker never eats. Besides the actual cooking all the knife and fork work is done in the kitchen. The viands, whether the meat or vegetables, are served at table cut up ready for transferring to the mouth. The pair of chopsticks used in eating are of wood or ivory, and both are held in the right hand. As shopkeepers here supply the Chinese Ambassador, there is an opportunity for the inquiring stranger to sample not only the more homely fare, but also the most aristocratic. To the former, I suppose, belongs the cuttle fish, which in China takes the place the herring does with us. To the latter belongs first and foremost the well-known birds'-nest shreds, the cost price of which to the merchant here is thirty-eight shillings a pound.

I give a receipt for making birds'-nest soup which may interest the ladies:— Take clean white birds'-nest shreds (or birds' nests) and soak thoroughly. Pick out all feathers. Boil in soup or water till tender, and of the colour of jade stone. Place pigeons' eggs below it, and add some ham shreds on top. Boil again slowly with

290

little fluid. If required sweet, then boil in clean water till tender, add sugar candy, and then eat, if you are a Chinaman; but if you are not, *don't*.

Sharks' fins, at fourteen shillings the pound, are another dainty dish to set before a king.

I must confess that I never had the courage to attempt either of these delicacies. I have, however, partaken of the sea slug, or *bêche de mer*. It is worthy of note that the most esteemed foods of the Chinese are all gelatinous, such as the birds'-nest soup, sharks'-fin soup, and sea-slug soup, which I have just mentioned. I have also partaken of Chinese tea. Tea is, so to speak, always on tap in this locality, and is offered to every customer at every shop. In fact, the Chinese are very hospitable in every way, and generally refused to charge even for the opium we consumed. They would also, after they came to know us, give us a present at parting, such as a cigar each, or some other token of goodwill. Ladies may be interested to know that the tea cosy is not used here. In place of it they keep the teapot warm in a wadded basket. The tea, served without sugar or milk, is in appearance as clear as sherry. Of course the tea the Chinese drink themselves and the tea they sell to us are two very different things. There is a legend, I hope without foundation, that the tea sent to Europe has already been used in China for cleaning carpets. But this cannot be true, because carpets in China are never cleaned. Tea shares with the opium pipe the proud characteristic of being one of the most popular medicines of the Chinese. But for ailments of an obstinate nature there are a few Chinese remedies to be had in these shops. It is noteworthy that practically no minerals are in use for this purpose, but only vegetable substances. There is a bottle bearing upon the label four hieroglyphics, which being interpreted, read *mao kan kiu tsiu*. This is a liquor prepared from the root of a kind of couch grass imported from Canton, and used as a febrifuge. Another favourite remedy is to be had in two forms. The bark of a kind of bittersweet, from the province of Szechuen, is sold under the name of *chuen kia pi*, and it is also to be had made up with the addition of spirit, and sold ready for taking in bottles bearing the mystic inscription, *u kia pi tsiu*.

Besides the teapot the counter of a Chinese shop has other quaint appendages. The hand balance for weighing opium consists of a brass scale pan suspended by silk threads from one end of an ivory rod. The rod is marked with two different decimally graduated scales, but why two I do not know. There is a moveable hanging weight which slides along either of the graduated scales. It is interesting to see the merchant posting his books. For this purpose he uses a writing brush which he dips in Indian ink, and holding it perpendicularly, traces the spidery Chinese characters with great rapidity in columns from top to bottom of the page. The ink is prepared by grinding on an inkstone with a well in it to hold water. For doing his sums he uses the abacus swanpan, or counting board. This consists of bone or ivory balls, sliding upon a series of wooden bars. The balls upon the first bar represent *units*, those upon the second bar *tens*, and so on. Up and down these bars the Chinaman sends the balls flying at lightning speed with the thumb and first finger of his right hand.

Our London friends have often brought out for our benefit their Chinese stringed instruments, and made Chinese music for us. Some of these instruments are played with and some without a bow. And there is a two-stringed instrument in playing which the bow passes between the strings. These same strings, by the way, are never of catgut, but always of wire or silk. A Chinese virtuoso wrote down for me the nine characters which represent the Chinese scale of nine notes, the last being the octave of the second, while the last but one is the octave of the first. He also obligingly read out the nine syllables by which they are designated, viz., *fan kung che chang i sze ho u liu*. When he played to us the pretty children of the boardinghouse keeper, who already learn to prattle Chinese as well as English, joined their voices in the words of a Chinese song. One day, while the talk ran on songs and music, the shopkeeper took us out into his back yard to see his pet singing-bird. It was a Mongolian lark (no pun intended), a bird valued at $25, or £5, even in China, and of course worth more here. It did not sing until made to do so by a curious process of decoying, consisting of the owner making motions with one hand to imitate the presence of another bird in the air outside the cage. This excited the poor shanma, which, after running up and down its limited dwelling several times, burst into melody. The Chinaman informed me, so tame was the bird, that he was accustomed to take the cage into Victoria Park and there give its inmate liberty for a time, and he could call it back to its cage whenever he pleased.

On their New Year's day they write Chinese New Year's cards for us. This anniversary falls, of course, on a different date to ours. It varies between January and February. Lamps are burnt before the household gods with a special kind of wick, and special oil made out of the seeds known as *chema*, which I believe is a kind of sesame, and which, curiously enough, are also used for salad. But its chief feature is the letting off at midnight of Chinese fire-crackers in quantities that would delight the heart of an anarchist. These pyrotechnic displays are not, however, confined to gay celebrations. They are also used at funerals. There has been but one Chinese burial in London within our limited experience, and our most vivid impression of it is that, as the procession was starting, vast bunches of crackers were set fire to—filling the whole street from end to end with noise and villainous saltpetre.

The Chinese religion may be said to be a Chinese puzzle. There are three religions in China, and everybody seems to belong to all of them, and, in fact, the worship of ancestors underlies them all. Here in London a room is set apart in every tenement for the family altar. We take off our hats on entering it as we should on entering a Christian church. At the back of the altar is a picture representing the deity to whom it is consecrated, or else a sheet of red or orange paper bearing his name. To the front of this stand a row of vases filled with sand. In some of these vases artificial flowers are stuck. In others joss-sticks are burning. I should explain that a joss-stick is simply a stick of incense, and diffuses a similar perfume to that used by Western nations. The blasphemous European uses it to light his pipe with, but the Chinese regard the joss-stick as sacred. Should you wish to extinguish one you must on no account blow upon it. That would be to defile it. You must put it out by shaking it to and fro. Besides the offering of flowers and of incense, an offering of food is never absent from the shrine. In Chinese London the food offered to the joss-house consists of a cup of tea and plate of grapes, apples, mixed biscuits and sweets. Upon funerals and other exceptional occasions mock money is burnt. The Chinese are too thrifty to make burnt offerings of real coin. Their mock money, otherwise known as joss paper, consists of three varieties. First there is a strip of plain paper pierced with holes; each hole represents one cash, a cash being a Chinese coin. Secondly, there are two qualities of wrappers decorated with tinfoil to represent silver, and in either of which the first sort must be enfolded when burnt in the oven. The cheaper of these two qualities of wrappers is merely a single sheet, and of these sheets five pairs is the quantity for one sacrifice. But if you prefer to use the more expensive variety, which is shaped like a cup, then you need only employ one pair instead of five. This same room which contains the objects of worship is also used because of the luck brought to it by the presence of the deity, for purposes of a different kind. This is the gambling saloon with its gaming table covered with Canton matting always packed with a dense crowd. The game with which the Chinese in all parts of the world are identified—the famous game of Fan Tan—is often seen here. It makes no great strain on the intellect. The apparatus consists of a brass bowl, a bamboo stick, and a number of those Chinese coins known as cash with the square holes in the middle by which they can be slung upon a cord for porterage. The method of play is as follows:—An unknown number of cash taken at random is partly covered with a brass bowl. The company then proceed to make their bets; there are four possible chances. When the bets are made the cashier proceeds to count out the coin into fours. To avoid any possibility of foul play he uses for this purpose the bamboo rod. It is obvious that at the finish there must be a remainder of either three or two or one or no cash at all. This is the winning number, and those who have staked their money on that particular result win, while the unfortunates who betted on the three losing numbers have to pay up. Such, in its most simple form, is Fan Tan. The Chinese make a large use of counters in their gambling games for the very good reason that their coinage consists almost entirely of small values. Therefore, while the cash represents the smallest unit, the next grade higher is a counter called the white pearl, which again is followed by the black pearl. These two look for all the world like a white and black button respectively. Then if you want a still larger stake, you may use chessmen, and lastly, highest token of all in value, comes the domino. This is usually wrapped in paper when used as a counter, and its fictitious value written on it. Besides real dominoes the Chinese have a kind of playing cards like dominoes. They are twenty-one in number, and in playing are divided into two suits. The eleven cards which constitute one of these suits are called *civil*, and the ten cards which remain for the other suit are called *military*. The reason for the pack consisting of twenty-one is that, as any mathematician will tell you, you can make exactly twenty-one different throws with a pair of dice, neither more nor less. The cards, therefore, represent every possible combination. It is a curious, and to me an inexplicable fact that in Chinese dice, and, therefore, on these cards, the numbers one and four are always red, while the two, three, five, and six are always black. Another kind of Chinese playing cards is called the "Ten Letter Cards." These do not appear to be very generally used, in fact the London Chinese assured me that they are only fit for children. But the fact seems to be, that in China they are peculiarly patronised by the *hakka* gipsies. There are thirty-eight cards in a pack, namely, four court cards,

> the ace of *kwon*,
> the ace of *sok*,
> two, three, four, five, six, seven, eight, nine, of *sjip*,
> two, three, four, five, six, seven, eight, nine, of *kwon*,
> two, three, four, five, six, seven, eight, nine, of *sok*,
> two, three, four, five, six, seven, eight, nine, of *tshien*.

Which barbarous spelling of the Chinese words must be excused on the score of my authority being a Dutchman, whose orthography I did not like to alter. The order in which I have arranged the cards is that of their respective values, beginning with the highest. Four persons generally play, and there are several games in each of which the number of cards dealt to the players is different. I shall not go further into details here, but proceed to another and far more generally patronised variety of Chinese cards. This kind is that most likely to be seen played in the gambling rooms of Chinese London. The packs consist of only thirty different cards, but there are four of each in the boxes in which they are usually sold. Some authorities, therefore, are in the habit of speaking of the pack as consisting of 120 cards, which I think is misleading. The thirty cards then are divided into three suits, to each of which there are plain cards, and a court card. The lowest suit is generally known among Europeans as the suit of strings, and its tenth card is called the *white flower*. The next suit in order is that of cakes, with its court card the *red flower*. Lastly comes the suit of myriads, with its court card the *old thousand*. This last suit is different in every way from the other two. In them the values were expressed as in our own cards by the varying quantities they bore of the object from which they are named. But in the suit of myriads each card bears a human figure, and its order in the sequence is indicated by a Chinese number at the top. The human figures, if you look at them closely, appear to have no legs. They are cut off short. This is because they are represented standing in their coffins, so I am told, but I do not know the story, which doubtless exists to explain this. The Chinese distinguished the principal cards by an index in the margin like our "squeezers." Our game of Poker seems to me the nearest we have to the Chinese games (which are various), played with the cards we are now discussing. But an attempt has been recently made to introduce one of the actual games of the Flowery Land, under the name of *khanhoo* into England. The desire of each player is to get such cards into his hand as shall make a better combination than those of his neighbour. The combinations admitted, and their values, vary with

CHINESE LONDON AND ITS OPIUM DENS

each game. The following list of five of them, arranged in their order, will give an idea of how the thing is done.

To hold 9 strings, 1 cake, 1 myriad counts 10 marks.

To hold 2 strings, 8 cakes, 2 myriads counts 11 marks.

To hold 8 strings, white flower, 9 myriads counts 12 marks.

To hold 1 2 3 cakes counts 13 marks.

To hold 9 strings, red flower, old thousand, counts 13 marks.

The three cards which make up this last combination are marked with red stamps. The game can be played with four players, or less, or more, but in the latter case extra packs of cards have to be brought forward. The number of cards dealt varies with each game.

JAMES PLATT.

23

E. C. MOORE, 'THE SOCIAL VALUE OF THE SALOON', *AMERICAN JOURNAL OF SOCIOLOGY*, 3, JULY 1897, 1–12

WHAT is the saloon in society? What is its social value? What are the demands which it supplies? are questions which have received a variety of answers. In general it may be said that these answers have fallen under two main heads, determined in each case by the point of view of those giving them. The patron of the saloon speaks: "It is a necessary feature of my life. It furnishes me with many things which I cannot get elsewhere. It does me no harm;" and his words savor of conviction. But another is heard: "I am opposed to the saloon and to the liquor traffic in all its forms. It is unnecessary; it is waste; it is more than that; it is positive evil and vicious in the highest degree. It represents no necessity and supplies no legitimate want." Diametrically opposed to each other, yet both have spoken from conviction and each has stated the truth as it exists for him. But there is no truth in a contradiction until it be resolved. Society has at least become conscious of the contradiction; its resolution can follow only upon a complete statement of its terms; and it is in the hope that certain partially neglected facts may herein be brought forward, which shall contribute to such a complete statement, that this paper is submitted.

The nineteenth ward of Chicago according to the school census of 1896 has a population of 48,280. It is a workingman's district and the population is typical of unskilled labor in general. The largest foreign elements in the ward are the Irish, German, Italian and Bohemian, stated in the order of relative numerical strength. Of those of foreign parentage about one-half are American born. As to moral condition, neither the extremes of vice nor of virtue are reached, while the general moral tone is rather healthful. It is believed that so far as population and worldly condition can be held to affect the saloon problem the conditions of the nineteenth ward are typical of the problem in general. A careful study of the saloons in the ward has been made, of which this does not profess to be a report. It is merely a statement of impressions gathered in the course of the investigation; the report itself belongs to a larger whole not yet completed in details. The laboratory method was employed. The saloons were visited, an attempt was made to escape that bane of social investigation—the psychologist's fallacy. In so far as possible, conditions were exchanged. Purse and scrip were left behind. The saloon became an integral feature of life. It was loafing place, news center, and basis of food supply in its free lunch counter; a complete orientation was made into its life. Trammeled neither by an abstinence pledge nor by a predisposition for its wares, it is believed that the freedom necessary to unbiased judgment was obtained.

It was assumed in beginning the investigation that an institution which society has so generally created for itself must meet a definite social demand; and that the demand was not synonymous with a desire on the part of society to commit suicide by means of alcoholic poison was taken for granted. The question became that of fixing the demand, of determining the social value. What does the saloon offer that renders it so generally useful, in the economic sense, to the great mass of those who patronize it? For it is use, not abuse, that it stands for. It does not personify "the vilest elements of modern civilization." It does not "trade in and batten upon intemperance." It supplies legitimate needs and stands alone in supplying them. It transforms the individual into a *socius* where there is no other transforming power. It unites the many ones into a common whole which we call society, and it stands for this union amid conditions which would otherwise render it impossible, and intemperance is but its accident. The evils it produces have been portrayed in glowing terms: "Men and women glorying in drunkenness and shame;" "The sotted beasts who nightly gather at the bar." The more uncommon particular has been declared the universal. The exception has been made the rule. If the evils of liquor drinking were in fact what they have been in imagination the human species would have become extinct in Europe within any three centuries since the rise of the Roman Empire. The man who speaks of drunkenness and intemperance only, when treating of drink in general, does not exhaust his subject. Indeed it may be questioned whether he reaches it. That intemperance is an exception can be proved only by careful observation. It is believed that the personal use of this method will support these statements. That great waste is incident to every movement of our social machinery cannot be doubted; that the waste is even greater here than elsewhere need not be denied. The machinery is still useful, though many refuse to look beyond its waste, and it will be employed until a better machine is invented.

Primarily the saloon is a social center. Few will deny this. It is the workingman's club. Many of his leisure hours are spent here. In it he finds more of the things which approximate to luxury than he finds at home, almost more than he finds in any other public place in the ward. In winter the saloon is warm, in summer it is cool, at night it is brightly lighted, and it is always clean. More than that there are chairs and tables and papers and cards and lunch, and in many cases pool and billiards, while in some few well-equipped gymnasiums can be found which are free to patrons. What more does the workingman want for his club? He already has all that most clubs offer their members—papers and cards and food and drink and service—and being modest in his wants their quality satisfies him. But his demand for even these things is not fundamental, they are but means to his social expression. It is the society of his fellows that he seeks and must have.

To say that the saloon is the workingman's club does not answer a single objection which its opponents raise; one must first prove the necessity of workingmen's clubs and of the kind that the saloon represents. The common laborer works ten hours per day, his pay is small. In many cases his family is large, at best his food would not be found sufficient for his gentler brother; add to this that his work is hard and his food poorly cooked, and the whole result will be a subnormal life. Given a human being, a center of life force, and among his first expressions will be a demand for society, nor does the family alone supply this want. History does not supply a single illustration of the self-sufficiency of the family. The social activity reaches beyond the immediate tie to the brother who is a brother only by courtesy. Social need outgrows the family and creates its own larger society, and this is what my workingman must do. He does not desert his family. He is not disloyal to them in seeking it, but he must find a larger circle in which to move. He must himself articulate in a larger life, and where shall he find it?

Does not the church offer what he seeks? In the first place four churches are somewhat inadequate to the needs of a population of 48,000, and yet if all places of worship in the ward, both Jewish and Gentile, be counted, four will be the net result. It is conceived that there is a difference between religious and social need— a difference between the organs of religious and social expression. The church is primarily devoted to worship. We seek *sociality*, and even a reconstructed church open seven days and nights in the week might fail to recognize our want. Indeed it may be questioned whether the church is called upon to note it. With us it does not, and our question remains unanswered.

But someone may say: "Are there not clubs where he can go?" No, and if there were they would offer conventions instead of freedom; must offer conventions of order of business, officers, etc., because of the inherent nature of clubs. The democratic element which is most essential—the absolute freedom to come and go and do as one pleases—cannot be incorporated into a club. But this reservation must be made, that in so far as the club expresses his vital interests, in the same measure does it become the institution which we seek. The trade union answers to this description. It is a much higher form of social expression than the saloon, and among its members it has supplanted the saloon in a large degree, but at present a very small percentage of workingmen belong to trade unions and their demand for social expression is not thus supplied; yet the reformer's greatest hope lies along this line, while his energies are largely given to more futile forms of social service. Of other organizations created for the purpose of ministering to this social need, most have been failures. They have come from the outside, splendid schemes to impress men, but alas! not to express them. But they succeed only as they express the human energy which they seek to convert to better uses.

Four churches, a few trade unions and impressive social forms cannot hope to meet the social needs of 48,000 people. Remember that there are no music halls or theaters beside. "What else have they but the saloon," and to the saloon they go. It was created for this purpose and still functions to this want.

The saloonkeeper is the only man who keeps open house in the ward. It is his business to entertain. It does not matter that he does not select his guests; that convention is useless among them. In fact his democracy is one element of

THE SOCIAL VALUE OF THE SALOON

his strength. His place is the common meeting ground of his neighbors—and he supplies the stimulus which renders social life possible; there is an accretion of intelligence that comes to him in his business. He hears the best stories. He is the first to get accurate information as to the latest political deals and social mysteries. The common talk of the day passes through his ears and he is known to retain that which is most interesting. He himself articulates in a larger social center composed of many social leaders like himself who, each representing his own following, together come to have a much larger power and place than the average citizen. My workingman is not too democratic to respect the ready intelligence, the power, and the better dress of the leader in his social center. They draw him to the saloon, and once there they continue to hold him. In addition the saloonkeeper trusts him for drinks—a debt of honor—yea more, he lends him money if in greater need. But the saloonkeeper is only one element in this analysis of attraction, and by no means the strongest. The desire to be with his fellows—the fascination which a comfortable room where men are has for him is more than he can resist; moreover the things which these men are doing are enticing to him; they are thinking, vying with each other in conversation, in story telling, debate. Nothing of general or local interest transpires which they do not "argue" out. Their social stimulus is epitomized in the saloon. It is center of learning, books, papers, and lecture hall to them, the clearing house for their common intelligence, the place where their philosophy of life is worked out and from which their political and social beliefs take their beginning. As an educational institution its power is very great and not to be scorned because skilled teachers are not present, for they teach themselves. Nay, verily, the apostle of the new education may welcome this as an illustration of education not divorced from social life by bonds of convention.

No one who is familiar with this life will deny the great educational value of the saloons, and this social expression, this freeing of human activity is rendered possible by the stimulant which the saloon offers. It stands not for social opportunity only. It affords also the conditions of sociality. "The first action of ethylic alcohol," says Dr. Kerr, "is vascular relaxation, commonly called exhilaration or stimulation, when a glow of warmth spreads over the whole system, when the heart beats faster, when 'happy thoughts' crowd in upon the brain, when all seems life and light and joy, when everything without and within wears a roseate hue." The heart beats more rapidly—there is an exaltation of the mind, a freeing of emotional life, pleasurable ideas, rapid thought, unusual merriment. Is it not a social ideal—a condition in which each one would appear before his fellow? Only there are different ways of reaching it. The demanding power of individuals is here wanting. The stimulus of books, pictures, and good music is absent. The constant stimulus of purposive intelligence is denied—a thousand things which stimulate to swift and happy thought in other forms of society are entirely wanting here. But human energy, which is after all the primal social fact, demands an avenue of escape and finds its conditions in the best way it can.

Moreover this stimulus not only supplies immediate social need. It has all the value for present-day civilization that stimulants have ever had in the formation

PLACES AND SPACES

of history. It helps to preserve the idea which as yet cannot become an act, and failing in its function must otherwise die. Such, psychologists tell us, is the value of the stimulant—to free the individual from the consciousness of the limitation which prevents the realization of his ideal, and to preserve his ideal for him and for society. It is here that the saloon gets its ultimate social value. The bacchanals were promoters of the Greek state, and the drinking of the Dark Ages contributed to the realization of the modern individual. Upon what beside shall the emotional life feed? or where shall it find its resting place of achievement, while the act itself is impossible save in the heightened activity of an exhilarated self? In this way it is believed that the saloon is aiding in the development of a higher form of society by preserving in its patrons a higher social hope. This is but a part of the social need to which it ministers, but by no means the least part.

There is another primal need which the saloon supplies and in most cases supplies well. It is a food-distributing center—a place where a hungry man can get as much as he wants to eat and drink for a small price. As a rule the food is notoriously good and the price notoriously cheap. And that air of poverty which unfailingly attends the cheap restaurant and finds its adequate expression in ragged and dirty table linen is here wanting. Instead polished oak tables are used and upon them reposes free an abundance such as to constantly surprise a depleted purse. That the saloon feeds thousands and feeds them well no one will deny who has passed the middle of the day there.

As to the physiological effects of the use of alcohol, the experiments conducted in the Yale laboratory, as they are reported in *Nature*, would seem to indicate that when the quantity of alcohol used is not in excess of 2 per cent. of the digestive fluid, digestive activity is aided by its presence. "Whisky can be considered to impede the solvent action of the gastric juices only when taken immoderately and in intoxicating quantities." It is believed that a large part of the ordinary beer drinking contributes less than 2 per cent. in alcohol to the whole digestive fluid—but the proof is almost inaccessible. Dr. Keeley declares that "in the laboring man a certain quantity of alcohol will preserve the body weight with the same foot pounds of labor, and with a given quantity of food; and if these other things are equal the absence of the alcohol will require more food, or a decrease either in the labor or in the body weight." He contends that its action is not to build up tissue but to prevent its breaking down. "It has an inhibitory action on cell metabolism." He adds: "I understand that these things are matters of demonstration, and that the everyday use of alcohol among laborers satisfactorily proves the value of the use and not the abuse of alcohol as a food—direct and indirect."

Such it is believed is the social value of the saloon. That it functions to certain social wants otherwise not supplied is our thesis. That its wares are poison is nowhere lost to sight, but that the poison appears in their abuse and not in their use is our contention. It is also admitted that social want is very inadequately supplied by the saloon. That a condition in which the idea can express itself in emotional terms only is essentially pathological. But it is believed that the saloon will continue to supply it as long as its opponents continue to wage a war of extermination

THE SOCIAL VALUE OF THE SALOON

against all that it represents, instead of wisely aiding social life to reach that plane where its present evils shall no longer be its accidents. The saloon is a thing come out of the organic life of the world, and it will give place only to a better form of social functioning. That a better form is possible to a fully conscious society no one can deny. When and what this form shall be remains for society's component units to declare. The presence of the saloon in an unorganized society is proof conclusive that society can wisely organize the need which it supplies.

It is hardly necessary to enlarge further upon the evils of the saloon in a protest against the predominance of one-sided statements in that very particular. They are many and grave, and cry out to society for proper consideration. But proper consideration involves a whole and not a half truth, and the whole truth involves its own power of proper action. In the absence of higher forms of social stimulus and larger social life the saloon will continue to function in society, and for that great part of humanity which does not possess a more adequate form of social expression the words of Esdras will remain true: It is wine that "maketh the mind of the king and of the fatherless child to be all one, of the bondman and of the freeman, of the poor and of the rich. It turneth every thought into jollity and mirth, so that a man remembereth neither sorrow nor debt; and it maketh every heart glad."

E. C. MOORE.

CHICAGO.

24

ROYAL L. MELENDY, 'THE SALOON IN CHICAGO', *AMERICAN JOURNAL OF SOCIOLOGY*, 6, NOVEMBER 1900, 289–306[1]

Preface

THE investigations of which this is a partial report were made under the auspices of the Ethical Subcommittee of the Committee of Fifty. "This committee, made up of persons representing different communities, occupations, and opinions, is engaged in the study of the liquor problem, in the hope of securing a body of facts which may serve as a basis for intelligent public and private action. It is the purpose of the committee to collect and collate impartially all accessible facts which bear upon the problem, and it is its hope to secure for the evidence thus accumulated a measure of confidence, on the part of the community, which is not accorded to partisan statements."

The investigations here reported were carried on from the Chicago Commons, a social settlement in the very heart of the industrial district, in one of the river wards of Chicago. It is probable that no better laboratory for the study of the social problems of America exists than this same district. Here, as from upturned strata, we can discover what have been the forces that brought about the present conditions, and some of the agencies now at work in the formation of the future.

I have sought to distinguish between those conclusions which the facts in hand fully warrant, and those to which they seem to point. Although, in the study of social questions, it is impossible wholly to eradicate the personal equation, I have attempted to do so as far as possible, by discussions with men of all classes, of all shades of religious and political opinions. Professors, ministers, business-men, settlement workers, police and sporting men, have, each in their way, rendered me invaluable service. In the homes and on the street corners, in the churches, saloons, and at places of amusement, at all hours of the day and night, and in all manner of clothes, I have gathered the facts which form the basis of this report.

I am especially grateful to Professor Graham Taylor, of the sociological department of the Chicago Theological Seminary, warden of Chicago

---

1 Published by permission of the Committee of Fifty.

Commons, and pastor of one of the churches of this district; and to Mr. John Palmer Gavit, editor of *The Commons*, who have willingly given their time to direct and discuss with me the details of the investigation. I would also acknowledge the courtesy of Joseph Kipley, chief of police, through whose order the special statistics in regard to the saloons and billiard halls were collected by the police department.[1]

The saloon in general

In considering the subject "Ethical Substitutes for the Saloon," it is essential that a careful study be made of the saloon itself, and that we seek first to determine the real nature of the institution in the abolition of which substitution may assist. We must try to ascertain the secret of its hold upon our civilization, tracing in the family, political and social life, and habits of the people the roots of this mighty tree whose shadows are casting an ever-deepening gloom over all other institutions. Above all we must try to lay aside for the present all preconceived ideas of the saloon, lest prejudice should keep from us the truth. It is only on the basis of precise observation of actual facts that our study can advance.

The popular conception of the saloon as a "place where men and women revel in drunkenness and shame," or "where the sotted beasts gather nightly at the bar," is due to exaggerated pictures, drawn by temperance lecturers and evangelists, intended to excite the imagination with a view to arousing public sentiment. I am not charging them with intended falsehood, but with placing in combination things which never so exist in real life; with blending into one picture hideous incidents taken here and there from the lives of those whom the saloon has wrecked; with portraying vividly the dark side of saloon life and calling this picture "the saloon." But it may be asked: "Are they not justified in doing so? Are not these the legitimate products of the saloon? By their fruits ye shall know them." Let one step into your orchard, and, gathering into a basket the small, worm-eaten, and half-decayed windfalls return to you saying: "This is the fruit grown in your orchard—as the fruit, so is the orchard." The injustice is apparent.

The term "saloon" is too general to admit of concise definition. It is an institution grown up among the people, not only in answer to their demand for its wares, but to their demand for certain necessities and conveniences, which it supplies, either alone or better than any other agency. It is a part of the neighborhood, which must change with the neighborhood; it fulfills in it the social functions which unfortunately have been left to it to exercise. With keen insight into human nature and into the wants of the people, it anticipates all other agencies in supplying them, and thus claims its right to existence. In some sections of the city it has the appearance of accomplishing more for the laboring classes from business interests than we from philanthropic motives. The almost complete absence of those things

---

1 To be published in the full report of the Committee of Fifty.

with which the uninitiated are accustomed to associate the drinking of liquor, and the presence of much that is in itself beneficial, often turns them into advocates of the saloon as a social necessity—an equally false position.

Hedged in on every side by law, opposed by every contrivance the mind of man could invent, the saloon persists in existing and flourishing—"it spreadeth like a green bay tree." The very fact of its persistence ought to cause us to realize that we have not yet struck at the root. The saloon in Chicago is restricted by every kind of law, yet it sells liquor to minors, keeps open door all night and Sundays, from January 1 to January 1. True, some of the down-town saloons close at 12 o'clock. But why? In obedience to the ordinance filed away in the archives of the city hall? Not so; but in obedience to another law—the law of demand. Those who in the daytime patronize the down-town saloons have returned to their homes and have joined the patrons of the saloons of their immediate neighborhoods. This is the law—and almost the only law that they will obey, and it is this law that we must face and deal with unflinchingly.

The saloon in workingmen's districts

When the poor, underpaid, and unskilled laborer returns from his day's work, go with him, if you will, into the room or rooms he calls "home." Eat with him there, in the midst of those squalid surroundings and to the music of crying children, a scanty, poorly cooked meal served by an unkempt wife. Ask yourself if this is just the place where he would want to spend his evenings, night after night; if here he will find the mental stimulus as necessary to his life as to your life. Is there no escape from the inevitable despair that must come to him whose long hours of heavy physical labor preclude any mental enjoyment, if his few leisure hours are to be spent in the wretched surroundings of a home, or, worse yet, of the ordinary cheap lodging-house, either of which must constantly remind him of his poverty? Are there not places in the neighborhood where the surroundings will be more congenial; where his mental, yes, his moral, nature will have a better chance for development? Are there not some in the neighborhood who have recognized and sought to satisfy the social cravings of these men, which the home at best does not wholly satisfy?

Yes, business interests have occupied this field. With a shrewd foresight, partially due to the fierce competition between the great brewing companies, they have seen and met these needs. The following table, made by a careful investigation of each of the 163 saloons of the seventeenth ward—a fairly representative ward of the working people—shows some of the attractions offered by these saloons:

Number of saloons	163
Number offering free lunches	111
" " business lunches	24
" supplied with tables	147
" " " papers	139

"	"	" music	-	-	-	-	-	-	-	-	8
"	"	" billiard tables	-	-	-	-	-	-	-	-	44
"	"	" stalls	-	-	-	-	-	-	-	-	56
"	"	" dance halls	-	-	-	-	-	-	-	-	6
"	allowing gambling		-	-	-	-	-	-	-	-	3

In the statement, now current among those who have studied the saloon "at first hand," that it is the workingman's club, lies the secret of its hold upon the vast working and voting populace of Chicago. That same instinct in man which leads those of the more resourceful classes to form such clubs as the Union League Club, or the Marquette Club; which leads the college man into the fraternity, leads the laboring men into the clubs furnished them by the saloonkeeper, not from philanthropic motives, but because of shrewd business foresight. The term "club" applies; for, though unorganized, each saloon has about the same constituency night after night. Its character is determined by the character of the men who, having something in common, make the saloon their rendezvous. Their common ground may be their nationality, as the name "Italian Headquarters" implies; or it may be their occupation, as indicated by the names "Mechanics' Exchange," "Milkman's Exchange," etc.; or, if their political affiliations are their common ground, there are the "Democratic Headquarters of the Eighteenth Ward," etc. As shown above, the "club-room" is furnished with tables, usually polished and cleaned, with from two to six chairs at each table. As you step in, you find a few men standing at the bar, a few drinking, and farther back men are seated about the tables, reading, playing cards, eating, and discussing, over a glass of beer, subjects varying from the political and sociological problems of the day to the sporting news and the lighter chat of the immediate neighborhood. Untrammeled by rules and restrictions, it surpasses in spirit the organized club. That general atmosphere of freedom, that spirit of democracy, which men crave, is here realized; that men seek it and that the saloon tries to cultivate it is blazoned forth in such titles as "The Freedom," "The Social," "The Club," etc. Here men "shake out their hearts together." Intercourse quickens the thought, feeling, and action.

In many of these discussions, to which I have listened and in which I have joined, there has been revealed a deeper insight into the real cause of present evils than is often manifested from lecture platforms, but their remedies are wide of the mark, each bringing forward a theory which is the panacea for all social ills. The names of Karl Marx and leaders of political and social thought are often heard here. This is the workingman's school. He is both scholar and teacher. The problems of national welfare are solved here. Many as patriotic men as our country produces learn here their lessons in patriotism and brotherhood. Here the masses receive their lessons in civil government, learning less of our ideals, but more of the practical workings than the public schools teach. It is the most cosmopolitan institution in the most cosmopolitan of cities. One saloon advertises its cosmopolitanism by this title, "Everybody's Exchange." Men of all nationalities meet and mingle, and by the interchange of views and opinions their own are modified. Nothing short of travel could exert so broadening an influence upon these men.

PLACES AND SPACES

It does much to assimilate the heterogeneous crowds that are constantly pouring into our city from foreign shores. But here, too, they learn their lessons in corruption and vice. It is their school for good and evil.

The saloonkeeper, usually a man their superior in intelligence, often directs their thought. He has in his possession the latest political and sporting news. Here in argument each has fair play. He who can win and tell the best story is, not by election, but by virtue of fitness, the leader. The saloon is, in short, the clearing-house for the common intelligence—the social and intellectual center of the neighborhood.

Again, some saloons offer rooms furnished, heated, and lighted, free to certain men's clubs and organizations. For example, a certain German musical society, occupying one of these rooms, fully compensates the saloonkeeper with the money that passes over the bar as the members go in and out of the club-room. In like manner some trade unions and fraternal organizations are supplied with meeting-places. A saloon on Armitage avenue has a bowling-alley, billiard tables, and club-rooms, in which nonpartisan political meetings were held during last spring's campaign. It is also offered to the people for various neighborhood meetings. In such a room a gay wedding party celebrated the marriage vow. It is, in very truth, a part of the life of the people of this district.

But the young man, where does he spend his evenings? Leaving the supper table he takes his hat and sets out from home, to go where? Let us follow the boy in the crowded districts—in the river wards of Chicago. As he comes out of the house into the street he is surrounded for miles with brick and mortar; not a blade of grass or a leaf of green to be seen. Placing his fingers to his mouth he gives a shrill whistle, which is answered by one and another of the boys, till the little crowd—their club—has gathered. Seeking to join informally such a crowd of the older young men, the only question asked on eligibility was: "Can you run?" Short words, but of tremendous significance. It is this: As soon as a small crowd of boys collects it is dispersed by the police. Having been arrested once or twice, these young men learned the lesson, and I was told "to scatter" at the word "jiggers," the warning note given at the sight of an approaching "cop." Driven about the streets like dogs by the civil authorities (whether it be necessary I am not now discussing); provided with no place for the healthy exercise of their physical natures, or even an opportunity to meet and tell stories, they have recourse to but one of two alternatives: to dodge the police, hiding in underground caves and under sidewalks until they become hardened against the law; or to enter the places the saloon has provided for them.

Thus again business interests have seized the opportunity that has been let slip, and have taken advantage of boys' necessities. Rooms, well lighted, furnished with billiard and pool tables, tables for cards and other games, are placed at the disposal of these boys. Five cents is charged for a game of billiards and a check which entitles the holder to a glass of beer, a five-cent cigar, a box of cigarettes, or a soft drink. The table shows 27 per cent. of these saloons thus equipped. Much less numerous are the saloons furnishing handball courts. These courts, models of attractiveness when compared with the neighborhood in which they are located, are used by young and old. Shower-baths are provided free. The boys must pass out by the bar of the adjoining saloon, where, heated by the game and feeling somewhat under obligations, they patronize the saloonkeeper. Some saloons have gymnasiums, more or less fully equipped. Bowling-alleys and shuffle-board are among the attractions offered.

For the large floating population of these districts, and for the thousands of men whose only home is in the street or the cheap lodging-house, where they are herded together like cattle, the saloon is practically the basis of food supply. The table shows that 68 per cent. furnish free lunches, and 15 per cent. business lunches. On the free-lunch counters are dishes containing bread, several kinds of meats, vegetables, cheeses, etc., to which the men freely help themselves. Red-hots (Frankfurters), clams, and egg sandwiches are dispensed with equal freedom to those who drink and to those who do not. For those desiring a hot lunch, clam chowder, hot potatoes, several kinds of meat, and vegetables are served at tables, nearly always with a glass of beer. The following amount is consumed per day in a saloon near here: 150–200 pounds of meat, 1½–2 bushels of potatoes, 50 loaves of bread, 35 pounds of beans, 45 dozens of eggs on some days (eggs not usually being used), 10 dozen ears of sweet corn, $1.50–$2 worth of vegetables. Five men are constantly employed at the lunch counter. The total cost of the lunch is $30 to $40 per day.

That the saloons are able to put out such an abundance, and of such variety and quality, is due to the competition of the large brewing companies. These companies own a very large number of the saloons in Chicago. Thus the cost of not only the beer, but the meat, bread, and vegetables, bought in vast quantities, is greatly reduced. Only a portion of those who drink patronize the lunch counter. The small dealers are forced into the competition by the larger ones. The general appearance of abundance, so lacking either in their homes or in the cheap restaurants, and the absence of any sense of charity, so distasteful to the self-respecting man, add to the attractiveness of the place, and are a wonderful help to the digestion. Here the hungry and the penniless find relief for the time, few being turned away until they become "steady regulars." I believe it is true that all the charity organizations in Chicago combined are feeding fewer people than the saloons. No questions are asked about the "deserving poor;" no "work test" is applied; and again and again relief is given in the shape of money, "loaned expecting no return."

Another function of the Charity Organization Society the saloon has taken unto itself and exercises more or less perfectly: the laboring man out of employment knows that in some saloon he is likely to find, not only temporary relief, but assistance in finding work. That these saloons pose as labor bureaus is evidenced by the names placed above their doors. The significance of these names is this: Men of the same trade, having common interests, make the saloon that represents their interests their rendezvous. To the "Stonecutters' Exchange," for example, men seeking stonecutters often apply. But information concerning positions is dependent more upon that gathered by the men themselves and made common property.

307

PLACES AND SPACES

Many a man has been "put on his feet" by just this kind of help, nor does he feel that he is accepting charity, but that he is as likely to give as to receive. He is asked neither his age nor his pedigree. His past history is not desired as long as he is in need now. Not a sense of obligation, but a real feeling of brotherhood; and this feeling, existing among these men to a degree not usually recognized, prompts them to aid each other. Grateful is he to the saloon that was his "friend in need;" bitter toward those who, without offering anything better, propose to take from him the only institution that has befriended him.

Scattered throughout the city, within easy reach of any neighborhood, are saloons offering a form of entertainment to the people not unlike the cheap vaudeville. Passing back of the screen, we enter a large room filled with tables and chairs; at the end of the room is a stage. While men and women sit around these tables, drinking beer and smoking, the painted, bawdy girls entertain them with the latest popular songs and the skirt dance. The regular vaudeville bill, including the comic man, acrobatic feats, cake-walks, etc., is presented. The character of the entertainment is but a reflection of the character of the neighborhood. In some communities no obscene word is uttered, and but little that is suggestive of evil is presented. It affords an opportunity for the hard-worked men and women to escape from their stuffy homes and thoughts of poverty into a clean, well-lighted room, where with their families they can enjoy an evening of pleasure. To see the hardened, careworn expressions on their faces gradually relax and melt away into expressions of simple enjoyment, as they laugh heartily at the jokes, might at first arouse one's sense of humor, but it would soon impress one deeply with the pathos of it all: with the thought that this little entertainment, cheap and vulgar as it is, seems to satisfy their longing for amusement. Patriotic songs are never missing, and I have heard them join heartily in the chorus. Cheer after cheer greets the names of our heroes, as they appear in the songs of the girls. The sense of the masses on the Cuban war policy could easily be determined by their applause and hisses at the saloon vaudevilles. These people have a sense of honor peculiar to themselves, and a careful observation of that which most frequently elicits their applause shows that an appeal to their sense of honor is sure to be well received. In ——'s vaudeville saloon it is estimated that 3,000 pass in and out between the hours of 8 P. M. and 6 A. M. Saturday nights. As has been stated, the character of these saloons varies with the neighborhood, and vulgar songs are frequently sung. The evil influence of some of these cannot be overestimated. Then too prostitutes often come here and mingle with the crowd.

A function, which should rightly be a civic one, the saloon has appropriated, and added to the long list of the necessities to which it ministers—that of furnishing to the people the only toilet conveniences in large sections of the city. In this respect the ordinary hotel is not better equipped than are the saloons. Moreover, either by their clerks or by signs, the hotels inform the man who habitually takes advantage of them that they are not for the use of the general public. We are behind European municipalities in this respect, and Chicago is especially deficient. Here is a field awaiting the efforts of some public-spirited man, a service by no means small, and one that would directly affect the liquor interests. Not that it will cause any man to cease drinking, but that it will remove a temptation from thousands of men who, of necessity, daily pass the bar which they feel under obligation to patronize. Nor will it longer necessitate the familiarizing of little boys with the evils of saloon life. Such are a few of the attractions which the saloon in the workingmen's district offers to its patrons.

While it is true that a vast army of the laboring men and boys of Chicago find the saloon the best place in their neighborhood for the development of their social, intellectual, and physical natures, they find there also things which appeal to their lower natures. Almost without exception the saloons exhibit pictures of the nude; in the higher-class saloons by costly paintings, in the smaller saloons by cards furnished by the brewing companies. As the saloon is "no respecter of persons," even in the best of them vile persons find entrance. That the youths are here corrupted is too well known. Our table reveals the appalling fact that 34½ per cent. of the saloons in this district are stall saloons. These saloons have set aside a large portion of the back of the building for private "wine-rooms," which, whether designed for this purpose or not, are used by prostitutes as places of assignation. There may be no definite business agreement between these women and the keepers of these saloons (I doubt if there is), but as a rule the saloonkeepers are compensated for the extra space and furniture by the money paid for drinks by young men attracted by these women. To set up the drinks to "the girls" is a custom; the women calling for "small beer" urge the men "to set 'em up" again and again; hence they are a source of revenue to the saloon. Their part in the profit is this: it furnishes them a suitable "hang-out," a place where they may secure customers for their inhuman trade, carried on, not in the saloon as a rule, but in their rooms, usually in the immediate vicinity, though occasionally miles away, lest they should be detected.

Again, as all through this study, exceptions must be made. These "wine-rooms" are not always used for illegitimate purposes. Where is the respectable young woman, who is but one member of a large family, all living, or rather existing, in a single room which serves as kitchen, dining-room, parlor, and bedroom for the entire family, to receive her young men friends? Is it strange that she takes advantage of these "wine-rooms"? Here her father goes; her mother and brothers are often there. They come here on cold nights to save fuel and light. Here, when a little tot, she used to come for the pitcher of beer; here, barefooted and dirty, she would run to hear the music of the German band; if she were pretty and could sing, many a bright ribbon did she buy with the money earned here. No, they are not all directly evil places, but the temptation is tremendous. How can a child, brought up in such a locality, forced to receive from the saloon even the common necessities and conveniences of life, grow up into noble and beautiful womanhood?

In about 2 per cent. of these saloons gambling is permitted. It is open and unrestricted, whenever sufficient "hush money" is paid. That more do not exist is simply due to the fact that the demand is not great enough for a larger number

PLACES AND SPACES

to thrive and pay the exorbitant "tax." The saloon, too, is in a very small number of cases, many times smaller than is usually believed, a rendezvous for criminals. There are low dives of indescribable filthiness, where vice is open and shameless.

Be it known, however, that there are in every neighborhood saloons free from any connection whatever with gambling or the social vice—places where indecency in conversation or manner is strictly prohibited, and drinking to excess not allowed. This is sometimes to secure "a better class of trade," and sometimes, incredible as it seems, to accord with certain principles and religious scruples of the saloonkeepers, who are not all archfiends of the evil one.

The saloon in business sections

The saloon in business portions presents a slightly different phase. While it is true that saloons in all parts of the city have about the same features, it is also true that in some certain features predominate, as the peculiar conditions emphasize that particular demand. Thus in the workingmen's district, the wretched conditions of home- and lodging-house life, and the failure of church and philanthropy to provide opportunity for social life, have turned over to the saloon this large field, from which it is reaping an abundant harvest. So in the business portions the lack of an adequate provision of places for business appointments has given the saloon an advantage which it was quick to take. Men who spend the day in the heart of the city come here for business and do not, as a rule, have time to sit around in saloons. Neither in the evening have the social features any special attraction for them. The majority of these men find in their homes and in the clubs to which they belong ample opportunity for social life. A larger per cent. than in the districts just treated enter the saloon just for the drink and pass out again.

The average business-man, aside from the regular duties of his office or place of business, has many appointments of a semi-business nature. Seeking a place for these appointments, other than his office, where constant interruptions must occur, he finds in many a first-class saloon a place altogether suited to this purpose. Here he may sit down, often in an alcove, at one of the polished oak tables with which this "drawing-room" is furnished, and discuss business at leisure. Some of these "drawing-rooms" are veritable palm gardens; costly paintings hang upon the walls; German orchestras, playing with exquisite taste, fill the air with music. Soft drinks are sold, and many an hour is spent in these places by those who may not know the taste of beer. In this connection it may be noted that soft drinks are expensive, because, as one manager said, "we are not here to sell soft drinks, and hope to force everyone to take beer or wine; there is more profit in them."

Not only are these used for business appointments, but separate rooms are sometimes furnished for the use of committees and small meetings of various character, no charge for their use being attached. There are in the city other places than the saloon for such appointments, but because of their scarcity and inadequacy need hardly be taken into account. Many business transactions take place in these saloons. The head of a department in one of Chicago's large wholesale houses assures me that certain of their best salesmen sell a large portion of their goods "over a glass of beer" in a neighboring saloon. The glass of beer in a business transaction has a function similar to that of the cigarette in diplomacy. Certain saloons, whose only distinguishing feature is their oddity and the novelties they present, owe their existense to a custom of long standing among wholesale merchants and others who take their "country cousins" to "see the sights." The music in some of these places is worthy of special mention. Orchestras, led by well-known musicians, attract people from all parts of city, people who come and spend the evening listening to the music. To the — — and — — young people come in great numbers, and when the theaters close these places usually fill rapidly. Clubs and fraternities here banquet their new members. Neither rowdyism nor anything other than good manners is public here.

The most distinguishing feature of the down-town saloon is the business lunch. But very few of the thousands who spend the day down town in offices or behind counters, live within several miles of their work. This means that it is both cheaper and more convenient, if not necessary, to get their lunch near their place of business. The liquor dealers have found it highly profitable to run restaurants in connection with their saloons. Because of their neatness, and at least the semblance of elegance and beauty, and of the music, which is of itself a strong inducement, they are patronized, not only by those who drink, but by hundreds who are willing to go where they can get the best for the least. The proprietor of one of the down-town restaurants said that he could afford to lose $30 to $75, or even $100, a day for the sake of advertising the beer under whose name and auspices his place was run.

That the saloons are able to compete with the restaurants so successfully is partly due to the fact that many of them are united under the control of the brewing companies—gigantic monopolies. Likewise, here the free lunch is well patronized. Hundreds, who breakfast and dine at their homes, especially those of sedentary habits, find sufficient for the midday lunch in that served with the glass of beer, usually several slices of cold meats, an abundance of bread, vegetables, cheeses, etc.

Here, as everywhere in Chicago, the social vice flourishes in connection with the liquor traffic. Here the proportion of the saloons in which the stall system is in vogue—which are used as houses of assignation—is relatively small. The saloons having any connection whatever with this evil all have a dance hall in the rear and a house of ill-fame above, all under one management. These, however, are not scattered throughout among the business blocks, as are the stalls in the workingmen's districts, but are clustered about certain streets, principally parts of Clark street, State street, Dearborn street, Custom House place, Wabash avenue, Plymouth place, and others. Suffice it to say that few enter these places who do not know the character of these saloons, so that in reality they amount to houses of ill-fame, with bar attachment.

PLACES AND SPACES

The saloon in suburban districts

In the suburban districts the saloon takes on still another character. The family saloon, the beer-garden, and the road-house are more in evidence. Throughout the entire city the saloons pose as family saloons, hanging out the sign "family entrance," but it is more particularly in the suburban saloons that one sees the families sitting together in groups. The main thoroughfare running through a suburban district is, so far as the saloon is concerned, a cross-section of the whole city, exhibiting the saloon in all its varying characters, both as to its moral tone and as to its social functions. The most delightful and apparently harmless feature of the saloon is the beer-garden Here is an instance where the words "saloon" and "beer-garden" are so loaded down with conflicting meanings and prejudices that they utterly fail to be of further service in conveying thought. To the German the word "beer-garden" carries with it no moral idea whatever; indeed, among them it is a highly creditable feature of their social life. To the temperance enthusiast it stands for all that is base and low—an equally erroneous conviction. These gardens are numerous in the suburban districts.

The ——, a typical German beer-garden, though scarcely comparable with the ——,[1] accommodates 4,700. During the summer an average of 3,000 gather at the ——, on the north side, every day, principally for the music. From a bandstand in the rear of the garden an orchestra renders exquisite music. This orchestra receives $125 per day for its services from 6 P. M. to 11 P. M. The waiters, most of them fine-appearing elderly gentlemen, dressed in black, serve beer, wines, and soft drinks to the people out in the open, while at tables beneath the roof dinners are being served. The garden is brilliantly lighted with Japanese lanterns hanging from the trees. The lights, the trees, the starry heavens above, the moon gliding now and then behind the clouds, soul-stirring music, now strong and full, now soft and sweet, make this a charming spot where lovers delight to come, where the business-man, returned from the crowded centers of the city, comes with wife and child, and the business cares float gradually away, borne on the lighter strains of music. Old men with their pipes find in this place a never-ending source of pleasure, and will sit by the hour philosophizing and reminiscencing over a single glass of beer. The people gathered here are in the main well-dressed and of more than the average intelligence. They are representative of the middle and upper classes of the suburban districts.

---

1 When Hyde Park became a local option district, the —— beer-garden, the most magnificent in Chicago, was flourishing near Washington Park. After a period, during which only soft drinks were sold, its owners, the —— Brewing Co., determined to turn this resort into a club, under the title ————. About four thousand certificates of membership were scattered all over the district. After a short but decisive fight with the Hyde Park Protective Association, the resort again became a beer-garden, without any beer, but still retaining its name and other attractive features. Thus it is at present, of necessity, a most excellent substitute. [Later, by a subterfuge, it has obtained a liquor license, and is a popular resort.—Eds.].

A young woman of strong temperance views exclaimed, after spending an hour in this garden for the first time: "Isn't it beautiful? Can it be, is it possible, that after all our ideas are wrong and these people are right?" It is not for our report to judge, but this is true that, while drinking to excess is seldom known here, a certain proportion of the patrons acquire in these beautiful and apparently harmless surroundings the progressive appetite which, with men of some temperaments, means the whole sad story of the ruined home and the drunkard's grave. Too much importance can scarcely be attached to the music rendered in some of these resorts. It is of the first quality and to be had every night for the nominal fee of $0.25. People, many of whom do not drink at all, gather here from far and near. The gardens draw their patronage mostly from those who own comfortable homes in the suburbs.

There are, of course, beer-gardens of all grades and qualities, but those for the poorer classes, the ten-cent and free gardens, are mostly in the form of open-air vaudevilles. In these the music is inferior, and the vaudeville bill, similar to that mentioned in a previous paragraph, is presented. They are much more numerous here than are the saloon vaudevilles of the city centers, and here no roof is necessary to keep out the smoke and dirt.

A unique feature of the suburban districts is the road-house. Buildings, interesting in their exterior architecture and well equipped within, are located along the road to the suburban districts. They are especially adapted to wheelmen and other pleasure-seekers wishing to stop for rest and refreshment.

As a general rule, funeral processions returning from the cemeteries that lie along the road to these suburban districts stop here for beer and refreshments. Drivers stop at the particular house of which they are regular customers, and the majority of the people in the procession stop and drink also.

An example of these is the —— ——, one of the many on the road between Chicago and Evanston. There are accommodations for wheels and carriages. A large room is furnished with tables and chairs, and either a glass of beer and light lunch or a dinner is served. Palms figure here as usual in the decorations. The bar-room is large and attractive. Above are rooms "free for private parties, balls, etc."

The adaptability of the saloon to the needs of a particular locality is a source of constant surprise and admiration, as it is also a cause of genuine consternation among Christian people who reflect at all upon the cautious institutionalism of the churches.

25

ANON, 'THE EXPERIENCE AND OBSERVATIONS OF A NEW YORK SALOON-KEEPER AS TOLD BY HIMSELF', *MCCLURE MAGAZINE*, 32, JANUARY 1909, 301–12

As told by himself*

ON Sunday, September 6, I noticed an advertisement in the New York papers, offering a "dandy" saloon for sale. Inquirers were directed to address an agent named James J. Cunningham. I looked up this man next morning, and found him very affable, even cordial. I had no definite idea of engaging in the saloon business, but Cunningham was very plausible. He described the place in question to me, dwelt on the proposition that here was a chance for an elderly, well-educated man like myself to get possession of a fine paying business for very little money, and explained to me that no experience was required to operate the business successfully.

It turned out that Mr. Cunningham had a partner, Mr. Pye, and it was the latter who attended to the actual work of showing places for sale to prospective buyers, and striking the bargains. So Pye was called up on the telephone, and it was arranged that he should meet me next day at Cunningham's office.

He did meet me, and accompanied me not only to the "dandy" saloon, but to several others that were also for sale. He gave me a lot of information about all these places. When we entered the "dandy" saloon, we found it crowded with people who were gaily spending their substance at the bar. Most of them were men of good appearance, and many of them were well-dressed and prosperous looking.

The proprietor, Frank Drugan, sat down at a table with us, and answered questions put to him. He said he had not been at all anxious to sell his place, for it had paid him very well. But he had just accepted a fine position under the Park Department, which paid him a salary of one hundred and fifty dollars

---

* The author of this article is a German, a man of education. His story is an accurate account of his experience in the business of saloon-keeping. For obvious reasons his name is withheld, and his associates here appear under fictitious names.—EDITOR.

a month, with little to do and the certain prospect of preferment; and as the municipal law forbade him to keep a saloon while in the city's employ, he was now obliged to sell it. The agent, Pye, confirmed this, and so did a friend of Drugan's who was called in.

In an aside Pye said to me that Drugan was "politics mad," like so many other Irishmen, and that that was really the reason of his being willing to sacrifice his fine place for a song.

Drugan produced some books and papers, which seemed to bear out his claims. He maintained that his profits from the saloon had been from fifty to sixty dollars a week. It was easy to see that Drugan was a hard drinker. He himself admitted this in conversation, and added that his wife had been very anxious to get him out of the business. This again was confirmed by Pye and Drugan's friend.

I inquired about the stock in the place, and was shown around the cellar, and allowed to inspect the glass cabinets that lined the walls of the bar-room proper. The rows of bottles of high-priced whiskies, brandies, cordials, wines, etc. and the piles of apparently filled boxes of cigars made a fine showing and seemed to represent a value of hundreds of dollars.

However, I did not make a decision that day. There were some other places advertised that I wanted to look at, and during the next two days I did so. Nothing came of this, and on Thursday I looked up Cunningham once more. He descanted again on the charms and advantages of the "dandy" saloon. Meanwhile he summoned Pye by telephone, and we should have gone together to Drugan's place, if my previous engagements had not prevented.

When Pye and I left Cunningham, he was under the impression that we were going directly to the "dandy" saloon, and he called Drugan to the telephone in the drug-store across the street from the saloon, and warned him to get ready for our coming. The druggist told me this a few days later, adding that Drugan, an hour or two afterward, had telephoned to Cunningham: "For goodness' sake, when is that sucker coming? My place is jammed with snide customers, who are eating and drinking and smoking me out of house and home."

I own a saloon without liquor

Of these goings-on I was not then aware. Suffice it to say that on a Friday morning, Pye took me once more to Drugan's place, and that I made as searching an examination of it and its revenues as I was capable of. The brewery beer book was produced, and from it I saw that forty half-barrels a week had been the average. He showed me the entries in his little receipt book, which apparently demonstrated that his receipts for the last three days had been, respectively, fifty-three, forty-six, and forty-nine dollars. I ascertained later on that these entries were bogus, and that his real receipts had been about forty per cent less.

As to the stock, that seemed to be untouched since my last visit. There stood the rows of shining bottles of liquor and wine; there were other rows of "wet goods"

PLACES AND SPACES

in their original packing; there were the cigar boxes in their old places. It seemed like a gratuitous insult to examine these things more closely.

At the urging of the agent, Pye, I made a definite offer to Drugan for his place. There was some haggling, but finally we agreed on a price, and Pye quickly filled out the bill of sale, stating that one thousand dollars had been paid for the stock, good-will, lease, etc. of the place. I drew my check for the amount, and handing that over to Drugan, I took possession of the saloon. Drugan passed over the keys to me, and calling out, "Tom," "Dan," he presented me to his bartender and porter as the "new boss."

Then he and Pye hurriedly left to cash my check. Both were visibly excited. Too late, I learned that this was because they were afraid I might quickly rue my bargain and telephone my bank downtown to stop payment on the check.

I did not examine my stock closely until the following day, when I found that most of what I had bought was in reality only "false front." That is, the bottles of wine, to all appearance in their original packing, were water; so were the bottles of whisky, brandy, kümmel, gin, cordial, vermouth, etc. The boxes of cigars were empty. The stock which I had estimated at two hundred and fifty or three hundred dollars was in reality worth about twenty dollars. So depleted was it, in fact, that there was not even enough liquor in the place to last a day, and I had at once to give an order for liquor to the agent who had regularly supplied the place, a young Hebrew. The porter and the bartender simultaneously informed me that the "beer was out"; that "number one, two, three, and four were run dry" (referring to the faucets at the bar); and when I made a hurried visit to the cellar, I found this true. There were only empty barrels. My predecessor had taken care of that.

The cold and haughty brewery office

I hastened to the brewery to order some beer. At the same time I wanted to inform the brewers of the change of ownership. When I arrived there I found the office crowded with a discouraged-looking set of men,—saloon-keepers come to ask some favor from the brewery management.

The office of the brewery, where I found myself, was arranged much like that of a bank. There were only a few chairs placed against the wall of the waiting-room, so that most of us were compelled to stand. Stout wooden partitions separated us from the clerks. The latter affected a very haughty demeanor. To questions they generally returned no answer whatever. It was a weary wait for most of us. One of the saloon-keepers, who appeared to be in trouble about his license, wanted to speak to the superintendent. "You can't see him to-day," was the curt reply. "When can I see him?" "Perhaps day after to-morrow." "But that is a busy day with me," said the crestfallen petitioner. "Can't help it—lucky if you see him then." The collector, too, was not easily approachable. "You must come back to-morrow morning," I was told, after waiting patiently for half an hour. "Be here punctually at half-past eight. That's the best time."

OBSERVATIONS OF A NEW YORK SALOON-KEEPER

The owners of the brewery were young men, knowing next to nothing of its affairs, and caring less. They conceived it to be their chief duty to spend its large revenues. The brains and moving force of the concern was a German who was styled the "superintendent." Although I was unable to have speech with him that afternoon, the clerks around the office assured me that all the beer I wanted would be sent to my place, especially as I had told them that I would pay cash for it on delivery, until a different arrangement could be made with the brewery. However, despite all their promises, the brewery did not send me any beer, and at six o'clock Friday evening I was obliged to close up my place, because I had no beer. This, I thought, was certainly a discouraging start.

The next day being Saturday,—the most remunerative day for the saloon-keeper,—I went to the brewery bright and early, accompanied by Drugan, the late owner. I wanted to settle things. After a long wait, I met both the collector and the superintendent. In Drugan's presence these two men informed me that I had been swindled and overreached by him and the agent, that it had been notorious that Drugan was head over heels in debt, and that his place was worth no more than the value of the stock—which I had found to be practically nothing. The whole matter struck them as a joke. Drugan stood by and said nothing.

The whole transaction had been a fraud. Drugan's appointment to a city job— as he now frankly admitted—was a straight lie; the saloon-agents had coöperated with him in putting up this game on me; and for their services they had received, so Drugan told me, not the legitimate commission of five per cent, but a full half of my $1,000. The brewery had begun its sharp and tricky relations with me.

Next, the brewery demanded a cash deposit of two hundred and fifty dollars. This, they told me, was to secure them against loss on their beer bills, their rent, and the license, the money for which they advance to the saloon-keeper. I gave them my check for two hundred and fifty dollars, but in addition had to pay them cash for my first order of ten half barrels, at the full rate of four dollars each. They sent the beer I had paid for, but did not give me a receipt for my two hundred and fifty dollars, a matter which caused me much trouble later.

The brewery and its "Man Friday"

I knew then, of course, what I know still better now, that the relations between the brewer and the saloon-keeper are close and complicated. In looking at a number of saloons, with an eye to purchase, I had found that every one of them was really owned by a brewer. The system under which I became the "Man Friday" of my brewery is practically universal in New York. The saloon is leased, the fixtures are supplied, and the license is paid by the brewer.

When I "bought" my place, I discovered that the brewery held a mortgage of $4,000 on its fixtures. These fixtures, when they were new, had cost perhaps $2,000. The fact that the mortgage was so much larger than the value of the property it covered made it practically certain it would never be paid off, and that the saloon would remain the property of the brewery. Another peculiar fact

317

PLACES AND SPACES

about this mortgage was that it was a "dead one"—that is, I paid no interest directly on it. To all intents and purposes, the fixtures that it covered constituted part of the brewery. I paid my rent to the brewery, but, although it was high for the locality—$1,000 a year—I paid no more than was stipulated in the lease held by the brewery from the owner. The brewery cleared $200 a year from advancing my $1,000 license and receiving back from me $25 a week for forty-eight weeks in the year. But the interest on the fixtures was apparently charged in the profits on the beer, where it could undoubtedly be well cared for—since, I have good reason to believe, they made 350 per cent gross profit on the beer at the price they sold it to me.

I take it, all things considered, that mine was a fair example of the average city saloon. Back of it, on hilly ground, rose a park, and in front of it was a plateau of rock, about sixty feet high, dotted with cottages and old-fashioned mansions. To right and left were residence streets of the humbler sort, and shops and stores. The saloon itself was cheerful and enticing enough, with its pretty plate-glass doors, its wide show windows, its bright mirrors inside, its bar and lunch counters, its glittering glassware, its colored placards and cosy back rooms. The "family entrance" was on the side street, and anybody who wished could enter that way without being observed.

A saloon-keeper's long work day

The saloon, whether profitable or not, was mine, and there was nothing to do but run it. So I started at once upon the routine life of a saloon-keeper. One of the first things I discovered about the business—contrary to all my expectations—was the long hours and the absolute lack of leisure. My saloon, like all others in that vicinity, was opened at five in the morning by the bartender and porter. At eight, sometimes later, I arrived from my home down town. And from eight in the morning until midnight or later I had to stay at my place. At one o'clock I sent away the bartender for his dinner and some sleep, until six, and during those five hours I tended bar myself. From six until midnight, the bartender, as a rule, ran the place. In the morning he and the porter were kept busy, cleaning the place, washing dishes and rinsing glasses, preparing the free lunch, serving it from eleven o'clock on, and waiting on early customers. There was a great deal of transient trade all through the daytime, especially from teamsters who passed by our place, and came in to get a drink or a cigar, while their horses got their fill of water at the trough outside.

The bartender's working day at the saloon averaged, therefore, fourteen hours, from five in the morning until one in the afternoon, and from six in the afternoon till midnight; my own hours were even longer, usually sixteen. It was seldom earlier than one in the morning when I got home, and to be at my place again at eight gave me less than five hours of actual sleep. Not being used to such hours, they quickly began to tell on my general health.

OBSERVATIONS OF A NEW YORK SALOON-KEEPER

The difficult problem of bartender

In the meantime, the matter of bartenders caused me anxiety. Tom Ryan, the bartender whom I took over with the saloon, seized the opportunity afforded him by several unavoidable absences of mine, to drink in excess, so that, early in the afternoon on the day of my taking possession, I found him in a state of advanced intoxication. While in this condition, he knocked down a regular patron of the place. The latter retaliated, and Tom issued from the fight with a badly split nose. He was bleeding freely, and went to the hospital to have his wound sewed up and dressed. When he returned, he presented a rather weird and ludicrous appearance.

It became known at once in the neighborhood that I meant to discharge him, and during that afternoon and the next morning about thirty men applied for his place. It was a peculiarity of the district, apparently, that about every second man either was a bartender or had been one at some time in his life. Most of the applicants had flattering testimonials to show, and almost every one made a point of assuring me that to engage him would bring his friends to my place as new customers.

From the lot I picked out an experienced German bartender, Henry Kurz by name, who had been seventeen years in the business, was known to almost everybody in the neighborhood, and had already tended bar in my place for a former proprietor. He showed me "recommends" of a high character. But none of them stated that he was honest. So I asked him: "Henry, are you honest?"

He smiled a sad and derisive smile. "As honest as any bartender. The really honest bartender does not exist. You can take that from me."

Well, there seemed to be a certain rugged honesty in his dishonesty, so I hired him, and he took off his coat and went to work for me. This was Saturday night, and the place was thronged. At the bar they stood three deep. There was joy at Henry's arrival. They all assured me that I was a lucky man; that my fortune was made; that Henry was so popular my trade would be doubled.

But from the first my receipts were smaller than they had been before his advent. I noticed, too, the disappearance of sundry bottles of French cognac. Two days later Henry got speechlessly drunk, so drunk that he fell down behind the bar, and the last time he was unable to rise. So I let him go, and only then, on taking stock, discovered that Henry had been robbing me right and left. Whole demijohns of liquor, dozens of bottles of wine, whole boxes of cigars, half a dozen bottles of brandy, half my store of glassware, etc., were gone. He must have operated with an accomplice on the outside.

My third man, an elderly personage of mild manners, was honest but slow and incompetent. My fourth, George Shrady, proved in every way acceptable, and him I kept till the last. The only trouble with George was that he was too decent a fellow for the business. He was respectably connected, had filled a responsible position for years with an oil firm in New Jersey, until it had removed to California, and had drifted into this new line while unable to obtain work of higher grade. His grandfather, a retired wholesale butcher, had offered to set him up in business for

PLACES AND SPACES

himself—"but not a cent toward your present line," the old man had said. Once a bartender, however, it seems difficult to get into any other business.

The average weekly wages of a "barkeep" vary between ten and fifteen dollars; few get more, except in hotels and other especially good places. Too many of them succumb to the perpetual temptation, and become drunkards.

This last remark also applies to the saloon porters, men who are employed to sweep the saloon and keep it and the rest of the premises in a clean and wholesome condition, prepare the lunch, run the lunch counter, tap the beer in the cellar, run errands, etc.

I had a wonderful specimen of this genus in my place. He had been nicknamed "Rip Van Winkle," because he possessed a strange faculty for sleep. He could sleep anywhere, and it took him only a minute to drop off into the land of dreams. I have seen him sleep five hours at a stretch, seated in a chair. He was a harmless inebriate,—lazy, irresponsible, with a continual craving for drink, but honest, clean-spoken, and with the remnants of respectability about him. He was a baldheaded man of forty-eight, but looked sixty. He had drifted away from his family.

"I'll make a hole in the water some day," he used to say. He had no will-power left. I tried at first to reclaim him, but at last became convinced that there was no stamina there.

A narrow margin of profit

After I had been running my place a few days, I began to make calculations as to whether it was a paying venture. I noticed that my money went faster than it came in. That, in a way, was but natural. A place with no stock needs restocking to begin with. I had to buy even such articles as a broom, a feather duster, bar brushes, soap, sapolio, etc. There was nothing in the place. The first week I had to buy fifty-four dollars' worth of liquor alone. I figured out my expenses per week as follows:

Beer	$100
Liquor	30
License	25
Rent	20
Free Lunch	15
Wages	15
Soft Drinks	5
Cigars	7
Gas	5
Sundries	10
Total	$232

Scanning the various items of this estimate, I could see that the best percentage of profit was made on the cigars. I paid only $1.50 and $2.50 a hundred for those I sold for a nickel, and $3 and $4 for those I sold for ten cents and fifteen cents. The next most profitable goods were liquor and "soft drinks."

320

OBSERVATIONS OF A NEW YORK SALOON-KEEPER

In places like mine, the sale of beer—the biggest item on my list—is, contrary to the popular impression, scarcely remunerative. There are several reasons for this. The chief one is the enormous sale of pitcher beer. Often this amounts to two-thirds of the whole amount sold. Customers come in all day, and during the evening as well, with tin cans, big pitchers, or other vessels of huge size, and invariably call for a "pint." And for the ten cents that is the price of a nominal pint, they expect their cans to be filled to the brim. They get much nearer a gallon than a pint, and what they pay for it does not even cover the cost to the saloon-keeper. Why, then, does he go on selling it at this rate? Because if he did not, he would practically lose the trade of these people in everything else. Their friends, too, would be persuaded to stay away and patronize some other place. Besides, there is much waste in drawing beer in glasses. My customers, like most workingmen, wanted as much beer for their money as they could get. Hence they generally demanded "schooners" at the bar, and they wanted no froth with their beer, taking exception if there was more than a finger's breadth of it on top of the big glass. "Give me my foam on the bottom!" was a common expression.

Thus it was that I made little money on the sale of my beer. And this even taking into account the large rebate allowed by the brewer. Nominally he sells his beer at four dollars the half-barrel. But from his weekly beer bill the rebate is deducted. This rebate varies from twenty-five to fifty per cent. Its exact amount is a matter of agreement between the brewer and the saloon-keeper. To a good customer, one who stands well, politically and financially, with the brewery, the rebate may be as large as fifty per cent. In my own case, the brewery collector informed me, the rebate would be thirty-two and one-half per cent, reducing my first week's beer bill of about one hundred and forty dollars to less than one hundred dollars, yet leaving me, according to my calculation, hardly any profit whatever, so far as beer was concerned. Of course, in neighborhoods where they don't "rush the growler," and sell only small or medium-sized glasses over the bar, the conditions are reversed. In such places the profits on beer reach from one hundred to one hundred and fifty per cent.

My customers, likewise, as a rule, took very large drinks of whisky—of a size about nine to a quart bottle. This grade of whisky cost me $1.90 per gallon, making the bottle stand me about forty cents. Nevertheless, this meant a profit of one hundred per cent, and over, to me. On the finer grades of whisky, brandy, gin, etc., my profits were larger. I gave my patrons what they called and paid for. That is, if they wanted Old Crow or Hunter whisky, they got it—at fifteen cents a drink. But many saloon-keepers fill the original bottles up with whisky costing them but $2.00 or so a gallon, and sell this for any brand of liquor that is called for. One of my competitors, for instance, told me in a burst of confidence that he had only one grade of whisky behind his bar and that only cost him $1.40 per gallon; he served it out at all sorts of prices from bottles bearing different labels.

321

PLACES AND SPACES

The free-lunch question

The free lunch was an expensive item. In my district only a free lunch could be served. No "business man's lunch" at ten or fifteen cents would go there. I was put to a daily outlay of between two and three dollars. And there was very little immediate and direct return. I remember one noon when I had a particularly appetizing hot lunch, a Jewish peddler came in. He ordered a "schooner" of beer, at five cents. He objected to the foam on top; he wanted it all beer. Then he sat down at a table, and during the next hour he ate three platefuls of my free lunch, and read all the newspapers in my place. He was one of the few Hebrews I ever saw inside my saloon.

The porter, under the bartender's instructions, usually cooks the hot lunch over a small gas range and slices the cold lunch, keeping the plates full and appetizing. The hot-lunch hours were from eleven to three. For this hot lunch we had a varying menu of pea soup, chowder, bean soup, lamb stew, beef stew, pork and beans, etc. There were some ten plates of cold lunch besides, consisting of bologna, liver sausage, spiced fish, pickled herring, smoked or shredded fish, sliced cabbage, onion, bread, pretzels, potato salad, radishes, etc. There is a big firm in Indiana which sends out, all over the East and Middle West, pork and beans in hermetically sealed gallon cans, at 90 cents a can, the minimum order being five dollars' worth; this can be very appetizingly prepared. Then there are several large firms in New York that make a specialty of supplying saloons with pretzels—at 60 cents for a large box, holding between two and three hundred. Other firms call and regularly furnish meat, sausages, etc. The saloon-keeper's free lunch saves many a poor fellow from starvation in hard times. A man may have a whole meal, with a big glass of beer or a "soft drink," for a single nickel.

Why saloons are open Sunday

I had counted on average daily receipts of forty dollars. But I had been obliged to get rid of a number of the old patrons, because their behavior was objectionable. Then about a score of customers had taken advantage of my inexperience and "hung me up" for considerable amounts. One man's bill was nearly ten dollars; another's almost seven; and several more owed between three and five dollars each. The first week I lost altogether about fifty dollars in this way, for these people soon left me and spent their cash elsewhere. Then a number of the best regular patrons lost their, jobs. They continued to drink, but "on trust." Hard times touch no other business man so quickly as the saloon-keeper.

My expenses were, as I have shown, $232 a week. I had counted, as I said, on receipts averaging forty dollars a day. Consequently, if I ran six days I could not hope to make more than my expenses—if as much. I was compelled to run Sundays to live.

A saloon week begins on Saturday, when the laboring men are paid, and from morning to midnight Saturday my bar was continually wet. But Sunday receipts average much more than those of any other day except Saturday, especially in a German-Irish district. On Sundays the "soft stuff" sales alone, to young fellows who had been playing tennis or baseball in the park close by or on the "boulevard," totaled as high as the whole of Monday's sales. Wednesdays and Thursdays I found to be the worst days, from a business point of view. On those days men and women would hand over nothing but pennies, nickels, and dimes, the larger coins and the bills being all gone. Vest pockets and stocking feet were being emptied of their "chicken feed"; the week's earnings were exhausted. Then came Saturday and Sunday again, with fresh money.

The politician's tithe

So I found very soon that it was necessary to keep open on Sunday in order to make both ends meet. When I had first taken possession of my place, Drugan, the former owner, had led me into a quiet corner, and said, after a few preliminary remarks: "You will have to pay fifteen dollars a month for police protection. Then you won't be interfered with on Sundays, unless there is a specific complaint against you, such as a letter, or unless some of the Central Office men should happen to butt in on their own account." I expressed some curiosity on the subject, and Drugan explained who the man was that acted as go-between. I heard that he was to be relied upon, that is, that he would actually turn over the bribe, for fair division; and I heard what amounts my neighboring competitors had to pay.

A day after my preliminary talk with Drugan, the go-between looked me up. He proved to be the secretary of a Democratic club.

"But why should I keep open Sundays at all?" I ventured to ask him when he had opened communication. "I don't much feel like risking arrests."

"Just as you please," answered the man curtly. "Only, in that case, you might as well shut up your place at once. It wouldn't pay."

This was confirmed, a few days later, by the collector of the brewery, and by a lawyer with a large experience in the saloon business, both of whom I talked with about the matter. Except in downtown business places, where conditions radically differed, a saloon-keeper, they maintained, could only make his place go by keeping open on a Sunday.

I learned about the captain of my precinct, and his methods of effecting excise arrests. One of his oldest and best officers lived near my saloon. This man said: "If you're pinched, it will be either through a letter of complaint reaching the captain—and that is something you can't guard against; or it will be through some Central Office men."

"Small consolation," I remarked.

I didn't pay any bribe, however, neither did I join the Liquor Dealers' Association (who attend for you to excise arrests), and on the second Sunday my bartender was arrested while serving a drink of whisky to a "plain-clothes man." He spent a very comfortable Sunday at the police station, playing pinocle with the officers in

PLACES AND SPACES

their own room, and next morning he was bailed out by a political friend. He was arraigned before a magistrate, who held him in $500 bail, to answer at the Special Sessions. I understand these cases seldom come to trial.

I learned something about the various methods employed by saloon-keepers to protect themselves against Sunday arrests. One must be "liberal." There is one saloon-keeper in The Bronx—his place is at one of the most densely frequented corners—who is popularly supposed to pay $3,000 a year for "protection." He can well afford it, though, as his net income is reputed to be at least $50,000. His place is often crowded in the small hours of the morning with men and women in a hilarious condition. There is a sort of "cabaret" performance in one room, where risqué songs are in vogue.

I was advised to see the district leader of Tammany Hall about the matter of protection. It is well to "keep on the blind side of him," I was told. To join two or three of the semi-political, semi-social Democratic clubs in the neighborhood is another advisable step. The secretaries of several of these asked, and obtained, initiation fees of me, and then urged me to buy some five dollars' worth of tickets for entertainments planned in the near future. In exchange, they promised to "look after" me in the way of police protection, and to furnish bail in case of excise arrests.

For a number of reasons, however, I made up my mind to keep my place closed hereafter on Sundays, even if to do so should spell heavy loss.

A hold-up by the "Graveyard Gang"

My experience, however, was not to be confined to a political "hold-up." I soon had an experience with the genuine article. During my first week as a saloon-keeper, I left my place a little after midnight to take the elevated railroad about two blocks away. As I stepped clear of the buildings adjoining my saloon, into a comparatively dark spot, two fellows rushed out upon me, and while one pinned my arms behind me with incredible swiftness and skill, his pal went through my pockets. Apparently they had been watching me through the windows of the saloon, for there were no false moves. The second man dived instantly for the left-hand hip-pocket in my trousers, and pulled out the forty-three dollars I had just put there—the receipts of the business for that day. Then both took to their heels, and were lost in the darkness of the little park near by. The whole thing had not taken more than ten minutes. There was nothing for me to do; it was so dark that I could give no accurate description of the robbers to the police. Yet it was fairly certain that the robbery was the work of members of one of the two gangs of young criminals who lived in that neighborhood.

One of these, known as the Graveyard Gang, has its hangout on top of a steep bluff that overlooks the neighborhood, from which point of vantage the gang can watch the land below and the passersby. They know all the people in the neighborhood and how much money they are likely to have in their pockets, their paydays, etc. Four of the members of this gang, the Rawlins brothers, I counted at first among the patrons of my saloon. Two of these boys had already, I found out,

324

"done time" in Sing Sing. Their parents (of Irish birth) were quite respectable people.

I soon learned that my case was not exceptional. I heard of several hold-ups during my short stay in the neighborhood. The second gang, mostly half-grown boys, with a youth named Billy McCoy for leader, are likewise a terror to peaceable citizens. One evening, while on my way to a restaurant for supper, I heard the details of their latest exploit. They had borne a spite against a Hebrew peddler. So they fell upon him, knifed him in various places, and inflicted painful and dangerous injuries from which the man has not yet recovered. If he does, he will be maimed and a cripple all his life. He was carried into a bakery the very moment I happened to pass, bleeding profusely. A great crowd had collected. "It's Billy McCoy's gang," somebody said. This happened but a stone's throw from the elevated station. These things are not only common, they are accepted as a part of the daily life of the section, and no adequate steps are taken to do away with such conditions.

The saloon-keeper and his revolver

The police afforded me and my place absolutely no protection. The men patrolling my beat rarely showed themselves until late at night, and then only to partake of a friendly glass at my expense. One night, when a terrific storm was brewing, we were just on the point of closing up, when in stepped the man from our beat, smiling all over his ruddy, handsome face. A moment later the storm broke loose, and rain began to fall in bucketfuls. The officer, secure against intrusion, took off his coat and sat down near the bar—drinking, smoking, and enjoying the blatant tunes that came screeching from the phonograph.

After I had been robbed in the way described above, knowing that I would get no adequate police protection, I consulted a lawyer as to whether I had not better exercise a saloon-keeper's privilege and carry a revolver to protect myself. The lawyer advised against it. He said I was not quick and "husky" enough to contend with these young criminals. They would put a bullet in me before I could draw my weapon, and if hunted down would plead self-defence. He counselled me instead to have a body-guard. So I arranged with my bartender, and he saw me every night to the foot of the elevated station stairs. This bartender, like nearly every other bartender, had carried a weapon ever since he had been in the business; and he told me of several instances in which it had saved his life. I had nothing but a baseball bat behind my bar for protection. I always stayed at my saloon with George and the porter until closing time, and never ventured out alone after dark—a sad commentary on the safety of life and property in that part of New York.

A "good drinking population"

The population in the neighborhood of my saloon was what is technically called in the saloon business "a good drinking one." It was made up of Irish and Germans in about equal parts, with a good-sized Italian section, and a few Americans thrown in. There were scarcely any Jews. Both Pye, the sales-agent, and Drugan, the late owner of the saloon, had dwelt on this last fact, saying that Jews were no drinkers and therefore "N. G. for our trade." There were a large number of grownup descendants of the Germans, Irish, and Italians, and on the whole I found them even better drinkers than their elders. Certainly they were better spenders.

When I saw the saloon for the first time, that is, when Drugan had stocked it up with bogus customers for my inspection, it was well filled with men of prosperous appearance and comparatively quiet manners. The actual patronage of the saloon I found to be of a very different class. An overwhelming majority of the people living near me were workingmen—day laborers, teamsters, furniture-movers, and mechanics; and of the last named many, when employed, earned high wages. But there was also an admixture of the criminal element, either living in the neighborhood, or "hanging out" in certain retired nooks near at hand.

Being German-born myself, and all my life accustomed to the moderate use of beer and wines, I had never had much sympathy with the movements against saloons and drinking. But here in my place, dealing mostly with men and women of either German or Irish blood, I was confronted by conditions that I had never suspected; in fact, could scarcely have believed possible. For to me the drinking habits of most of my patrons appeared frightful. Intemperance, intoxication pursued to the point of senselessness—and this not once in a while, but frequently or daily—was common. I think I am not overstating the fact when I say that my unmarried patrons spent about seventy-five per cent of their earnings in drink. Among the married men there were wide differences, largely owing, I daresay, to the greater or lesser restraining influence of wives and children; but even the married men, I believe, spent an average of at least twenty-five per cent of their wages in this way, and many of them much more.

Four quarts of whisky a day

Some of my regular patrons habitually consumed their four quart bottles of whisky a day, not reckoning the beer, etc., that they drank besides. One-, two-, or three-bottle men I counted by the score among my regular customers. And it seemed to me that the character of their toil made hardly any difference. There were, for instance, many marble-cutters living in my district. Their hours were not long; their labor was not exhausting; their pay was very good. Yet nearly all of them had dissipated habits. On the other hand, there were hard-working teamsters, furniture-movers, carpenters, bricklayers, etc., who were comparatively temperate.

There were curious types among them. One bricklayer, a man earning good wages, on coming home Saturdays, always provided liberally for his family. Then, his mind freed of that responsibility, he would issue forth, dressed in his best clothes, on a "glorious drunk." He would return home late Sunday night or early Monday morning, with not a cent left. This was his practice, regular as clockwork. When intoxicated, this man button-holed everybody, paid for drinks for his auditors, and told rambling stories that had neither beginning nor end. By his baleful eye he held men spell-bound, like the Ancient Mariner, for hours and hours.

Then there was a teamster, Fred Reynolds by name. He spent all his wages on drink. His weekly earnings probably averaged twenty-five dollars; on Sunday nights he never had a cent left. His clothes hung about him in tatters and he wore neither socks nor underclothes.

A little German there was, a cripple, pale and thin. This man was an expert piano-mover, despite his dwarfish size. He was always drunk or half drunk; always smiling, chipper, and in good humor. He drank like a fish, oceans of beer, and never seemed to eat anything.

A painter, another German, was a regular customer. He also was very good-natured, and never quarreled. But he would not tolerate interference with his drinking habits. One boss he had had, an American, who had objected to his drinking during working hours. "Well," said Fritz, "I am not your slave, and if I cannot drink when I feel like it, I'll stop work." And he did.

As a rule, they fiercely resented interference, even when it was manifestly for their own good. It made them violent and abusive. There was one man, for example, Joe Rumpf, of German parentage, a good fellow at bottom, a very hard worker, and of extraordinary strength, who had married an Irish wife with whom he lived very unhappily. The principal cause of their disagreements seemed to be a "star boarder," who had aroused his jealousy. The couple were Catholics, and a divorce was out of the question. When his domestic difficulties began to weigh on Joe's mind—as they generally did on Saturday nights, after liberal indulgence— he would pull out an ugly-looking dirk and threaten to do for the whole family, "star boarder" and all. In this mood, he madly resented any sort of interference. He drank until he fell down like a log, sleeping off his stupor in some corner of the saloon.

It interested me to study drunkenness in its various stages, as it presented itself to me among my patrons. Many became quarrelsome, pugnacious, boisterous, vindictive; others despondent, melancholy, talking of their wrongs. Of course, racial traits have much to do with that. Drink accentuates them. Some of my patrons became coarse in their talk and rude in their habits when drunk, while others, particularly those of German blood, became sentimental. With a very large proportion of these men to drink in excess was their only recreation, their only pleasure, from week's end to week's end.

From my saloon experience I judge that this class of our population differs from those better placed and better educated chiefly in its lack of restraint.

A degenerate second generation

One of the most surprising and unpleasant observations I made concerned the second generation—the adult American-born sons of Irish or German fathers. These

PLACES AND SPACES

men, as a rule, not only shared the drinking habits of the latter, but usually outdid them. Besides that, many of them were not only more dissipated than their elders, but were also very frequently shiftless, indolent, and unreliable. And not a few of them were criminally inclined, even when their fathers were strictly honest and respectable. I found this to be the case, too, among the young Italian-Americans and Jewish-Americans of the second generation. While the old folks still remembered their early religious teaching, and felt its restraining influence, these influences, in the majority of cases, seemed to be entirely removed from the younger men. Scarcely any of them belonged to any church. They scorned, almost without exception, the faith and practices of their elders; they scoffed at every form of worship; and they ridiculed those of their number who gave way, on these points, to home influence. A number of them seemed to me to be wholly devoid of moral sense. As a rule, their parents had very little control over them.

Here are a few illustrations, taken from among my younger patrons. Johnny Ackerman was the son of an Irish mother and German father; a handsome boy, only nineteen. He earned good wages as a plasterer, averaging about twenty-five dollars a week. But he was very dissipated, and spent his earnings on drink and amusement, working often but two or three days out of the six. Saturdays and Sundays he usually drank hard, frequently consuming three bottles of cheap whisky at one sitting, till he dropped senseless. Although still a youth, his health was already completely undermined. He defied his parents when they remonstrated with him, telling them that he would "cut out for himself" if they interfered with his pleasures.

One of the best of my patrons, but likewise a queer type in some respects, was Pat Skelly, born of Irish parents. He was a widower, with two pretty little daughters, to whom he was always gentle, even when in his fiercest mood. He was an excellent marble-cutter, making his six or seven dollars a day. He frequently went "on a spree," though, and then for days and days he would do nothing but drink, drink, drink. At such times his handsome face, originally smiling and tanned, assumed a brick-red hue, and his fine, dark eyes stood out, lobsterlike and scowling. And the more he drank the more contentious he grew.

Another specimen of the second generation was Jack Fuddihy, who held some sinecure under the city government. Having nothing to occupy his mind or body, he became a chronic sot, hanging around the saloons of the district when out of money, waiting Micawber-like for something—or rather somebody—to turn up at the bar, and guzzling innumerable small beers and big whiskies between his rising (at ten in the morning) and saloon-closing time. Twenty-four hours after drawing his semimonthly pay he would have not a red cent left.

Then there was Drugan, Mike Drugan. Only thirty-five, he had been bartender for fourteen years, and for ten years of that time had never drawn a sober breath. He was married and had several small children. His regular daily allowance of whisky was three quart bottles—the beer, wine, etc., do not count. This man's face was of an ashen hue, and the more he drank the grayer it got. Yet he was always able to talk, to draw beer, to mix drinks, to count out change, and to find his way home to bed.

328

OBSERVATIONS OF A NEW YORK SALOON-KEEPER

The "honest workingman" as seen in a saloon

In my experience with the workingman and mechanic, I became unpleasantly aware that my estimate had flattered him. "Honest" is a relative term; one cannot expect a very delicate perception of honesty from men whose rude natural instincts have never been "toned down," so to speak. But here, in my numberless conversations before or behind the bar, I found that "honesty" was laughed at and derided. It was always the clever rascal that was praised and admired. When they commented on newspaper stories, their sympathies nearly always, it seemed to me, were on the wrong side—on the side opposed to truth and justice. Their moral standards were, from their own admissions, deplorably low. I don't want to be understood as meaning that there were no exceptions. There were, notably among the men of the first generation (that is, those born across the water); but these were, after all, only exceptions.

Thus, I was astonished to find, even among those of my patrons who were evidently well-disposed toward me, that they could not find it in their hearts to condemn the swindle that had been practised on me by Drugan and the agent who sold me the saloon. They smiled and said it was a "smart" thing to do. Likewise, I got nothing but good-natured banter for allowing myself to be "hung up" by some of my patrons.

"Drugan would never have let them do that to him. He would have gone after them with a big club, and would have knocked the stuffing out of them, but he would have made them pay."

This is what one of my stanchest adherents said to me, and then he urged me to do the same. That the mere act of cheating a man, of failing to discharge an honestly incurred debt, is dishonest, I could not convince my friend, whose morality was no higher than that of the district where he had passed all his life.

My patrons were not choice in their language. They used habitually terms and phrases that elsewhere would not be permissible. But they were so used to them that they were scarcely aware, I think, of their original meaning. With all this loose talk going on, it was rather astonishing to me that my patrons, one and all, were respectful to me, at least so far as words went. They addressed me indiscriminately as "Pap," "Pappy," "Doc," "Colonel," "Boss"; but never a word of abuse did they give me.

The saloon-keeper in the hearts of the people

What place does the saloon-keeper hold in the hearts of this class of the population? Speaking from my experience, a very large one indeed. When a saloon changes hands, the news travels with incredible speed. Within a few hours the whole district knew about me, and I was discussed at every fireside in all my bearings and dimensions. And one question trembled on every lip: "Is he an easy mark?" The reply must have been, on the whole, in the affirmative, for my popularity was at once established. Half the population, I think, must have been lying awake nights,

PLACES AND SPACES

trying to solve the problem of "how to hang me up." Having successfully "worked Pap"—as they called me most frequently—they must have spread the news of this "easy mark" among their friends, even in far-away parts of the city.

A couple of teamsters came up to my place all the way from down town on a Sunday evening. They did not have a penny between them, but looked to me not only to supply them with their Sunday beer, whisky, and cigars, but even with carfare to return home. I had never before set eyes on either of them, and when they told me that it was Jack Rawlins (one of my most undesirable patrons) who had told them about me and my place, I was not prepossessed in their favor. But they felt heartily and truly aggrieved when I refused to meet their expectations.

There is a sort of familiarly affectionate feeling for the saloon-keeper among these people. He has often been called the "poor man's friend," and his place the "poor man's club," and I must say there is a kernel of truth in this.

All the drinkers at my place, with very few exceptions indeed, opened their hearts to me and George, the "barkeep," even when not encouraged to do so. They would tell their secrets, their troubles, their entanglements, their domestic woes, their afflictions. And the drunker they got, the more confidential they became.

There were many calls for charity. Whenever a case of distress became known in my neighborhood, it was to my place that the first appeal was made. I recall one pitiable and very deserving, case. It was that of a piano-maker, a German of middle age, with a large family depending on him. This man had formerly earned large wages, but had been out of work for eleven months. His savings went first, next one valuable after another was pawned or sold, and then came absolute want, and on top of it sickness in the family. A number of my patrons responded quickly and nobly to an appeal for help, and there was one more happy family that Saturday night.

A family drunk for thirty cents

A great deal of "rushing the growler" was done at my place, and all over the district, in fact. I had occasion to observe the evil effects of this drinking by women and children all through the day and evening. True, it is an inexpensive mode of becoming intoxicated. On thirty cents a whole family of topers can become drunk, for with twenty cents for beer and ten cents for cheap whisky they obtain as much as their husbands or sons for many times that amount. Many of the women that came with huge cans to be filled, bore not only the stamp of dissipation, but of degradation as well. And with their children it would be worse. It was hard for me to understand how these mothers could send their young daughters for beer. Often I would turn girls away, telling them to explain to their mothers that children could not be served with drink in a saloon. Then they would be quite mortified, saying they were no longer children, which perhaps was the truth.

One woman, with an appearance of some refinement still clinging to her, came regularly every afternoon to get her allowance of liquor—twenty-five cents' worth of Old Crow. I inquired about her and found that she was the wife of one of my

330

patrons. So I spoke to him about it in confidence; but he became very angry, telling me it was none of my business what his wife drank, as long as she paid for it. Poor woman, the stamp of the drunkard was already on her delicate frame.

Once for all I had instructed both my bartender and porter to refuse to serve out drink to any children that came to the saloon door, and so far as my observations went this order was obeyed. It was not my way of thinking alone that made me strict on this point; the law, as enforced by the Gerry Society, is severe in this respect, and offences are punishable not only by a large fine, but by jail. But the behavior and the words of most of the children who were thus refused showed me that elsewhere they did not meet with the same cold reception. And nearly all these children, girls even more than boys, saw absolutely no wrong in venturing into a saloon frequented by men who were by no means choice in their language. To them the saloon was a place of delight. They would linger around my doors all day and all evening, trying to catch glimpses of the inside.

Can a saloon-keeper discourage drinking?

I made it a point not to encourage my patrons to drink, merely as a matter of principle. Of course, many saloon-keepers act differently. What the view of my district was on this point, I discovered soon enough. I remember the case of two strangers—both just in from the far West—who dropped in one afternoon. They at once began to spend money liberally. One of them, a man of about fifty-five, baldheaded but very active, pulled out a big wad of five and ten dollar bills, and declared his intention of leaving this roll at my place. He invited everybody to drink with him and was in that stage of intoxication when a man becomes careless of money and does not keep track of it. He handed me a ten dollar bill in payment of his first round, and when I gave him his change, would not accept it, swearing it was not his. He proposed champagne, called for the best in the house, and was with difficulty persuaded by me, after a while, to stop this reckless waste of money. I heard one of my regular patrons characterize my conduct as that of a fool. He spoke to me aside. "You must humor these two," he said, in a reproachful tone. "Let them spend their money here. If they leave, they are sure to spend it elsewhere." Certainly the business offered never-ending problems and temptations.

I and 2,500 others go out of business

But I had no intention of continuing in the business. After I had been in my saloon only a few days, I made up my mind that its patronage was not of a kind I wanted. I then notified the brewery of my intention to sell the place, at a sacrifice, to somebody better qualified and more accustomed to deal with the particular class of people from which my customers were recruited. I acted frankly and honestly toward the brewery people. I asked them to assist me in disposing of the place, since I understood that a large brewery has always some men on hand for such a purchase. But the brewery took no notice of me.

PLACES AND SPACES

In the meanwhile I was having an unpleasant experience of another kind with the brewery people. They had, as I have already said, required an advance deposit of two hundred and fifty dollars from me. They not only did not treat me fairly in matters connected with this deposit, but they neglected, after promising several times to do so, to give me a proper receipt for my money. Finally, I consulted a lawyer who has an extensive acquaintance with saloons. This lawyer, after considerable effort, got the brewery at last to give me a receipt for my deposit. But even this receipt was couched in such general terms that it meant practically nothing.

"Is this the kind of receipt you give your customers?" asked my lawyer. "A receipt stating merely that this two hundred and fifty dollars was received by you 'on account of the place on—Street?' Why, that engages you to nothing. If my client accepts this as a valid receipt, his two hundred and fifty dollars are gone."

"Yes, that is the only kind of receipt we give under such circumstances," said the brewer. "It's our way of doing business."

The outcome of it all was that I instructed my lawyer to begin suit against the brewery for the recovery of my two hundred and fifty dollars. Then it turned out that the brewery made a claim to this money of mine on the plea that it must go to pay for the rent of the saloon after I should quit it.

I had now made up my mind that whatever happened, I would not go into the business for another year, consequently I informed the brewery that I should vacate the saloon, at the latest, by midnight of September 30, the date when my license would expire. The effort of the brewery to hold me for the rent, my lawyer informed me, was entirely unwarranted, inasmuch as I had signed no lease nor any other papers.

In the meantime I made extraordinary efforts to dispose of my saloon to somebody else, even by sacrificing half or two-thirds of my purchase price. But I was unsuccessful. All over Greater New York saloons were closing up at this time; there were consequently numberless chances of getting hold of such places at one's own figure, or at no expense at all.

As the last of September approached, the number of saloons known to be going out of business increased rapidly. Hard times had struck the town the past year, hundreds of thousands of breadwinners were out of employment, and the saloon-keeper was first of all affected, because it is on the laboring man that he has chiefly to depend for his custom. On the night of September 30 there were closed, in Greater New York, no less than 2,500 saloons of every kind out of a total of about 9,000. One single brewery that I know of lost three hundred customers that night. The brewery that supplied me lost one hundred and fifty.

For one of that one hundred and fifty I can say that when the load of worry, disgust, and financial loss that had pressed down upon him, through his short experience of nineteen days as a saloon-keeper, finally rolled off his shoulders, he felt as if he had got rid of the Old Man of the Sea.

I had been drawn into the business by a gross form of conspiracy to defraud, yet I have no remedy—so I have been informed by the district attorney—because of the extreme difficulty of getting convincing evidence in this kind of case. I consequently have lost my first $1,000. The brewery now holds a good share of my

$250 deposit to cover an imaginary obligation which I never assumed, though I may secure this eventually by lawsuit. And I have lost utterly, of course, the credit given to dishonest customers during the course of my business.

I found in my short experience that it was almost impossible for me to make money decently in the business. I lost patronage because I refused to allow my saloon to become a hang-out for criminals, and a place of assignation; I lost a big source of revenue because I refused to encourage hard drinking among my patrons; and finally I lost all possibility of a margin of profit by refusing to pay politicians a monthly bribe to break the law.

There may be, and doubtless there are, saloons in this and other cities, where it is possible for a man to own and run one and yet retain his self-respect; saloons frequented by respectable and well-bred persons. But, to judge from what I have heard in conversation with saloon-keepers of the better sort during my experience and since, such places must be very scarce.

26

HUTCHINS HAPGOOD, 'MCSORLEY'S SALOON', *HARPER'S WEEKLY*, 58, 25 OCTOBER 1913, 15

An ancient landmark, a relic of one phase
of American life that has passed

McSorley's saloon happens to be situated in New York City, on Seventh Street, near Third Avenue, within a stone's throw of the historic Cooper Union, but it might have been, as far as its spirit is concerned, placed almost anywhere in this great country of ours.

It is the type of saloon that is passing away, but is represented by isolated examples, here, there, and everywhere, which still persist.

This famous saloon—and what old town has not its famous saloon?—is sixty years old. John McSorley, its founder, dead these three years at the age of eighty-seven, was one of the historical figures of our town. His horses were as good as those of Commodore Vanderbilt. The quaint portrait of old Peter Cooper hangs on his saloon walls, also an old play-bill announcing a comedy by Harrigan and Hart called "McSorley's Inflation". An old copy of the *New York Herald*, framed on the wall, announced the assassination of President Lincoln. The walls are covered with old New York and national reminiscences. There is a striking portrait of John McSorley, of his cabinet officers and of the members of his Chowder Club.

A one-hundred-years-old safe, an ancient slanting ice-chest, old solid chairs and tables, a sedulous care manifested to keep the place as it always was, help to establish an atmosphere of tradition and permanence. Entering the saloon one seems to leave present day New York and to find oneself in a quieter and more aesthetic place.

John McSorley's son now owns the saloon, and his one pious passion is to maintain the spirit of the place and the spirit of his father. He regards his father as one of the great moral characters of the age and he wouldn't change a thing in the old saloon, nor fail in the slightest degree in carrying out the old man's ideas. Even old John's cats are still happily basking in ancient love, and still gaily boxing for the delight of the McSorley worshippers.

Old John McSorley walked every morning at five o'clock for thirty years to the Battery bath, and opened his saloon at seven. He drank steadily and soberly from the age of thirty to the age of fifty-five and for the last thirty odd years of his life he neither smoked nor drank. He had had enough. No one can sit quietly in his saloon and open his senses to the moral atmosphere without feeling that there is a personality there—a personality respected and cherished by McSorley, son.

Father McSorley sold ale and practically nothing else. If he sold whiskey occasionally, he insisted on its being good and taken "neat".—no mixtures for him. His ideas of drinking were as solid as his ideas of furniture. Nothing flashy for him. Son McSorley does the same, and he sells good ale, too, and a lot of it for five cents.

No woman ever passed or passes the threshold of McSorley's saloon. The dignified workingmen who sit quietly for hours over one or two mugs of ale look as if they never thought of a woman. They are maturely reflecting in purely male ways and solemnly discoursing, untroubled by skirts or domesticity.

"Drunks" have never been welcome in McSorley's saloon. They often tried and tried to brace in with a bold look, but McSorley and his son had an instinct for them and for panhandlers and always gently rejected their nickels. The old man used to sell once to some young mechanic, to whom, if he tried to be a "regular", the old man would give a lesson in deportment and then send back to his job.

The spirit of McSorley's is to welcome the drinker of a mug or two during long hours and discourage the "flash" party who spend much but seldom and drive away the quiet, constant ones. No matter how many diamonds and money a light and well-dressed stranger may possess, he cannot get a real welcome at McSorley's, and on no account is he admitted to the back room at lunch time, unless he will content himself with a sandwich and a mug of ale and not disturb the habits of the serious workingmen.

McSorley's closes always at midnight. Under the law it could be kept open till one o'clock, but old John McSorley wanted to go to bed at twelve, and so his son does, too. The tradition is as zealously maintained as in any aristocratic old French family.

RAW onions and ale—these are the staples, and both are strong and pure. Rembrandt would have delighted in McSorley's and I think that Velasquez would have found his account there, too, as our own John Sloan does. The wives of the men who go to McSorley's know where the husbands have been. There is no mistaking a McSorley onion.

Old John McSorley was, among his other qualities, a good deal of a prophet. He used solemnly to warn his brother saloon-keepers that if they yielded to the wiles of the devil, for the sake of immediate gold, the liquor license would be raised on them. And, behold, since his early time, the license has gone from $75 to $1,400 a year. The toll on the wicked is great and heavy, and unfortunately involves the good, for we are all brothers in misfortune.

Since the breweries got possession of the saloons, they exact so much of the profit that the poor saloon-keeper is often forced to do shoddy and careless and hasty; or in other words, evil things, in order to live. But McSorley, son, owns his

PLACES AND SPACES

own saloon, and, strong in the spirit of his father, maintains the ways of balance, form, and virtue.

IF there were more saloons like McSorley's in the country, and fewer of the other kind, there would probably now be no strong temperance movement, attacking the price of the grape or the corn—that element of civilization recognized from Plato to Omar as emphasized by Fitzgerald and accepted as a stimulating spark kindling our poetry, our literature, our temperamental sociability, inciting our fancy, and warming the world in which we live.

McSorley's saloon is, as I have said, mainly frequented by quiet workingmen who sip their ale and look as if they are philosophizing. It is true that the saloon in general today—(good and bad) is the principal place in which ideas underlying the labor movement originate, or at any rate become consciously held. It is there where men talk over, think, and exchange feelings and ideas relating to their labor and their lives. The social philosophers take their fragmentary thoughts and construct them as to programmes and systems.

SOME of these programmes and projected systems are extreme, some unbalanced. Now, it is probable that in McSorley's saloon the thinking workingman takes more things into account than he does in a brutal, hasty and violent saloon of the more frequent type. There is a correcting conservation in the atmosphere of McSorley's which tends to eliminate from the worker's feeling and thought that which is hastily considered.

The heavy, solid chairs, the rich, dark colors, the trailing mementos of the past give pause to the headlong spirits, tending to take away what is unbalanced.

Yes, as one sits in McSorley's saloon, watching the subtle cats, conscious of the old slanting ice-chest, aware of the quiet workingmen sipping their genial ale, wrapped in the shadows of tradition, one feels a little solemn, as in a quiet retreat, though not too remote from human nature's daily luxuries.